Praise for *The Glorious Deception: The Double Life of William Robinson aka Chung Ling Soo, the "Marvelous Chinese Conjurer"*

"Mr. Steinmeyer's book is like his illusions: a presentation of the seemingly simple in a progression which leads to delight."

—David Mamet

"A lush new biography . . . When [Steinmeyer] describes the performances of Chung Ling Soo, you simultaneously thrill to them from the best seat in the house and watch the trap doors work from underneath the stage. . . . *The Glorious Deception* is a true detective story and a sparkling cultural history."

—Teller

"Captivating . . . In Steinmeyer's capable hands, Robinson becomes a walking, talking illusion and a reminder: never trust appearances when in the presence of a magician."

—*Kirkus Reviews*

"In this affectionate and informed biography, Steinmeyer tantalizingly picks along the trail of the magician's life. . . ."

—*Publishers Weekly*

"Wry and colorful depiction of magical entertainment before and after the turn of the century . . . Steinmeyer has done an awe-inspiring job. . . ."

—David Regal, *Genii*

Praise for *Hiding the Elephant*

"Like Mr. Steinmeyer's own magical creations, this book is provocative, entertaining, and original."

—Ricky Jay, author of *Learned Pigs & Fireproof Women*

"Simply the finest, best-told, most graceful history of the Golden Age of magic I've ever read. It belongs on that elite shelf of historical explorations, like *Longitude* or *The Professor and the Madman*, which are so entertaining, so informative that the reader with no prior interest will feel educated and enthralled on every page."

—Glen David Gold, author of *Carter Beats the Devil*

"A delightful new book. Steinmeyer is a modern master. He writes with wit."
—Michael Pakenham, *Baltimore Sun*

"A wonderful new book. . . . A wonderful history of stage magic and the performers who made it."

—Jon Carroll, *San Francisco Chronicle*

ALSO BY JIM STEINMEYER

Hiding The Elephant:
How Magicians Invented the Impossible and Learned to Disappear

The Complete Jarrett

Two Lectures on Theatrical Illusion

The Magic of Alan Wakeling

The GLORIOUS DECEPTION

THE DOUBLE LIFE OF WILLIAM ROBINSON, aka CHUNG LING SOO
the "MARVELOUS CHINESE CONJURER"

JIM STEINMEYER
author of HIDING THE ELEPHANT

CARROLL & GRAF PUBLISHERS
NEW YORK

THE GLORIOUS DECEPTION
The Double Life of William Robinson, aka Chung Ling Soo,
the "Marvelous Chinese Conjurer"

Carroll & Graf Publishers
An Imprint of Avalon Publishing Group Inc.
245 West 17th Street
11th Floor
New York, NY 10011

AVALON
publishing group incorporated

Copyright © 2005 by Jim Steinmeyer

First Carroll & Graf edition 2005
First Carroll & Graf trade paperback edition 2006

Library of Congress Cataloging-in-Publication Data is available.

ISBN-10: 0-78671-770-X
ISBN-13: 978-0-78671-770-5

9 8 7 6 5 4 3 2 1

Book design by Maria E. Torres

Printed in the United States of America
Distributed by Publishers Group West

CONTENTS

INTRODUCTION

This is a story about secrets, and one man who lived a life ruled by deception.

William Ellsworth Robinson was a magician who found his fame in the years that bridged the nineteenth and twentieth centuries. He was recognized for his inventions and originality. And he also made his fame with slavish imitations. He prized loyalty and secrecy. Yet his early success was based on a brazen mixture of opportunism and espionage.

His business acquaintances described Robinson as a loyal husband. He was almost certainly a bigamist. We know that he was also a devoted father. Yet he abandoned his first children. Friends remembered him as calm and philosophical, although he sometimes exploded in bursts of temper, worthy of his upbringing in Manhattan's rough-and-tumble Bowery.

Offstage, he was respected for being plainspoken and refreshingly honest. Onstage, he became known as one of history's most successful impostors.

Early in his career, William Robinson chose the title Man of Mystery. It looked impressive on a playbill, and it suited him perfectly.

Deception is usually a negative term, but occasionally it can prove to be positive and uplifting. That's a magician's goal: to sweep together a series of tiny lies, overstatements, optical illusions, and false clues, constructing an enchanting deception for the audience, showing them something they never thought possible. The magician earns an audience's trust through his ability to mystify. There's no question that William Robinson was not simply one of the most fascinating performers in history but one of the world's greatest magicians. I believe that his deceptions were beautiful masterpieces, worthy of any artist, and decades of stunning reviews and eyewitness accounts make this case.

Robinson's story has achieved renown for his curious death, one of the great tragedies of the stage and an astonishing mystery that perplexed his colleagues. But the headlines of that event have created a deceptive fog, a swirl of secrets that have clung to this talented magician for many years.

—m—

No delight is more transitory than a magic trick.

The creation of an illusion is a basic element of all theater. In the moment, it can be a refreshing and unexpected mixture of logic and emotion: an example of that fresh gust of wonder that lies within every discovery.

But a great illusion is only partly a performance. It is created by suggestions made by the magician, and it takes form within the minds of his audience. A moment later, after the experience is over and the wonder has passed, that same trick is often remembered as a puzzle to be solved or dismissed. For many people, a magic show is recalled as a childish indulgence. It's human nature to avoid deception. Paying for the privilege, offering one's time and attention for the purpose of being fooled, can be a special annoyance. Even worse, it can seem to be a sort of self-deception.

For centuries, magicians have puzzled over this dichotomy. Is magic a universal art, like music or dance? Is it a skillful novelty, like plate spinning or ventriloquism? Or is it a puzzle, a mere intellectual exercise?

I believe that there's a simple answer. A lot of magicians are obsessed with puzzles. Others have just been spinning plates. But over the course of a long history, a few magicians have actually become artists.

In my 2003 book, *Hiding the Elephant*, I wrote about a distinct period in entertainment history when magic mixed with art, and a number of its practitioners were remarkable, inventive artists. From the 1860s to the 1920s, magicians confronted an entirely new range of optical illusions for the stage, and this inspired a burst of creativity and changed the way they performed.

William Robinson belonged to this same period and faced the same opportunities. It was a revolutionary era in show business, just as minstrel, circus, and variety saloons were being stirred together and distilled into a new concoction called vaudeville. Robinson was trained by one generation of magicians—the old masters like Herr mann the Great and Harry Kellar—and then became a pioneer for the next generation, men like Harry Houdini and Howard Thurston. In many ways, Robinson would be considered one of the great transitional figures in the history of magic if he weren't remembered today for suddenly becoming someone else.

—⚬—

As in *Hiding the Elephant*, my point of view is that of a magician. My background is not that of a performer but a designer of illusions used by other magicians: onstage, for television specials and Las Vegas shows, or on Broadway. I've been fortunate to work with many of the great magicians of recent years, developing new effects for their shows. My job has also involved a study of the techniques used by past magicians. Today, the business of magic is very different than it was in William Robinson's day, involving new technologies and materials, and all these improvements have provided new opportunities to deceive an audience.

But in other ways the business of magic is very much the same as it was a century ago. Audiences aren't really intrigued by technology. They're interested in fantasy, and the best tricks involve everyday objects in extraordinary fairy tales: catching silver coins from the air, animating playing cards so they crawl out of a deck, producing a pretty assistant from a wisp of smoke in a glass cabinet. The same tricks that mystified our grandparents impress us today.

By modern standards, William Robinson's magic might seem a bit slow or deliberate, but it's only a question of fashion, the same way films made fifty years ago move at a different pace from today's movies. The accounts of his performances suggest that Robinson was uniquely charismatic and mystifying and would match any of the greatest magicians performing today.

Of course, we magicians are notoriously close-mouthed, but the real reason we guard our secrets is not to protect them from being known by the audience, but to protect the audience from the secrets. The methods used by magicians are simple and uninteresting. Magicians prize basic, dependable techniques for their illusions, but they also realize the corrosive effect when an audience understands those crude secrets. These bare technical details are terribly deflating.

Still, I've chosen to tell this story by explaining some secrets, and I am hoping to take the readers into my trust. I believe that an understanding of these secrets provides insight into the achievements of some remarkable magicians, as well as into William Robinson's world and his creations. Just as it's impossible to understand a composer's life without listening to his music, or a painter's achievements without seeing her paintings, it is impossible to appreciate Robinson's mastery of secrets without explaining how he found the world of magic, and how he left it.

Any good magician seeks to surprise, and comes to value the twist that instantly catches the audience off guard. So it's a fitting tribute to William Ellsworth Robinson that his story starts with a figurative wave of the wand, at a performance of the greatest Chinese magician who ever set foot on a British stage. It was less than a century ago, a remarkable time when wonders were still a commodity, and could be acquired for the price of a theater ticket; when a boy from Manhattan could become a true man of mystery.

—Jim Steinmeyer

Chapter I

THE WOOD GREEN EMPIRE

A ll the World's a Stage.

Inscribed in the plaster and finished in gold leaf, those five famous words appeared over the proscenium at the Wood Green Empire in north London, in the smooth white halo that formed the focal point of the theater and surrounded the bloodred, gold-tasseled curtain.

It was a typically artistic touch for a Frank Matcham theater. Built in 1912 on the High Road, the Wood Green Empire was one of the last designs of the noted architect. Matcham's many "Music Halls," "Empires," "Palaces," and "Hippodromes" dotted all of Great Britain and were carefully designed to accommodate variety entertainments, following a precise formula of seats, balconies, lobbies, and exit doors. Traveling from city to city, the Edwardian music hall performers— continually rearranged and reassembled like puzzle pieces for that week's entertainment—were pleased to arrive at the Matcham houses. They admired the modern loading doors that opened directly onto an alley, the full-sized orchestra pits, generous dressing rooms with slate tables, convenient bathrooms, good acoustics, modern electric lighting, and the deep stages that could show off any act to its best advantage. Some of the theaters were even equipped with special rooms for the horses or sea lions popular in animal acts.

To music hall patrons, Matcham theaters represented the epitome of Edwardian design. The lobbies were lavish and exotic, with mosaic floors, crystal fixtures, and arched staircases fitted with thick Axminster carpeting and polished brass handrails. The dress circle offered an elegant oak bar stocked with bottles of scotch and gin, taps of stout and ale. The cantilevered steel balconies, built without vertical posts, guaranteed that every spectator had a clear view of the stage. The auditoriums were decorated as Moorish temples, rococo palaces, or renaissance castles, filled with tight whorls and broad curlicues of filigree, scrollwork, cartouches, carved elephant heads, richly painted friezes, goddesses smiling benignly from the tops of their caryatid columns, and glittering stained glass set within oval domes. It was all finished in soft, rich hues: burgundy or forest green plush, mahogany-colored velvet curtains, glowing rose-colored marble, alabaster, and burnished gilt trim.

The design of the Wood Green Empire continued Frank Matcham's tradition of indistinct fairy-tale décor, all translucent white, warm cream, gold leaf, and red plush. There were eighteen hundred and forty seats. By all accounts, on the night of March 23, 1918, at the nine o'clock Saturday show—the second performance of the evening and the last show of the week—every seat was filled and a handful of latecomers stood in a neat line in the back of the stalls, leaning against the upholstered railing and contemplating their programs. Every one of them was there to see the star attraction, "Chung Ling Soo, The World's Greatest Magician, in a Performance of Oriental Splendor and Weird Mysticism, assisted by Miss Suee Seen, presenting in rapid succession the most Beautiful, Baffling and Interesting Series of Illusions ever submitted to the Public."

The patrons naturally expected to be amazed and astonished. Instead, every member of that audience, nearly two thousand people, watched as Chung Ling Soo's spell was unexpectedly broken. They were the eyewitnesses to a final explosive act—the climax of the strangest tragedy in stage history.

—⁂—

At 9:00 p.m. promptly, there was a clatter in front of the stalls as the musicians took their places in the orchestra pit. The lights dimmed, and Mr. Forbes Russell, the musical director at the Wood Green Empire, stepped to the podium, his head bobbing above the railing at the front of the stage. He nodded to his musicians, gave the upbeat, and the audience was treated to a brief overture—in honor of their star attraction Mr. Russell had selected the latest Denmark Street "Chinese" melody, which allowed him to use the gong and marimba, specially installed that week to provide the proper oriental accents.

Then the music hall acts began. Tom Keno, the "Pattering Comedian," dashed onto the stage to offer a few minutes of quick laughs. The Three Osrams, an Australian acrobatic act, were next; then Annie Rooney, "In a Bright Entertainment"; Ruby Roya, a dancer who billed herself as "The Radiant Revue Girl"; and Will H. Fox, who sat at a piano and offered comedic monologues that slid smoothly into his original songs filled with puns and topical references. The printed program boasted that Fox had performed his specialty "over 16,000 times."

Like most music hall acts, these first five turns each ran only ten or fifteen minutes long. The art of the music hall was in assembling these short performances into a well-composed program of ascending wonders—the first act was often deliberately sacrificed to the stragglers, who arrived with their glasses of beer and awkwardly stumbled through the rows of spectators, high-stepping over each set of knees as they searched for their seats. Those ten minutes were devoted to grabbing the audience's attention and settling them down. Then a few flashy or fast-moving acts could impart enough energy to carry them through the mediocre performances that, of necessity, filled out the center of the program. The idea was to build steadily to the big finish, the most anticipated attraction. When the local music hall was lucky enough to engage a star for the week, a closing act whose name could be proclaimed in extra-large type at the top of the bill, invariably the whole show seemed infused with a magical, electric energy. The anticipation seemed palpable; every burst of applause seemed to crackle with excitement, every joke seemed funnier, every song brighter and more memorable.

Just past ten o'clock, Will H. Fox stood at his piano bench, and in response to a flurry of laughter and applause, he bowed deeply, scanned the audience with a broad smile, and marched to the wings with a grand, purposeful stride as the front curtain dropped. There was a brief pause as the orchestra picked up their instruments and Forbes Russell raised his baton. Then the gong echoed through the Wood Green Empire, followed by an energetic flurry from the violins—a convincing oriental crescendo—to announce the star attraction. The curtain rose on a beautiful silk backdrop, painted in shades of blue and white in a recreation of that famous scene found on china services, the arched boughs, curved bridge, and distant pagoda of the famous Willow Pattern. This silk curtain swept open, showing a row of Chinese assistants standing in line, bowing to the audience. Behind them, another round curtain opened, revealing a blue and white scene behind it, then another, and another: nested concentric circles creating the illusion of the Willow Pattern coming to life. As the stage was gradually revealed, the audience saw a final row of Chinese assistants, flanking one final upright circle in the center of the stage. The assistants turned and bowed, the kettledrums rumbled with anticipation, and the disc was raised to show a tall, handsome, swarthy Asian man posed in profile. This was Chung Ling Soo.

The Marvelous Chinese Conjurer.

Soo turned to the audience and walked slowly to the footlights with a kind of bowlegged swagger, shifting his weight from leg to leg beneath his gold embroidered silk robe. He bowed to the center, to the left and to the right, and then slowly removed his cylindrical mandarin hat, which was taken by a waiting assistant. With a fixed smile he opened his robe, turned on his heel and tossed the robe back off his shoulders; another assistant stepped behind him to catch the garment with a flourish.

Beneath the embroidered robe, Soo was dressed simply, in dark silk pants and a loose oriental tunic, in an artistic contrast to the bright scenery and the colorful robes worn by his assistants. Like any virtuoso, Chung Ling Soo began his show in gradual steps, with small, elegant exercises in conjuring. He tore a strip of tissue paper into dozens of separate pieces, which he wadded at his fingertips. Blowing on the torn bits, he opened the bundle, slowly, slowly, to reveal that the pieces had fused back together again. He held the strip high in the air, and then dropped it from his fingertips so it fluttered to the floor. In his small movements, Chung Ling Soo exhibited a regal grace. He changed a vase of ink into a vase of water, and made a purple silk handkerchief disappear on one side of the stage and reappear on the other, tied securely between two yellow handkerchiefs.

The magician was almost completely bald, with a small patch of hair at the back of his head, ending in a long black braided queue. He never spoke during his performance. At several points, one of his main assistants, Kametaro, offered the few necessary words of explanation, apologizing that Chung Ling Soo could not speak English. Soo listened intently to Kametaro's words, eyes half closed, smiling and nodding in casual agreement. After almost 18 years in the British music halls, Chung Ling Soo had never needed any words. He was a master of pantomime, accentuating every illusion with his dramatic poses and expressive gestures. His eyes twinkled as he performed, and with a cocked eyebrow or a crooked smile, he perfectly conveyed what was then thought to be the oriental sense of humor.

As a sign of his stardom, Chung Ling Soo was not merely a ten-minute act on the music hall stage; he performed half the program, a full fifty-five minutes of magic. After establishing his credentials with the audience as a master of sleight-of-hand deceptions, he smoothly transitioned to larger and larger wonders. The curtains opened on five wooden crates, each filled with glass bottles of stout. Soo moved from crate to crate, examining the contents and indicating pleasure at the discovery. With a casual gesture, he directed his assistants to stack the crates. When the heavy boxes were assembled into a tall column, a fabric canopy was whisked over the tower of stout. Seconds later the fabric was drawn away and the boxes and bottles had disappeared. In their place was one gigantic, six-foot-tall bottle. Soo registered his delight, rubbing his hands together before reaching over to the oval label on the bottle. He looked out at the audience with a wink—there was one more surprise in store—then swung open the label like a door. Inside the bottle was Suee Seen, the co-star of the show and Soo's wife, a delicate Chinese maiden with a pale white face and narrow dark eyes: a living porcelain doll. Offering the magician her tiny hand, she stepped from the opening in the bottle and bowed, palms pressed together, first to Soo, and then turning to acknowledge the applause of the audience.

By 10:30, Chung Ling Soo was well into his program, and the pace of the illusions quickened, a sign of his innate showmanship. He held up an arrow attached to a long white rope, and then loaded both into the barrel of a rifle. Suee Seen took her place on the opposite side of the stage, standing in front of a large round target. Soo lowered the rifle, pointing it directly at the Chinese princess, and fired. The arrow and rope flashed across the stage, passed through her body and impaled itself in the bull's eye of the target. Suee Seen, her eyes tightly shut, released a short, sharp scream of surprise, which precisely mirrored the audience's reaction. The rope was threaded through the center of her body! Soo slowly approached her and, whispering in her ear, tenderly convinced her to open her eyes. He slowly led her forward to the footlights, demonstrating to the audience that the white rope had passed through the waist. Soo tugged it to and fro as she looked down in amazement. Pulling the rope free of her body, Suee Seen regained her composure, smiled sweetly, and skipped into the wings.

Moments later, Soo's wife entered again, now in a different bright silk costume, and hopped onto a wide table in the center of the stage. A tall metal cylinder, some two feet across, was lowered over her, covering her completely. Soo clapped his hands, the cylinder was lifted, and in her place was an enormous orange tree, its branches filled with green foliage and ripe fruit. Soo and an assistant reached up to the branches of the tree, picking handfuls of oranges and placing them in a basket. Using a mighty, underhanded pitch, Soo tossed each orange into the audience. The oranges were propelled to the back of the theater, to the far corners of the balcony, to specific seats in the dress circle as the audience clamored for their souvenirs. Each orange had a small red paper label tied to its stem, a portrait of the magician. One of the last oranges was tossed straight up the aisle, where the spotlight settled on Suee Seen herself, magically rematerialized and standing in the midst of the audience.

Music hall habitués would have seen Soo's show before, at Wood Green or many of the other halls in the area, and they remembered some of his most popular illusions, determined this time to watch the performance even more closely. During his years on the stage, through trial and error Soo had added many new features, concentrating on a large repertoire that he tailored to his own personality. Of course, he had imitators. After he had become established in the halls, there were many other magicians who pretended to be Chinese, donning yellow greasepaint and glossy black wigs, squinting and grinning at their audiences, or yammering some pidgin gibberish. Soo prided himself on the authentic and indulged in none of the standard clichés. The public knew that he was the real thing. Some in the audience that night probably recalled the newspaper scandal, about a dozen years earlier, when another "Chinese" magician appeared in London and started performing under a deceptively similar name comprised of Chinese syllables. In a bid for publicity, the imitator had offered an affront to Chung Ling Soo and Suee Seen, accusing them of merely pretending to be Chinese. Chung Ling Soo and company arrived at the designated newspaper office, prepared for a magic duel, but at the last moment his detractor had lost his nerve and failed to show up. Ever since then, Chung Ling Soo had possessed the press's endorsement and the public's confidence.

During the years of the Great War, Chung Ling Soo's name had become a sort of trademark for miracles. British soldiers at the front had begun to turn it into a catch phrase. Faced with a typically impossible military order, they might mutter under their breath with an exaggerated Cockney accent: "An' jus' 'oo do you think *I* am? *Chung Ling Soo!*"

The Chinese Ring Trick was one of his specialties, included in his show for many years. Suee Seen held a stack of a dozen large, heavy metal rings, each about eight inches across. She handed each of the rings to various members of the audience, gesturing that they be examined carefully for any breaks or gaps. The rings were collected again and tossed up to the stage where Soo began to link them together into a large chain. First two rings, linked and unlinked as he held them at his fingertips. The process seemed effortless: steel rings softening to melt through each other, then hardening again. He tossed the rings high into the air and linked them, with a clang of steel against steel, as they descended. He linked three rings, then four, five, and six. Soo interlocked the rings in a number of places, forming woven chains or impressive knots of steel. Finally he assembled all of the rings in a line and then folded them together again, forming a jumble of steel loops that hung like so many keys dangling from a single ring. He paused only briefly for applause. With a final shake, the rings came loose again, miraculously dropping to the stage, separate and single.

At 10:40 that night at Wood Green, the tone of Chung Ling Soo's show shifted dramatically. A beautiful silk curtain, emblazoned with the imperial Chinese dragon in green and gold, obscured the stage. The orchestra took up an ominous march, which was suddenly repeated, in muffled tones on stage, with chimes and drumbeats. The curtain was raised on an elaborate setting, featuring a wide oriental archway. A phalanx of Chinese soldiers, in leather and bronze plate armor, marched though the arch toward the audience, beating the time on their native drums. Two of the soldiers rested long rifles on their shoulders.

As the line of soldiers parted, another line of assistants appeared through the archway with an elaborately carved ebony and gold palanquin. Carrying the palanquin forward by its horizontal handles, they set it on the stage and opened the door to reveal Chung Ling Soo seated inside. As he stepped out, the audience saw that he had donned the elaborate headdress and the quilted robe of a Chinese warrior. His face was fixed in a somber gaze, as if lost in thought.

His assistant Kametaro stepped forward to address the audience in broken English. "Ladies and Gentlemen, if you please . . . Chung Ling Soo now demonstrates how he was condemned by the Boxers during the rebellion, and executed by firing squad. How he defied their bullets! And again, tonight, on our stage just as in Peking many years ago."

Chung Ling Soo took several deliberate steps away from the footlights, removing himself from the action.

Kametaro continued his instructions: "Two gentlemen on stage, please. Two men who know something of guns, who have loaded bullets." He scanned the front row of spectators for audience

Poster advertising the bullet-catching feat, showing five gunmen.

members who were willing to help. That night there was a bit of hesitation, so Kametaro continued with flattery. "Do we have any British soldiers in our audience, any brave young men who know their guns, please? Surely you would be willing to step up here, on behalf of the audience."

One soldier in uniform stood up and made his way from the side of the auditorium to the stage. Seated in a different spot in the auditorium, another young man—also a soldier but out of uniform—decided to join him. These two volunteers were quickly handed the rifles to examine.

The British soldiers, blinking uncomfortably in the spotlights, discovered that their experience with guns was actually of little value. Chung Ling Soo's rifles were muzzle-loaders, two old-fashioned weapons that were markedly different from the automatic rifles they had been trained to use in the British army. They peered down the barrels, checked the trigger, and nodded in agreement. Yes, they were real guns.

"Now, please select two bullets. Real bullets, you'll find." From a box of bullets, each soldier selected one and held it up in the spotlight so the audience could see. The bullets were large round slugs, about the size of marbles. Suee Seen stepped up to the men, holding a small metal cup in her hands, and she signaled for the men to drop the bullets inside. Kametaro continued, "Miss Suee Seen shows you the two bullets. Could we have two gentlemen in our audience mark them? A scratch or a mark that you will see again. . . ." She stepped off the stage and down the stairs, locating two gentlemen seated on the aisle who agreed to mark the bullets. She reached into the cup, lifting out the first bullet, and handed it to a man along with a small knife so he could scratch an identifying mark into the soft lead. The second bullet was given to a second spectator, and the marking repeated.

The Chinese assistants talked them through the procedure as the audience watched intently. First, a tin of gunpowder was shown and some of the powder was sprinkled onto a small tray. "Real gunpowder? Is it real?" Kametaro asked. One of the soldiers smelled the powder. Kametaro carried the tray of powder forward, touching a lighted match to it. The powder exploded with a white flash and a small acrid puff of smoke. "Yes, real powder," he answered his own question. Kametaro poured a charge of gunpowder into each of the two rifles. The Chinese assistants followed with the cotton wads. Each rifle held a metal ramrod beneath the barrel; these were unsheathed, and, as the soldiers from the audience supervised, each charge and wadding was tamped down.

In the aisle of the theater, the marked bullets were dropped into the cup with two sharp pings, and Suee Seen quickly returned to the stage, where she tipped the contents into the hands of the waiting volunteers. Each British soldier took a bullet, looked over the marks so they would recognize them again, and dropped their bullets into the barrels of the rifles. The Chinese assistants followed with another cotton wad, which was rammed in place. They set the ramrods aside on the table and then positioned the percussion caps on the guns. With another rattle of the native drums, Soo's cast escorted the young soldiers to the side of the stage so they could watch the finish of the illusion.

"Ladies and Gentlemen, silence please. Silence for Chung Ling Soo," Kametaro warned. He pointed ominously at the men seated on the aisle. "Two bullets! You have seen to it that the bullets were marked." Then pointing to the side, to the volunteer soldiers, "And you seen the guns loaded. Now silence, and watch closely. Watch, everyone."

Chung Ling Soo backed slowly into place, to the far right of the stage, from the audience's viewpoint. He stood just several feet in front of the curtain. An assistant handed him a porcelain plate, which he gripped tightly between his hands. Meanwhile, the Chinese riflemen took their positions on the opposite side, duplicating a chilling execution by firing squad. They slowly lifted the rifles to their shoulders. Between the riflemen and the victim stood Kametaro, well back of the firing line, his sword drawn and raised over his head, awaiting the final signal.

The Chinese magician paused dramatically, drew a deep breath, and then raised the plate until it was in front of his chest. Holding his pose for a moment, he created an incongruous picture—his small porcelain plate brandished like a shield. It was a reminder of the odd Boxer cult that had inspired the Chinese rebellion in 1900, reported in a series of lurid newspaper headlines around the world. According to the Boxers' mystical beliefs, they were impervious to foreign bullets. Now Chung Ling Soo would demonstrate how his magic surpassed even the claims of the Boxers. He braced himself, looking down to widen his stance, and then took another deep breath. With a quick nod to Kametaro, he signaled that he was ready.

Kametaro lowered his sword sharply. The Chinese riflemen, who had been posed, immobile, guns pointed in careful aim, squeezed their triggers.

The last drumbeats ended as the riflemen took their positions. Chung Ling Soo's audience sat in breathless silence. There had been no music from the orchestra to break the tension. The prolonged stillness only accentuated the two sudden, almost simultaneous cracks from the rifles. The sharp explosions echoed off the hard white plaster and gold filigree of Frank Matcham's theater, and drew an involuntary gasp from many in the audience. It was 10:45 p.m.

—ᵐ—

An audience was lucky to see the gun illusion. For 12 years, Chung Ling Soo had included Condemned to Death by the Boxers in his shows, but it was performed erratically, unexpectedly, as a special dramatic feature, and only at the whim of the star. He never presented it on a matinee, which was arranged for children and families. The gun trick was seldom advertised, and almost never promised on the playbill. Later that Saturday night, as the audience stood on the sidewalk outside the Wood Green Empire and discussed what they had just seen, they studied the fine print of their programs. Even allowing for the romantic titles that magicians used to advertise their specialties—The Mystic Bottle was the illusion in which little bottles became the giant bottle, The Living Target was the rope and arrow trick—they found no mention of the gun illusion.

Like any good joke or a popular song, a great magic trick not only surprises its audience but also reaches its climax by fulfilling expectations, by completing every element of foreshadowing. It ends by achieving a magical but perfectly logical ending. For a dozen years, even though the situation had seemed impossible, Chung Ling Soo's porcelain plate did manage to stop the bullets. Upon the crack of the rifles, Soo thrust the plate forward, then twisted it upright in his hands—from a shield to a tray. The audience heard the snap as the bullets hit the porcelain, then the rattle as they whizzed around like a roulette ball in a circle within the lip of the plate. He stepped toward the footlights, offering the bullets to the two volunteers from the audience. The men would dip their fingers into the plate, pick up the two lead slugs, and identify the marks as Soo smiled with relief. For many years, that was the inevitable, theatrical climax of Condemned to Death by the Boxers. Soo then offered hearty handshakes to his volunteers—first a western handshake, then a Chinese handshake, clutching his own hands and bobbing them up and down in front of his chest—as the men were escorted back to their seats and the orchestra sounded a triumphal chord. Sometimes he awarded his volunteers the bullets as mementos. Occasionally he gave away the plate.

If everything had proceeded as planned, Chung Ling Soo would have continued with the finale of his show. His popular fire-eating feat was scheduled next, and it climaxed when the burning embers in his mouth were instantly transformed into a shower of colored silk ribbons. Then the curtains would have swept open, revealing a large metal globe set within a raised stand. Showing the metal sphere empty and then closing it again, he would have magically produced a line of costumed actors from its interior. In the program it was called The World and its People.

—⁂—

At 10:45 p.m. on March 23, 1918, as the shots rang through the theater, Soo reeled, twisting slightly to his right. His shoulders arched. He dropped the plate, which smashed against the wooden stage floor.

His assistants, familiar with the clockwork precision of his performances, watched dumbfounded. Used to the rhythm of the show and anxious to get backstage to their next costume change, they turned to see the nightmarish scene. Soo shouted out a few words—the company onstage and spectators in the first few rows heard him distinctly—and then backed up several steps toward the wings as his knees began to buckle. A technician from the wings rushed on, catching the magician's shoulders and easing him to the ground. It was only when Soo fell onto the stage, his eyes wide and his mouth contorted into a tight grimace, that his assistants noticed the dark stain on the front of his robe.

Chung Ling Soo's cast rushed to him. Some, like his wife Suee Seen, ran on from the wings, crouching by his side. For several uncomfortable seconds, the music hall patrons watched the clutch of nervous actors leaning over Soo's crumpled figure and listened to the murmurs and overlapping, barked orders—frantic commands that were being echoed by stagehands behind the curtains. After hearing Soo call out, the stage manager signaled for the curtain to be lowered, which spared the audience the climax of the tragic scene. Seconds later, the white Bioscope screen fell quickly into place, and the projectionist in the booth took his cue; the latest silent newsreel from the War Office started with a flicker. Several minutes later, the film abruptly stopped, and the orchestra instinctively took up their instruments for the obligatory "God Save the King." The audience rose in an uneasy chorus before pushing their way out the doors and into the cool spring night.

—⚏—

It was only with Monday morning's newspapers that the nearly two thousand spectators at the Wood Green Empire, along with the rest of London, learned the truth. Chung Ling Soo had died, just hours after he fell, from his unexpected gunshot wound. The imaginary execution that they watched that night—the examined guns, the marked bullets, the methodical process of loading the rifles with powder—now seemed insidious and horrifying because it had proved to be real. The audience had eagerly watched every detail of the illusion, seduced by Chung Ling Soo's miraculous abilities. They expected a logical, magical, happy ending, not the tragedy that they had witnessed.

—m—

At first, the casualty seemed completely inconceivable. Soo's own staff was shocked by his death and could offer no explanations, neither for how he successfully caught the bullets every night, nor for how he failed on the last night. Magicians around the world were mystified. Harry Houdini, fulfilling a long engagement at New York's Hippodrome Theater—he was making an elephant disappear twice every night—dashed off a note to a colleague attempting to analyze what happened on the Wood Green stage. "From what cabled accounts I have read, it seems as if there were something peculiar about the whole affair, and as soon as I get details will let you know. There are only two ways it could have happened. One is a failure of exchange . . . or mixture of bullets." Houdini, who had been badly fooled by his friend Chung Ling Soo, included the most sinister possibility. "[If] one of the men instead of loading the trick cartridge would substitute one of his own . . . that would be murder."

—m—

Slowly, painfully, the details of Chung Ling Soo's death became known from public testimony, reports in the newspaper, or letters between his friends and associates: how he caught the bullets and why he chanced to fail in one show. These revelations led to the complicated history and relationships of this music hall star. Like the fine silk threads from his precious robes, his secrets began to unwind and fray, destroying beautiful patterns that had been carefully woven over the course of a long career. The very first clue, the thread that had quickly unraveled, was heard by a handful of spectators seated near the stage on that Saturday night. Although Chung Ling Soo, the "Marvelous Chinese Conjurer," had never uttered a word from the stage during his long career, a moment after the rifles sounded, he cried out quite audibly to the people around him, in perfect English, "Oh my God. Something's happened. Lower the curtain."

—⁓—

Houdini was not alone in thinking there was something suspicious and sinister about Soo's death. A number of the Chinese magician's associates attempted to braid together the confusing threads of the tragedy, and invariably wove plots of murder, revenge, infidelity, and betrayal. Or, strangest of all, there was speculation of a sensational public suicide, the result of many deceptions that had led to self-doubt and fatal despair.

An odd coincidence provided part of the solution to Chung Ling Soo's mystery. Few people realized that his career had not started in Imperial Chinese splendor, but in the cheapest dime museums and the most notorious variety stages, with a lifetime of secrets that were alternately guarded, hoarded, stolen, hijacked, or purloined. The ascendancy of the Marvelous Chinese Conjurer could be explained in five words, and they had been in plain sight of the Wood Green Empire audience, the gilded letters that had framed his last performance.

As the quotation continued from Shakespeare's *As You Like It:*

> All the world's a stage
> And all the men and women merely players:
> They have their exits and entrances;
> And one man in his time plays many parts,
> ... Seeking the bubble reputation
> Even in the cannon's mouth.

Chapter 2

HARRY HILL'S SALOON

A
udiences have never noticed that the most glorious deception in any theater isn't a stage illusion, a plot twist, or a
special effect, but the theater itself.

Nineteenth-century theaters appealed to the public with their
lush, exotic décor. Finished like marble palaces, the interiors gave the
impression of comfort, permanence, and security. But many theaters
in the Victorian age were little more than rough wooden ware-
houses, simply framed and then slathered with plaster inside that
could be deceptively painted like stone. Even this pretense stopped
at the curtain line. Above the stage, the flies, or the tower to raise
and lower the scenery, consist of a tall dusty shaft filled with dry
timber and enormous sheets of painted fabric. Curtains, carpeting,
and upholstery were all highly flammable.

From the early 1820s, the artistic preference was for gas lighting,
which consisted of open flames behind glass fixtures. Even at the
end of the century, when electric lights were used onstage, the gen-
erators, early lighting elements, and fabric-wrapped copper wires all
tended to overheat, spark, or short. Electricity certainly wasn't considered safe.

Fortunately, theaters only housed their audiences for several
hours a night—the illusion of safety fleetingly put to the test. Theaters
burned and theater fires were dreaded by all show business professionals. History records that many famous theaters—like Drury
Lane in London, Niblo's Garden in New York, or McVickers in
Chicago—were actually successions of theaters, continually restored
and rebuilt upon ashes.

Added to the mix were the treacherous flashes of ego or adrenalin found in any performance. It wasn't uncommon for the cast or crew to be overtired, underprepared, yet still emboldened by a kind of raw energy. Some actors found fearlessness in a bottle, but most came by it naturally. All theater professionals felt it and came to rely upon it. On any given night, the star might sing his song with an extra twinkle; the sword fight would be enacted with bloodthirsty thrusts that were never there in rehearsal; the stagehands would work adventurously at double speed. Foolish decisions were made, as well. In the darkness behind the scenes, obvious mistakes were ignored, all for the sake of the show.

Harry Hill's famous Concert Saloon was one of the rowdiest dives in New York. It was a two-story wood frame building on Houston Street near Crosby in the Bowery. A lantern on the porch, with red and blue colored lenses, illuminated the two entrances. A large door admitted men for twenty-five cents each. A smaller door was for the ladies, who could enter free of charge. Actually, no *lady* ever set foot in Harry Hill's Saloon, but it was regularly filled with waitresses, dance hall girls, and prostitutes. Inside, there was no attempt at glamour; the interior walls had been knocked down—still showing the various heights and wallpapers of each small room—to make a large open space that served as a dance hall, barroom, variety theater, Punch and Judy show, and boxing ring. In the next room was the billiard parlor. With a little perspective, we can see Hill's notorious saloon as a transitional experiment in entertainment. It was a sort of petri dish where several features were combined and developed. As a sports parlor, it anticipated the appeal of sporting events and hosted, on its uneven wooden stage, the first New York match of the great pugilist John L. Sullivan. As a variety theater, Hill's provided the training ground for a number of singers and actors, decades before pretentious, high-flown terms like vaudeville or music hall had entered the public consciousness.

Of course, like any petri dish, it was also a dirty, steamy little collection of vermin and on any given day was not fascinating so much as deeply unattractive.

Harry Hill straightened his vest, marched to the edge of the curtained platform against the wall of his saloon, and held up a hand. "Order! Order!" But his customers were typically drunk and rambunctious. "Order, the lot of yer!" he growled. "I'll crack the skull of any man who can't settle down! Be quiet, I say! I want a little respect for the dearly departed, or I'll teach yer about respect, right here!"

The owner of this peculiar establishment was a square-jawed ex-fighter who wore black dye and Macassar in his hair and an enormous diamond stud on his shirtfront. Harry Hill was born in Epsom, England, in 1816 and worked at the race track in his early years. He was brought to Astoria, New York, in the early 1850s to manage a large stable, and then several years later came to the east side of New York City as a horse dealer. He also gained a reputation as a wrestler, boxer, and sportsman. He opened his saloon on Houston Street, "the resort of sporting and betting men," although, according to the *New York Times*, "the men who frequented this place were almost exclusively bad characters, and were either pugilists or men who would go anywhere to see a fight."

Hill never managed to improve the clientele, but he kept them in line with a list of posted rules and his own helpful advice: seats were for women, foul language was not allowed, a round of drinks was obligatory at the start of any dance, and "take a little wine for thy stomach's stake." The most important decree was that no trouble take place within his patchwork walls, which meant that the local pimps, prostitutes, thieves, and drunkards who filled his saloon were all obliged to step outside before beginning a transaction, planning a crime, or picking a fight.

That was fine with Hill. He went to church on Sunday and prayer meetings on Wednesday, donated to charity, and wrote bad poetry, which was ostentatiously read to his glassy-eyed audiences once a week. The *Times* described Hill as "a queer combination of the lawless, reckless, rough and the honest man." He was famous for

Harry Hill, the infamous saloon owner in
Lower Manhattan.

protecting his drunken customers by taking money away from
them, and then returning it when they sobered up. On one occasion,
an intoxicated guest pulled Hill aside and entrusted him with an
$84,000 bankroll for safekeeping. The next morning, the man had
forgotten all about it, although he had a hazy recollection of having
been at Hill's. When he returned there, Harry Hill surprised him by
producing the roll of money, handing it to the man and advising him
to leave New York City before he took another drink.

Hill's rules were strictly enforced with fisticuffs, and evenings at his
saloon consisted of the proprietor strutting in patrol, defining wide circles around the room, shushing the troublemakers, offering seats to
the ladies, or pulling offenders by their collars out to the pavement. He
had an amazing effect on his customers, the same way that a great lion
tamer seems to hypnotize wild beasts, and his Concert Saloon earned
a reputation as the most lawful den of iniquity in the city. The bawdy
evenings and rough clientele became tourist attractions; out-of-town
ministers might arrive in search of material for their next sermons, and

slack-jawed visitors from the Midwest were given a taste of the New York they'd read about in lurid crime magazines.

The saloon was open and serving liquor all night, attractions which required hefty payoffs to police officials. Still, it was publicly shut down several times in response to crusading city politicians. Later, after the headlines had been printed and the moralists appeased, the red and blue lantern would quietly be lit up again. By most accounts, after the bribes, protection money, and court cases, Hill still wound up with almost a million dollars after two decades as a saloon owner, although he lost much of it to wagers, bad investments, and impetuous loans to his loyal friends.

Pounding with his fist on a nearby table, Harry Hill quieted the room. "That's better! I hope that yez all said a prayer for the poor souls in Brooklyn, may the good lord protect 'em!" There was a murmur of agreement. "Tonight, we're going to start the show with a special song. Our stage manager Jim Campbell has composed a sad ballad about the Brooklyn fire."

It wasn't much of an introduction, but Jim Campbell took his cue and pushed aside the curtain. Jim Campbell's real name was James Campbell Robinson. He was 43 years old, with sandy red hair, a curled moustache, bright blue eyes, and a ruddy complexion. The father of three children, including William Robinson, he was a real professional—a favorite at Harry Hill's—and he knew instinctively how to deliver a performance. The pianist offered eight bars, Campbell cleared his throat and began to sing in a clear tenor.

> I sing the tale of misery, of terror and of death,
> That makes this life a burden to the ones in sorrow left;
> That sent, thro' many a household, sore misfortune swift and dire;
> Of the dead and living heroes of that fearful Brooklyn fire.

—◆—

Campbell's song was taken from the recent headlines. On the evening of Tuesday, December 5, 1876, the popular actress Kate

Claxton was appearing in the melodrama "The Two Orphans" at the Brooklyn Theater, when a backdrop behind the scenes caught fire. It was eleven o'clock, and the audience had just returned to their seats for the last act. In the wings, a "moonlight cut scene," a painted profile of canvas and netting, had been accidentally pushed against a kerosene lamp as the crew was moving some canvas flats. At first, no one noticed. The show was long and complicated, with a great deal of scenery and a large cast; at that moment the stagehands were busy. When the glow was first seen, just a small flame licking up the edge of the fabric, a stage carpenter attempted to strike off the burning section with a pole. It should have been an easy job, but the flames extended beyond his reach. A group of carpenters argued over the next option. The scenery could have just been pulled down, but this would have, in turn, brought down the canvas for the scene being played onstage, sending it falling onto the actors. The front curtain could have been dropped and the entire stage cleared, but at that moment the fire seemed so insignificant that they feared that would only create a panic.

Those brief moments of raised voices backstage occupied a critical interval. As the carpenters made their plans, a draft blew the fire vertically, where it jumped from scene to scene across the grid, high above the stage. Now enormous sheets of canvas were wrapped with flame. The technicians knew that the theater was lost.

Unfortunately, "The Two Orphans" was a popular show and the Brooklyn Theater was filled with nearly a thousand people, as many as four hundred in the balcony. The audience had cheered each melodramatic duel and sobbed when Kate Claxton's blind orphan was reduced to begging for coins on the snowy Paris streets. The Broadway playwright and producer James Steele MacKaye arrived that night to watch Kate Claxton in her famous role, and, unable to find an available seat, he'd been given a chair in a corner of the orchestra pit. The theater was an impressive three-story brick structure, just six years old, which had been built on an L-shaped lot at Washington and Johnson streets in Brooklyn. But like every theater of the time, it was simply a vertical space

lined with layers of flammable materials and packed with customers. There were no emergency exits, just five narrow doors
leading in to the auditorium.

From his seat in the orchestra pit, a strange flash of light at the
side of the stage caught MacKaye's attention. He crouched down to
peer into the flies, where he saw a strip of flame climbing upwards.
He calmly stood and stepped over the railing of the orchestra pit,
walking up the aisle with the intention of alerting an usher. Meanwhile, the curtain was quickly lowered and Mr. Thorpe, the stage
manager, stepped out from the wings to explain the situation. But
the dark smoke, quickly rolling over the heads of the audience, had
already been noticed. Neither MacKaye nor Thorpe was heard.
Shafts of orange flame began pushing through crevices in the
scenery, illuminating the auditorium like bursts of hellish lightning.
As one, the spectators realized their fate, raised their voices in desperate shouts, and made frantic scrambles for the doors.

The next day the *Brooklyn Union* had difficulty conveying the
appalling suddenness of it all. "To the uninitiated it is impossible to
show how rapidly the flames will spread when once under headway
upon a stage. The frame upon which the scenery is supported is
wood of the lightest description, and if the theater has any age what-
soever, is as dry as tinder; the canvas is cotton painted, and therefore
highly flammable; the ropes, the unused scenes lying against the
walls, the numberless gas jets feeding the flames, the light timber,
all of these make a fuel upon which the flames feed with astonishing
rapidity. . . . In less than ten minutes from the time the fire was discovered the stage was enveloped in volumes and vast sheets of
flame, while the roar and crackling was awe inspiring."

The section of seats on the main floor, the most expensive seats,
was small and these patrons were able to find the exit and leave the
theater. MacKaye was one of the first out the door, although he
found himself standing in the cold without his coat. Similarly,
almost everyone in the dress circle escaped, although in the panic a
number fell and were injured in the crush. The actors and technicians behind the scenes, who found themselves surrounded by the

inferno, might have been luckiest of all. Almost all of them survived, by using the stage door that led directly to Johnson Street.

But the gallery, the upper balcony of cheaper seats, was filled with families who had entered up the stairs through two narrow doorways. They were doomed. The newspaper reported, "The panic that possessed these poor beings is something too intense to be described. The whole mass struggled to the doors when a huge block occurred. The young and the weak were knocked down and trampled upon and at the doors the people were literally wedged together. . . . Many losing their senses, becoming frantic, insane through fear and utterly despairing of life, leaped into the raging flames beneath."

Thirty minutes later, the brick wall behind the stage collapsed into Johnson Street, which only fed the flames with a fresh blast of air. The Brooklyn fire brigade, surrounding the building and dousing it with water, could do little else but watch helplessly. Ninety minutes after the initial flames, the building had been reduced to an empty brick shell, and the flames continued to roar.

The fire struck when other shows throughout Manhattan were just lowering their curtains and showmen and stagehands were gathering in the bars. Several panicked telegrams were dispatched across the East River, and the news of the disaster was passed, from stage door to stage door, up and down Broadway and the Bowery. The jeweled society audience attending the latest revival of "The School for Scandal" stepped out of the Fifth Avenue Theater and onto a sidewalk ringed with newsboys peddling their extras. "Brooklyn Fire! Tremendous loss of life!"

As the sun rose the next morning on the Brooklyn Theater, it revealed a crowd of people, cold, raw, tear-stained, muddy, and covered with soot. Many were there in desperation, searching for family or friends, listening to the rumors that percolated down the sidewalk, and eager for real news. Their misery was shared by a steady stream of citizens from Manhattan, stunned by the disaster and following the black smoke in the sky. They arrived on ferries, passing beneath the stone towers of the uncompleted Brooklyn Bridge.

As soon as the light allowed, policemen, firemen, and members of the thirteenth regiment of the National Guard began the grim task of searching for bodies. They were found, stacked like layers of cordwood, beneath the stairways, surrounding the doors, pressed against the hallways. By noon the morgue was filled, and a nearby brick warehouse had been requisitioned for more bodies. In all, two hundred and ninety-five victims were located, and one hundred and three were buried in a common grave at nearby Green-Wood Cemetery; some were never identified. At that time, it was the most devastating theater tragedy in the United States.

—⁓—

The fire had horrified the country and devastated the cities of Brooklyn and New York. It also inspired important reforms in fire safety, seating plans, and exit doors. Steele MacKaye, who had seen the fire from his vantage point in the orchestra pit and then witnessed its devastation from the sidewalk, began his own experiments with fireproof scenery and later patented a folding theater seat, to help widen each aisle for an evacuation. Every theater in the city felt the tragedy at its box office; the winter season of 1876–77 collapsed and many shows were canceled.

The night of the fire, Jim Campbell had made his way across the East River to Brooklyn as soon as he heard the news. A week later, at the Little Church Around the Corner on Twenty-ninth Street in Manhattan, he attended the funeral of the two actors who had lost their lives in the fire, Henry Murdoch and Claude Burroughs, from the Brooklyn Theater Company. The last verse of Campbell's "Brooklyn Fire!" explained:

> Our country's known some glorious deaths, that made our heart's
> blood freeze;
> Our soldiers at the cannon's mouth, our sailors on the seas;
> But fame's bright scroll, all glittering o'er, no prouder names can
> boast
> Than Murdoch and brave Burroughs too, who died while at their post.

Jim Campbell stretched the point by praising the two actors' "glorious deaths . . . at their post," or comparing them to heroes "at the cannon's mouth." When the fire was first seen, Murdoch and Burroughs foolishly ran up the backstage stairs to the dressing rooms, no doubt to retrieve their clothing, and became trapped by the flames; their bodies were found in the wreckage. Real heroes of the fire had been identified, like the young man who was passing by the theater when the alarm sounded, and ran inside to save others and perished himself; or the suave doorman who had led the evacuation and was trampled by the crowd. Still, Campbell can hardly be blamed for his emotional overstatement, or for lionizing the actors. "The Brooklyn Fire!" became a popular favorite that propelled the singer/composer through the local theaters, and was sold as sheet music for parlor pianos.

―∞―

Harry Hill thought of himself as a sportsman, an entrepreneur, and a poet, but he didn't pretend to be in show business. That's why he had hired Jim Campbell as his stage manager. Campbell contracted the acts, organized the programs, and kept the shows running smoothly through the evening.

James Campbell Robinson had been born in 1833, of Scottish parents living in New York. As a young man he married Sarah Titus, also from New York and born in 1840. His first son, William Ellsworth Robinson, was born on April 2, 1861, in Westchester County, New York. The family settled on the lower east side of Manhattan. A second son, Edward, was born in 1863 and a daughter, Maud, in 1871.

James Campbell Robinson's early show business experience had been in Charley White's touring minstrel show, traveling across the country in horse-drawn wagons. Minstrel shows were, by the end of the Civil War, highly formulaic productions: songs, jokes, acts, and sketches built upon a line of black-faced clowns—coarse caricatures of the lazy Negro, the wily Negro, the dandified Negro—and organized in separate acts. The usual formula was to open with the minstrel line, a semicircle of chairs with the two musicians, "Mr. Tambo" and "Mr. Bones," seated on either end of the row. They mocked the grandly formal master of ceremonies, the "interlocutor," who sat in the center and introduced each specialty. Everyone in the line, in turn, contributed to the music or comedy. The first act ended with a rousing song.

The second act resembled a variety program, with the curtain rising and lowering on different routines, dances, impersonations, political monologues, and comic stump speeches, with an occasional novelty act like a juggler or ventriloquist. An especially sentimental song might be given its own showcase during this act.

The finale of the show was a one-act farce, incorporating the entire cast. Often these were parodies of current plays, operas, or Shakespeare—the grander the subject, the sillier the result. Much of the humor derived from inserting the comic "Ethiopians" into these roles, burlesquing high culture and punning real song lyrics or scripts. Invariably, the farce ended happily with a grand cakewalk, a high-stepping musical parade of the entire cast around the stage.

Each minstrel troupe had its specialty. Leavitt's minstrels boasted an especially large line; the Christy Minstrels were known for the quality of their music, having introduced many Stephen Foster songs; Primrose and West offered opulent costumes; and the San Francisco Minstrels were renowned for their wild improvisational comedy. Charley White's own specialty was the "Darkey Play," which closed the show. This gradually became the focus of his performance, and White wrote dozens of these farces during his career.

Minstrel shows are remembered today for the offensively racist characterization of blacks: white comedians in burnt cork, rolling their eyes, simpering and drawling. By the late 1880s and '90s, talented African-American performers like Bert Williams and George Walker had ironically found success by "blacking up" and learning the proper lazy Southern accents, so they could appear in minstrel lines and dazzle the audiences with their skills.

These seat-of-your-pants tours of the 1860s were an education for

James Robinson—traveling by buckboard, unpacking at a dingy hall, arranging the scenery, and then performing in the show. It allowed the ambitious young performer to learn a great number of skills which would serve him through his career. Some of his early song titles probably date from compositions around this time. There were sentimental songs about the troops, like "The Boys that Shoulder the Guns" and "The Heroes who Fought on Both Sides," a Negro comic song—they were called "coon songs" at that time—called "Uncle Ben's Fight Wid De Debbil," and a melodramatic tearjerker, "Angels Watch O'er Her."

James Campbell Robinson specialized in character impersonations and dialect singing. Certainly he mastered the drawl of the stereotypical Negro, but also an Irish brogue, Scottish burr, and the broad accents that defined the "typical" Hebrew, Dutchman, or Italian. He dutifully studied ventriloquism, hypnotism (mesmerizing volunteers from the audience and putting them through comic paces), and became an adept magician, traveling with a small case of tinplate and wooden apparatus for his tricks, and the traditional gold-fringed table outfitted with secret shelves and trapdoors. When Punch and Judy shows became a fashion in America, he bought a set of puppets and advertised that he was available for engagements.

Early in his career, he dropped his last name and became Jim Campbell, which he may have adopted in imitation of the successful Campbell family of New York minstrels. He also worked as H. J. Campbell or Professor Campbell. Using the title "Professor" was a fashion for magicians and hypnotists, suggesting an impressive scientific background. In 1872, when Charley White organized his own small theater, White's Atheneum, at 585 Broadway, he hired Professor Campbell to perform Punch and Judy for his audiences.

Jim Campbell listed himself as "theater actor" on an 1870 form, but it was around this time that he started working as a stage manager for Harry Hill. This was the most successful engagement of his career, and arranging the performances at the Houston Street Concert Saloon—pleasing the motley customers, the performers, and

Hill himself—must have called for enormous quantities of tact, talent, and gritty resolve. The two shows, at 9:30 and 11:15, usually consisted of ten or twelve performers in quick succession. Hill's crowd naturally preferred lady singers, dancers, or acrobats. Then the stage was cleared, and the entertainment closed with a "Grand Boxing Match."

Of course, on any given night, Jim Campbell could dip into his bag of tricks and put on most of the show himself, even ducking into the puppet theater to please the crowd with the violent slapstick of Punch and Judy. His experience with so many skills does suggest a mastery of none, and Campbell's career seemed to gravitate toward second-class entertainments, as indicated by his special status at Harry Hill's.

Confident in his stage manager's talents, the saloon owner encouraged Campbell to accept the occasional outside engagement, singing his latest songs, performing his magic act, or appearing in a role in a downtown melodrama. "Remember, You Have Children of Your Own" was a "motto song" Campbell had written for his friend Frank Lewis, who was billed as "The Great Motto Vocalist." In this case, the motto was part of a lushly sentimental lyric, typical of the Victorian era.

> In your path thro' life each day, you will meet along the way,
> Fellow mortals upon whom this world doth frown;
>
> They were once to someone dear, so don't pass them with a sneer,
> But speak a kindly word in cheering tone.
> You know not what's in store for the loved ones you adore.
> Remember, you have children of your own.

It's easy to imagine this song sending the part-time poet Harry Hill to reach for a handkerchief, and holding the ruffians at his saloon in rapt attention.

—m—

William Ellsworth Robinson
in his twenties.

James Campbell Robinson did have children of his own, and, not surprisingly, he encouraged them to go into show business. Much of his attention fell on his first son, William Ellsworth Robinson, who was fifteen years old in 1876. Billy, as he was called at home, was tall, handsome, and thoughtful. He shared his father's gray-blue eyes, as well as his literary and organizational skills. But he hadn't demonstrated the sparkle or the oversized personality that Jim was hoping to see, the innate presence of a great actor, who attracts every eye as he steps into a room.

Billy was fascinated by many technical aspects of show business, and would have picked through his father's assortment of props and costumes, the ventriloquist dummy, and the magic tricks. Jim wanted him to boldly try them out in front of audiences, anxious for the boy to enter the inevitable school of hard knocks that was necessary for success in show business. Billy's tendency was to rehearse alone, in front of a mirror, testing and rejecting, mouthing the words quietly to himself.

He didn't like the sound of his voice and wasn't comfortable singing. He was a quick study with dialects, but didn't like telling jokes. The hypnosis act called for a loud, gregarious personality, far beyond his abilities. The Punch and Judy puppets bored him.

He also wasn't interested in just doing some magic tricks, like his father. Billy Robinson had decided to become a great magician.

Chapter 3

THE PALACE OF MAGIC

As Billy Robinson pursued his interest in magic, he suffered the growing pains of any beginner. He was drawn to the technical side of magic, studying secrets, obsessively practicing his sleight-of-hand effects, or fussing over the small touches of his special apparatus. But unlike most boys, Billy had three amazing inspirations. One was his father, a seat-of-his pants theater professional who knew a bit about magic and a great deal about showmanship. Even when he wasn't asked, Jim Campbell teased and tutored his son, showing him how to reinterpret the coarse tricks into engaging entertainment.

The young Robinson's second inspiration was found in a string of impressive magicians who came through New York, touring their wonders. Billy saw the latest magic illusionists—direct from their successes in London—in popular museums like Barnum's or the old New York Coliseum. He saw the Englishman Robert Heller, who had considerable success in America, playing a long run at the Globe Theater on Broadway in 1876. A skillful pianist and humorist as well as a magician, Heller was a popular entertainer who titillated audiences with his scandalous posters, composed in enormous capitals, and tiny letters at the end of the phrase, "GO TO HELLer's."

Billy Robinson was also fortunate to see Signor Blitz at the end of his career. A small, rubber-faced man with feathery white sideburns, Blitz had been born in 1810 in either England, Moravia, Germany, or Poland; he was vague about his background, and, it now seems, probably was not the first performer to adopt the Blitz name. Still, his show was a popular success for decades in America. Blitz offered a circus-like collection of skills. He was a ventriloquist, plate spinner, and magician, and also exhibited "Learned Canary Birds" that performed a number of humorous tricks, like riding in a tiny cradle or firing a diminutive cannon.

Robinson's final source of inspiration, which might have initially meant the most to a shy boy like Billy, was a thick book of secrets that had just been published in London. It was a wholesale collection of secrets—including specialties of Heller and Blitz—and provided important lessons that would last a lifetime.

—⚏—

Modern Magic was written by Professor Hoffmann and first published in London in 1876. Even today, bibliographies of magic use the year 1876 as a dividing mark: books before and after *Modern Magic*. The volume similarly defined two generations of magicians. The older generation, who had developed and guarded these secrets, saw the publication of *Modern Magic* as anathema. "The conjurers stood aghast, their treasured mysteries were revealed to even schoolboys . . . the author laid bare the secrets of the professionals, and ransacked the dealers' stores for apparatus to explain and expose," wrote Sidney Clarke, a historian of the art. One magician said that "Hoffmann deserves to be hanged," and another that "the golden days of magic are over. The world will be as full of magicians as the Jersey coast is of mosquitoes."

The younger magicians, the neophytes who had been counting their pennies, desperately leaning across the counters in the magic shops in search of secrets, felt very differently about the book. It gave them instant access to the world of magic. Clarke explained how its publication "had an almost incalculable effect in revolutionizing and revivifying the art of conjuring and improving the status of the conjurer. [Since *Modern Magic*,] the improvement of the quantity and quality of tricks and illusions has been most marked."

Hoffmann was a pen name. The author's real name was Angelo Lewis. He was born in 1839 and became smitten by magic as a boy

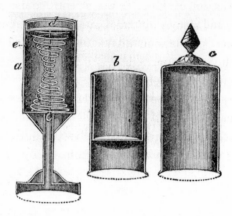

The trick coffee vase, diagrammed in *Modern Magic*.

growing up in London, but the art always remained a hobby. Through his school years, he frequented a magic and toy shop in Holborn and attended the performances of itinerant Victorian conjurers like Professor Anderson and Professor Taylor. He studied the brief secrets explained in the *Boy's Own Book*, as well as classic French and German texts on the art of conjuring. When a publishing opportunity from Routledge came along, Lewis, who became a lawyer but dabbled in writing, decided to write a book about his hobby.

Modern Magic could only have been written by an amateur, someone enthusiastic but oblivious of the oppressive hierarchy of secrets.

In 500-plus pages, Hoffmann explained the popular effects being used by professionals and gave clear advice about organizing a show. His text began, "To Make the Pass," offering seven methods for the secret maneuver essential to all card trickery, and then "To Force a Card," and "To Make a False Shuffle," and proceeding with dozens of card tricks. The chapters moved on to coin tricks and watch tricks, producing candy from a handkerchief or a cannonball from a hat. He explained The Chinese (Linking) Ring Trick, The Coffee Trick (a canister of coffee beans changing to liquid coffee; white beans changing to sugar, and a vase of bran changing to hot milk), trick tables, living heads, and disappearing assistants. The final explanation was for The Aerial Suspension. This illusion, the levitation of a lady, had surprised London audiences the previous decade. Hoffmann diagrammed the metal harness, and the placement of the springs and catches that were responsible for the mystery.

Many magic dealers felt betrayed, and when the final book appeared, they were forced to lower the prices of their apparatus; they could no longer appeal to the precious value of the secrets. As the years passed, however, they found that *Modern Magic* had brought them a steady stream of new customers, in search of the special apparatus that had been described in the book. Some professional magicians shrugged off *Modern Magic*'s appeal. John Nevil Maskelyne, the leading magician in London, owned and operated his Egyptian Hall theater in Piccadilly. He was a pragmatic showman and a clever inventor. When the book appeared, he told Hoffmann, "I am glad that you have written your book. Now that you have explained all the old tricks, conjurers will have to invent new ones." It was a typically cagey remark from Maskelyne. Of course, not "all" the tricks explained were "old," and Maskelyne himself lost several of his secrets to Hoffmann's text, but he was too clever to admit it.

The sensibilities expressed in *Modern Magic* were purely Victorian. When Hoffmann suggested palaver, it dripped with propriety, as in the introduction to the old Cups and Balls effect. This sleight-of-hand trick consisted of little cork balls, which appeared and disappeared from beneath three metal beakers.

Ladies and gentlemen, in an age so enlightened as our own, it is really surprising to see how many popular fallacies spring up from day to day. . . . Many people have asserted, and, among others, the celebrated Erasmus of Rotterdam, that a material object can only be in one place at one time. . . . I must beg you to observe that I have nothing in my hands, except my fingers, and that between my fingers there is nothing save a few atoms of the mysterious fluid, which we call the atmosphere, and through which our jolly old Earth spins so merrily along.

To get the proper effect, one must picture a typical student of the art, an awkward teenage boy, carefully mouthing these words.

Hoffmann's advice to his fellow magicians was of the same fashion. He advocated slow and deliberate presentations, avoiding undue humor. "The program should consist of a series of ten or twelve groups of tricks. . . . Between each of the items, there should be an interval of one or two minutes (filled up by music), while the operator leaves the stage and makes the necessary preparations for the next trick. The few minutes' break is always acceptable to the audience (who are apt to become fatigued by too long protracted attention)." One can only imagine the danger of society ladies growing faint from the magic.

Stanley Collins, a London society performer, never quite forgave Hoffmann for his treachery, but he did admit many years later that *Modern Magic* had proven to be as misleading as it was inspiring. "With all its claptrap vases, ridiculous boxes and similar rubbish, [it] was long out-of-date and old-fashioned when it was written for urchins. There was certainly nothing 'Modern' about it." Actually, Collins was only partly right. *Modern Magic* perfectly captured mid-Victorian conjuring. It incorporated Robert-Houdin's innovative creations from 1850s France, and gave hints about the latest London optical marvels of Maskelyne and Tobin, circa 1870. But the book is filled with the silly accoutrements of Victorian culture, which had been subverted to magicians' goals: small metal tables with velvet-draped tops, fussy little trays, containers, decorative metal covers, cones, "reticules," and boxes. Any of these would have looked perfectly ordinary in a cluttered Victorian parlor, and for a short period of time when the book was written, they did.

The real fault of Hoffmann's book is that, for almost a century and a half, it has nudged every magic show in the direction of a Victorian relic—forever freezing the art in the 1870s.

—m—

There is no good record of Billy Robinson's earliest shows; in later years he wrote only vaguely of some of his favorite tricks. But we have his primer, his treasure map, and gospel in *Modern Magic*, the book that represents the state of the art in 1876. Based on Professor Hoffmann's book, and articles Robinson later wrote about magic, we have an excellent idea of what he performed as a teenage conjurer.

These shows were informal, family entertainments, not what you'd expect to see at Harry Hill's saloon. Billy Robinson performed at private parties, picnics, or on school programs. Often his job was to entertain the children, and for a half-hour performance, he might have earned fifty cents or a dollar. He traveled with his props— including the table his father used for his own magic—in a small trunk and recruited his younger brother Edward Willis Robinson to assist, carrying on the apparatus, secretly pulling on strings, or making the necessary preparations backstage.

He opened his show with a short address, the fashion of the time, in which he invited his audience to enjoy his "little experiments, which endeavor to prove that seeing is believing." Writing years later, Billy Robinson explained his philosophy: "Don't bore your audience with a lengthy opening speech; make it short, pointed and effective, and don't try to impress them with the idea that you are superior to them . . . rather, let them think that you are the same flesh and blood as they, simply an ordinary mortal who has selected the art of magic as a calling." This relaxed approach suited Billy well, as he was never a comfortable speaker or comedian. His goal was to get to the magic.

His first tricks—omitted when performing at a church function— were with playing cards. In his nimble fingers, the cards passed from his hand to his pocket, changed values, disappeared and reappeared. He proceeded with the Rising Card effect, in which a number of cards were selected by members of the audience, and then shuffled back into the deck. The deck was then placed, upright, in a small holder. One by one, the selected cards rose from the middle of the deck, sliding up into view, as if lifted by an invisible finger.

Borrowing a quarter from a boy, he asked its owner to scratch a mark into the edge so he could identify it again. Billy wrapped the coin in a handkerchief, and then showed the audience a large ball of wool yarn, before dropping the yarn into a clear glass vase on his table. The hank was shaken out. The coin disappeared. Taking the end of the wool from the vase and handing it to a boy in the crowd, Billy instructed him to unwind the ball of yarn. As the boy pulled and pulled—invariably the children started laughing at this laborious process—the ball of wool became smaller and smaller. When it was unwound, a coin clattered free from the center of the wool and was discovered in the vase. Robinson asked that the vase be taken over to the coin's owner. The boy reached inside, removed the coin and identified his secret mark.

Picking up a hat, the magician then proceeded with The Shower of Money. Half-dollars were caught in the air—they seemed to become visible just as the magician's fingers closed around them—and dropped, one by one, into the hat. "You see, magicians have no need of a mint. There's silver anywhere you look." Actually, the coins were called "palming coins," purchased at a magic shop. They looked like shiny half dollars but were thinner and easier to handle for the necessary manipulations. One after the other, the coins clinked into his improvised bank. He stepped down into the audience, deftly removing a coin from behind the ear of one little girl, the nose of a boy, or squeezing a coin from the tips of a gentleman's moustache. It was a virtuoso performance of palming and misdirection, allowing Billy to exhibit his sleight-of-hand skills. Picking up a long, slender wand, he stabbed at a spot in the air and was surprised to see a half-dollar suspended from the tip of the wand. He deposited his coin into the hat, and then repeated the process. He used the wand as a diving rod, catching silver coins at its tip as he reached under the elbows of the children, into their coat pockets, or beneath a little girl's hair ribbon. By the end of the trick, he had managed to discover several dozen coins. "It's a good idea to combine both the sleight of hand and mechanical methods," he later wrote about this routine, advocating the use of the tricked wand that produced coins. "All methods are good, but should not be abused and made to do all the work."

Like many beginning magicians, Billy Robinson had spent hours studying sleight of hand from the popular textbooks, and then rehearsing the maneuvers in front of a mirror so that he could perform them faultlessly. But authors like Hoffmann didn't address the mistakes or missteps that could occur during a presentation. At one show, Robinson faced down a boy in his audience who seemed to think that the point of the show was to try to catch the magician. After several taunts and whispers, Billy stopped the show to rebuke him. This silenced the boy for several minutes. During his next trick, as Billy made a coin disappear, the boy decided to strike back. "Oh, you've got it in your palm," he said loudly. The magician masterfully transferred the coin to his pocket as he swung his body to cover the motion. In the middle of an uninterrupted routine, the maneuver would have worked perfectly. But once the audience had been directed to study the movements of his hand—modern magicians call this adversarial relationship "burning," as the audience's eyes relentlessly watch every movement—it was hopeless. "Oh, now you have it in your pocket," the young boy insisted, stopping the show with gales of laughter. Billy Robinson learned that he was obliged to charm and mystify in equal doses. The tricks were easy to learn. Human nature was a much more difficult lesson.

For the finale of his show, Billy offered to demonstrate a lesson in magical cooking. A shallow chafing dish was set on his table. He broke two eggs inside, and then added a spoonful of flour, a vial of spirits, and a pinch of pepper. Touching a match to the inside of the pan, he set fire to the entire mixture. Billy slammed the lid on the pan, pausing dramatically while the flames were extinguished. When the lid was removed, two gray pigeons were found inside, perched on the edge of the chafing dish.

—⁂—

Reading *Modern Magic* would convince anyone that a magician should be a metalworker. Many of the best pieces of equipment described—like the Wizard's Omelet Pan that was Robinson's finale—were handmade of soldered tin, nickel plated, or "japanned" black with shiny lacquer. They took considerable skill to construct and were costly pieces of apparatus. Billy Robinson couldn't have afforded the Omelet Pan that was displayed on the shelves of Martinka's magic shop, at 493 Sixth Avenue in New York. But according to one of his associates, after Billy completed his public schooling, he took a job in a brass foundry. He learned to work with sheet metal, shaping and soldering it, and became a meticulous craftsman.

In the late 1870s, when Robinson showed his handiwork to Francis and Anthony Martinka, the Austrian immigrant brothers who ran New York's largest magic manufacturing company and magic shop, they were impressed. Robinson was brought into the shop to work on special projects, and access to New York's newest magic shop gave the young man a privileged position in the world of magic.

The Martinka brothers were slightly round, with receding hairlines and enormous handlebar moustaches. They played the roles of German toymakers, organizing a factory of incredible devices, delighting in their secret projects and adding to their list of customers. The key to the business's success was Mrs. Martinka, Francis's wife, a congenial hostess to visitors, but a shrewd businesswoman who supervised each project with an iron hand. She was also responsible for the creation of any fabric props—trick sacks and tablecloths—and the construction of the special tissue paper flowers used by magicians.

There was something spooky and magical about the very premises on Sixth Avenue, a sort of city-bound Aladdin's cave. The building had originally served as a "rope walk," where the rigging for sailing vessels was made. Later it had been a coal and wood yard, and then a skating rink. But first-time visitors were certain to be disappointed. From the street, the business seemed to occupy a tiny sliver of the ground floor of a dingy old brick building. On the second floor was a Chinese restaurant. A narrow window displayed various pieces of apparatus, and above the door, in gilt lettering, was the improbable title, "Palace of Magic."

"One glancing at Martinka's would believe it but a narrow booth-like hole in a brick wall," according to a newspaper account. Just beyond the door was a small customer room, surrounded by glass counters and shelves of apparatus. Through an arch was a window-less room with additional shelves of apparatus. The Martinkas' shop front boasted the latest tricks and books. They had a number of copies of Hoffmann's *Modern Magic* in August 1876, for example, just months after it had been published in London. Few customers ever saw beyond this room.

The surprises began just behind these displays. The property widened as it extended back. There was a tall stock room filled with small apparatus, then a room packed with large crates of apparatus, a paint bench, workroom, and offices. Behind this, in a still wider space, were the lathes, saws, and drills. "The store, starting with a mere slit in the wall, reaches 200 feet deep into the brick bowels of the block, and spreads out to a width thrice that of its beginning," a visiting reporter marveled. The workshop was lined with a row of "illusion closets," small rooms with solid oak doors, each closed with a padlock. In these rooms were the special projects under con-struction for professional magicians. Each prop would be taken from the closet for work in the shop, and then locked away at the end of the day or when a visitor was invited inside for a tour.

New effects were tested in a tiny theater that seated about one hundred people at the back of the Martinkas' property. This was the fabled "Palace of Magic," a dark little room with a raised stage and an upright piano. Out-of-town professionals were welcomed here, and they might be encouraged to perform a little something for the cognoscenti of New York magicians who regularly gathered there.

Customers appreciated the Martinkas' old-world sense of honor and their willingness to tackle any challenge, regardless of the com-plexity. All the work was concealed from curious eyes, and visiting magicians were guaranteed privacy to discuss their latest plans. Rival magicians were deftly, seemingly effortlessly, steered around each other as they arrived to check the progress of their latest illu-sions. One of their commissioned illusions consisted of a room-sized cabinet that produced optical illusions through the use of reflec-tions; it was "the largest illusion ever made," according to Francis

The little theater of magic, at the back of Martinka's shop.

Martinka. The apparatus required a glass mirror about seven by ten feet, which had been ordered from a glass manufacturer. For the proper optical effect, the mirror had been specially made with its silver backing applied in a series of narrow, parallel stripes. It was a difficult, unusual job and the mirror, which reportedly cost two thousand dollars to manufacture, was too large to be brought into the shop, so the illusion was gradually assembled on the sidewalk over the course of several days. Acting nonchalant, never betraying the delicacy of the apparatus or the secret of its use, the staff chose off-hours to uncover the mirror and work on the trick, "never long enough to allow people to get an inkling of what was going on." When it was finished, they breathed a sigh of relief, then packed it in enormous crates and shipped it to the waiting magician.

In the early years of their business, one of the Martinkas' best customers stepped into the office, closed the door, and described an ingenious little device that he had been shown in London. Magicians technically distinguish such important little accessories as "fakes," something that's seen but is camouflaged to look like something else, or "gimmicks," something that is always concealed from the audience.

He described a hollow, metal finger painted flesh color, with rounded clips at the base, so that it could be gripped between the performer's real fingers. Technically, this was a fake. It took the form of a sixth finger. A silk handkerchief could be hidden inside the hollow finger. If the performer's hand was kept in motion—waved up and down—the hand appeared empty and the audience wouldn't notice the extra finger. A series of careful manipulations allowed the finger to be slipped away and the handkerchief extracted. The Martinkas took measurements of the magician's hand, sculpted and painted the fake finger in a secret corner of the shop, and delivered the tiny prop in a tightly wrapped package. Years later Francis Martinka explained how the sixth finger had bamboozled the other magicians when they saw the handkerchief tricks that were made possible. The company could have sold hundreds to their customers, but they refused to divulge the secret for over a year, "in keeping with strict business principles."

—⁂—

One day, as Robinson was hunched over a workbench at the Martinka shop, Mrs. Martinka careered down the narrow corridor, stopping only to pound on each doorframe with her open hand. "Heraus! Heraus! Heraus!" He was familiar with the drill; an important visitor had arrived and Francis wanted privacy in the shop. Billy wiped his hands with a rag, covered his work, slipped the drawings in a drawer and walked toward the back door. Hearing laughter, he turned to see Francis Martinka, thumbs in his vest pockets, leading a tall, angular man down the hallway. The visitor was wearing a fashionable maroon coat, buff-colored trousers, and a bright gold silk cravat. He was flourishing a gold-topped cane in one hand and held a soft Homburg hat in the other. He looked, Billy thought to himself, exactly like Mephistopheles, dressed for a stroll in the park. His expressive face was trimmed with a shock of black hair, parted severely in the middle, a pointed goatee, and a long waxed moustache. Two dark eyebrows bobbed above his coal-black twinkling eyes. Billy recognized him from the newspaper engravings and lithographic posters.

It was Alexander Herrmann, the greatest magician in the world.

Chapter 4

THE GREAT HERRMANN

The Herrmann family was a dynasty of magicians. Samuel Herrmann was born in the last years of the eighteenth century, a Russian-Polish Jew who settled in Altona, near Hamburg, Germany. By 1820, he was working as an itinerant magician, performing card tricks and imitations of bird whistles through little towns in Germany, Alsace-Lorraine, and France.

The family name has been debated for many years; it may have originally been Grosskopf or Rindkopf. It's also been suggested that Samuel was not the first magician in the family, but learned the art from an older brother. Samuel's sons later implied that their father was actually a physician who practiced in Hanover, and performed magic as a hobby. This was an exaggeration, perhaps intended to add status to the family. Samuel and his wife, Anna Sarah Meyer of Hamburg, had sixteen children. The oldest, a son named Compars, was born in 1816, probably in the town of Patesen in the old Kingdom of Hanover. Their youngest child, a son named Alexander, was born in 1844 in Paris. These oldest and youngest sons became two of the greatest magicians of the century.

In keeping with the mysterious origins of the family, even the name Compars or Comparse is suspicious. In German and French, it is a technical term for a supernumerary or confederate in the theater, which suggests that it was not a given name but one he assumed during his years in show business. He often appeared as Professor Herrmann, or later with his name simplified to Carl Herrmann. Although Compars never credited his father with his education in magic, he must have been Samuel's pupil, and early in his career shared his father's ability for lively bird imitations.

Carl Herrmann toured Europe in 1847, and the following year at the Adelphi and Haymarket theaters in London, billed as "Herrmann of Hanover, Premier Prestidigitateur of France." He followed with tours of the British provinces and returned to Europe again. His little brother Alexander was working with Carl as early as 1851, when the boy was just seven. He was levitated above the stage, supposedly suspended by a single hair from his head, which was pinched in the magician's fingers, and also appeared as the blindfolded "clairvoyant" in Carl's version of Second Sight. The official family history is that Alexander joined the show in 1854, when he was ten and Carl was performing in St. Petersburg. Alexander later romantically claimed that he either "ran away" or was "kidnapped" by his oldest brother. Actually, their father at first objected, but gave his approval for Alexander to join Carl as his assistant.

Early in 1861, the year that Billy Robinson was born, Carl Herrmann first came to the United States. By that time, he had abandoned many of the mechanical effects borrowed from Robert-Houdin's show, and concentrated on sleight-of-hand mysteries. His magic delighted the critics and filled theaters across the eastern United States. Carl Herrmann was dark and devilish, with a wild mane of hair and a broad brow, deep-set eyes, and a full, curled moustache and goatee. He appeared onstage in a full swallowtail coat. A Boston critic praised his performance, noting that "everything is artistic and you cannot but feel that you see before you one who relies but very little on humbug," which seems a surprising compliment for a magician. "Herrmann is something of a humorist, too, and he often makes an entertainment more palatable by the incidental business and the introduction."

In September 1861, at the Academy of Music in New York, the youngest Herrmann—he was billed as Monsieur Alexander—was introduced to the crowd during Carl Herrmann's performance. He demonstrated his ability to throw cards into the audience. He could take ordinary playing cards and throw them, with a sharp snap of the wrist, so that they spun out in wide arcs from the stage. Alexander was able to deliver the cards accurately to any individual seat in the theater, or send them against the back wall of the auditorium, where they ricocheted against the plaster with a loud crack. It was a brilliant display of strength and juggling that brought the crowd to its feet. On November 30, 1861, the brothers presented their magic before President Lincoln in Washington.

Carl and Alexander performed together and separately through the 1860s and into the 1870s, bouncing between Europe, South America, and the United States. There's no question that young Alexander had acquired his brother's skills. But if Carl was dark and fascinating—the aging, scheming Old Scratch, who spoke with a slightly indefinable German or Russian pronunciation—Alexander was the bright, witty Mephistopheles, whose words bubbled with good humor and sparkled with his Parisian accent. He was billed as the "Comique Necromantique."

Between 1871 and 1873, Alexander performed at London's Egyptian Hall, a tiny, fusty theater in Piccadilly that had originally served as a museum for Egyptian artifacts and was adorned with weird cartouches, scarabs, hieroglyphics, and gilded papyrus-leafed columns. Alexander always referred to the engagement as his triumphant "one thousand nights." Alexander's career was simmering just as his older brother's was cooling. The brothers declared a truce, neatly dividing up a map of the world. Europe was left to Carl. America would be Alexander's.

—m—

The popular caricature of a magician—the tall, slender man in knee breeches and a long tailcoat, the goateed, devilish performer with flashing eyes and coarse black hair, the graceful roué who flexes his long, tapered fingers and announces, "et voilà!" as the rabbit is pulled from the hat—that is Alexander Herrmann. He was America's favorite magician for over twenty years. Even more than a magician, he became a celebrity and a man of the theater. One of Alexander's favorite sayings was, "Great magicians are born, not made." It was certainly true in his case.

When Alexander returned to America in 1875, he became acquainted with the dancer Adelaide Scarsez, a red-haired beauty with an hourglass figure and bright blue eyes. She had been born in 1853 in England of Belgian parents. Adelaide had appeared at the Folies Bergère in Paris and cities in America as a Hungarian Dancer. Her other specialty was a novelty act in which she appeared on stage in tights, performing trick-riding stunts with a high-wheeled penny-farthing bicycle. The official story—for the press—is that Adelaide and Alexander first met on the ship to America during the magician's voyage. In fact, they had met years earlier during Herrmann's engagement in London, and Adelaide had been smitten with the elegant magician. New York City's Mayor Wickham married the couple on the steps of City Hall in March 1875. Herrmann thanked the politician by reaching into the mayor's coat sleeve, withdrawing a roll of bills, and presenting them back to Mayor Wickham with his thanks.

"M'lle Addie," as she was billed on the programs, performed her bicycle act dressed as a pageboy to assist his sleight of hand, or took the dramatic part of the enchanted Slave Girl, levitated in midair. On a stage, she had the same magnetic appeal as her talented husband. Adelaide was a talented actress and dancer, and a quick study.

—⚯—

By the time he was in his early twenties, Billy Robinson was something of an expert on magic. He sought out any magic show he could find. Most were the temporary attractions at the variety theaters or dime museums—the urban predecessor of the sideshow. But Alexander Herrmann only performed at first-class theaters. In New York, Herrmann worked at Niblo's Garden or the Academy of Music, and tickets might be a dollar, or a dollar fifty, the same price as last week's opera or the latest melodrama. After finishing at the Martinka shop, Billy Robinson ran to the box office and bought the very best ticket he could—close to the stage and on the aisle, so he would be

Alexander Herrmann, as he dressed for his stage performance.

sure to have a perfect view of the legendary Herrmann magic.

Every minute of the Herrmann show was an inspiration. Robinson watched Herrmann's elegant entrance, the way he pulled off his gloves, rolled them into a ball and made them disappear at his fingertips. He studied the way the great magician scaled cards into the audience. He nodded with appreciation as Herrmann found a cannonball in a borrowed hat, changed the cannonball into a rabbit, and finally held the rabbit in his hands and seemed to pull it apart into two live, kicking rabbits. "You'll forgive me," he told the audience with a smile, "I've been told not to split hares, but I find zee Americans like it very much!"

After years performing magic, Billy Robinson still suffered with his patter, hesitating before every joke. By contrast, Herrmann's worst puns were delivered grandly, and enhanced with a Gallic shrug and a slight frown; this made it seem as if the great magician had just tasted something unpleasant. The audience smiled at the pun and his reaction at the same time.

One of Herrmann's favorite effects, The Mysterious Orange, was a perfect exhibition of his skills.

Stepping into the aisle of the theater, he approached a lady, bending over to reach into her corsage. His fingers seemed to pluck a walnut from the flowers. He tossed this to his black assistant, named Boomsky. A bit farther up the aisle, Herrmann stopped at a gentleman, stroking his hair at his collar and finding a lemon. Boomsky took this is as well. From beneath the beard of a third gentleman he found an orange. As Boomsky placed these three items on Herrmann's table, the magician borrowed a white dress glove from a man, and returned to the stage.

The object of the experiment, Herrmann said with a smile, was to invisibly pass the glove into the center of the walnut. He rolled the glove between his hands and the bundle seemed to become smaller and smaller. Shaking the glove open to take another look, he discovered that it was now tiny, the size to fit a doll.

Herrmann feigned concern, looking over the footlights to apologize and explain that he thought the glove might be a bit too small now. The spectator grumbled his agreement. Herrmann dutifully pulled at the glove between his hands, attempting to stretch it, and asked what size the spectator wore. The man called back to him, "Size seven." "Fifteen and a half?" Herrmann responded. "Gracious, zat is a large size, sir!" Before the man in the audience could correct him, the magician opened his hand, disclosing a gigantic glove, several times the normal size.

He rolled the glove between his hands again, and then opened them to show that the glove had disappeared. Then he picked up the walnut, which disappeared as he bounced it between his hands. He picked up the lemon, appeared to toss it into the air, and it also vanished.

"Of course, zey are not really gone. You will see a logical explanation, and it is all so very simple," he told his audience with exaggerated seriousness. "Zee glove has gone into my walnut, my walnut into my lemon, and my lemon into my orange."

He picked up the orange in one hand, and a small knife in the other. Cutting open the fruit, the audience was surprised to see that the orange was hollow, just an empty peel with the lemon inside. He withdrew the lemon, then cut open the rind, twisting it in his hand so the peel formed a long spiral curl. Inside the lemon was the walnut. Cracking the walnut, Herrmann proudly showed a white interior. It was the tightly folded glove. Proudly removing the glove from the shell and carrying it back to the owner, he returned it with a deep bow.

The orange trick called for masterly palming and careful

switches of one glove for another. During the course of the effect, the orange had been exchanged for a specially prepared peel, containing the lemon and walnut and then carefully sewn shut again. The first changes of the glove, and its eventual disappearance, were accomplished by sleight of hand. Late in the illusion, he introduced a trick table. As he picked up the lemon, his fingers pushed it through the traps in the tabletop. Using his skills at pantomime, he appeared to hold the lemon in his hand, then toss it into the air, where it disappeared.

When Herrmann showed the glove inside the walnut, it was a duplicate white dress glove that had been placed there before the show, when the halves of the shell were glued shut. He switched this glove for the spectator's glove, just as the audience applauded and he stepped into the aisle. It was a beautiful, poetic effect and it was accomplished with a classical understanding of the art: sometimes making the secret maneuvers one step ahead, sometimes one step behind, establishing a strong rhythm of sleight of hand, then changing techniques and using a mechanical table at a critical moment to keep the audience off guard.

Another popular trick, originally from his brother Carl's show, involved a large shawl. Alexander Herrmann stood on the rundown, the ramp at the front of the orchestra pit, and handed the shawl to a lady in the audience, asking that she draw it through her hands to assure herself that there were no pockets inside it. Taking the shawl back, he brought both his hands beneath it. In an instant, a round flat shape seemed to appear beneath the fabric. Herrmann drew away the shawl and revealed a shallow glass dish, about a foot across, filled to the brim with water and goldfish. "Perhaps, Madame, you did not notice this!" He handed the dish to an assistant, and then drew the shawl through his hands again. "You like my magical way of fishing, no?" He threw the shawl over his arm and produced a second and third bowl of water the same way.

The secret was that each bowl had been sealed with a specially shaped rubber cover, which was stretched over the mouth of the bowl to seal in the water. The bowls were then turned upright and tucked into narrow pockets inside the magician's jacket. Beneath the cover of the shawl, Herrmann's fingers deftly lifted each bowl from its pocket and righted it. The rubber cover would be carefully pulled away, and the bowl of water taken from beneath the shawl.

Herrmann had an intuitive skill with such small effects, but sometimes the delicacy of his touch and the nonchalance of his flourishes worked against him. At one performance, as Herrmann removed the rubber cover from the first bowl, it slipped from his fingers and fell to his feet with a loud, disconcerting plop. Herrmann blinked slowly, and reached down without hesitation. "Ah, my beret. I always wear it when I perform zis treek!" He picked up the sloppy, wet, black piece of rubber, and placed it on his head with the same aplomb as a king donning his crown. Then he produced the second and third bowls from beneath the shawl.

Both Herrmann and Billy Robinson had been born the sons of competent magicians. But there was something indefinable and larger than life about Herrmann, far beyond Robinson's abilities. He could learn all the tricks, he could rehearse the secret moves, but he could never summon Herrmann's magnificent sangfroid. He realized that much of Herrmann's talent was far beyond his reach.

That accident with the rubber cover would have crushed Billy Robinson if it had occurred during one of the young man's performances. "Great magicians are born, not made."

—◊—

Early in 1883, Billy Robinson met a pretty, shy blonde girl who lived on Suffolk Street in Manhattan. Her name was Bessie Smith. He was 21; she was just 16.

Bessie had been born in London and was the only child of Isidor and Henrietta (Kitty) Smith, two German immigrants who arrived in New York in 1869, when Bessie was just three years old. Henrietta died shortly after their arrival. Isidor, a professional hairdresser, raised Bessie, and they lived with her aunt and uncle.

Bessie had probably seen a performance of the "Man of Mystery" during one of his Manhattan shows at a school or party, and she was quickly smitten with the young magician. Billy impulsively offered his hand in marriage and whispered of a career in show business.

William Robinson and Bessie Smith were married in a civil ceremony on February 22, 1883, in Manhattan. Jim Campbell Robinson, the groom's father, served as a witness.

To a determined magician like Billy, his interest in Bessie was not a sign of love so much as securing a partner who would contribute to his success. A magic show is a combination of large props that must be packed and transported in heavy, dirty crates, and small intricate props, which must be repaired, guarded, and nursed backstage. A magician working by himself can only carry, set up, and perform a limited range of miracles. But adding a devoted assistant working in the wings, carrying trays on stage, preparing the next tricks, and then changing costumes to appear on stage, the Robinson show would be all the more impressive. Bessie, young, starstruck, and infatuated, never understood just how much Billy was devoted to his magic, and how little he was devoted to her.

Shortly after their marriage, Bessie realized that Billy was disloyal. Evidence suggests that Billy had continued a relationship with another girl—she may have been a young servant living with the Robinsons. In December 1883 a child named Annie was born into the Robinson family. Bessie was not the child's mother.

Jim and Sarah Robinson quickly assumed care of Annie A. Robinson, and raised their first grandchild—their decision may have been an effort to salvage their son's marriage. Bessie was devoted to Billy's career and had determined to become a loyal partner, but her husband's carelessness confused and frustrated his young bride.

Robinson soon found himself intrigued by another mysterious lady—in a much more innocent way. She was named Thauma, a freak of nature who offered the magician an important secret.

—∽—

Billy Robinson pushed his way inside the exhibit room and shouldered through the crowd. He was determined to be in the front row at the little theater in the Eden Musée, standing just behind the painted metal railing. "Please take your places, gentlemen. Ladies, step forward. There's room for everyone. You'll all have a good view," the exhibitor, C. H. Senauer, explained as the room filled and the spectators jostled for position. There was a rustle as coats were opened, hats removed, petticoats settled, and paper-wrapped bundles set on the floor. Then a long moment of anticipatory silence, and Mr. Senauer began his introduction.

"This afternoon I'm pleased to introduce a lovely young lady, a strange young lady, a fascinating young lady. She was named for the goddess of mystery, Thauma!" As he spoke, the exhibitor paced slowly from side to side, just behind the horizontal handrail. He was sizing up the audience. He was taking advantage of this slow, dramatic introduction to look into the eyes of each person—there weren't more than twenty or thirty standing in neat rows at the railing—and watch for any troublemakers: the boy with a paper spitball, the drunken man ready to begin an argument. "Yes, Thauma is a mystery. But she will be charmed to meet you, and you will remember her," he dropped his voice to a hiss, ". . . for the rest of your life."

The Eden Musée opened early in 1884 and was New York City's most glamorous dime museum, a dark three-story building of gables and columns on Twenty-third Street between Fifth and Sixth avenues. Dime museums were the urban predecessors of sideshows, a sort of pay-as-you-go collection of wonders. The wax museum formed the central area. A gallery of smaller theaters and exhibit rooms promised a rotating collection of wonders and required an additional nickel or dime for admission. At the Eden Musée, audiences could see a real electric chair, play a game of chess with Ajeeb the wind-up mechanical chess player, or enjoy a concert by a Hungarian band. A dozen years later, the very first Edison motion pictures were projected in a small theater at the Eden Musée. Dime museums were also proving grounds for the latest trends in magic. The small theaters and short shows were ideally suited to the latest stage illusions or untested sleight-of-hand acts that would never have been booked at the downtown theaters of Broadway.

Thauma was intriguingly billed as a freak of nature. Robinson knew better. Thauma was not a person. She was an illusion invented by Dr. Lynn, a popular magician who had toured around the world in the 1860s and '70s. C. H. Senauer had been hired by Lynn to exhibit his effect in New York. Thauma had already been exhibited at the Crystal Palace in London and the Folies Bergère in Paris, where she was teasingly billed as "Où est le Corps?" or, "Where is the Body?"

Robinson squinted in the glare of gaslights in the Eden Musée's tiny theater; half a dozen lamps framed the curtained stage for Thauma, and these brightly illuminated the room. Mr. Senauer stepped to one side and pulled a cord, drawing back the red plush curtain. There was a gasp. Billy Robinson leaned forward and fixed his stare beyond the lights.

The little stage was hung with dense black drapery. Thauma was an attractive young lady with dark curls pulled up in a bow. She wore a tight-fitting bodice with a low, scooped neckline, trimmed in lace, which complemented her décolletage.

Her body stopped at her waist.

She appeared to have been sliced so neatly, so perfectly, that the spectacle was strange, grisly, and awe-inspiring all at the same time. Compounding the illusion, Thauma was "sitting" on a child's swing, a horizontal plank of wood that hung from cords on either side. Her waist was pressed against the swing, and her hands, raised alongside her face, held on to the cords.

The exhibitor gave the swing a push, and it rocked back and forth. Finally he held out his hand, stopping the swing, and gave it a shove laterally so that it rocked right and left as the lady smiled innocently. As the swing settled, Thauma gripped the cords tightly in her hands and lifted her half body straight up, so that she was suspended several inches above the plank of the swing. Mr. Senauer slipped his hand between her body and the swing, waving it back and forth to demonstrate how the mysterious half lady was isolated in space. As

Thauma, the living half lady, at the Eden Musée.

he stepped away, Thauma lowered her torso again; it landed on the plank with a dull thump, and she winked at the audience.

The half lady, rocking back on her swing just several feet away, fascinated Billy Robinson. He knew that Thauma's brief performance had been polished in Paris and London before she was exhibited in New York; his textbooks had taught him to idealize European magic. She answered questions from the audience and recited a few lines of poetry to the applause of the audience. Billy was lost in thought. He squinted at the stage, and then slowly held up his hand, vertically, to one side of his face, shielding his eyes from the row of lamps, studying the optical illusion.

"Thank you to Thauma, and to our audience for your patronage today," Mr. Senauer concluded, flipping the curtain closed again. The audience picked up their parcels and pushed toward the exit. Billy knew that, in those few minutes at the Eden Musée, he'd seen something amazing and important.

Chapter 5

OLIVE PATH

Variety entertainment was being scrubbed clean in the 1880s. The short, punchy acts associated with the Bowery were being revised, expanded, and repackaged for the great American public. Jim Campbell and his son William Robinson were lucky enough not only to witness that transformation, but to be pushed along in its wake.

The saloons like Harry Hill's had earned terrible reputations for their police raids, beer-sodden clientele, blowsy waitresses, and frowsy entertainments; the evenings were only fit for men, but never gentlemen. The legendary story from these dives (the author Douglas Gilbert suggested that it might have happened at New York's Volk's Garden) concerned one manager's shouted introduction for his establishment's next act. "Now, gents, Miss Beatrice McWhorter will sing 'Beneath the Moonlight.'" Whereupon a drunken patron suddenly pulled himself from his chair and managed to rattle the hall with the pronouncement, "Beatrice McWhorter is a whore!" As he collapsed back into his seat, the manager continued, unfazed, "Nevertheless, Miss Beatrice McWhorter will sing 'Beneath the Moonlight.'"

The man who is given credit for polishing variety until it shone, and then throwing the doors open to women and children, was a short, swaggering former minstrel and circus clown named Tony Pastor. Pastor was born on New York's Greenwich Street in 1832. Having spawned a natural performer and an irrepressible ham, his parents gave up on various attempts at giving him a conventional education. When Pastor was still a boy he was considered a prodigy, performing with the minstrel troupe at Barnum's museum in New

York. He toured with circuses and learned show business from the sawdust up: acrobatics, comedy, and even trick horse riding. Before he was twenty years old, he had donned the polished boots and lace-trimmed jacket of the ringmaster in an Ohio circus, and then graduated to the role of featured clown—at the time, there was a tradition of the singing clown, who opened the show with a comic song.

By all accounts, Pastor's voice was never better than a husky baritone, but the circus ring had taught him how to sell a song to his audience, acting it expressively with facial expressions and poses. By 1860, he was back in New York, working at a circus in the Old Bowery Theater, then moving smoothly into the fledgling variety saloons, and finally settling at the American Concert Hall, or, as it was commonly known to its loyal public, "444," its address on Broadway. One night, early in the Civil War, instead of concluding the show with the expected comic song, he stood at the edge of the stage and belted the verses of "The Star Spangled Banner." This was long before the melody was appointed the national anthem; it was commonly hurrahed during parades and rallies for the Union troops. A visitor to the theater recalled, "Tony sang the first verse amid the most intense silence." The audience was shocked to hear politics swept onto the variety stage. "He then asked the audience to join in the chorus. It was tremendous. I thought the roof of the building would fly off." Pastor's programs at 444 made him famous: comic songs, especially songs about the feminine charms, mixed with melodies honoring the Union cause.

In 1865 Pastor left to form his own traveling troupe, then returned to the city several months later and settled in the Bowery at the old Minstrel Hall, now renamed Tony Pastor's Opera House.

Pastor's famous reforms came slowly, and his early shows were designed to appeal to cheering, hooting, beery men. But as his variety theater moved uptown—first to 585 Broadway and then to Fourteenth Street at Union Square—he deliberately placed himself shoulder to shoulder with fine hotels and in competition with Broadway theaters. Pastor made a determined effort to appeal to the best class of people. His ideals were captured in his advertising,

"The resort most cherished by the ladies, children and the cultured mass of amusement seekers." The theaters were cleared of the stench of liquor or the blue haze from cigars, well lit and neatly upholstered. The shows were carefully arranged to appeal to everyone, without a hint of vulgarity. Pastor's was a place where "one may laugh without blushing," according to the *New York Dramatic Mirror*.

The magic word, reportedly first used by the producer John W. Ransone, was "vaudeville." The origin of the title isn't clear. It may have been assembled from the French words for "voice of the city," or a term for the ballads from the Vire River in Normandy. If the word seemed mysteriously classy or continental, this probably served to differentiate it from the sawdust-on-the-floor variety, beer, and boxing saloons of the mid-1800s. Real vaudevillians never treated it as a foreign word, but immediately appropriated it into their jangling slang and even spelled it "vodvil." Tony Pastor, who is often credited with inventing vaudeville, avoided using the title for much of his career, feeling that it was unnecessarily sissy and French.

Like many supposedly brand-new things, early vaudeville was suspiciously similar to its predecessors in entertainment—patrons found a mixture of features which had been cherry-picked from establishments like Harry Hill's, circuses, dime museum novelties, and the farces and musical numbers popularized in minstrel shows. Pastor preferred to structure his show around balladeers and comedians, but he included acrobats and jugglers—magicians seldom worked at his establishment—and then concluded the evening with his corps de ballet and a short comic play.

Through the 1880s, the vaudeville bill took shape: the musical farces were dropped and the show was built around variety stars. Tony was famously supportive of performers, and he discovered many future stars, including the most famous chanteuse of the era, Lillian Russell. Pastor, the old ham, remained an attraction on any bill. Dressed in a blue velvet jacket, or white tie and tails, he would saunter to the center of the stage. The "little general," as his friends knew him, had a bull-like neck that was barely contained inside his stiff collar, and a shiny black moustache, waxed and rolled into long, horizontal points. "Well, here I am again," he grinned to the crowd across the footlights, and then launched into a series of the latest comic songs. His voice was raspy, and his dance steps awkward, but his audience cheered him on, just as the host of a grand party receives the affection of his guests.

—꿈—

When Pastor boasted of respectability, he was attacking the old-style entertainments personified by Harry Hill. For decades, Hill's dirty, crime-ridden saloon in the Bowery had been an easy target for moralists and politicians, but the fashion for vaudeville was the final insult. Variety performers, who had always been willing to work for very little money, aspired to the bright lights and prestigious shows at Tony Pastor's tamer, friendlier theater, and Pastor's formula for vaudeville naturally spread to more theaters and beer halls throughout the city. Variety had been stolen out from under Harry Hill, and the saloon on Houston Street was left with the dregs.

Earlier in his career, Hill had instinctively fought back against these problems, using his connections and his capital to attract new acts and pay needed bribes. But by the 1880s, the old saloonkeeper had unwisely covered loans for his friends and tied up his money in a number of bad investments, like his own hotels in Flushing and steamboat ferries between Flushing and New York City. In 1886, when a new, crusading administration swept into City Hall in New York, Hill's famous Houston Street Saloon was shut down once again, and never recovered. Harry Hill, nearly bankrupt, moved to Harlem and opened a small bar on piles at the corner of the Harlem Bridge. "But even here," the *New York Times* reported, "the police followed him and interfered with him wherever they could." By the end of his life, in 1896, Harry Hill had been reduced to managing a tiny shack of a bar in Corona, Long Island, welcoming each patron with a hearty slap on the back and reciting his poetry for the barflies.

Professional photograph of William
Robinson, magician.

William Robinson was circling New York with his magic show, performing in union halls, at church functions, or for private parties in one-night engagements. He had assembled a long, complicated program of magic, featuring his new wife, Bessie: "Robinson, the Man of Mystery, The World's Marvelous Enchanter, Assisted by Mlle. Bessie, in . . . 'Scenes of Enchantment.'"

The title, "Man of Mystery," was Robinson's version of the traditional superlatives attached to a magician's name. Robinson began signing his letters with the pompous salutation, "Mystically thine, W. E. Robinson." He grew his moustache long and curled the ends with wax. On stage he wore black knickers, silk hose, and a formal tailcoat, in the style of Herrmann. Photos of the Man of Mystery show a pleasant, sandy-haired entertainer, with squinting eyes and a tight smile.

The tricks for Robinson's new program consisted of the solid, dependable material that he had learned from *Modern Magic* or behind the counter at Martinka's shop. He caught coins in the air, cut up and restored two handkerchiefs at the same time—a red and white one—apparently mixing up the pieces as the handkerchiefs came together again so the red handkerchief ended up with a white center, and the white with a red one. He performed his cooking routine, as well as The Chinese Rings. This was a trick that Robinson introduced as a rare feat from the Orient, just as the instructions from *Modern Magic* recommended.

Not surprisingly, he also included some of Jim Campbell's old specialties, like ventriloquism, which Billy billed as "Robinson, the Man of Many Voices, with his Comical Companions." This part was performed using several of his father's carved dummies, and borrowing Campbell's dialect comedy and broad accents.

For another section of his show, Billy performed as "Robinson, the Famous Spiritualist," in which he demonstrated some of the famous mind-reading tricks and "So-Called Spiritualistic Manifestations" of the séance room. He magically produced writing on several blank school slates, showed how mysterious forces tipped tables, and predicted a number freely selected by a member of the audience. For the finale of this section, he demonstrated how he could be tied inside a cabinet and, when concealed by a curtain, produce the standard raps and rattles associated with a séance.

The subject of Spiritualism was a popular feature in magic shows. The religion had begun in America in the late 1840s with a popular notion that spirits could communicate with the living through an organized séance. The movement had attracted millions of devout believers, as well as a number of scoundrels who were happy to take a few dollars and produce a "message" from the great beyond—a whispered greeting at the séance table or the ringing of a bell in a dark room.

Billy billed his tricks without any pretensions of real ghosts, calling them "So-Called Spiritualistic Phenomena . . . Produc[ed] by Natural Means." Actually, he had come to the subject with a genuine interest. His family, like many others of the mid-1800s, was open-minded on the subject. Jim, Sarah, and the children were raised

Roman Catholic, but they followed the latest accounts of Spiritualists. Through the 1870s and '80s, Jim Campbell Robinson and his
son Billy were curious enough to attend occasional séances. While
sincerely interested in the cause, the magician in Billy realized that
most séances were filled with fakery. These underhanded tricks provided inspirations for his act.

"Mademoiselle Bessie" was given prominent billing by her
proud husband, but she was only incorporated into a few tricks.
She was featured in a "Beautiful and Poetic Vision, An Arabian
Night's Dream," in which she was levitated over the stage. With
her elbow resting lightly on an upright wooden pole, she appeared
to sleep, stretched horizontally, in midair. The scene was
enhanced with various music cues, and Billy draped bits of costume over the sleeping Bessie, so she appeared as Red Riding Hood,
a Scotch Lassie, or An Angel Asleep in the Clouds. Later in the
program, Bessie also assisted with "The Marvelous Living Pictures," a hand shadow act in which husband and wife held their
fingers before a small spotlight and created silhouettes of the Rol-
licking Irishman or the Cat Duet.

"Scenes of Enchantment" was an example of Billy's full education
in magic and his devotion to Herrmann's style of performing, a two-
hour show of assorted wonders. The program was a slavish imitation
of Herrmann's show, from the Spirit Cabinet to the levitation
trick—it was Herrmann and his wife Adelaide who had presented
the levitation with the odd addition of costumes. Billy Robinson
even copied titles from Herrmann's program, like an extended series
of tricks called the "Soirée Magique!"

To an ambitious young performer like Billy, the drumbeat of his
playbill, "Robinson, Man of Mystery . . . Robinson, The Man of Many
Voices . . . Robinson the Famous Spiritualist," would have been a
source of pride. Ironically, this "master of all trades" approach was
what vaudeville managers avoided. Robinson was forced to pare down
his act, but the result attracted little attention. An 1885 *New York
Times* review noted a special benefit at Koster and Bial's which
included Robinson, Man of Mystery, but the young magician earned

no special praise, just the acknowledgment that he "went through a variety of conjurer's tricks."

Bessie enjoyed being on stage and was an attractive addition to the act. But a magic show involved backbreaking work, long hours of rehearsal, and the inevitable nauseating mistakes—stage nerves mixed with faulty planning—and these were hard lessons for a beginner.

When the Robinsons discovered that Bessie was pregnant with her first child, Billy supplemented his income with more dependable work. The New York City directory for 1884–85 lists William Robinson as the head of the household at 14 Suffolk Street, just several doors away from Bessie Smith's father. Robinson's occupation is listed as teacher.

On February 10, 1885, Billy and Bessie's son was born. Unfortunately, the baby's arrival quickly put a strain on the marriage. Even the child's birth certificate shows uncertainty—a week after the birth, the baby had not been given a name. He was later called Elmore.

Now that she was a mother, Bessie was not available to leave home and assist her husband's magic act. Billy was forced to simplify the performance, or work with another showgirl who was willing to learn the duties of assistant.

—⁂—

When Harry Hill's infamous Saloon closed in 1886, Jim Campbell, Hill's longtime stage manager, suddenly found himself out of work. Campbell was nearly 53 years old. A resilient, pragmatic performer, he was always ready to return to the boards, dust off an old act, or write a new song that might propel him back through the halls to make a little money. A lifelong bibliophile, he was able to perform on Lyceum—a sort of educational vaudeville developed for smaller cities. As Carl Sunshine, he delivered an entertaining lecture titled, "The Rambles of a Literary Vagabond."

Jim Campbell was surprised to receive an offer from an ambitious young Boston vaudeville entrepreneur, named B. F. Keith. Keith wasn't looking for just an act. He was looking for a stage manager.

Benjamin Franklin Keith was born in 1846 in Hillsboro Bridge, New Hampshire, and raised on a West Massachusetts farm. He saw his first show, a traveling entertainment, when he was seventeen years old, and became obsessed with show business, analyzing it like a science during his first jobs in the industry. In 1882 Keith settled in Boston and leased a small storefront on Washington Street, where he installed his own dime museum attractions. "Baby Alice" was his first real star, a small baby, supposedly three months old, who weighed only one and a half pounds. Keith charged ten cents admission to see tiny Alice; his hall was filled with curious spectators for two weeks and his cashbox jingled with dimes. In 1885, working with a Providence, Rhode Island, producer named Batcheller, he opened the Gaiety Theater in that city.

It was at the Gaiety that Keith made his first innovation. He had noticed the pleasant feeling in a theater when the show was running, and also the dark, dreary atmosphere that pervaded when the curtain came down and the audiences were moved in and out. "Did you ever notice the hesitancy on the part of early comers to a playhouse to assume their seats in the auditorium, how they hang back until reassured by numbers?" he wrote years later, explaining his discovery. "I was always maneuvering to keep patrons moving up and down stairs in view of passersby on the sidewalk for the specific purpose of impressing them with the idea that business was immense."

On July 6, 1885, Keith's Gaiety began a policy of Continuous Performance. The theater opened at 10:30 that morning, and closed at 10:30 that night. Acts were repeated throughout the day. There was no start to the "show" and no end; the audience filed in and watched until they were satisfied, then left the theater. Keith's big stars performed twice a day, and other acts were asked to perform three or four times, to fill out the bill. One performer, who was giving a brief lecture on an arctic exploration, was confused by the new system. "Why, Mr. Keith, I can't go out there and make that talk over again," he protested. "The same people I talked to before are still in the house." Keith convinced him to return to the stage. He did, and people all over the auditorium stood up and began to leave. But new patrons quickly filled those seats. Keith reported, "The gentleman who lectured soon saw the point."

Continuous performance was a remarkable success. Although it exhausted the performers and scrambled the traditional pacing of a show, it attracted the public, who came to think of vaudeville as a modern convenience, accessible virtually any hour of the day: entertainment as hot and cold running water.

In August 1887, Keith opened the Bijou Theater in Boston. The Bijou was a beautiful theater decorated in red and gold, with a round Moorish arch surrounding the stage, and it became a showcase for Keith's continuous vaudeville, which was revolutionizing show business. "Two things I determined at the outset should prevail in the new scheme," Keith later wrote. "My fixed policy of cleanliness and order should be continued . . . and entertainment would directly appeal to the support of ladies and children."

Supervising the backstage required diplomacy, professionalism, a full knowledge of the acts, an iron hand, and a magnificent sense of timing. Jim Campbell's tough-as-nails stage experience, honed after years in old-fashioned variety, was perfectly suited to the latest innovation in vaudeville. Campbell began work at the Gaiety Theater in Providence, and then moved to the Bijou Theater in Boston.

—⁂—

At one of his variety engagements in New York City, William Robinson met Olive Path. Olive was a showgirl, a dancer and chanteuse—one of a group of young ladies who formed the ballet in an early variety show or formed the chorus in the play. She was more resolute than most, because she had a lot to overcome. She was not the voluptuous beauty—tightly packed into a spangled leotard and cotton tights—that the 1880s audience expected. Instead, Olive was tiny, well under five feet tall, with a slender figure. She had the narrow gray eyes, round cheeks, and thin red lips of a porcelain doll. Photos, throughout her life, show a diminutive lady with a child-like face of indeterminate age—anywhere between twelve

Showgirl Olive Path, nicknamed Dot.

and forty. Like every experienced actress, she made it a habit always to lie about her age.

She was born in Cleveland, Ohio, in 1863, and her real name was Augusta Pfaff. Her father and mother, John Pfaff and Mary Steele Pfaff, were both born in Germany. John and Mary immigrated to New York in 1851, and then moved to Cleveland, where John worked as a confectioner. Mary raised their nine children.

By 1880, the family was living in Elyria, Ohio, and John Pfaff was a saloonkeeper, which may explain the 17-year-old Augusta's involvement in show business. Several years later she had worked her way to New York City. She had anglicized her name: Pfaff became Path, and Olive may have been chosen as especially poetic for an entertainer, like Rose Garden or Lily Field.

In any case, William Robinson would always call her Dot, because of her diminutive size. She would call him Will.

On stage, tiny Dot Path was confined to the ends of the line of showgirls, placing the fuller, prettier girls in the middle of the stage. Or she was chosen for the child's role in the play that closed the program. But Dot was the ideal size for a magician's assistant, fitting easily into cabinets, suitably light and slender for the levitation illusion. She was also, by her early twenties, a tough professional, stoically enduring cramped dressing rooms, drafty, dusty stages, and theatrical lodgings. She was capable of quickly packing a trunk and, belying her size, determinedly maneuvering it down the stairs in bumps and crashes, and then twisting and tugging it across the floor to the loading door of the theater.

William Robinson fell in love.

Chapter 6

THE BLACK ART

B en Ali Bey stepped onto the stage with a long, loping stride. It took only four paces to reach the center of the small platform, and then he spun on his heel, cocked a shaggy white eyebrow, and glowered beyond the footlights.

Sitting in the front row, watching with curiosity, Will Robinson's first impression was that Ben Ali Bey looked ridiculous. There was nothing modern about this magician: none of the polished, cutaway-coat sophistication, the London and Paris niceties that had been imported to New York City by Alexander Herrmann. Instead, Bey was a strange German concoction of theatrical mysticism: equal parts *Thousand and One Nights* and a Berlin costume shop. He was dressed in a long skirt and full robe of soft white fabric, adorned with colorful embroidered panels and any handy bits of gold braid, lace, and fringe. Atop his head was a bizarre turban wrapped around a pointed wizard's cap. The magician held a twisted white-painted wand in one hand, his other thumb tucked into the colorful cummerbund that encircled his full belly. Bey growled his introductory talk in German, his long, snow-white beard pointed aggressively at the audience and bobbing up and down with each harsh syllable. Billy Robinson couldn't understand a word of it—he had only learned a bit of German from the Martinka family—but the audience listened closely and chuckled in response to his jokes. Billy expected the worst. This sort of melodramatic, fairy-tale magic had been out of fashion for over a generation.

His 1886 European trip was an extravagance for the young New York wizard. Robinson must have intended it as a deliberate assault on the world of magic, a pilgrimage to the trendsetting capitals where he could witness the latest experiments in the art. More important, Will Robinson intended to acquire a few secrets that would give him a head start back in New York, a chance to premiere the latest innovations from Europe. The trip was also his attempt to escape a failing marriage and the tedium of a stalled career—he left Bessie and Elmore behind.

Robinson had worked his way east, first stopping in London. There he was able to see the famous Maskelyne and Cooke theater of magic at Egyptian Hall in Piccadilly, a creaky, fusty little auditorium decorated with painted Egyptian hieroglyphics. Egyptian Hall served as a laboratory for great magicians, where the latest European innovations premiered. In Paris he stopped at the famous Théâtre Robert-Houdin, founded by France's leading magician. Jean-Eugène Robert-Houdin had died over a decade earlier; a rubber-faced French magician named George Méliès was the current proprietor of the theater, and presented the master's famous tricks in the elegant Louis Quatorze–style theater.

While the famous theaters of magic in London and Paris had been inspiring to Billy Robinson, they had also been instantly familiar. Robinson still worked with the Martinkas on special projects, and he had appealed to the New York magic dealers to underwrite his journey. The Martinka brothers' business depended upon regular trips to Europe, where they copied the latest ideas for their catalog or arranged to import the latest apparatus. Robinson was obliged to visit the Carl Willmann factory in Hamburg, where the finest metal apparatus was manufactured. Willmann's specialty was spun brass props (shaped from sheet metal as they were turned on a lathe, not merely hand-bent and soldered together) that were then heavily nickel-plated so they shone like the finest silver service. Willmann's bright metal vases, urns, lamps, cages, and tables were highly prized by magicians around the world, and exclusively imported into the United States by the Martinkas.

Robinson, Man of Mystery, quickly established his credentials at the neat little Willmann factory, examining their products with a careful eye and passing along the latest improvements from America. He also placed a large order for the Martinka shop, ensuring that their shelves would be filled with the finest glittering apparatus for the magicians of New York. Carl Willmann had seen the strange act of Ben Ali Bey the previous season in Hamburg, and he told Robinson that the act had caused a unique stir among German magicians. He urged his American visitor to attend the Passage Panoptikon, a Berlin version of the Eden Musée, consisting of a small theater with adjoining waxwork exhibition, where Ben Ali Bey was performing.

—∞—

Ben Ali Bey nodded to the pianist, who took his cue and began to play the entry march from *Aida*. The curtains opened on a strange stage setting. It didn't look like a magic act, Robinson thought to himself. Raised above the stage was another, smaller stage—a heavy wooden platform about twelve feet across, lifted on trestles so it was about two feet over the stage floor. This small stage was surrounded by drapery; a fabric ceiling and curtained back and sides of inky black velvet enclosed the performing area. Painted columns with elephant heads and a painted mural of the Nile River added to the pretend oriental motif. A row of gas lamps on the stage floor enhanced the illusion with a bright halo of light.

Ben Ali Bey continued his introduction by leaning down and pointing, with his wand, to the platform of his miniature stage. As a fellow magician, Robinson knew exactly what the white-robed wizard must have been saying: he was demonstrating how this platform stage was held aloft by the row of trestles. Bey waved his wand in the open space between the floor and the raised platform, and Robinson filled in the words. "As you can see, there are no trapdoors of any kind used."

The German magician stepped up a small ladder, mounting the

raised platform. He paced right and left in the darkened cave, taking purposeful strides, giving the appearance of a fairy-tale wizard in his dark dungeon. Then the piano trilled. Bey pushed up his long, full sleeves and held his white wand high in the air. There was a quick, rough command from the magician. "Kommen!" And then a small, four-legged wooden pedestal table appeared standing beside the magician. Robinson instinctively drew in his breath. He wasn't sure what he'd just seen. There had been nothing on the stage just a moment before, and then the brightly painted table appeared, with barely a flicker of motion.

Bey reached over to slowly pick up the table and turn it over in his hands. He banged it on the stage, demonstrating with a thump that it was solid, carved wood. The magician didn't pause for applause. He moved steadily onward, oblivious of the audience and their stunned reactions. The pianist began playing Beethoven's *Turkish March*.

Ben Ali Bey, the inventor of a new form of magic, Black Art.

Bey tapped his wand on the floor and instantly two large, polished metal urns appeared on the stage. The magician carried them forward, showing them to the front row of the audience. He kept up his chatter, obviously urging the spectators to examine the urns. They were just empty metal containers. He replaced them on the stage and, with overstated solemnity, reached into a pocket in his robe and withdrew two small beans. The audience laughed. It was something out of Jack and the Beanstalk. Bey held the beans carefully in his hand, giving every impression that they were precious and mysterious. He dropped the dark coffee bean into the first urn, and the audience heard it clatter to the bottom. The small white bean fell into the second urn. He quickly placed covers atop each urn, and there were more spells, waving the wand around the empty metal urns. When the covers were removed, seconds later, one urn held steaming hot coffee, and the other was filled with cubes of sugar.

Not pausing for applause, the German magician marched to the other side of his stage and held a cloth in front of his little wooden table. When the cloth was whisked away, a stack of cups and saucers had appeared. He ladled out coffee and served it to lucky members of the audience.

Bey's show was a long one, and it included two intermissions so that the magician could set more new tricks on his small stage. In a section titled "Indian Magic," Bey produced a small barrel, showed it empty, and set it upright on a table. He reached inside and withdrew enormous bouquets of flowers, one after another. Finally, an enormous snake rose from within the barrel, weaving in the air and snapping its jaws at Ben Ali Bey. The snake disappeared into the barrel again. The magician picked up a number of large toy balls, placing them into the barrel until it seemed to be filled. Finally he lifted the barrel and tipped it forward. There was nothing inside.

One of his prettiest effects consisted of apparently blowing a large soap bubble, and then fanning it about the stage until it settled on a small porcelain plate. He repeated this with a second, third, and fourth bubble that were all magically stacked into a pyramid of glassy spheres at the end of the illusion.

To a magician like William Robinson, the show was weird, unsettling, stimulating. It was nothing like the conjuring the Man of Mystery had studied, and that was part of the appeal. It was as if Ben Ali Bey were a real wizard who had arrived in Berlin and was playing the part of a stage magician—keeping his powers in check and performing tricks with balls, urns, and borrowed watches. He seemed to have an endless supply of wonders, one phantasmagoric image after another. He didn't perform tricks, but real magic, and magic in abundance.

The white wizard paced the stage, talking continuously, conducting it all with his wand the same way a maestro stands before an orchestra and summons music. As the show built to a crescendo,

Ben Ali Bey showed a large framed slate, placed it on an easel, and made a chalk drawing of a skeleton. The drawing came to life, dancing a jig. A lady appeared from an empty treasure chest; it was the magician's daughter Sulamith, dressed in a gown as exotic as her father's costume. The magician removed his own head and placed it on a table to one side, and then instantly restored it to his shoulders, stepping forward to take his bow.

Near the end of Ben Ali Bey's strange, dream-like demonstration, Will Robinson recognized something familiar: the darkness in contrast with the light, bright colors on stage. He held his hand to his eyes, blocking out the glare from the row of gaslights: Thauma! Looking beyond the patch of darkness on Bey's tiny stage, he suddenly understood exactly what was happening. It was not merely a mystery; it was a miracle.

—∞—

Of course, Ben Ali Bey was not a real wizard. He was not even a trained magician. He was an actor, born Max Auzinger, in Munich in 1839. In the early 1880s, during a performance of the play *Donatin Morlay* at the national theater in Berlin, he was serving as the stage manager as well as playing several character parts. One scene was the spectacular rescue of the heroine from the dungeon. Auzinger had used dense black velvet drapes, part of the theater's stock scenery, behind the prison window.

According to the script of the play, a Negro slave was to climb down a rope and appear at the window to release his mistress, saving her in the nick of time. A German actor in black makeup played the slave.

Auzinger was watching from the wings when the black-faced actor appeared at the window. The stage manager waited for the audience's roar of approval. There was no reaction. Auzinger positioned himself to look at the actor through the window. Only a row of teeth and two beaming eyes were visible, floating in front of the inky darkness of the curtains.

The secret became known as Black Art—a nice mixture of a technical term as well as a magical one—and it depended on an ingenious optical effect. A black object "disappeared" when it was in front of a black background because there was no visible shadow to distinguish one surface from another—or more properly, the shadow was being swallowed up in the blackness. The color formed a perfect camouflage. Auzinger's first tests were with black cloth attached to the walls of his daughter's doll's house. He placed a tiny white porcelain angel in the doll's house, covered it with a scrap of black fabric, and watched the angel disappear.

Realizing the magical quality of the secret, Auzinger applied it to a conjuring act. He performed it for the first time in June 1885, billing himself as Maxistan A-Uzin-Ger, but the act was not a success. He teamed up with a German magician named Charles Arbre and, as part of Arbre's show, restaged the act as Ben Ali Bey. After several months of false starts, Auzinger left Arbre, produced the act in Hamburg, and then in Berlin at the Passage Panoptikon.

To obtain the perfect result, the German magician tested the blackest of curtains and carefully arranged the gaslights on his stage. White and bright colors were perfectly visible within the setting, and seemed to glow against the dark background. An important part of the secret was the row of lamps beneath the stage, called dazzlers. These were shielded so they didn't throw light on the performance area, but instead were positioned to shine into the eyes of the audience. The dazzlers provided a curious illusion, seemingly brightening the act—audiences remembered the brilliant sparkle of lights on Auzinger's stage—but they actually darkened the performance area by causing the spectators' pupils to contract.

Once the drapery and lights had been arranged, Auzinger had the power to make anything invisible. An assistant swathed in a special costume of black coveralls—with matching black gloves, boots, and a hood with black mesh eyeholes—could not be seen by the audience. The assistant could carry forward the table, which was similarly covered with a large black sheet. As Auzinger waved his wand, the sheet was rapidly pulled away, causing the brightly painted table to appear. When the black-clad assistant stood near Auzinger and manipulated round glass spheres, it seemed as if bubbles were floating. A black hood quickly slipped over Auzinger's own head gave the appearance that he had been decapitated.

—m—

Max Auzinger's account of his discovery—the accident of the black-amoor in the dungeon—sounds suspiciously neat, especially from an experienced old showman. In fact, the origin of the illusion is probably much more complicated. The secret had been in use for many years before the alleged discovery, incorporated into several small tricks. For example, Robinson himself had employed a table, borrowed from his father's old act, that used black fabric on the top to conceal several small trapdoors. Jim Campbell later told his son that he had first encountered Black Art when he saw a popular performer named McAllister in America. McAllister used a setting with a black tabletop and a wide black shelf behind it. A black-wrapped bundle, sitting on the table, was invisible to his audience. During the course of his act, he cleverly inserted this bundle into a borrowed hat, later reaching in the hat, secretly unwrapping it, and producing the traditional string of flags, toys, and finally a rabbit.

In the 1860s, the use of black-wrapped props and assistants was an important secret in Pepper's Ghost, an elaborate stage effect that was first produced in London. Pepper's Ghost involved light-colored objects reflected in a large sheet of glass, giving the audience the effect of translucent ghosts onstage.

Years before Auzinger's scene in the dungeon, the secret of Black Art seemed to have been completely understood by the British magician Dr. Lynn. Some time in the early 1870s, when working at the London Aquarium, Lynn produced a weird puppet effect called Living Marionettes. It consisted of the heads of actors attached, at the neck, to tiny, articulated puppet bodies, about a foot tall. The effect was hilarious, and became a popular parlor amusement. When Living Marionettes was described in an appendix to Professor Hoffmann's

Modern Magic in 1880, the text noted that the illusion was accomplished by draping the actor's real body in black. "It will be noticed that the drapery is entirely of black, and that the eye is deceived by the absence of any break in the color of the drapery, as to distance."

In the late 1870s, Lynn first introduced Thauma at the Folies Bergère in Paris: this was the illusion that Robinson later saw in New York. In fact, the lady was not deformed, but was a complete actress, from head to toe. A specially shaped wooden torso, cut off at the waist, was strapped beneath her bodice, and concealed beneath her costume. Her actual torso and legs were draped in black fabric, which matched the black draperies behind her. Just as Thauma's body was suspended on a small wooden swing, her legs, concealed in the invisible darkness behind her, were also suspended on a matching velvet-covered swing. Her back was arched and her legs extended horizontally, away from the audience. The bright lights surrounding the frame of Thauma served to create the illusion of perfect darkness.

The ingenious Dr. Lynn had discovered Black Art long before Auzinger, and there's even evidence of Lynn's inspiration. In 1862, working as Hugh Simmons, Lynn toured the Antipodes and Japan. In Nagasaki, Japan, he was the first western magician to perform in that country, and he reportedly learned several Japanese magic tricks and juggling feats. In Japan, the traditional form of puppetry is Bunraku. Japanese Bunraku consists of small, elegant puppets operated by puppeteers directly behind the puppets and swathed entirely in black. Although Bunraku operators were never intended to be completely invisible, the artistic conceit was that the black costuming, in combination with the dark background, isolated the puppets on their stage and created a powerful illusion. Bunraku would have had a memorable effect on the English magician Simmons, and led to similar effects, like his Living Marionettes and Thauma.

—⟋ⱦⱦ⟍—

Shortly after Auzinger's success with Black Art, Charles Arbre, his previous associate, plundered the secret, copying the Ben Ali Bey act and presenting it under the name Ben Azra El Muz. Arbre also sold the secret—including curtains, props, and costumes—through a Hamburg magic dealer named Lischke.

When Will Robinson shielded his eyes from the pinpoint lights that surrounded the scene, he was able to distinguish the black against black surfaces on stage—that was the secret of Thauma at the Eden Musée and Ben Ali Bey's miraculous show at the Panoptikon. By rights, the discovery was Auzinger's. But show business never functioned by such polite, rarefied rules. Robinson's understanding of the secret was enough, in his own mind, to entitle him to copy the act. As the old German actor fought off competitors across Europe, he was unaware of the ambitious young magician racing back to America. William Robinson would stake his claim for Black Art in the New World.

—⚇—

Performing nine minutes of Black Art would be much more difficult than presenting two hours of "Scenes of Enchantment," Robinson's own show of tried-and-true, comfortable classics of magic. Working secretly at the Martinka shop, Robinson made the tables and boxes that appeared and disappeared. For a glowing skeleton that would appear floating in space, break into pieces, and then reassemble itself, he used papier-mâché for the bones, and then painted them with layers of thick white enamel so they would shine in the dark setting. "This is one of the most expensive stage illusions, costing several hundred dollars to properly stage it with the best drapery and accessories," Robinson wrote many years later. "Unless such are used, the proper illusory effect is lost. In magic as well as in other business, cheap apparatus is dear at any price."

Black Art only worked when every element functioned properly: the scenery, the gaslights, the wardrobe and props. If a piece of drapery fell out of place, if the gas operator in the wings of the theater missed his cue and fed too little fuel to the dazzlers, if a blackrobed, invisible assistant carelessly thrust an arm in front of the white-garbed magician, the entire illusion collapsed. There was no glib remark, no sudden bit of sleight of hand that could rescue the act. The only way of achieving the illusion was through careful planning and rehearsal. It was a meticulous ballet in which the visible and invisible danced together.

For the first time in his career, Will found himself perilously dependent on an assistant. The unseen half of the act had to share his precision and commitment. He found such an assistant in Olive Path—tiny Dot, who took the assignment soberly and understood quickly the potential of Black Art. Dot sewed costumes and packed the props. She practiced each move with Will, night after night, standing behind him and studying their magical choreography in a large mirror at Martinka's. Their rehearsals were all the more exciting for their late-night, locked-room subterfuge. It was now Will and Dot's precious secret, and it seemed as if they were the only two people in America who knew it.

Dot Path proved to be determined and resilient. She didn't object to the long hours encased in her black velvet costume, or the endless adjustments and experiments as Will second-guessed each decision. She was devoted to show business in a way that young Bessie Robinson had never been.

After Robinson's return from Europe, he neglected his wife and family. Will and Bessie didn't file for divorce—a long, expensive process, and unavailable to Robinson, who was raised a Roman Catholic. Like many couples of the day, they decided to ignore their marriage and quietly cancel it. Bessie took the baby, Elmore.

Will spent his time working exclusively on the new act, constantly thinking about improvements, rehearsals, and little Dot.

—m—

Jim Campbell understood the importance of his son's new act. He secured a booking for Black Art at the Keith theater where he was working as stage manager. On Monday, August 8, 1887, William Robinson appeared as Achmed Ben Ali on the stage at the New

Century Museum in Providence, Rhode Island, with Olive Path as his invisible assistant. It was a prestigious booking at one of the country's first vaudeville theaters, under the direction of vaudeville's most innovative manager, B. F. Keith.

There is little question that Robinson's Black Art act—as Achmed Ben Ali—had been taken from Auzinger's performance as Ben Ali Bey. But Will's name Achmed Ben Ali was also derived from Achmed Ali Bey, an early vaudeville acrobat. Billy Robinson, searching for the perfect exotic name, borrowed bits and pieces from various performers. On stage, he had simplified Auzinger's stage setting, eliminating the raised platform so that it could be set quickly in a vaudeville program. Achmed Ben Ali wore a wig of long, dark brown hair, a full beard, a long Egyptian headdress, and a full white robe. Unlike Auzinger, Robinson performed his wonders silently, to musical accompaniment.

Tables appeared and floated across the stage. An orange tree seemed to grow suddenly from a small seed. A staff was transformed into a serpent, which slithered offstage. Apples poured into one basket quickly disappeared, then reappeared across the stage in another basket. A rabbit, tossed into the air, vanished in a flash. A skeleton appeared suddenly, and bits of it became disconnected, floating in space. Finally, Achmed Ben Ali seated himself atop a slender pole—the thickness of a walking stick—defying gravity. As the audience applauded, he suddenly disappeared while airborne, leaving the wooden pole standing upright on the stage.

Olive Path worked in perfect concert with the white-robed wizard. Peering through the eyeholes in her black hood, she hit each mark, was ready with each black container, and deftly handed Will the necessary props, supporting the magician like a guiding spirit.

Jim Campbell also watched over the act carefully from his post in the wings. He had introduced his son to the gasman at the theater, instructed him on how he should rehearse the act and write up the cues to ensure that the act was dependable in any theater. Based on his decades in show business, Keith's new stage manager suggested late summer for his son's debut. It was a slow period in the theater, and a good way to try out the act. But by all accounts, there was no tryout needed. Achmed Ben Ali became the talk of the city and filled the Gaiety, show after show, with jostling crowds. The *New York Clipper* recorded that the magician offered "new and remarkable feats, and the rush to see him is great." He was extended for another week, and then another. The initial engagement ran for a full month, and secured him bookings at Keith's other theaters.

So, ironically, it was Achmed Ben Ali that became the star, not William Robinson, Man of Mystery. Robinson found the disguise surprisingly comfortable. Becoming someone else was a delicious deception. The magician had never been at ease speaking onstage, feigning the sophisticated, witty remarks that were expected to accompany a magic show. By playing the part of the Egyptian mystic, hiding behind dark makeup and a beard, he wasn't expected to smile, chatter, or engage the audience. His pantomime skills carried the act. The magic spoke for itself.

Dot, similarly, discovered that being invisible was liberating. She

William Robinson in costume for the Black
Art act.

was no longer burdened with the role of the simpering little girl, forced to pad her costumes so she could stand next to the busty, leggy beauties that attracted the attention of the crowd. Her hard work carried the act. Her talent spoke for itself.

Offstage and out of costume in Providence, Will and Dot began introducing themselves as Mr. and Mrs. William Robinson. This made it easier to travel together and share a hotel room. It avoided explanations and smoothed over introductions. Dot knew about Bessie, left behind in New York, who was no longer interested in being Mrs. William Robinson. So Olive Path took the role, onstage and off. There was something romantic and intriguing about this deception, as well: yet another secret they shared between themselves, and kept from the rest of the world.

Chapter 7

HARRY KELLAR

B efore they left Providence, Rhode Island, Will and Dot were determined to put their next illusion, The Cocoon, on stage. The couple was convinced that it would be an effective follow-up to the Black Art act.

The Cocoon was the invention of the French magician Buatier deKolta, and it was first presented at Egyptian Hall in London on May 2, 1887, while Robinson was at work on his Black Art act in New York. The Cocoon was a mechanical masterpiece. It was artistic, intellectual, and beautiful to watch, a perfect model for late-Victorian magic.

Ironically, deKolta was never a graceful performer. He was short and plump, with long shaggy hair and an unkempt beard. He had a tendency to wear oversized clothes and struck odd poses as he operated his magic; he suggested less a ballet dancer than a workman attempting ballet. His genius lay in inventions, and those inventions were striking and original. Audiences overlooked the awkward performances for the genius of his tricks. His fellow magicians studied deKolta as the great innovator of his generation, the man who set trends in magic.

The fact that William Robinson had built the first American copy of The Cocoon, just months after its European premiere, suggests that he had made some powerful friends in London during his European trip. Robinson obtained a description of the trick and the secret from an unknown but well-connected magician who saw the performance at Egyptian Hall and was clever enough to study the details in deKolta's patent, which had been granted on March 1, 1887. It was a complicated bit of machinery, and Will must have begun building it in New York, before he and Dot took Black Art to Providence.

When The Cocoon was finished, Jim Campbell informed his son that this ingenious trick was perfectly unsuited to a vaudeville show, where acts were set quickly onstage, and it was difficult to rely on trapdoors or special scenery. The Cocoon was just too much for Keith's stage at the New Gaiety Theatre. When Robinson finished his engagement as Achmed Ben Ali, he convinced the manager of the Westminster Musée, a dime museum in Providence, to try out The Cocoon. It was a chance for Will Robinson to perform again as the Man of Mystery, wearing his cutaway coat and high collar.

At the Westminster Musée, Robinson began The Cocoon by stepping from the wings, trailing a long red satin ribbon that he held in his hand. He stretched it across the stage, about seven feet above the floor, by looping it over hooks on each side wall. To each end of the ribbon he attached a small bag filled with sand, so the ribbon would be stretched taut. He then picked up a frame of lightweight wood, about three feet square and a foot deep, with paper stretched on one side of it. The frame was, essentially, a shallow box with a paper bottom. He stood the frame in the center of the stage, with the paper side facing the audience, and pulled down the ribbon so that it could be looped under two hooks at the top of the frame. The small weights on the end of the ribbon pulled the frame into the air, so that it was suspended over Will's head.

He now picked up a large black crayon and drew a sketch of a silkworm on the paper. Stepping away from the frame, he commanded a transformation, uttering a few magic words. The paper tore open—like a drumhead that was stretched too tightly and burst—revealing the pretty, lavender, oval-shaped cocoon within the frame. The cocoon seemed to fill the entire frame.

Robinson pulled away the box-like frame, leaving the cocoon suspended on the ribbon. He slid a stool beneath the cocoon, and stepped to the side of the stage, lifting the weights so the ribbon went slack and the lightweight cocoon was slowly lowered to the stool.

Stepping back, he commanded the final transformation. The

cocoon slowly opened, revealing a lady tucked inside it. This was Dot Robinson, dressed in a pretty butterfly costume. She was helped from the cocoon and the duo took a bow.

The Cocoon was a wonderful choice for the Man of Mystery act. Will proudly built it around the diminutive Dot, which meant that the apparatus was delicate, light, and impossibly small. When the cocoon opened and Dot was tucked inside, it was a genuine surprise and a perfect climax for this pretty, dream-like fantasy. The apparatus fit her like a glove, which also signaled Will's intention to keep working with her.

Unfortunately, The Cocoon was too complicated for Mr. Bingham, the manager of the Westminster Musée. There were several secrets responsible for the effect. At the beginning of the trick, the silk cocoon, with the lady inside, was pushed up through a trapdoor in the stage and secretly inserted into the paper frame. This happened just before the frame was lifted up onto the ribbon.

Several fine steel wires, arranged so they would be invisible against the backdrop, helped to lift the frame and cocoon. The wires allowed Robinson to demonstrate that the paper frame was virtually weightless. When the cocoon was revealed, the ribbon—and the concealed wires—lowered the cocoon to the stool and Dot was found inside.

Will and Dot were frustrated by their failure to find a home for The Cocoon. They were proud of the trick and proud to be the first performers to bring it to America. By the end of September, a magic dealer in Chicago was advertising plans for "Buatier's Cocoon," and they realized that other magicians would soon be performing this trick. They packed up the apparatus, and accepted an engagement for Achmed Ben Ali at Keith's Gaiety Musée and Bijou Theatre in Boston.

—⁓—

Black Art proved to be an even bigger success in Boston than it had been in Providence. Achmed Ben Ali appeared at the Bijou on October 17, 1887, and the Robinsons were extended, week after week, as crowds returned and told their friends about the unusual

Egyptian mystic. Keith's continuous entertainment meant that they were stranded in the theatre for most of the day, awaiting their next show or repacking the props for the next performance.

The *New York Clipper*, a theatrical journal, took notice of the act, reporting that, "Achmed Ben Ali is certainly the best feature that has ever been presented at a museum in this city. His illusions are really amazing, and he ought to prove a 10-times winner for manager Keith. The latter means to make him so, if he can, and when Manager Keith starts out with cold-blooded determination to do a thing, he appears to have the facility of getting there."

Achmed Ben Ali was one of Keith's first stars, and the act should have guaranteed a long, successful career for the Robinsons. But by the time they reached Boston, Will and Dot had been tempted by other offers.

Both Alexander Herrmann and Harry Kellar—American's number one and number two magicians, and two fierce rivals in the theater world—sent representatives to see Achmed Ben Ali's new act and report back to the master wizards. Kellar himself came to see the show before it left Providence, and he made it known that he was interested in the act as a feature of his upcoming tour.

Of course, when Robinson worked at the Martinka shop in New York, he had met Kellar when the magician stopped in have his props repaired or to examine the latest apparatus.

Unlike Herrmann, he was a completely home-grown wizard. Harry Kellar was born Heinrich Keller in Erie, Pennsylvania, in 1849, and as a boy held a series of jobs in his hometown and for the Erie Railroad. He ran away from home when he was eleven, sold dry goods and worked at a printing press in Cleveland, and sold newspapers in Lower Manhattan. Young Henry became a ward of The Reverend Robert Harcourt, who received the boy's pledge that he would finish his education and study for the ministry. But in upstate New York, Harcourt took Henry to see a performance by a Buffalo magician who worked under the name The Fakir of Ava—his real name was Isaiah Hughes. The boy watched as the Fakir supposedly smashed a borrowed watch and made it reappear again as he fired a

Harry Kellar, the popular American
magician.

pistol, caught silver coins from the air, and changed paper shavings
into milk and sugar. Henry had never imagined such things; he was
completely enchanted by the magic and haunted by the idea of
becoming a magician.

During the Civil War, Henry and Reverend Harcourt were living
in Buffalo, New York, and the boy was employed at a nearby farm.
One morning he saw a newspaper advertisement placed by the Fakir
of Ava. The magician was looking for a boy assistant. Henry ran two
miles to the Fakir's farmhouse and applied for the job. He later
learned that it was the Fakir's little black and tan terrier that was
responsible for the interview. The other boys who had applied found
the dog snarling and snapping at their ankles. When Henry pushed
his way through the gate, the dog dashed up to him, wagging his tail.
The Fakir of Ava considered that a fine judgment of the boy's character, and awarded Henry the job.

After his employment under the Fakir, Keller set out on his own in
1867, at age 18, performing in small communities throughout the

Midwest. Keller struggled from town to town. He lost all his money, had props and clothes attached by the local sheriff, hopped on freight trains, and pleaded to local printers for tickets and handbills necessary for his shows. In Beaver Dam, Wisconsin, he rented a small hall on the second floor of a building. When he stepped onto the stage, he realized that his meager audience was made up entirely of creditors. They weren't interested in the magic. They were waiting for the magician. At intermission, he lowered his props out of the window on a rope, and then climbed down the rope and ran to the train station.

In LaCrosse, Wisconsin, his luck suddenly changed. The Davenport Brothers, the originators of the séance act, were working in town and looking for a road manager. Keller was ready to accept any job. He signed on, and toured for two years with the famous Spiritualists. The Davenports guarded their secrets, but Kellar watched them closely and privately made his own experiments with the cabinet, quickly learning the method for their act—once inside their wooden cabinet the brothers skillfully loosened the ropes around their wrists and ankles and caused the séance manifestations. He also learned to distrust the brothers. After organizing their tours through the eastern United States and Canada, Keller left when William Davenport insulted him, calling him his "servant."

Keller built a new show around a copy of the Davenports' act, although he always informed his audience that his séance was the result of pure trickery, not spirits. He changed his name to Harry Kellar—altering the spelling of his last name to avoid confusion with the magician and mind reader Robert Heller—and with a partner named George Fay toured through the southern United States, into Mexico and South America. Then, working with a succession of different partners, Kellar accomplished two full world tours with his magic, making and losing several fortunes.

Kellar had exceptional taste in magic. Although not an innovator, he had begged or stolen the greatest illusions in magic and brought them to his audiences. He made regular trips to London to study the latest effects of Buatier deKolta or John Nevil Maskelyne, and then copied the illusions for his audiences. Maskelyne always felt a chill when he saw Kellar's face in his audience, his pencil poised over his notebook; he had rebuffed Kellar's offers to buy his tricks, but the American was persistent. In the early 1880s, Kellar purchased a pirated copy of Maskelyne's card-playing automaton, Psycho. This was a little mechanical man, sitting atop a glass cylinder in the center of the stage, that seemed to think and answered questions by striking a bell or picking a playing card from a rack beneath his hand. Psycho even played members of the audience in a game of whist. He often won. Kellar managed to demonstrate Psycho before Queen Victoria before bringing the automaton back to the United States.

In 1884, when he returned to his native country, Kellar found that his main competition in magic was Herrmann the Great. Herrmann was well established, and had defined the look and character of a magician: the swaggering, devilish man of the theater. In contrast, Kellar was a big man with an open face and clear blue eyes. By the 1880s, his light brown hair had almost disappeared, and his oversized moustache gave him the appearance of your favorite uncle about to show you a trick, or a charming con man. Kellar was never sanguine about his competition. After several run-ins with Herrmann, he came to think of Herrmann the Great as a pompous fake, flaunting his sophisticated European connections. It rankled Kellar, and only made him work harder.

—⁓—

In fact, there were a lot of things about Harry Kellar that Will Robinson didn't admire. Kellar was a solid, sober showman, but he wasn't really a skillful magician. He had thick, stubby fingers and performed sleight-of-hand magic awkwardly. Sleight of hand had always been considered a badge of honor among magicians, and Herrmann's classical effects were especially admired. To a student of magic like Will Robinson, Kellar's lack of ability was an embarrassment, like a singer who couldn't hold a pitch.

Instead, Kellar specialized in presenting mechanical effects. When he caught silver coins from the air—a trick he had first seen performed by the Fakir of Ava—he couldn't palm the necessary stacks of half-dollars. With typical determination, Kellar had a special, flesh-colored metal holder made for him by the Martinkas. This device contained the coins, and special metal tabs soldered to the side of the holder allowed Kellar to clip it between his fingers.

But as the Robinsons and Kellar talked business, after one of the vaudeville performances, Will came to respect Kellar's hard-headed resolve and his legendary perfectionism. Over dinner with the Robinsons, Kellar surrounded the young magician with a flurry of magic gossip and a hundred technical questions. The breathless conversation flattered the young magician and also kept his head spinning: Where did the Martinkas get the hinges for his Spirit Cabinet illusion? Why was German brass of a better quality than American brass? Kellar was fascinated to hear about The Cocoon and asked the Robinsons if it was an illusion he could use in his show.

When Herrmann's name danced through the conversation, Kellar froze and his eyes flashed. "He's a thief," he told the young couple, and his words hardened into a long, brittle monologue about his rival. According to Harry Kellar, Herrmann was trying to steal away one of Kellar's supporting acts, a magician and juggler named D'Alvini. Herrmann, he told them, was ready to plunder anything: an employee, an idea, or a dime. In order to drive the point home, Kellar darkly hinted that Herrmann was also interested in the Black Art act, and he let those words hang in the air as Will and Dot exchanged glances. Robinson had never heard the world's greatest magician discussed in such bilious terms. It seemed undignified and unbecoming of Kellar.

If Will and Dot thought they had fooled Kellar with the Achmed Ben Ali act, they were mistaken. Kellar knew all about Auzinger, Hamburg, deKolta, black velvet, and the special gas lamps. He knew that Black Art was the latest idea, and that he'd have to bring it to his audiences. He wanted to make a deal.

Part of Kellar's flattery of the Robinsons worked against him. The Robinsons hesitated, waiting for Herrmann's offer. They knew that he'd had a report on the show, and that his route would be nearing Boston at the beginning of November. But their dreams were crushed when they opened an issue of the *New York Clipper* and found a flashy advertisement topped by a portrait of Alexander Herrmann. It announced the magician's new 1888 season for "The Prince of Prestidigitateurs" with his two new illusions: Black Art and Le Cocon.

Will squinted and read the fine print in the ad: "The only original Black Art and Le Cocon in the United States will be seen at the 5th Avenue Theatre, Niblo's Garden, NYC, Globe Theatre, Boston, Hooley's Chicago, Academy of Music, Philadelphia, Grand Opera House, Cincinnati, National Theatre, Washington, Ford's Theatre, Baltimore. August Next, will start on a Grand Tour of California, Mexico and Cuba."

It didn't really matter that Black Art and The Cocoon had already been seen in the United States, that Will and Dot had spent months on these effects to establish them as their own. Herrmann had the name and the long list of prestigious engagements. Herrmann was the star, and he'd laid claim to these mysteries as any conquering hero claims territory.

In fact, Herrmann had just stolen the ideas faster and more efficiently than Robinson had stolen them. Alexander and Adelaide Herrmann had been traveling through Europe the previous year, just like Will, searching for new effects. They both stumbled on Auzinger's new act, and they decided to bring it to America. Herrmann may have purchased the Black Art act from Lische in Berlin, the dealer who sold copies of Auzinger's act. The apparatus for The Cocoon was from a London or Paris magic dealer. In fact, Herrmann had taken possession of both props in the autumn of 1887, while Achmed Ben Ali was still appearing in Providence.

Herrmann's ad announced that he wouldn't be interested in the Robinsons' services. Even worse, the ad was intended to discourage Kellar from using Black Art and The Cocoon—they were now Herrmann's tricks. In a different situation, William Robinson might have been emboldened by the challenge: he was now competing, head to head, trick for trick, with the Great Herrmann. The Robinsons had been patiently waiting to make their best move. But suddenly, Will and Dot felt like the game pieces on a chessboard, being jumped, circled, and outmaneuvered by the world's greatest magicians.

—⁂—

Before the end of the Robinsons' Boston run, an envelope arrived, adorned with engraved angels and a disembodied hand pointing to the letters, "The Wonderful Kellar, Monarch of High Class Prestidigitation." Inside, the Robinsons were surprised to find an offer from Kellar: sixty dollars a week for Black Art, The Cocoon, Dot's work as an assistant, and Will's services backstage.

Of course, Kellar had also seen Herrmann's *New York Clipper* advertisement, and read that Herrmann was featuring the same two tricks, and planning to tour the western states and Mexico. But the Robinsons underestimated the cold gleam in Kellar's eyes when he spoke of Herrmann, his terrier-like ferocity when he had his hackles up. America's second-greatest magician was determined to make a reckless charge, head first, at the greatest— following the same route and using the same tricks as ammunition. His offer wasn't logical. Kellar was declaring war, and he needed Will and Dot as his allies.

Achmed Ben Ali's review, predicting a "ten times" success for Keith at the Bijou, was prophetic. Achmed Ben Ali was extended, again and again, and ran exactly ten weeks. Just days after he closed, one theatrical journal already felt the loss, writing, "he ought to come back." A few weeks later, in January 1888, the Robinsons joined the Kellar show.

—⁂—

Harry Kellar didn't like Robinson's choice of name: Achmed Ben Ali. Kellar had been to Egypt, he told Billy Robinson, and he knew that

Egyptian magicians aren't very good. No, Achmed Ben Ali shouldn't be an Egyptian.

But India had a great tradition of magic. During his travels, Kellar had seen the tricks of the Indian street fakirs. So he decided that Robinson would portray a white-robed Indian magician, performing magic more miraculous than any Indian magician ever dared. Kellar awarded his new co-star an authentic Indian name: Nana Sahib, the name of the mysterious Indian rebel who had led the revolt against the British in 1857.

With the addition of the Robinsons, Kellar's show was especially successful. In addition to Kellar's tricks with borrowed handkerchiefs, watches, and coins, he presented his impressive Cabinet Séance, the growth of two rosebushes from seeds, mind-reading tricks, and several mechanical automata—the card-playing Psycho and a cornet-playing life-sized figure named Echo. The musician P. C. Shortis presented a program of banjo favorites. Nana Sahib, billed as the "East Indian Necromancer in Oriental Occultism," was Billy and Olive Robinson with the newly rechristened Black Art act. As Billy worked in pantomime, Kellar stood at the footlights, giving a running commentary of the act, building up each trick and dramatically recounting his adventures in India. A special feature of the evening was Kellar performing the Cocoon illusion, with Olive Robinson as the pretty butterfly and Billy backstage, operating his apparatus.

The programs gave no clue that Nana Sahib was actually portrayed by an American magician, but included the credit, "Mechanician: William Robinson." Another important addition was Mrs. Harry Kellar. Eva Medley was born in Australia and was an accomplished cornet soloist. She had first met Kellar in Melbourne, Australia, during his tours, and corresponded with him for several years. In 1885 she came to the United States and toured with his show, giving cornet solos under the name Eva Hewitt. On November 1 of that year, they were married in Kalamazoo, Michigan. Harry was 38 years old; Eva was 24. Mrs. Kellar had a handsome face, a square jaw, and dark, chestnut-colored curls; her voluptuous, tightly corseted figure was the ideal at the end of the nineteenth century. Eva was also a gossip, and, fueled by a drink or two, was capable of creating the sparks for a smoldering argument, tinged with a blue streak. She was a valuable part of the program and a colorful member of Kellar's traveling company. It was Eva, hidden behind the scenes, who operated Echo's mechanism, giving the effect that the mechanical man was playing the cornet.

That spring, the Kellar show marched through the Midwest. The production traveled by rail. The show manager booked the halls, relying on his relationship with theater managers and his experience with each city. The percentage was negotiated with the house manager. The goal, of course, was to assemble a list of cities like pieces of a puzzle, so that transportation was easy and the company was given enough time to set up the performance. Advance men placed ads and distributed colorful lithographic posters, which were plastered on blank walls and fences, announcing the show. Kellar had commissioned beautiful new posters portraying Nana Sahib—the artist took license with the image, showing a bare-limbed, wide-eyed wizard, stumbling out of his cave of wonders.

The cast and equipment for the show arrived in each town by train. The illusions, draperies, and costumes were carried in heavy cases. At the train station, they were transported to the theater by horse-drawn wagons. It required a full day to set up the show for the week's engagement; Kellar's men depended on a good local stage manager who knew the backstage of his theater and could supervise his crew of technicians. Philip Claudi, nicknamed Barney, was Kellar's stage manager. He supervised as the show was unpacked, curtains were hung, and trapdoors were cut in the stage. Like all magic show proprietors, Kellar carried several cases of tools and building materials; invariably, the apparatus in the cases became jostled, dented, and broken. In addition to supervising the local stagehands, checking Kellar's props, and setting up the Black Art act, Billy Robinson was also responsible for checking the props and making the necessary repairs. Metal props were polished. Wood cabinets were waxed, hinges oiled, and springs tightened. Kellar's famous perfectionism

A poster advertising Nana Sahib's appearance with Kellar.

made Robinson's job even harder. He was constantly anticipating the
boss's checks and double checks.

Dot followed to the theater, setting up the dressing room, airing the
costumes, and preparing all the props for the Black Art act backstage.

Mr. and Mrs. Kellar went directly to the hotel to handle any interviews and check the local advertising. Kellar arrived at the theater in
the afternoon, after the unpacking was finished. He first visited the
box office and checked the ticket sales, then stepped into the auditorium. As he made his way down the aisle, he always called "Barney!"
and his stage manager answered, "Yes, Boss!" Kellar then came onto
the stage, testing the acoustics by loudly laughing his way through a
dirty bit of doggerel: "'Tis well to love, but oh! How bitter / To love
a girl and then not fit her! Eh, Barney?" Kellar's stage manager called
out from the wings, "Yes, sir! And then not git her!" They both guffawed, and Barney took the boss on a tour of the stage, showing how
the illusions had been installed, his marks on the stage, the best route
to Kellar's dressing room, and the position of each prop backstage.

—ↄↄ—

With his newfound success, William Robinson had managed to reinvent his life, ignoring his previous relationships and responsibilities. Annie A. Robinson, his six-year-old child, was being raised by his parents while Jim worked for the Keith Theatre. She was pretty and precocious. Jim Campbell, Annie's doting grandfather, couldn't resist the opportunity to teach the little girl a dance and a few songs, showing her off to friends at the family's home in Boston. Annie seemed to be a natural.

In 1888, Bessie Robinson met a seasoned vaudeville performer named Hugh Vitalus Lee. Lee was then 42 years old—twenty years Bessie's senior—born in Kentucky and earning a living with a professional, dependable, if uninspired magic act. Hugh Lee fell in love with young Bessie. Already an experienced magic assistant, she immediately joined the act. One of Hugh and Bessie Lee's featured tricks was the levitation that she had learned with Billy Robinson.

Hugh and Bessie wed, or started telling people that they were married, and continued living in Manhattan. In addition to her son Elmore, Bessie gave birth to a daughter Yetta in 1889, and several years later another son, Vitalus.

Although Billy Robinson had been unable to balance a family life with a show business career, Hugh and Bessie Lee managed very nicely, like many other vaudevillians. It was a sign of Billy's restlessness, and Hugh's maturity.

—ↄↄ—

One of Kellar's favorite effects was called the Enchanted Casket. A half dozen finger rings were borrowed from members the audience. Kellar attempted to load them into the muzzle of a pistol, but found that the rings were too large to fit. Using a mortar and pestle, he crushed the rings into misshapen lumps of metal, then slid them into the pistol. Kellar took aim at a small wooden chest suspended in a stand at the side of the stage. He fired the gun. There was an explosion and the smell of gunpowder.

He removed the box from the stand and unlocked it to find another, slightly smaller box inside. This was repeated, revealing box after box, until six or eight nested boxes were revealed. Inside the smallest one—just several inches square—was a tiny nosegay of flowers with dangling ribbons. Tied to each ribbon was a borrowed ring, now fully restored.

Kellar untied the rings and returned them to the spectators, but it was discovered that one ring was still missing. Kellar proceeded with his show, showing a large wine bottle made of dark glass. Miraculously, he poured several small glasses of different drinks from the bottle, including lemonade, whiskey, and crème de menthe. These drinks were all handed across the footlights, so the audience could taste them. When the bottle was emptied, Kellar picked up a small hammer and broke the bottle open. Inside was a live guinea pig. This invariably received a big laugh from the audience, who suddenly contemplated what they were drinking from the bottle. Kellar's final surprise was that the guinea pig had a ribbon tied around its neck, and a gold ring knotted to the bow. This was the missing ring, which was returned to its owner.

The Enchanted Casket was a combination of several old tricks—the Nest of Boxes and the Inexhaustible Bottle—but Kellar had a number of neat touches and used beautiful apparatus for the illusion. His nest of boxes was expertly made from beautiful hardwoods. The special table, which was responsible for inserting the bouquet of flowers and rings into the boxes when the audience least suspected it, was equipped with a neat brass mechanism: a tiny, spring-powered elevator.

Will Robinson was particularly intrigued by the pistol. As far as the audience was concerned, this was the least interesting part of the trick, but typical of Harry Kellar, he insisted on a unique, beautifully made trick pistol that would give exactly the right effect.

It seemed to be a short pistol with a tube for a ramrod beneath the barrel. After the borrowed rings were secretly taken backstage, duplicate rings were crushed and jammed into the barrel, then the pistol shot at the wooden box. In fact, the upper barrel had been permanently blocked in back, and the spark from the cap was redirected down to the empty ramrod tube. Will Robinson was responsible for setting it every night for the show. A blank charge, of just powder and wadding, was inserted into the narrow ramrod tube. During the show, Kellar slid the bits of metal into the barrel along with gunpowder and wadding. But when he fired, the upper barrel was never discharged. The audience heard the report, saw the flash near the muzzle and smelled the powder. They never realized that the shot was fired from the small tube just beneath the barrel.

Every night, as Will secretly prepared the gun for the performance, emptying the barrel and loading the ramrod tube with a charge, he told himself that it really was a perfect illusion. In fact, it was much cleverer than it needed to be.

Chapter 8

NANA SAHIB

Harry Kellar was notoriously hotheaded. Unlike his wife, he did not argue; he exploded, stomped, and raved. Once, after a performance, a spectator visited Kellar backstage and indicated that he knew the secret of one of his trick boxes. When he left, Kellar dragged the magic box—an intricately made prop—into the alley and smashed it to bits with an axe. He told his stunned crew, "Now we'll build one so that no one will know."

On another occasion, during the solemnity of a levitation illusion, Kellar was making graceful gestures over the floating lady when he noticed the back curtain move suspiciously. He slowly stepped to the curtain, opened his large hand and delivered a firm wallop, smacking the bulge in the curtain at head height. There was a loud yelp from behind the curtain. Kellar kept up his graceful gestures and returned to the trick. He never discovered who was sneaking about backstage.

There was something warm and deflating about his temper—the boss as a buffoon—unless one was on the receiving end of the lightning bolt. Invariably Kellar came to his senses, gushed apologies, pledged friendship, and offered heartfelt slaps on the back. Often, deeply chagrined, he mumbled his regrets as he handed over a new pocket watch.

—⁓—

By the middle of 1888, Kellar's temper was fixed squarely on Alexander Herrmann.

The first problem proved to be D'Alvini. A well-liked performer, D'Alvini billed himself as "The Jap of Japs," but he wasn't actually Japanese. He was born William Peppercorn in London, England. He worked as a gymnast and juggler in traveling circuses, and then learned a bit of conjuring. In 1866, traveling through the Orient, he assembled a group of Japanese acrobats and jugglers, which he called the "Tycoon Troupe." D'Alvini had a mane of black hair and a large, expressive face. Wrapped in a kimono and wearing an odd, triangular hat, he looked vaguely Japanese to his audiences in Europe or America.

He was a clever magician and an amazing juggler; one illustrated bill shows him balancing a tray of glasses and a small oil lamp on a bottle; the bottle is balanced on his forehead. A favorite trick was to spin a silver dollar into a large porcelain basin so that it rotated around the inside edge of the bowl. Picking up the basin in his hand, he kept the coin rattling and revolving merrily with slight twirl of the wrist, like the perfectly timed twists imparted by a plate spinner.

In 1887 D'Alvini worked for Kellar for just four months before leaving to join Herrmann; this departure was around the time the Robinsons were added to the show, and the D'Alvini incident may have added to Kellar's determination in signing the young couple.

Adding insult to injury, Kellar was convinced that D'Alvini had taken secrets with him, for shortly after he joined Herrmann's company, Alexander Herrmann began exposing the fraud of Spiritualism from the stage, pointing out various secrets of the cabinet séance act.

The problem of exposures was a slippery slope. A number of magicians had campaigned against the deceptions in the séance room. Kellar exposed Spiritual tricks in his performance, demonstrating the secret of the floating table, and he had testified before the Seybert Commission, a group investigating the claims of mediums. Kellar fooled the investigators by producing writing on a blank school slate. The difficulty with Herrmann's séance revelations is that they came perilously close to Kellar's bread-and-butter act. There's a good chance that these tricks did not come from D'Alvini, and there may have been no offense intended. But Kellar—always mindful that he was the second best—assumed the worst.

The feud between the magicians publicly boiled over into the newspapers in May 1888. Herrmann had been signed to perform a benefit for the New York Press Club, to be presented at the Academy of Music. He proposed an exposure of Spiritualism. Kellar quickly volunteered his own services, adopting an altruistic tone. The *New York Dramatic Mirror* reported, "Kellar, not being at all of a jealous disposition, and being quite as anxious as Herrmann to benefit the Press Club, is perfectly willing to participate in the entertainment." Kellar was quite an expert at Spiritual frauds, and was well aware that Herrmann was a newcomer to the subject. His séance demonstrations relied on his glib showmanship. To Kellar, the benefit was a chance for score settling and public one-upmanship.

Herrmann was too clever to accept. First he seemed to consider the offer, studiously asking for an outline of Kellar's proposed demonstration. But when he received it, he shrugged to the Press Club that his rival intended only "a juggling performance." He demurred at working with Kellar.

The tickets had already been printed with both names, but the Press Club had no alternative but to apologize to Kellar and explain that he wasn't welcome. Herrmann had been the first signed; he had the more prominent name. Kellar complained bitterly and seemed to feel that Herrmann had used his outline to structure his own performance. "Herrmann and I are friends no longer," he told the *Philadelphia Inquirer*.

William Robinson had been oblivious of the latest of Kellar's outbursts about Herrmann. Nana Sahib was a hit with audiences, and the week-to-week travel, the unpacking, performances, repairs, and packing up again meant that Will and Dot were busier than they had ever been. But unexpectedly, Robinson found himself in the center of the tussle.

In June, both Kellar and Herrmann were playing in Boston. One night, Herrmann's tour manager, Edward Thurnaer, and a Greek author named T. T. Timayenis appeared at the stage door at the Boston Museum, where the Kellar show was being set up by his staff.

They found Will and made him a promise of double his salary if he would leave Kellar and join the Herrmann show with his Black Art act. Thurnaer and Timayenis also whispered tempting offers to work for Herrmann to several other assistants.

Kellar heard of the visit and fumed. The next day, on the sidewalk in front of the Adams House, he saw Timayenis engaged in another sales pitch to Robinson. Kellar stormed across the street, blindsided the author, and knocked him to the pavement.

Timayenis looked up and tried to talk his way out of it, "Oh, Kellar. I be so glad to see you!"

"You lie, you miserable, craven-hearted Greek; you are not glad to see me," he said, pulling the author into the gutter.

Robinson stood back in the sunlight, watching open-mouthed. The Great Kellar, red-faced, spitting, and stammering, offered windmill punches in the dusty street. For months, Will had been stumbling between the train stations and the dressing rooms, or the stages and the hotels. He'd never understood just how important he had become. America's greatest magicians were fighting over him.

—m—

Herrmann had been performing Black Art since the end of 1887, when he saw Robinson at the Bijou Theater in Boston. He advertised it lavishly in his playbills, but his performance wasn't as effective as Robinson's Oriental Occultism. Herrmann's Black Art was arranged in a dramatic sketch. Herrmann played Dr. Alcanthara, a Faust-like scholar. Madame Herrmann portrayed Judith, his vision. Other characters included a Slave, an Angel, and Mephisto, who arrived magically to enchant the scene.

The highlight of the act was the decapitation of Madame Herrmann, but it seems that the entire sketch was mannered and unappealing. It didn't have the simple, stark staccato of mysteries—played directly to the audience and building the audience's applause—that Robinson had achieved with Nana Sahib. Herrmann made plans to change his presentation. A January 1888 ad in the *New York Dramatic Mirror* announced that Herrmann would be appearing with "Huka Agha, the Oriental Fakir," indicating an intention to find an assistant who would play the part and copy Robinson's success.

When the tour started, there was no Huka Agha. Herrmann lazily dropped his plans to change the act and soldiered on with his usual Black Art, realizing it was a near miss. In truth, the master magician had little interest in these full-stage illusions. He preferred to buy them, ready-built, rather than conduct all the experiments himself.

So Thurnaer and Timayenis were dispatched to purchase the best product. When confronted, Herrmann brushed it off. Thurnaer's offers were "simply a business transaction." Timayenis, he insisted, was not working as his agent. Timayenis's presence that day is a puzzle. He had written a publication for Herrmann, an 1887 souvenir booklet called *The History of the Art of Magic* that was sold at Herrmann's shows. But Timayenis was also a strident anti-Semite and the author of a famously malevolent book titled *The Original Mr. Jacobs*. Why he would have befriended Herrmann—who never denied his Jewish heritage—is mysterious. The answer probably lies in Herrmann's stardom and hospitality, and in Timayenis's opportunism.

When it was all over, Kellar grumbled to a reporter, "Herrmann is the most unprincipled man I ever met, and I think he'd lie for a 3-cent piece." He explained how his rival tried to hire away Robinson by doubling his salary, but insisted that Robinson, "my Black Art man, wouldn't work for Herrmann for $1000 a week, as we know too much about his dirty, mean ways of doing business. And, to show my appreciation for [Robinson], I raised his salary $75 a week more than I paid him last season, or $15 more than Herrmann offered him."

The swagger was pure Kellar. But the end result was interesting: Kellar not only matched Herrmann's offer, but paid Robinson even more to stay, and then boasted of his largess in print. The situation suggests that Kellar's Black Art man was not just amused by Herrmann's overture, he was deeply flattered and seriously tempted.

Will Robinson had just received his pocket watch from Kellar.

—᠁—

Incredibly, just as Kellar and Herrmann were squaring off, they found themselves locked in a professional dance. In 1887, Kellar had signed with Michael B. Leavitt, the respected American theatrical manager, for tours of the western United States and Mexico. Leavitt was also managing Herrmann on his tours, and intended to take Herrmann through the West and Mexico several months before Kellar. These were the dates Herrmann had announced for Black Art and Le Cocon in his *New York Clipper* advertisement. Both magicians had toured through Mexico years before, with great success.

Leavitt booked Herrmann in Mexico City September 12, and the manager then urged Kellar to postpone his Mexico trip from September 1 to October 1. Kellar understood that Leavitt was using Herrmann to skim the cream off the top. He sent his business manager to Leavitt, pleading to break their contract so that Kellar could negotiate his own tour of Mexico.

"I was pretty hot and made up my mind to make a fight of it," Kellar later told a reporter. Kellar paid Leavitt's $500 forfeit fee, breaking the contract, but Leavitt pointed out the fine print in the contract: each individual booking required a $500 forfeit fee. Kellar exploded, and Leavitt agreed to tear up the contract in return for a new tour with Kellar the following spring.

Now without management, Kellar signed the Orrin Brothers to represent him in Mexico, urging them to secure the Nacional, the largest theater in Mexico City, for two weeks from September 1 to September 11. He planned to neatly outmaneuver his rival by beating him to the capital city.

Herrmann heard of Kellar's plans, and pushed Leavitt to let him go to Mexico directly, canceling some of the California dates. "This I objected to," Leavitt wrote, "for Herrmann was very strong in the

West. He was so insistent, however, that I saw I would lose him if I held out." Herrmann booked himself into the Teatro Principal, a smaller showplace, intending to open August 26, a full week before Kellar.

Kellar was emboldened by the challenge. In an effort to gain an advantage, each magician had pushed back his schedule, week by week. But now Kellar reached an impossible conflict: a two-week engagement at Heuck's Theater in Cincinnati. He was contracted to appear from August 5 to 18—leaving barely enough time to reach Mexico City. Kellar knew that Heuck wouldn't cancel, and Kellar didn't want to risk publicizing the fact that he was breaking engagements to make his assault on Mexico—that would only alert Leavitt and Herrmann.

Kellar contacted Heuck and offered him an irresistible deal. The contract called for them to divide the gross receipts. Kellar suggested that he would pay Heuck the full receipts for the first week, the 5th to the 11th. Then Kellar would take the receipts for the second week, August 12 to 18. Technically this fulfilled their 50-50 split. Heuck greedily agreed; every manager understood that the first week of an appearance was the most profitable.

Meanwhile, Kellar had the Orrin Brothers quietly secure the Nacional for the week beginning August 17, one solid week before Herrmann's opening. The theater wasn't available. The Spanish National Opera had booked it. But Kellar was desperate to see his plan put in place, so he agreed to share the bill with the Opera. In Cincinnati, Kellar played the first week at Heuck's, paid the manager the gross receipts, and promptly informed him that he was packing up his show and would not play the second week. Heuck was shocked, but couldn't object; the theater manager had already been paid in full.

The subterfuge worked perfectly. The Kellar show, with Nana Sahib, Olive Robinson, Mrs. Kellar, and P. C. Shortis, banjo soloist, raced across the border into Mexico and opened on August 17.

Kellar's instincts were right; as the first great magician to play Mexico City that season, he filled the theater and attracted glowing reviews. Kellar spoke in English and Spanish. Newspapers commented on his beautiful scenery: plush curtains of red, emerald green, and copper, all trimmed in lace. The paper noted his elegant evening clothes, the mysterious dark chamber of Nana Sahib, and the intricate mind-reading automata—mechanical men who performed for the audience. There was also special praise for the poetic feat titled From Chrysalis to Butterfly, Kellar's title for The Cocoon.

Harry Kellar's show closed in Mexico City and continued to Guanajuato, Aguascalientes, and San Luis Potosí. Despite the frantic planning, Herrmann's shows in Mexico City were delayed. The Herrmann posters, important for advertising, were held up at Juarez. Herrmann convinced many of the managers to change the routing (increasing the railway expenses) and send them zigzagging across the country. Because Leavitt was paying expenses and splitting the gross receipts with Herrmann, the magician could afford to be extravagant. "Extra baggage in Mexico is a rather serious item of outlay, and the Herrmann paraphernalia was not alone bulky, but very heavy," wrote Leavitt. "This was not enough to suit his ideas so he began to buy all sorts of curios, bric-a-brac, odd furniture and other articles designed for use in fitting up his house in New York, until his excess baggage amounted to several thousand pounds."

Herrmann finally premiered in Mexico City on September 30 at the Teatro Principal, conducting his program in an enchanting mix of Spanish, English, and French. Once again, the critics swooned, paying particular attention to Herrmann's artistic sleight of hand. The Cocoon illusion and D'Alvini's humorous juggling were also singled out for praise. Herrmann promoted his show with an early morning performance in the Volador Market. With reporters in tow, he approached a lady selling eggs. As he picked up the eggs in his hands, she was surprised to see that they had changed into walnuts. Squeezing them in his hand, they became eggs again, to her great relief.

Kellar was ready to leave Mexico until he was told that Herrmann had been boasting to the press how he had driven his rival from the country. "This raised my Pennsylvania Dutch, and I determined to

Harry Kellar and Dot performing The Cocoon.

make it warm for Mr. Herrmann." Much like sacrificing the profits in Cincinnati, Kellar was no longer making business decisions. He was settling scores. He returned to the Teatro Arbeu in Mexico City, playing opposite Herrmann at the beginning of October, and then moved to Puebla and Veracruz, effectively blocking Herrmann from his final engagements in those cities. A Mexican newspaper commented on the "rivalry between Herrmann and Kellar," noting that they each gave good shows, with excellent supporting acts and beautiful, talented wives. "The combat was equal; none of the opponents had the advantage over the rival."

Leavitt insisted that Kellar's tour of Mexico was less than successful, as Leavitt controlled the best theaters, which he had reserved for his man Herrmann. More than likely, the frantic tour was messy for both magicians. After returning from Mexico, Leavitt met Herrmann in Kansas City to settle their account. "The bill of extra expenses that Herrmann had prepared for me was a most amazing affair. The litigation that ensued increased the ill-feeling already engendered, and our subsequent relations were not pleasant." Leavitt also wrote, "Herrmann always disliked his business opponent [Kellar] intensely, and was forever talking about him with bitterness." Years later a Chicago newspaperman recounted Herrmann's "hatred for his rival in business and enemy, Kellar. Herrmann once asked me if I would be so kind as to never mention his name in connection with Kellar."

Kellar reciprocated, seeming to have difficulty with the name Herrmann. He began calling the magician Mr. Niemann, insisting that he was simply using his real name rather than his professional name. "All Niemann knows," Kellar told a reporter, "is what he picked up from the original and bona fide [Compars] Herrmann, whom he once assisted and who is now dead, and from D'Alvini, who is now with him but who used to be with me."

For years, Alexander Herrmann suffered from the rumor that he was not actually related to Compars Herrmann, the great magician of Europe. The accusation seems to date from an 1889 lawsuit between Herrmann and the theatrical manager George Lederer over disputed money. It was whispered that the young Alexander had been hired as an assistant, and then acquired the Herrmann name. Researchers have since demonstrated that the two magicians were brothers, and both part of the Herrmann family.

Kellar was delighted to repeat the rumor, again and again, calling into question Herrmann's ties to the great family of magicians. Kellar may have also appreciated the nasty German pun in the name "Niemann." It can be roughly translated as "nobody."

After the tour, Will and Dot returned to the United States feeling exhausted by Kellar's maddening chase, but exhilarated. The Robinsons spent several weeks in Boston, with Will's parents and his daughter Annie. Jim Campbell was working at Keith's Bijou Theater.

Dot had purchased several exotic costumes in Mexico and began planning a new specialty for their return to vaudeville, a small practical act that would be easy to tour. But in a Boston machine shop, Will saw an elaborate, impractical idea that quickly attracted his attention.

Benjamin B. Keyes was an inventive amateur magician and machinist who built special props for circus acts and conjurers. For the last year, Keyes had been working on a new idea, a levitation illusion. His inspiration had been an act called Edna, invented by the magician Will B. Wood, which had played dime museums in Pittsburgh early in 1888. Wood's Edna was billed, "The Only Human Being who Walks in Open Space . . . No Glass, Wires or Ropes Used."

Edna floated across the stage, right and left, while turning in the air and striking various poses. Keyes looked at the illusion as a puzzle. He was fascinated with machinery, so he started his experiments with the most important piece. He reasoned that a special metal corset made the illusion possible. The corset would be strapped beneath the clothing of the floating lady. A perfectly round metal belt encircled her waist—it was actually a rotating ring within another ring. This meant that the corset could be firmly attached to a horizontal support behind the lady. When the support was hidden, it would give the impression that the lady was floating. But because of the rotating belt, the lady would be free to pirouette, making twists and turns in the air.

B. B. Keyes made sketches of how he envisioned the metal corset—magicians call it a harness—which had to break apart for the entrance of the lady and be fitted with neat bearings so that it revolved easily. When Will Robinson met Keyes and saw the plans, he suggested the rest of the solution.

Wood's lifting machinery, which made Edna float, was concealed behind the curtains. But Will realized that Black Art would perfectly conceal the lifting device, and give a large range of motion on stage. A large, rolling derrick covered in black fabric could be hidden behind the lady. The derrick would lift her, turn her in somersaults, and float her from side to side across the stage.

Little Olive was the most important piece of the puzzle. The corset was a bulky, complicated device, and it needed to be precisely fit to the lady. Dot's slender figure was a great advantage. The trick also called for a resilient floating woman: being dashed from side to side or spun in the metal corset caused bruises. Many ladies would have refused the job, but Dot was ready to endure the long rehearsals.

Keyes and Robinson called the illusion Astarte, after the mythical goddess of love. Will cabled Kellar with information about the levitation, explaining that it was something he was developing for his own performances with Dot. Harry Kellar was thrilled, but urged him to finish it so it could be performed in the Kellar show when the tour resumed at the end of the year.

Kellar had always been fascinated with the idea of levitation and was continually searching out the best mechanism to accomplish this illusion. He knew of Wood's act, and trusted Robinson to develop a good piece of apparatus. Kellar was willing to pay the necessary costs so that he could use it in his tour, and magnanimously offered that the apparatus would remain the property of Will and Dot after it was used on the Kellar show. This was only logical; it had been specially built to fit Mrs. Robinson.

Astarte was packed and loaded onto a freight car when the Robinsons joined Kellar at the end of 1888. But the new levitation proved to be a daunting challenge.

Keyes's beautiful little metal corset only worked when it was attached to an enormous, heavy contraption to lift and turn the lady. The crates were bulky and difficult to move. The trick required extra draperies, special lighting, hundreds of pounds of dirty iron counterweight, and steel tracks positioned on the stage. Rehearsals were slow and difficult, coordinating Will's movements—wheeling the heavy derrick from side to side—with Dot's dainty pirouettes in the air. The costume was a particular problem. Dot fussed with various arrangements, attempting to cover the corset while still allowing it to twist and turn. Unless the costume was perfectly tailored, she seemed to be wearing a barrel beneath her dress, and the trick became laughable.

When the show reached New York City in January, Kellar and Robinson determined to make a full-scale assault on Astarte. Will took pieces of the equipment to the Martinka shop early in the

Dot Robinson and Kellar with the Astarte
levitation.

morning to make repairs. Dot bought different fabrics to experiment
with the costume. For two weeks, the magicians spent their days
locked in a room at Dockstader's Theater on Broadway. The premiere was announced, and then delayed. Kellar nervously paced the
perimeter of their cold rehearsal room. Dot and Will studiously
drilled the choreography of the flying lady. On February 25, 1889, it
was ready.

The curtains swept open on a bare, black-draped stage. Olive
walked on from the wings, dressed in a bulky pageboy's costume.
She handed Kellar her cloak, and he knelt by her side, reaching down
so that she could place a foot in his hand. With a sudden toss, he propelled Olive into the air. The movement, according to a review the
next day, was one "that would assist a lady to mount a horse." But
several feet above the stage, Olive miraculously stopped moving.
She was floating in space.

Little Olive turned and seemed to walk along an invisible horizontal line, then revolved in somersaults and pirouettes. She dove

through the air, describing a wide circle; she offered a few airborne steps of a Spanish Dance, and then quickly turned over and walked upside-down across the stage. Kellar picked up a large metal hoop decorated with hanging ribbons and passed it over the floating lady with graceful swoops, demonstrating that no wires were used. Finally he took her hand and gently pulled her to the ground again, as if he were catching a wayward balloon, and she took her bow.

Even after its premiere, the work on Astarte continued. The invisible apparatus rumbled, betraying its presence. The corset rattled and jammed. Olive's costume was a continual source of trouble. Not every reviewer was enchanted with the delicate Astarte, and several commented on the lack of illusion. The *Chicago Herald* wrote, "Her waist is a third larger than any other portion of her body, and this gives a clue to the whole business."

—m—

In addition to the Robinsons, Kellar added to his company a husband-and-wife team of mind readers, Charles and Martha Steen, and a group of folk dancers called the Spanish Students. Nana Sahib was still included, and in March 1889, when the show was near New York, Will Robinson incorporated a special new trick into the Black Art act.

His six-year-old daughter Annie was recruited for a special appearance that week, a unique version of the Indian Basket Trick. The Basket allowed Will to indulge in a bit of dramatic acting. Kellar was thrilled to welcome the little girl into the show.

She was introduced to the audience as Annie Lloyd. She marched to the center of the stage, where Nana Sahib placed the girl in a large wicker basket. With wild-eyed fury, the mystic picked up a long sword and pierced the basket, again and again. Kellar stood at the edge of the stage, objecting to the spectacle. Annie, inside the basket, offered a series of plaintive screams. Finally Kellar waved away the savage Indian conjurer, and carried the basket to the front of the stage. He opened it, paused, then tipped it forward and showed that the little girl had disappeared. "Here I am, Mr. Kellar," Annie laughed, running in from the back of the auditorium and jumping into his arms.

—m—

After two seasons with Kellar, Will and Dot left to join Herrmann's show, taking their Black Art act and the elaborate Astarte apparatus.

Their departure was inevitable. The Kellar show was always second best. Herrmann was Robinson's long-time inspiration, and Will was flattered and haunted by the tempting offer from the great magician. He had always admired Herrmann's devilish sleight of hand, his clubby manners with the reporters, his mysterious nonchalance. He was at the top of the profession, and to Will and Dot he seemed to be the ideal employer.

But there might have been another motive behind the couple's departure from Kellar. One associate later hinted that Robinson left for personal reasons. Perhaps Annie's appearance with the show led to a discovery: Will and Dot were not married, and could not be married. Theater professionals were always accused of loose morals, and a hotel manager or small-town constable could have created a local scandal for the Kellar show.

The problem may have also been a practical one for Kellar. Will and Dot had been unprofessional for posing as a married couple. Important illusions like Astarte had been built around Dot. If she were simply a sweetheart, not a wife, could Kellar really depend on her part in the show?

In fact, Will and Dot had a committed professional relationship as well as a personal one. Robinson's first marriage had neatly dissolved. Hugh and Bessie Lee continued working in vaudeville, later settling in Ohio with their two children and performing on the Gus Sun Circuit, one of many small vaudeville chains across the country.

Elmore, Bessie's son with Will, didn't fit into the new Lee family. Unlike little Annie, he wasn't welcomed into the Robinson family. Hugh and Bessie Lee had Elmore placed in a Pennsylvania orphanage, and William Robinson lost track of his son—a sad casualty of his parents in show business.

—∞—

One night, after Will and Dot left the Kellar show, there was an odd accident on stage. Kellar was performing The Enchanted Casket, using his specially made trick pistol. He had crushed the duplicate rings and loaded them into the barrel of the gun with gunpowder and wadding. He aimed at the box and fired. But on this evening, there was an especially loud report from the gun, and bits of metal were fired across the stage, embedding themselves in his hardwood casket, tumbling through the curtains at the side of the stage, and peppering the brick wall in the wings. Kellar froze for a moment, muttered something under his breath, and then proceeded with the trick, unlocking the boxes and returning the borrowed rings.

After the show, it was Kellar who exploded. He and his stage manager, Philip Claudi, examined the gun and tried to discover what had gone wrong. Their best guess was inferior workmanship. Somehow the plug in the back of the gun had worn away, and the spark accidentally connected to the upper barrel. The full charge and the broken bits of ring had actually been fired out of the pistol.

Fortunately, no one had been hurt, but Kellar cursed the damned pistol that had damaged his drapery and the finish on his wooden casket. In fact, neither Kellar nor Claudi ever knew exactly why the gun misfired. Kellar promptly took the prop outside the stage door and destroyed it. For the next shows, he improvised with a much simpler trick pistol, and finally dropped The Enchanted Chest from his shows.

Chapter 9

ABDUL KHAN

A lexander Herrmann was admired for his offstage bonhomie, and there are dozens of stories of his improvised tricks, which he used to delight newspapermen or attract attention on the street.

Herrmann's reputation for impromptu tricks preceded him and sometimes created problems. Once when he was traveling in America, he found Ben Nye, the humorist, staying at the same hotel. Nye had never met Herrmann, but instantly recognized his devilish features and had heard of his taste for practical jokes. As Herrmann walked through the dining room, he stepped over to Nye's table, attempting to make a magical introduction. Herrmann delicately lifted the lettuce on Nye's salad plate, plucking a woman's diamond ring from the leaves. "Dear me, Mr. Nye, you are very careless with such valuables," Herrmann muttered, expecting Nye to gasp in amazement. Instead, the humorist calmly picked up the ring, saying, "Yes, I am, but it's of no consequence. I'm a very wealthy man, and I have more of these at home. Here, waitress, is a little present for you." He presented the ring to the girl attending his table. Herrmann tried to explain the joke to the waitress, following her to the kitchen and soliciting the help of the proprietor before she reluctantly turned over her gift. Herrmann and Nye became fast friends and the magician delighted in telling this joke on himself.

—∞—

We have a number of accounts of Kellar rehearsing—trying out material, making changes, losing his temper, and struggling to master a new routine. But Herrmann seems never to have worked at his magic. He didn't worry or plot the way Kellar did; he didn't indulge in red-faced fits if a prop failed during the show. He was prone to shrug and laugh, knowing that he could carry his audience smoothly over any unfortunate mistakes. He trusted his staff to set up the show in the theater. Herrmann arrived shortly before curtain time, put on his greasepaint, and touched up his graying goatee and eyebrows with black makeup. Then he donned his silk hose and patent leather pumps, his white linen shirt and tailcoat. He methodically filled the specially tailored pockets with small props, packets of cards, and rolled handkerchiefs. As the orchestra played an overture, he nodded to his assistants and the stage manager, put on his gloves, picked up his wand, and sauntered into the spotlight. He spoke and wrote excellent English, but as he walked onto the stage his Parisian accent—"it iz my plai-zir, lad-iez and gen-tle-men"—was concentrated to a sticky, attractive confection.

When Will and Dot Robinson joined the Herrmann show in the autumn of 1889, they found their job a wonderful luxury. The cast and technicians stayed in the best hotels, ate at fine restaurants, and traveled in well-appointed Pullman cars. They appeared in prestigious theaters for top ticket prices and met the finest actors and managers. Offstage, Herrmann the Great surrounded himself with Oriental antiques, lounged in an iridescent Turkish silk dressing gown and Moroccan slippers, and was continually wreathed in the perfumed smoke of Persian tobacco. During their tours, the Herrmanns spent lavishly—and often unwisely—purchasing fine clothes and good wine, and collecting a number of exotic pets that traveled with the company: a cage of canaries; a screeching parrot; Sandow, a trick monkey; Lily, a Mexican chihuahua; and two St. Bernard puppies named Why Don't You? and Trilby.

The Robinsons were happy to join the menagerie. After two years of backbreaking work, performing Black Art in continuous vaudeville and traveling with Kellar's show, they had reached the pinnacle of magic as cast members in Herrmann the Great's company.

Dot Robinson, billed as Florine in
Herrmann's show.

Madame Adelaide Herrmann was an elegant companion. She'd
begun her career as a dancer, had performed a bicycle act, and had
even been shot out of a cannon, but she had gradually assumed the
role of the show's prima donna. Offstage, Madame Herrmann handled
many details of the tour, made creative decisions about her husband's
magic, and exhibited a facility for business beyond Alexander's. She
quickly formed a bond with Dot, a sort of mother-daughter relationship. But William Robinson found Mrs. Herrmann difficult and imperious. He was the show's backstage director, which meant that his
priorities and orders sometimes conflicted with Madame's.

Critics agreed on her importance to the show. When she was
onstage, Adelaide was much more than Alexander's assistant; she
was a co-star, presenting several of the illusions by herself. She
appeared during her husband's act wearing a riding coat, vest, and
men's trousers, which was especially daring.

During the Cremation illusion—a melodramatic sketch in which
the victim seemed to be burned alive—she donned a long white

gown and took the part of Josephine. Wrapped in a shroud and placed into a coffin, she was set afire. As the burning figure crumbled to ashes, a tableau appeared behind the gauze on the other side of the stage: Josephine was clinging to a cross, in devout prayer.

William E. Robinson was credited on playbills as "Stage Director" or "Mechanician." He and Dot appeared as cast members in Herrmann's illusions such as the Cremation; Dot, in red tights and a sparking doublet, was Le Diable, and Will played Charcot with a French accent. In La Stroubeika Persane, an escape illusion, Will played Ivan Ivanoff with a thick Russian accent. He was shackled to a board and enclosed in a curtained cabinet for several seconds. When the curtains were pulled away, Princess Stroubeika, played by Adelaide, was found shackled to the board in his place. Robinson was discovered standing in the back of the auditorium.

In a comic sketch called Elixir Vitae, Robinson took the part of The Patient, and his lines were tinged with a flat Scottish burr. He marched into the scene, complaining about a headache to Dr. Sever, played by Herrmann. The Patient was seated in a chair and a metal helmet was placed over his head. True to his name, the Doctor picked up a huge knife, cutting off the patient's head and placing it on an adjoining cabinet.

The dramatic and comic parts were a refreshing change for Will, who was never comfortable speaking in his own voice on stage and could never have competed with Herrmann's glib jokes. Herrmann's preference for placing the illusions within short sketches meant that Robinson was expected to be an actor, not a magician. He effectively disappeared within the roles.

The Robinsons' famous Black Art act was given a place of honor on the playbill, advertised as "New Black Art." The program explained, "The most complex and seemingly supernatural feats prevail throughout this act; objects and figures materialize and do their master's bidding. Mirrors of gigantic shadows vanish like lightning." Will was able to combine several of Herrmann's previous Black Art tricks with the best of his Nana Sahib material. He presided over it all in his colorful robe and white turban. But when the Robinsons first joined the show, Herrmann wrinkled his nose at the name of the fictional magician: no, Robinson's original choice, Achmed Ben Ali, would never do. Not unexpectedly, Herrmann also sniffed at Kellar's suggestion, Nana Sahib.

When Alexander was a young man, he told the couple, he had performed in Constantinople for the Pasha. He knew all about oriental magic and oriental names. He suggested a perfect, authentic title for a wizard: Abdul Khan. By that time, Robinson had adopted so many identities, accents, and names that he was happy to agree with Herrmann's suggestion. Abdul Khan was the new feature.

—m—

Early in 1890, the Robinsons brought their elaborate Astarte illusion to Herrmann's show. Alexander Herrmann renamed it Florine, Child of the Air. Florine was Adelaide Herrmann's pet name for Dot. The levitation was an ideal feature for Madame Herrmann. She introduced the effect and then tossed little Dot into the air, caused her to turn somersaults, and finally passed the hoop around Florine, who floated in graceful circles around the darkened stage.

The new name for the levitation illusion hints at a sore spot with Kellar. When the Robinsons left with Astarte, Kellar felt cheated out of a feature illusion. Although he hadn't paid for the machinery, he had made a considerable investment of time and publicity, and he expected that Astarte would be a longtime feature.

In the fall of 1889, Kellar rented Will B. Wood's original illusion, Edna. Wood had performed it in dime museums the previous year and had filed a patent for the invention. This was the effect that had originally inspired Keyes and Robinson to create Astarte. Wood's harness was far too small for the buxom Mrs. Kellar—who had no intention of being lifted upside down and spun about—but it was the perfect size for the teenage daughter of the Steens, the husband-and-wife mind-reading team that appeared with Kellar. Kellar billed the effect as Edna, the Human Orchid, Wood's original billing, and even used Wood's engravings for his newspaper advertisements. This name change signaled his association with Wood and was a back-handed slap at Robinson's Astarte. Kellar now had the original.

Kellar loved the floating lady, but the illusion was a nightmare for the stage technicians: heavy, complicated to set up, and difficult to transport. When the Steens left the show in 1890, Kellar stopped using the illusion, and Edna the Human Orchid was returned to Wood's show.

The following season, Kellar's tour was suspiciously simple and austere. The show was filled out with a long mind-reading sequence involving Mrs. Kellar—she sat blindfolded in a chair and solved complicated mathematical problems or identified numbers added by the audience. Kellar's old Spirit Cabinet feature was given star billing. Kellar's show was suffering from the loss of the Robinsons' versatility and creativity. Harry Kellar knew it, and, true to form, he fixed his eye on his rival and schemed his next move.

—m—

As a man of the theater, Herrmann wanted his own theater—the same way that the actor Edwin Booth and the playwright Augustin Daly had their own Broadway showplaces with their names on the marquees. In 1888, he partnered to manage a theater in Philadelphia, but the venture was a failure. Two years later, he tried again, building a new theater on Fulton Street in Brooklyn. Herrmann's theater was intended as a home for his show when he was in New York and—rented out to other producers—a source of income when he was on the road. It was a typically grand, misplaced idea for the wizard, and the project dragged on for months. The *New York Times* reported that the quality of the construction was inferior, and "complaints have poured into the Building Commissioner's office in regard to the alleged careless workmanship." The plans were rejected, but somehow construction continued, using the old plans. In the summer of 1890, when Herrmann had invested a small fortune in the building, and the construction was nearing completion, the rear wall of the theater collapsed into a pile of rubble. No one was hurt, but the accident left Herrmann with a lien of $27,000 against his property. The magician was typically sanguine about his debts. His associate M. B. Leavitt wrote, years later, "Professor Alexander Herrmann was a man who, although his earnings were enormous, was perpetually hard up for ready cash, and always relied upon me to advance sometimes as much as five thousand dollars or more, when we had a contract in contemplation. This was a safe investment . . . Herrmann's business was of the sure-fire type, and could be counted upon to win without fail." His career bumped along, from liability to prosperity, and back again.

As he was abandoning plans for Brooklyn, Herrmann discovered that he could lease Dockstader's Theater, a small, ornate upstairs theater on Broadway at Twenty-ninth Street. This was, coincidentally, the theater where Robinson and Kellar had premiered Astarte the previous year. Herrmann spent extravagantly on the interior, which was refinished in cream and salmon pink, with decorations in gold leaf and draperies in deep red plush. On October 11, 1890, Herr-mann's Gaiety Theater officially opened. A month later, on November 6, he opened his own magic show in his new showplace. For the occasion, he included Prince Awata, a Japanese juggler, on the program.

While Herrmann's show at the Herrmann Gaiety Theater was drawing holiday crowds, a new show opened at an adjoining auditorium, the Fifth Avenue Theatre. Sardou's Cleopatra premiered on December 23, with Fanny Davenport in the role of history's seductive princess. Unfortunately, Miss Davenport had neither the sparkle nor the figure to play the famous Egyptian—she was, in the words of one reviewer, "a cumbersome and unwieldy temptress." During the scene in which she was carried onstage in a rolled carpet, the audience began snickering; the bundle resembled a python swallowing a cat. Much of the play's appeal was due to its elaborate scenery and expensive special effects, designed to conceal Miss Davenport's inexperience: there was windblown dust, bending palm trees, and blasts of flame.

On January 2, 1891, the curtain fell on the performance of

Cleopatra and the audience filed from the auditorium. Fifteen minutes later, as the night watchman was making his rounds at the Fifth Avenue Theatre, he discovered a small fire under the stage. It was reportedly the result of a smoldering cigarette. He called for help in the street, and at 11:55 the first alarm was sounded. When the fire chief arrived, he sounded a second, third, and fourth alarm, realizing that the wood and fabric inside were quickly fueling the fire and that the Fifth Avenue would be lost. By 12:15, the fire was showing at the windows, and then, seconds later, through the roof. Suddenly, there were six loud explosions, in quick succession, as the gas tanks for *Cleopatra*'s pyrotechnic special effects ignited. The blasts sent flames bursting through the roof, and blew out the theater entrance on Twenty-eighth Street, sending showers of sparks tumbling over the adjoining buildings.

The Herrmann show had also concluded by the time the alarms had sounded. Herrmann's Gaiety Theater shared a brick wall with the Fifth Avenue Theatre and was quickly endangered by the spreading flames. Firemen arrived at Herrmann's, trudging up the stairs, dragging hoses and axes; they broke through the wall in an effort to spray the flames with water. Madame Herrmann took all the animals from backstage—their personal pets as well as the rabbits and doves that took part in Herrmann's magic. Meanwhile, Will shuttled Herrmann's props out of the way of the firemen, avoiding the water from the fire hoses, and gathered them in a corner of the theater. Dot gathered the costumes and the precious Black Art props and folded the velvet drapes so they could be packed in hampers.

Meanwhile, sparks were jumping to the roof of Herrmann's theater. The firemen quickly doused them with water before they ignited. Herrmann's crew worked for hours, saving the one-of-a-kind magic props that were necessary for their shows. The latest effect, Stroubeika, was quickly carried to the street. The board-and-shackles construction was a mechanical masterpiece, involving hidden springs and levers to make the escape. Robinson knew that it would take many hundreds of dollars and months of work to replace the illusion. When the firemen told the Herrmanns that their theater was safe, the crew collapsed, wet, dirty, and exhausted from their labors.

Guests across Broadway, in the Sturtevant House Hotel, were surprised to watch burning embers blow across the street and lodge in the edges of the hotel's mansard roof, starting small flames. Everyone in the hotel was safely evacuated. By 1:30, as the flames were being extinguished at the Fifth Avenue Theatre, the firemen turned their full attention to the hotel. A corner of the Sturtevant House's roof collapsed, and the building suffered water damage, but the structure was saved.

There were no fatalities in the disastrous Fifth Avenue Theatre fire—the theaters were empty before the fire began—but the auditorium and neighboring businesses were completely destroyed. The walls were pulled down and it was rebuilt the following year.

Herrmann had unwisely insured his new theater for only $5,000— he told reporters that he had expected to take out an additional $50,000 in insurance that very next day. In the confusion, the morning newspapers reported that Herrmann's theater was probably lost. But luckily, the damage at Herrmann's Gaiety Theater was confined to the broken wall and splattered water. Herrmann's theater reopened two days later, and the magician played an additional five weeks on Broadway, then took his show on the road again.

He returned to the theater only several times over the next few years. The rest of the time other producers leased it for their plays. Eventually, Herrmann tired of securing leases, signing contracts, and working to keep the enterprise profitable. He gave up the lease on the theater in the spring of 1894. It was retitled St. James' Hall, and then a succession of names—the Jonah, Theater Comique, the Princess—before it was demolished in 1907.

During the summer months, when theaters were unpleasantly hot and touring shows took their breaks, the Herrmanns would travel to Europe, retire to their mansion in Whitestone, Long Island, or steam around New York on the rented yacht Alexander had christened *Fra Diavolo*.

Both Will and Dot were in their late twenties, and had little regard for the creature comforts so essential to the Herrmanns. When they returned to New York each summer, Will unpacked his books. He took advantage of the tours to scour bookshops in every city and gather an impressive library on magic. Any available money was spent on ideas for their own show. The Robinsons looked at their work with Herrmann as a way to earn money and plan their career as professional magicians. Starting with the costumes from Mexico—a skirt and vest trimmed in fringe for Dot—they assembled an act called South American Mysteries. Will did the magic, including material from his original act with Bessie, and favorites from Herrmann's show. Dot assisted and also demonstrated some trick shooting, in the style of Annie Oakley. They performed in the Catskill Mountains, where New Yorkers went to escape the summer heat. At the new resort hotels, the crowds were enthusiastic and the acts could be a little rough around the edges; it was the perfect spot to try out new material.

One summer around 1890, the Robinsons settled in Boston with Jim Campbell. Will had decided that his next act should be the famous hat trick, in which many different objects were taken from an empty hat. Years earlier it had been the specialty of a British magician named Hartz, who called the routine Devil of a Hat. Will was devoted to the classic tricks, and decided to improve Hartz's act for vaudeville.

Robinson set to work at the shop of Milton Chase, a Boston magic manufacturer. He spent weeks working on the special props for the act—half of the secret was the use of expandable props that could be packed tightly but sprung open when released from the hat, and the other half consisted of tables equipped with ingenious, spring-loaded trapdoors, to deliver the bundles into the hat at specific moments. Will wanted everything perfect. He made two additional small tables, using polished metal and clear glass tabletops. The tables were trimmed with small dangling prisms that decorated the

William E. Robinson, the Man of Mystery.

table like fringe around the edge. The prisms were actually cut from metal and were nickel plated; Will called them "glitters." He had a special set of tails made with concealed pockets. When the act was finished, he arranged for a tryout at Keith's Bijou Theater, the site of his previous success. Robinson was given a safe spot on the first show in the morning, at 10 o'clock, when there would be few people in attendance. Theater professionals called it "the milkman's show."

Robinson was still surprisingly ill at ease on stage with his own act. Will's teeth were small and discolored, and this was a definite disadvantage for a performer. He avoided smiling on stage, but this made him look unnecessarily stern. He was not at his best speaking to the audience, so he eliminated the idle chitchat that traditionally accompanied tricks: "I call your attention to this hat. I wear it myself, so I can assure you that it contains nothing." Aware of his strengths and weaknesses, he worked silently so he could concentrate on the illusion. For music, he chose a deliberately aggressive march to keep the pace lively.

Will stepped on stage with various bundles tucked into his special pockets. He picked up the hat and showed that it was empty. With a flourish, he reached inside and produced strings of flags. Skillfully sliding the next package from his pocket to the hat—magicians call these essential bundles "loads"—he produced more flags. He continued with a quick succession of toy dolls that seemed to fill the hat several times over. Reaching back into the hat, he found bouquets of flowers, glass bottles, and metal goblets.

Unfortunately, Robinson's mechanical table misfired. A metal ball, the size of a cannonball, was supposed to be propelled forward into the hat as Robinson momentarily passed the table—a maneuver that required a treacherous bit of timing. Instead, the ball was sent careering across the stage, crashing into one of his glass-topped tables. Will dashed to catch the table, but only managed to knock over the matching table. The hat trick ended abruptly with bits of glass scattered on the stage and laughter ricocheting through the theater. Robinson skulked offstage, unable to voice an apology or joke his way through the accident. Afterward, Keith wasn't interested in the hat trick.

Robinson's expertise in the workshop worked against him. A complicated act like that should have been built in stages, with each part rehearsed and perfected before the final apparatus was constructed. Will was supremely confident at the workbench, but couldn't summon that confidence on stage. His glass-topped tables and twinkling "glitters" were a theatrical version of putting the cart before the horse.

Despite his frustrations as a magician, there's no question that Robinson had become a great assistant. Standing next to Herrmann during a performance, his impulses were inspired. One of Herrmann's tricks was a simple mechanical mystery using two small metal cages. A canary in one cage disappeared and instantly reappeared in the cage across the stage. One evening, the canary accidentally escaped through a flap in the side of the cage, flying into the audience. The magician couldn't proceed with the trick until he had the bird in the mechanical cage. Robinson quickly dashed down the steps, grabbing the bird as it landed on a seat in the theater, and then carefully carrying it back to Herrmann.

All eyes were on the little bird that had been rescued and returned to the stage, but as Herrmann reached over to Robinson for the canary, he found that his assistant had palmed the bird in his other hand. "Go on with the trick," Will whispered, and Herrmann instantly appreciated the ruse. The magician acted as if he took the bird in his closed hand, carrying it to the footlights, cradling it delicately in his palm and stroking its feathers. Meanwhile, Robinson nonchalantly stepped offstage with the bird concealed in his hand.

Herrmann was a masterly actor with such tricks, and he deliberately took his time with the subterfuge; many in the audience actually thought that they saw the bird in Herrmann's hand. "Ah, zee little bird is mad! I shall make him fly, and you shall not see him go!" With a grand flourish, Herrmann opened his hand, showing that the bird was gone. Instantly, the bird reappeared in the cage across the stage.

Little Olive Robinson had also become an invaluable part of the show. She was an ideal assistant. Unlike Madame Herrmann, whose duty was to look graceful and refined, Dot was willing to wrinkle a costume or push her way through a splintered trapdoor for the sake of a trick. A journal for magicians proclaimed her "the queen of assistants . . . pretty, graceful and quick, with brains enough for two," and explained that Dot was "not over[ly] in love with magic, which seems to be the disposition of every conjurer's spouse, [but] she puts her whole heart and soul into her work." Dot left the tricks to Will, but accepted any challenge and mastered any performance that was required. Herrmann often told her with admiration, "Dot, after zey made you, zee mould was broken!"

In the autumn, the Herrmann company would reassemble again in New York before setting out on tour. Will and Dot's plans for their own act were put on hold and they turned their attention to making repairs on Herrmann's tricks or rehearsing the new feature for that season. The salary was respectable, the Herrmanns were appreciative, and the work was a pleasure. The Robinsons, however, were becoming luxuriously bored.

—◊◊◊—

It took Harry Kellar two and a half years to calculate how much he needed William Robinson for his show, and the best way to get him back. Kellar did it by offering new ideas. He knew this would tempt the ambitious young magician. Kellar returned from his London vacation in 1891 with sketches of the latest tricks that he wanted built for his show, and a plan of just how the Robinsons would be incorporated into it. Besides, Kellar told himself, the Robinsons were of even more value now: they'd just spent several seasons with Herrmann the Great, working with his show and sharing his secrets.

Chapter 10

OUT OF SIGHT

When the Robinsons rejoined Kellar early in 1892, the boss was attempting to improve his show on every level: better material, new advertising, and a more polished performance. He was determined to break out of the second-class theaters and reach Herrmann's level of success. Kellar even hired a well-known New York stage director to critique his performance and offer suggestions. The name of this clever director has been lost, but it was said that Edwin Booth, America's greatest actor and a friend of Kellar, had personally recommended him.

The director asked to see Kellar at work, and the magician offered a front-row seat for that evening's performance. No, the director told Kellar, he'd rather sit in the back row of the theater, to take in the whole production. When the curtain went up on the show, he watched carefully and took notes. At intermission, Kellar's company manager, Dudley McAdow, approached the director to ask what he thought.

"Your man has a fine show," the director told McAdow, "and I have no idea how he does those things. But that moustache . . . ! He's got to shave off that ridiculous brush moustache. The audience doesn't respect him because he looks like a cheap dialect comedian." McAdow groaned, "Impossible. Kellar loves his moustache. He's always brushing it and trimming it. It's his trademark, and it's on all of his advertising. He'll never shave it off."

The director shook his head. After the show, when Kellar wanted his opinion, the director was quick to offer praise for every element of the production. "And, Mr. Kellar, from the laughter and interest from those down front, I assume that your patter is also very good. Of course, from where I was sitting, you couldn't be heard. But I suppose there's nothing to be done about that." Kellar asked him what he meant. The director explained that, no matter how loudly the magician spoke, his beautiful moustache would only muffle his voice. It was a simple matter of acoustics.

Kellar contemplated the remark, furrowed his brow, and told him, "Come back tomorrow night, and then tell me what you think." The next evening, everyone was surprised when Kellar walked through the stage door; he had shaved off his prized moustache. The director told him that he heard every word and the show was now perfect.

The company laughed at how easily the boss had been hornswoggled. A series of beautiful new lithographs featured the cleanshaven wizard. His wonderful crooked smile was now shown to its best advantage and seemed to complement a dishonest twinkle in his blue eyes. A decade later, when L. Frank Baum wrote *The Wizard of Oz*, his title character was described as a bald, clean-shaven, plain-speaking

Harry Kellar's new appearance, without his
prized moustache.

middle-American con man. There's little question that Baum modeled the Wizard after America's prominent magician Harry Kellar.

—⚏—

Harry Kellar's winning offer to the Robinsons included his grand plan for a permanent magic theater. Kellar had leased an auditorium in Philadelphia that he renamed Kellar's Egyptian Hall. The name was stolen from Maskelyne's famous Egyptian Hall, the magic theater in London.

This was actually Kellar's second venture in theater management, and his second Egyptian Hall. In 1884, he had leased the Masonic Temple in Philadelphia, called it Egyptian Hall, and performed there for an impressive six months. But shortly after he left the theater, it burned to the ground when one of the exhibits in the adjoining waxworks caught fire. Kellar always considered Philadelphia a good city for his show and fondly remembered his success at Egyptian Hall. He told one colleague that he had only one superstition: when he occupied his own theater, he would call it Egyptian Hall to bring him luck. At the end of 1891, he secured the lease on the Concert Hall on Chestnut Street and opened his second Egyptian Hall for an indefinite run.

He was right about Philadelphia audiences. The show was a success and he quickly added additional matinee performances. The Egyptian Hall was an ideal space to develop new material and rehearse the new ideas he had seen in Europe. Will and Dot rejoined the show near the end of his run in Philadelphia, in the spring of 1892, presenting their levitation illusion, now billed as Astarte, The Maid of the Moon. Kellar also performed The Cocoon. The Robinsons' Black Art Act was billed under the boss's preferred name, Nana Sahib.

After playing seven months in Philadelphia, Kellar took his show back on the road. In October, the company returned to Egyptian Hall for an additional three months.

Robinson offered an invention of his own to Kellar, a disappearing lady that Will called Out of Sight. The apparatus consisted of a simple bentwood chair and a twelve-foot-tall rectangular frame of timbers, equipped with a drum and a crank. Mrs. Kellar was seated in the chair and then securely tied to the seat and seatback with ropes. Additional vertical ropes were attached to the framework. By turning the crank, the chair and its human cargo were lifted off the stage, until Mrs. Kellar was dangling some five or six feet in space. Kellar stood to one side and fired a blank gun at the chair—six shots in a row. There was a sudden puff of smoke and the chair tumbled to the ground, as if the bullets had split the ropes. The chair was empty. The lady was gone.

Robinson's original idea was slightly different. He called it Gone, and it was an ideal effect for a dime museum or sideshow, where he could install a special set to accomplish the effect. A large sheet of glass covered the front of the rectangular framework, and a matching piece of scenery was suspended overhead, so it could be reflected in the glass. Gone was a clever idea, but impractical for a touring show, so Will eliminated the glass and incorporated Black Art, renaming the improved trick Out of Sight.

In Kellar's show, the illusion played against a black velvet curtain. The chair was raised in the air until it was framed inside the upright rectangular timbers. As the chair dropped—the lady was actually strapped to a concealed seat and released the chair so it fell beneath her—a roll of black fabric, at the top of the frame, was quickly pulled down by rubber straps. The fabric blocked the audience's view of the lady dangling in the framework.

The combined effects of the chair falling, the black fabric snapping in place, and the puff of smoke were timed perfectly to give the impression that Mrs. Kellar disappeared in midair.

Robinson may have first devised Out of Sight for Alexander Herrmann. On several occasions, Herrmann said that his favorite illusion was deKolta's Vanishing Lady. In this classic effect, the lady was seated in a chair and covered with a large sheet. When the sheet was pulled away, she had disappeared. Artfully done, the trick was a masterpiece. But, as Herrmann explained to one writer, the trick became "too well known. Its great success proved its ruin. Irresponsible bunglers took it up and made a fiasco of it." Out of Sight was clearly devised as an improvement on deKolta's trick—lifting the chair in the air and eliminating the sheet, so she seemed to vanish as everyone was watching. But Robinson was surprised to find that Herrmann wasn't interested. As always, the magician hesitated with new material. He was a great fan of the original trick and doubted if Robinson's would be better. When Robinson told Kellar about Out of Sight, he grabbed the idea, asking Will to build it for the show. For Kellar, part of the illusion's appeal was hearing that Herrmann had failed to understand the idea and had carelessly dismissed it.

—m—

Kellar also brought several new ideas back from London. Flyto was the creation of the British magician Charles Morritt. A large upright cage was brought on the stage. It was about the size of a phone booth, with sides of vertical bars. A young lady entered the cage and the magician pulled down roller blinds on all sides, obscuring her. Kellar fired a pistol and the blinds flew up. Instead of the lady, inside the cage was a uniformed soldier. The soldier stepped out of the cage and seconds later the missing lady was found standing at the back of the auditorium, where she took her bow.

But that was just the first surprise. Kellar attached the empty cage to two chains dropped from above. The roller blinds were pulled down and the cage was lifted high into the air. A second empty cage was wheeled in from the wings. The lady ran up onto the stage and entered this cage. The blinds were pulled down. Another pistol shot. The blinds flew up on both cages. The lower cage was now empty, and the lady had been transported into the hanging cage. The entire illusion was accomplished in seconds, and left the audience breathless.

Kellar also included a trick called Cassadaga Propaganda. He'd seen it performed by Maskelyne in London and copied it for his own show in America. Cassadaga Propaganda (it was named after the famous Spiritualist camp in upstate New York) was an entirely different type of spirit séance. Kellar showed a small, lightweight wood

Kellar's poster for the small spirit-cabinet trick.

cabinet, about three feet square and a foot and a half deep. The cabinet was first seen resting on the seat of a chair. Kellar showed a thin sheet of glass, placing it across two trestles. He then stepped over to the tiny wooden spirit cabinet, lifting it effortlessly and placing it atop the sheet of glass. The doors of the cabinet were opened and the interior was shown to be empty. When a bell was placed inside and the doors closed, the bell rang in answer to questions and then tumbled from the top of the cabinet. Similarly, a slate was placed inside and a chalk message was written on its surface. The spirit even played a hand of euchre opposite three members of the audience by indicating which card should be played for each trick.

Cassadaga Propaganda was an ingenious illusion derived from deKolta's Cocoon illusion. The tiny spirit cabinet had Dot Robinson concealed behind the back wall. She was curled up on a narrow shelf. A series of fine steel wires—invisible when the cabinet was carefully lit—extended from the back of the cabinet to the flies overhead, where they were attached to counterweights. The weights made the prop virtually weightless. Kellar could lift the little cabinet, and Dot behind it, casually depositing it on the sheet of glass. Dot could then reach through the curtains in the back of the cabinet to ring the bell and write messages from the spirit world.

Kellar knew that it was an ideal feat for the Robinsons. Will had experience working with the necessary steel wires and counter-weights. Dot was the perfect assistant for the illusion, as it required someone tiny and agile.

Like any Maskelyne trick, there were several neat touches incor-porated into Cassadaga Propaganda. At the beginning of the routine, the cabinet was seen resting on a dining chair. Actually, the back of the chair was spring-hinged to fold down, out of the way, leaving room for Dot on her secret shelf. As Kellar picked up the cabinet, the springs returned the chair back to an upright position, eliminating the hiding place.

One night, as Kellar picked up the small cabinet and prepared for the séance, the spring jammed and the chair back remained hori-zontal. Kellar glared down at the chair and his face reddened. If he had simply moved along with the trick, placing the cabinet on the glass, the audience wouldn't have noticed. But his temper got the best of him. He cocked his leg and gave the offending chair a swift kick, sending it tumbling into the wings, where it landed at Robinson's feet. That was Kellar's way of telling his master mechanic to fix it.

—m—

During one engagement, Kellar recruited Will and Dot for a unique bit of magic. The magician had become embroiled in a controversy with a local Spiritualist named Cary. Cary claimed to be a material-izing medium, capable of producing hazy white ghosts in the dark-ened séance room. Kellar claimed that such feats were frauds. To prove it, he promised his audience that he would produce ghosts more realistic than Cary's, and by purely natural means.

Kellar's Spirit Cabinet was a large wooden box, like an armoire, raised off the stage on short legs. The front and back were closed with doors and the top was open. A committee from the audience examined the cabinet carefully for trick panels; the spectators then took seats at the side of the cabinet and behind it, to ensure that no one could sneak in from any direction. The stage lights were lowered. Kellar called for the spirits, and a series of knocks and raps were heard from the cabinet. When the doors opened, two white gauze-covered spirits had materialized. One was tall and one was short. The ghosts hopped down from the cabinet, walked to the footlights, and took a bow.

The ghosts were the Robinsons. When the curtains had first opened on the spirit cabinet, Will and Dot were suspended above the cabinet, hidden within a large black velvet bag that dangled from a black rope. The illusion was performed in front of a black velvet backdrop. Just like Nana Sahib's Black Art act, the black bag was completely invisible when the stage lights were carefully adjusted. During the séance, as everyone in the audience watched closely, the bag was slowly lowered into the open top of the cabinet. Once inside the cabinet, Will and Dot pushed the black bag open, adjusted their ghostly costumes, and opened the front doors.

Kellar was delighted with the deception. Will had also made a serious study of Spiritualism's tricks, and like many magicians he found them disappointingly simple and crude. Kellar's improvised séance convinced Will that an inventive magician could make real money performing marvels in the séance room.

Unfortunately, in 1893, Robinson was presented with just such an opportunity.

—◊—

Zanzic was a tall, slender, dark-haired magician. His real name was Robertstein or Brenner, and he also worked under the name Henry Andre. Zanzic had been born in New Orleans, the son of a Creole fortune-teller. He was six years younger than Will, an old friend from the days when they were both starting out in magic and used to meet at the Martinkas' shop. His associates thought of Zanzic as unstable: accident-prone and filled with half-baked schemes. He certainly had the skill to be a good magician. But for Zanzic, the adrenaline of a performance was like a strange, addictive sort of poison that made him giddy and stupid.

When the Columbian Exposition opened on Chicago's lakefront in 1893, drawing millions of tourists to the city, Zanzic organized an impressive get-rich-quick plan. He would open a full-scale Spiritualist parlor in Chicago and outdo the ragtag mediums at their own game. Zanzic planned on using state-of-the-art magic to lure the tourists and charging exorbitantly for the séances.

Zanzic's banker, Jack Curry, arranged the funds. Sam Bailey, a Boston magician, was recruited to help run the operation. Zanzic courted his old friend Robinson, realizing that his creativity was the key to the plan. Will foolishly agreed to do it.

The partners rented a house on the North Side of the city, and reportedly spent five thousand dollars tricking it out with the finest illusions. Robinson treated the house as a laboratory for his ideas. In the séance room, a trapdoor was installed in the floor, which was above a fully equipped workshop. Before the séance began, blank school slates could be bolted together and sealed with wax. In the darkened room, they would be handed through the trapdoor where accomplices would open them, chalk a message, and seal them again so they could be returned to the séance. Another parlor in the house was double lined with black velvet on every wall. Two assistants, dressed in black velvet costumes, could manipulate gauzy fabric that had been colored with phosphorescent paint. The gauze started in a black bag. By slowly withdrawing the glowing fabric, causing it to float around the room, and using it as a veil to drape over a black-clad assistant, a ghost would slowly seem to appear in the room.

Zanzic even hired private detectives to uncover information about their scheduled clients; in the darkness of the séance room customers would be amazed to hear the ghosts whispering names of their dearly departed relatives, hometowns, and street addresses.

As a magician, Robinson had been determined to give the best, most dumbfounding show for the money. But he should have realized that the elaborate plans were unnecessary. In the séance room, most of the illusion is created in the minds of the eager spectators, who are happy to interpret a momentary flash of light as a recognizable ghost, or a few raps as a message from the spirits. Once the Chicago Spiritualist parlor was opened, and the medium Zanzic was in charge, the enterprise spiraled down to a desperate, larcenous con game.

One of their clients was a wealthy old German businessman, who returned for séance after séance with various health complaints, and personal questions for the spirits. He paid the mediums handsomely, so Will and Zanzic finally arranged to materialize a vision of his departed wife. The magicians found a young lady who matched the description, draped her with gauze, and produced her in the darkened room. The businessman sobbed his approval, and after the séance, as he paid the medium, he hinted that he would be anxious to spend an hour with his wife's spirit—alone.

Zanzic negotiated a hefty fee, auditioned a prostitute, and installed a bed in the séance room. The following week, the German was reintroduced to the spirit of his departed wife as Zanzic left the room and pulled the door closed. As the magicians were counting their money and gloating over their success, there was a scream from inside the room. They burst in to find the girl in tears. In the midst of his spiritual ecstasy, the poor man had suffered a heart attack and dropped dead.

The magicians dressed the man and carried the body to the street, hoping to deposit it on the sidewalk unnoticed, so it could be discovered later. Unfortunately, the businessman's servant had accompanied him to the séance and was waiting outside for his employer. When the accomplices appeared with the body, the servant went to phone the police. Hopelessly trapped, Zanzic explained the situation, paid off the police, and quietly abandoned the scheme, escaping from the city. It was a wonder that Zanzic, Robinson, and the entire gang weren't thrown in jail.

Several years later, Will Robinson created a new magic act for Zanzic, importing new apparatus he had seen in Europe. The act may have been intended as a final payoff to his maddening friend for the Chicago scandal. Naturally, Zanzic had little success with the new act, and was plagued by horrible accidents on stage. In 1897, he was working as an actor in a melodrama. Zanzic played the villain, and at the climactic moment, the heroine was to fire at him with a revolver. The gun was loaded with a blank charge. But one night Zanzic stood too close to the actress, and the burning powder exploded against his face. He lost his left eye in the injury, and reportedly returned to fulfill another performance that same evening.

In 1899, he was booked to perform his magic act in vaudeville at Proctor's Pleasure Palace in New York City. One of his tricks was a copy of Kellar's mystery with the borrowed rings and the nest of boxes. He intended to slip the duplicate rings into a large, antique pistol, then fire it at the box across the stage. Zanzic searched for weeks to find a pistol that looked just right. The day before his premiere, he found just what he wanted in a second-hand shop on Third Avenue. He bought the gun, but never thought to check if it was loaded.

On the day of the show, he planned to use only a percussion cap under the hammer to give a small explosion when the gun was fired. He loaded the crushed rings into the barrel and pointed the pistol at the little wooden box. As he steadied the gun, he'd managed to wrap a finger of his left hand around the barrel.

The gun exploded with "a report which would have been creditable to a small cannon," according to the *New York Times*. The performer bowed, smiled, and rushed to the wings. The curtain came down.

At the hospital, Zanzic lost his left index finger to the second joint. "If the man escapes lockjaw and blood poisoning he will recover in three or four weeks," the *Times* concluded. A trade journal for magicians reported the following month that the magician was "getting over it nicely and will soon be able to do business again."

—m—

In 1894, Robinson returned to more innocent deceptions. For a friend at Coney Island, he suggested a sideshow exhibit titled The

Muscle Dance. At the Chicago Columbian Exposition, a dancer named Little Egypt had drawn crowds to the midway with her Middle Eastern belly dancing. Her undulations were popularly known as a Muscle Dance. Robinson's idea was to have a small tent with a garish banner advertising the forbidden entertainment. The barker outside cautioned that the show was only for gentlemen, no women or children allowed. As the crowd drew close, they were promised that the dancers performed completely naked, without a stitch of clothing to obscure their natural beauty.

The price was only ten cents, and when a line of salivating gentlemen had queued up inside the tent, they were given one final caution. The show was for amusement purposes only. If they felt it wasn't worth a dime, their money would be cheerfully refunded. With that, the curtain was opened on a small table. Three empty mussel shells sat on the table, and three tiny pink mussels flopped back and forth on the table, in time to the music. Robinson animated them with a thin piece of thread, invisible to the audience. Almost always, the men laughed, and most of them agreed that the joke had been worth a dime.

—m—

In April 1894, while Kellar was playing in Chicago, a celebratory dinner was held for Herrmann in the same city, at the Auditorium Hotel on Michigan Avenue. It was officially Herrmann's thirty-fifth year in show business, and Herrmann was toasted and praised for his contributions to the theater. Attending as a guest that night was William Robinson, "the machinery man of the Kellar company," according to a newspaper account, who had worked for Herrmann in previous tours. "A warm friendship continues to exist."

Reading this report the next day, Kellar may have been curious about that warm friendship. Herrmann had just introduced a series of new illusions in his show. One trick, called Escape from Sing Sing, was created to capitalize on a recent prison break in the headlines. Two small jail cages were used, and the prisoner disappeared from one and reappeared in another. It sounded suspiciously like Flyto, the illusion Kellar had purchased in London.

Even worse, Herrmann's Mysterious Swing consisted of a wooden swing in a raised rectangular framework. Madame Herrmann sat in the swing. Herrmann fired a pistol. The swing crashed to the stage and the lady was gone. This sounded identical to the illusion Robinson had built for Kellar, Out of Sight.

—m—

William Robinson's old friends had noticed how easily the magician had neglected his previous life—ignoring Bessie and his children, pretending to be Dot's husband. It was a different kind of trickery from a magic show. Will surrounded himself with deceptions, and these provided continual reminders of how inconsistent and untrustworthy he could be. For Dot, it was personal. She'd chosen to be a part of the illusion; she was always aware that their relationship was built on a lie.

But a new, precarious level of deception had worked its way into Robinson's professional career. As the secret supplier to the great magicians—the man who knew everything about the art, devised the ideas, built the apparatus, directed the shows, and worked onstage or backstage to produce the perfect results—he was equally invaluable to Kellar and Herrmann. They jealously wanted him in their companies. But part of his service was also espionage. He shuttled illusions, like Black Art and Astarte, between magicians, and he also shared inventions, like the Flyto illusion or Out of Sight. According to a fellow magician, Will had "double-crossed" both of his employers.

Supplying ideas or information was his graceful dance from one partner to another. But as Will and Dot waltzed back and forth, from Kellar to Herrmann, everyone began to realize that Robinson's services were desirable in part because the stage manager had become so untrustworthy.

Chapter II

THE MARVELOUS BULLET CATCH

The summer of 1894 was unbearably hot in Manhattan. After weeks of sweltering weather, the *New York Herald* organized a Free Ice Fund to distribute cooling 25-pound blocks of ice to the poor throughout the city. Herrmann volunteered his services to raise money for the Free Ice Fund, and a benefit performance was announced for Wednesday, August 1, at the beautiful Metropolitan Opera House, a yellow brick building at Broadway and Thirty-ninth Street.

That evening, the Opera House was filled with glittering New York society, including Judge Henry Gildersleeve, New York City Mayor Gilroy, and the vaudeville entrepreneur Tony Pastor. William and Dot Robinson, on break from the Kellar show, watched from two seats on the aisle. Their old boss had never been better. The program was a mixture of Herrmann favorites and new illusions. The magician scaled playing cards into the upper balconies of the Opera House. Madame Herrmann presented a series of elaborate dances, a new feature that she had introduced in the show the previous year.

Finally, Herrmann showed a large cheval mirror, seven feet tall. Adelaide stood on a narrow shelf in front of the glass, admiring her reflection. Herrmann placed a tiny screen around his wife, blocking her from view. He pointed out how the audience could see above and below the mirror at all times, as well as to the right and left of the screen. Seconds later he tipped the screen back. She was gone. The mirror was turned and rolled offstage, with no clue to the mystery. Herrmann called it After the Ball, a title borrowed from a popular song.

But it was Herrmann's finale that had brought crowds to the theater and filled the cashbox of the Free Ice Fund: the Marvelous Bullet Catching Feat. He would catch six bullets, the newspaper announced, fired from the high-powered rifles of the National Guard. It was a feat that Herrmann had performed only several times in his career—only for special shows or benefits.

The Robinsons craned their necks as the band played a march and Corporal Albert Veltenheimer led his six riflemen onto the stage. A committee of prominent New Yorkers, headed by Judge Gildersleeve, examined six bullets in their cartridges. Spectators were asked to scratch identifying marks into the bullets and then drop them into a small metal tray. Herrmann stepped onstage. He was dressed grandly in a tailcoat, with yellow silk breeches and a matching vest. Each soldier opened his rifle and Herrmann stepped along the line of riflemen, peering down the barrels to ensure that there were no other bullets inside. Then the soldiers dipped their fingers into the tray; each withdrew a marked bullet and held it over his head.

A long runway had been installed at the Opera House, extending from the stage a full thirty feet into the auditorium. The gunmen marched down the runway, so they were completely surrounded by the audience, then turned and faced the stage.

A newspaper drawing of Alexander Herrmann catching a bullet in New York City.

"Load!" the Corporal commanded, and the six riflemen slipped the bullets into the barrels and snapped the guns closed. Two riflemen in front lay on the ground. Two kneeled. Two stood.

Herrmann picked up a small glass dish and carried it to a nearby table. Then, taking his position in the middle of the stage, he faced the gunmen. Another command from the officer, and the riflemen placed their guns at their shoulders, finding a clear shot at the magician.

General O. O. Howard of the National Guard, who had helped organize the event, was surprised to see Herrmann standing alone on the stage that way. When the illusion was explained to him, he assumed that Herrmann would have stood behind a screen, or be surrounded by some trick apparatus responsible for the effect. Herrmann held both hands up, his palms facing the gunmen, leaning forward with his chest out. He nodded. Corporal Veltenheimer gave a sharp command, "Fire," and six loud cracks pierced the air in the Opera House. The audience gasped. Three ladies, in their theater seats, fainted at the spectacle. Herrmann's hands instantly grabbed through the air in front of his face as his hands closed into fists. The smoke cleared. The magician was still standing. There was a long pause—deathly silence. As the audience was doubting what they'd just seen, wondering if Herrmann could really have caught a projectile, he slowly stepped to the table, reached down, and dropped six bullets into the glass dish.

The delicate clatter of the lead bullets against the plate formed an astonishing climax. The audience burst into applause. But the magician, looking pale and relieved, quickly held up his hand for silence. The corporal marched to the dish, picked it up, and carried it into the audience. One by one, each bullet was identified by its mark. The theater erupted in a roar of approval.

Adelaide was terrified of the Bullet Catching Trick. To calm her fears, Herrmann had repeatedly shown her how it worked. She could rationalize that her husband would be safe. And she was experienced at dangerous tricks; she had, after all, been shot out of a cannon herself early in her career. But the sight of six riflemen taking aim at Alexander as he stood, alone, in the center of the stage, was too much to bear. She locked herself in the dressing room. Only when the shots rang out and the trick was completed did she rush onstage, throwing herself into his arms.

The Robinsons joined the ovation, standing, applauding, and whistling. Herrmann had never been better, William thought to himself, and the Bullet Catching Trick was nearly perfect.

—m—

The famous gun trick dates from the 1600s, but its popularity can be credited to Philip Astley, a British horseman who is remembered as the founder of the modern circus. In the 1760s, Astley presented the trick by galloping around the circus ring atop his horse, brandishing a sword. A marked bullet was fired at him from the ringside. The showman slashed the saber through the air, then dramatically rode to the edge of the crowd to show the result: he had apparently caught the bullet on the end of his sword.

By the late 1800s, the trick had become a standard effect with magicians, although one with a deadly reputation. The most chilling account was found in one of magic's most influential books.

The French magician Jean-Eugène Robert-Houdin had performed at his own small theater in Paris in the 1840s and '50s and was responsible for a number of innovations in the art, including new techniques for tricks and artistic presentations. It was this French magician's influence—imitated and imported across the Channel— that defined the Victorian style of conjuring in *Modern Magic*. Robert-Houdin had a short but glittering career, and in his retirement he wrote a succinct volume on sleight-of-hand magic and another textbook on the techniques and secrets of stage deceptions. But Robert-Houdin's lasting influence consists of his dramatic autobiography, titled *Confidences d'un Prestidigitateur*. The book was published in France in 1858, and then translated into English and published the following year in London and Philadelphia.

The *Confidences* reads like the very best nineteenth-century novels, filled with picaresque adventures, brushes with royalty, earnest ambition, and remarkable twists of fate. The book was responsible for inspiring generations of young men, from John Nevil Maskelyne, the British magician entrepreneur who opened his own theater in London, to Harry Houdini, the dime-museum escape artist from Manhattan.

According to Robert-Houdin's book, his career in magic was the result of a fortuitous accident. Although fascinated with conjuring, he had been trained as a watchmaker, the profession of his father. Stricken by food poisoning, he collapsed by the side of a country road in France and was rescued by an itinerant magician traveling in his wagon. The magician, Torrini, nursed Robert-Houdin back to health. During the long journey and the convalescence, Torrini explained his sad story. He had once been a famous showman, summoned for command performances before such dignitaries as Pius VII and the Sultan of Constantinople. His name was known throughout Europe.

I was at Strasbourg; I was performing at the theater and everyone was anxious to see my touching scene, which I had named "The Son of William Tell." My son Giovanni played the part of Walter, the son of the Swiss hero, but instead of placing an apple on his head, he held it between his teeth. On a given signal, a spectator, armed with a pistol, fired at Giovanni, and the ball lodged in the heart of the fruit.

Torrini detailed his own particular secret for accomplishing the feat. Moments before it was loaded into the gun, the marked bullet was switched, using sleight of hand, for a special bullet:

A chemist had taught me how to make a metallic composition bearing an extraordinary resemblance to lead. I had made balls of it, which, when placed by the side of the real ones, could not be detected. The only precaution necessary was not to press them too hard. When [rammed] in the pistol, they fell into an impalpable powder, and did not go further than the wad.

Many years later, Robert-Houdin experimented with this secret. The bullet was molded of hollow wax, mixed with soot to give it a dark, metallic look. The wax bullet was crushed in the barrel of the pistol and the magician was careful to stand a great distance away.

When the gun was fired, the loose bits of wax, heated by the explosion, never reached him. The secret was simple and it should have been safe. But having presented the effect some thirty times, Torrini suffered from a showman's overconfidence, that strange mix of numbness and fearlessness. In Strasbourg, he made a small mistake: "I had taken all possible precautions. The false bullets were contained in a small box, of which I alone had the key, and I only opened it at the moment of action. That evening I had been peculiarly careful; then how can I explain the frightful error? I can only accuse fatality. So much is certain, a leaden bullet had been mixed with the others in the box, and was inserted in the pistol.

> Conceive the horror of such an action! Imagine a father, with a smile on his lips, giving the signal which will deprive his son of life. It is frightful, is it not? The pistol was fired, and the spectator, with cruel adroitness, had aimed so truly that the bullet crashed through my son's forehead. He fell forward with his face to the ground, rolled over once, or twice, and....

Torrini served six months in prison, convicted of "homicide through imprudence." His life in ruins, he began touring the countryside, slowly rebuilding his career, when he happened across the ailing Robert-Houdin.

Jean Robert-Houdin's memoirs read like a novel because he had masterfully fictionalized entire chapters of his life. After years of searching playbills, newspapers, and town records, authors in the twentieth century determined that there never was a Torrini. By inventing his mentor, the author avoided the embarrassment of explaining how, as a prosperous, well-educated watchmaker's son, he had been attracted to the disreputable world of show business. Torrini became the perfect device, allowing Robert-Houdin to define the old style of show business, first giving credit to and then differentiating himself from the traditional touring conjurers. The accident explained why Torrini looked on Robert-Houdin as a son, trusting him with his secrets. It also foreshadowed the climax of the book, in which Robert-Houdin capped his own successful career with a successful reprise of Torrini's trick.

Although there was never a Torrini, Giovanni, or William Tell illusion, Robert-Houdin was right in casting the gun trick as a dangerous experiment. He must have based his story on the actual death of Madame DeLinsky, the wife of a Polish magician. In November 1820 the couple were performing in Arnstadt, Germany, before the family of Prince Schwarzburg-Sonderhausen. They had planned to include the gun trick, in which Madame DeLinsky faced six gunmen. The DeLinskys thought they had found a perfectly simple secret for their illusion. They solicited the gunmen to be their confederates. The guns were loaded with paper-wrapped cartridges, and a soldier usually bit the end of the charge to open it. DeLinsky's soldiers were told to secretly bite away the bullet and insert a blank load in each rifle. Accustomed to loading a gun but unaccustomed to taking part in a performance, one of the gunmen reverted to his usual routine, and accidentally placed his bullet in the barrel. Madame DeLinsky faced the firing squad, was shot by a single bullet through her abdomen, and died two days later. Many in the royal party fainted when they saw her fall. The magician DeLinsky was driven mad from the shock.

In America, Carl Herrmann introduced his own version of the gun trick. A rifle, a shotgun, and a pistol were shown and loaded with marked bullets. These were then fired at him by three members of the audience; Herrmann succeeded in catching all three bullets on a plate, but also displayed a bloody wound on his hand. He cleaned it by dipping his hand into a bowl of water, and then lifted the bowl to scatter it toward the audience. It had turned into a bowl of pink rose petals.

In 1876, Professor Hoffmann included a matter-of-fact description of The Charmed Bullet on page 409 of *Modern Magic*.

The charge of powder was loaded into the gun, and a round lead bullet was shown. The performer had it marked with an identifying scratch. The bullet was dropped into the pistol, followed by a small paper wad. Using the wooden rod, the bullet was rammed into the pistol. The performer then took his place some distance away, the gun was fired, and the marked bullet was caught between his teeth, or alternately against a china plate.

Hoffmann included none of the trick's grisly history, but matter-of-factly described the preferred secret, which was safer than Torrini's wax bullets. The bullet was a lead ball, slightly smaller than the bore of the pistol. A short metal tube, closed at one end, was painted to match the color of the wooden ramrod. This metal "fake" was palmed in the magician's hand. He secretly dropped this tube into the barrel of the gun just before the bullet was inserted. The bullet naturally fell into this tube. The magician then pushed the ramrod down the barrel, making a tight fit between the ramrod end and the secret tube; when the ramrod was pulled out, the bullet and the tube were carried away with it. Observant spectators might have noticed that the ramrod seemed to grow an inch or so in length: this was the addition of the metal tube on one end. "The performer, however, prevents the possibility by holding the rod by that end, thereby concealing the tube with his hand." The pistol was handed to the spectator, and the magician returned to the stage. "During his short journey [he] gains possession of the bullet. This is effected by sharply drawing away the ramrod with the left hand, thereby leaving the tube open in the right, and allowing the ball to roll out into the palm." The empty gun now held only a powder charge, and the magician was ready to magically produce the bullet, palming it in his fingers as he picked up the plate, or slipping it unobtrusively into his mouth, using the misdirection of touching his lips with a handkerchief.

This was probably the method used by Signor Blitz when he performed the gun trick in the 1830s, shortly after his arrival in America. Blitz found that this dangerous feat brought crowds to see his show. The secret seemed simple and foolproof; after all, the magician knew whether he had successfully withdrawn the bullet, and would only proceed with the trick once this had safely been accomplished. But during a performance in New York City, as Blitz turned his back and marched to the stage to extract the bullet from the ramrod, his eager spectator took the opportunity to drop a handful of tacks down the barrel of the gun. Blitz extended his left hand, asking the spectator to aim for it. When the gun exploded, several of the tacks tore through Blitz's hand. The remaining tacks were driven into the wall behind him.

Antonio Blitz, who caught bullets during
his career in America.

In future performances, Blitz and his company were determined to watch the spectators closely. One evening, just as Blitz prepared to catch the bullet, his assistant signaled him that the gunman had made a suspicious motion. Blitz stopped the performance, took the gun, and tipped it over. A brass button fell from the barrel. When the audience recognized what had happened, the spectator "was then booed and hissed as a reward for his dastardly conduct."

Something about the life-and-death challenge of the trick inspired the worst elements in Blitz's audience. During a performance in Savannah, Georgia, Blitz was preparing to catch the bullet when a spectator suddenly stood up and brandished his six-shooter, garrulously insisting that the magician attempt to catch those six bullets as well. Signor Blitz faced down the spectator, calmly talking him out of shooting, until the spectator put away his gun and resumed his seat.

The experience exhausted Blitz, who felt that no mere trick was worth those hazards. He later wrote, "[T]he gun trick became attended with so much danger that I found it necessary, for self-protection, to abandon it."

Will Robinson never saw Blitz catch a bullet; the veteran performer had stopped using the trick before Robinson was born. But Robinson had studied Blitz's 1871 autobiography, *Fifty Years in the Magic Circle*, which described the magician's misadventures performing it; Will circled the chapter on the bullet-catching trick. The young magician had also dog-eared the pages of Robert-Houdin's *Confidences* and had compared Torrini's tragic, poetic story—in those days, read as fact—with the technical description of The Charmed Bullet in *Modern Magic*.

William Robinson knew how the gun trick was performed, and he knew exactly why magicians feared it. Alexander Herrmann's performance of the Marvelous Bullet Catching Feat was especially astonishing and memorable.

—⁓—

Will and Dot returned to the Herrmann show in the fall of 1894. No doubt Kellar's suspicions and tantrums played a part in their decision. Ultimately, their choice was not just business, but also personal. The Robinsons liked the Herrmanns. They considered them friends and enjoyed traveling with them. They had learned to work around Alexander's friendly nonchalance and Adelaide's cool grandeur. In a newspaper interview the year after their return, Alexander's little Florine gushed about her employers. "Our home [when we're not touring] is in the Herrmann manor in Whitestone," she said. "I have never met a man any kinder to anyone than Mr. Herrmann is to us. He treats us as if we were his family. In fact . . . I feel almost as if I were his daughter." Dot described how much they enjoyed acting in the show, or standing in the wings, watching Herrmann's tricks. They seemed to have an idyllic life on the road. "The Herrmanns live in their [railroad] car in a city. [We] stay in a hotel, sleep until noon, go out and see the sights. No, nothing could induce me to leave his company. I am treated too well."

Unfortunately, as soon as the Robinsons joined Herrmann's show, they landed squarely in the middle of another battle with Kellar. In September 1894, Kellar had contracted with the Queen's Theater in Montreal. When he arrived, he was chilled to see Herrmann's lithographs pasted next to his own. Herrmann had always found success in Montreal—it was easy for him to intermingle French and English in his patter—and when he heard that Kellar would be at the Queen's Theater, he booked his own show into the Academy of Music.

Kellar and his manager, Dudley McAdow, decided to fight. They took out large newspaper ads in red ink and sent bill posters to paper over Herrmann's lithographs—a dirty trick that forced Herrmann to ship more posters and then to hire his men to paper the city for a second time. "Frankly, the result far exceeded my expectations," McAdow told the *New York Dramatic Mirror*. "From the opening night, our receipts were away ahead of Herrmann's." Reviews suggest a tight professionalism in Kellar's show—which was partly attributable to William Robinson's last two years, building Kellar's new illusions and supervising his new routines. But in the same two years, Herrmann's show had rattled apart. Alexander Herrmann was typically interested in the small magic tricks and comedy; he left the full-stage illusions to his staff. "The Escape from Sing Sing . . . would have been a success only for the fact that the curtains on one of the cages would not work exactly right and the prisoner was seen going out through the back of the cell," the *Montreal Gazette* reported. As for Herrmann's Mysterious Swing, the paper thought, "there was nothing mysterious about it. The black curtain that is supposed to go up and hide Madame Herrmann from view stuck half way up, with the result that the illusion was completely spoiled."

William Robinson, the new stage manager, was now responsible for the repair and operation of all of Herrmann's illusions. His work was cut out for him.

Chapter 12

ESCAPE FROM SING SING

I n addition to their jobs running the Herrmann show backstage, the Robinsons immediately took starring roles in Herrmann's illusions.

One new feature was The Artist's Dream, which consisted of a large painting of a lady that was covered with a cloth. When the painting was uncovered, a real lady stood before the painting, and the image of the lady had disappeared from the canvas. Herrmann and Robinson developed a dramatic scene to surround the effect. Madame Herrmann played the artist—a man—who is hard at work on the canvas of his dead sweetheart. Will played Barney, a comic Irish servant. Herrmann was Mephistopheles, dressed in a red doublet and feathered cap. He appeared magically in the middle of a thunderstorm to enchant the painting. Little Florine played the lady who stepped from the painting. At the end of the scene, as Mephistopheles laughed menacingly, the lady disappeared and mysteriously returned into the two-dimensional canvas.

In the Asiatic Trunk Mystery, Dot was sealed in a cloth bag and then locked within two nested trunks. The trunks were placed in a curtained cabinet. Seconds later, Dot was free, and another assistant was found locked within the trunks.

For The Escape from Sing Sing, introduced the previous season, it was now William Robinson who took center stage. He wore a convict's uniform of horizontal black and white stripes. The distinctive uniform had actually been designed at Sing Sing Prison in Ossining, New York, so that any escaped criminal would be easy to find.

The audience watched as Herrmann led the convict onto the stage at gunpoint, shoving him into the small cage and slamming the cell door. He pulled down red roller shades on all four sides of cage, hiding the convict from view, and then fired his gun. When the roller shades flew up, the audience saw that the cage was empty and the convict had disappeared. Seconds later, he was found standing at the back of the auditorium.

The illusion was accomplished by having another assistant who doubled for Robinson. Dressed in the same uniform and cap, with matching moustaches, they looked almost identical. The quick action of the illusion prevented the audience from getting a clear look at the convict.

Will's double was led into the cage. Will's job was to duck out the stage door and dash down the alley of the theater to the front entrance. There, an usher was waiting with an open door. He would enter the auditorium and make his spectacular reappearance. He timed it carefully to arrive in the lobby just before the convict disappeared on stage.

One evening, he turned the corner of the alley and ran into two local policemen on their beat. To them, the situation was clear. The police grabbed him and took him down to the local station, despite his protests that he was expected at the Herrmann show and was "part of The Escape from Sing Sing." Herrmann was perplexed by Robinson's disappearance, but smoothly improvised a new ending to the illusion and continued with his show. By the end of the performance, Dot was frantic, and Adelaide and Alexander realized that their stage manager must have suffered an accident. Together, they inquired at the local police station. There they found Robinson locked in a real cell, still wearing his convict's uniform, pacing up and back and swearing loudly. Herrmann exploded in laughter. He explained the situation to the police chief, arranging Will's release. As the tour continued, the magician never missed an opportunity to needle Robinson about his failed escape.

Another of Herrmann's new illusions was called Ya Ko Yo, or The Chinese Immigration Made Easy. It was first premiered at Herrmann's Theater in New York, when Robinson was working with Kellar. On stage were two large cabinets, decorated as pagodas. One pagoda was

labeled "Peking," and the other "San Francisco." Both were suspended
from ropes and attached to a large beam scale over the stage. At the
beginning both pagodas were empty, so they dangled, perfectly balanced, above the stage floor.

Herrmann grabbed the edge of the cabinet labeled "Peking," pulling
it down to the stage. A smiling "Chinaman" with a long black queue
skipped onto the stage and dashed inside. Herrmann closed the doors.
Slowly, one rope seemed to tighten as the other went slack. The scale
tipped, lifting the "Peking" cabinet and lowering the "San Francisco"
cabinet to the floor. Opening both containers, the audience saw that
the Chinese man had arrived in "San Francisco."

For Will Robinson, becoming Chinese was no more difficult than
playing a Russian or an Irish man. It was another cue in the show,
another quick change of costume. He donned the silk pants and
jacket, colored his face with yellow makeup, soaped and darkened
his moustache so it could be reshaped to an Oriental droop. Like any
of these parts, Will used a formula of stereotypes: rounded shoulders,
tiny bows, and facial features tightened into a grimace. It was the
best he could do. He'd never seen a real Chinese magician.

—m—

Robinson's most interesting role was that of Alexander Herrmann.

Will Robinson had inherited his father's skills as a mimic and
could master almost any language. Although he was always self-con-
scious about speaking onstage with his own voice, like many actors
he lost his inhibitions within a good role. Backstage, he delighted the
cast with Herrmann's Parisian purr, delicate hand gestures, mincing
steps, and tortured puns: "Don't be afraid. Ziss is a horse pistol. I
know. I raised it from a colt!" When Herrmann saw the impression,
he found it hilarious. But he also knew that Robinson was a good
magician, capable of performing many of his own tricks.

There's a legend that Herrmann took advantage of Robinson's
skill, regularly recruiting him for this impersonation. A friend of
Will's later insisted, "On more than one occasion, after inspecting

the house through the inevitable spy-hole in the act drop, Herrmann, disgusted with the paucity of the audience or not feeling up to it, would instruct Robinson to don his dress clothes and make up as Herrmann . . . go out and fool the crowd."

The story seems to exaggerate Herrmann's indifference and Robinson's abilities. It couldn't have been a regular occurrence. But we do have a good record of at least one such impersonation.

On December 3, 1895, Herrmann was performing his magic act at the California Theater in San Francisco. At the same time, he was across town at Mechanics' Pavilion, riding one of his high-stepping stallions at the Pacific Coast Association Horse Show. Herrmann traveled with his own horses, and he couldn't resist the opportunity to attend the show. The newspapers reported on Herrmann's marvelous feat, concluding that it was truly the work of a master magician. Herrmann dismissed the feat, disingenuously suggesting that his program allowed for various breaks—like his wife's dances—that allowed him a little time to leave the theater. The actual secret—William Robinson—wasn't exposed until much later.

—⁂—

Kellar still bristled at Herrmann's successes. The Bullet Catching Trick, which made headlines when Herrmann performed it in New York in 1894, must have particularly irked Kellar. On March 6, 1895, the *New York Times* announced a plan to hold a grand magical exposition at the Metropolitan Opera House, the same theater where Herrmann had performed his feat. George Lederer, Herrmann's former manager, explained that the exposition would feature a number of famous magicians and "explanations by some of them of certain illusions produced by their rivals."

The *Times* added suspiciously, "Prof. Herrmann, who has a number of suits pending against Mr. Lederer, will not be one of the exhibitors." But, of course, Kellar's name was prominent. "If Prof. Kellar accepts the offer made to him to join in this exposition he may, among other things, expose the shooting act of Prof. Herrmann, in which the latter poses as a target for a number of soldiers with loaded carbines."

Of course, there never was a Magical Exposition, and there may have never been plans for one. The article was probably devised by Lederer and Kellar, two of Herrmann's sworn enemies. They wanted to take the wind out of the magician's sails.

But their threat didn't discourage the magician from performing the Bullet Catching Trick at several other special performances, where Will was entrusted with the secret. In January 1896, Herrmann presented it at the Baldwin Theater in San Francisco. He repeated it four months later, on May 18 at Palmer's Theater in New York, another benefit for the Free Ice Fund. On June 18, "Herrmann's Celebrated Shooting Sensation" was performed at the Olympia Theater as a benefit for the *New York World*'s Sick Babies Fund.

Herrmann's secret was typically simple and bold. The National Guardsmen were recruited as confederates and carefully rehearsed in their parts. The six cartridges—lead slugs attached to brass shells—were shown to the audience and the lead bullets were marked with scratches. They were then dropped into a small metal tray.

The tray was one of Herrmann's magical devices. Pushing a small lever, a depression in the tray slid from one side to another, switching the six marked bullets for six blank shells. The leader of the guardsmen picked up the tray and made the switch as he brought the bullets to the stage.

Each rifleman reached into the tray and withdrew a bullet, holding it high. But Herrmann had rehearsed them to hold the bullets with the brass shells pointing up. In this way, their fingers concealed the fact that there were no bullets on the ends of the shells.

As they loaded the blanks into the rifles and took their positions for firing, the tray was taken backstage and the six cartridges recovered. Robinson pried the lead bullets from the brass shells. When Herrmann reached into the wings for the plate, Will dropped the six bullets down the magician's coat sleeve.

Herrmann took his position with his hands raised before him. When the rifles were fired, he closed his hands into fists. As he

Herrmann's bullet-catching feat in San Francisco.

approached the table, he slowly brought his hands together and lowered them. The six bullets slipped out of his sleeve and into his hand just before they tumbled onto the glass plate.

In San Francisco, Herrmann performed the trick in a different manner. He wore a full white poet's shirt, suggesting that he was ready for a duel. Herrmann held the white porcelain plate vertically between his hands, pointed at the gunmen, like a target. Herrmann had secretly been handed the bullets, which he concealed in his fingers at the edge of the plate. When the guns were fired, he released the bullets as he twisted the plate so it was horizontal. The rattling bullets seemed to have been stopped in midair by the magician.

The trick seemed foolproof. Herrmann himself examined each rifle to ensure that there was nothing else in the barrels. Once the trick tray was operated, each rifleman was presented with a blank. Robinson, backstage, could examine the tray and ensure that all six real bullets were recovered. This was the final guarantee that each rifle held a blank. Robinson signaled that the trick was safe by handing the bullets to Herrmann.

But Herrmann still considered these performances foolhardy, and the trick was performed only seven times, always for charity. In 1896, with a sense of his own mortality, he promised his wife that he would never repeat the Bullet Catching Trick again.

—m—

Throughout 1896, Herrmann suffered from chest pains. The magician was a habitual smoker and his doctor insisted that he had a "smoker's heart," recommending to his patient that he permanently give up cigarettes. "Oh, zey won't hurt me. I only take a puff on a cigarette now and zen," Herrmann told his doctor.

His health problems made him think about retirement. He told the *New York Dramatic Mirror* that he had a nephew, Leon, who was "very clever." Leon was in school in Europe, but Alexander promised that he would be brought over next season to tour, "with a view to have him become my successor."

During a break in the show's run in the spring, the Robinsons vacationed in London, meeting the local magicians and attending Egyptian Hall, the Maskelyne theater. They returned at the end of June, in time to travel with Herrmann the Great to upstate New York for the strangest engagement of his career. When he first presented The Escape from Sing Sing—the illusion was based on a real escape in 1893—he came to sympathize with the prisoners in the famous jail. For over a year he petitioned the authorities to allow him to donate his services "to give the poor fellows a little pleasure." The show was arranged for July 4. The Herrmanns, with a group of a dozen friends and associates, left New York City early that morning on a train, arranged specifically for the purpose by the New York Central Railroad. There was no possibility of performing his full show—no room for his large illusions. Herrmann took several suitcases of props.

When Herrmann's group arrived, almost 1,400 prisoners—wearing the rough gray and black bars that Will donned every night for the magic show—were seated in the new chapel, listening to popular melodies played by their prison orchestra. A number of seats in front were reserved for Herrmann's guests. Madame picked a chair in the front; tucked into the crook of her arm was Fidget, their tiny black-and-tan Dandy Dinmont terrier. Beside her sat Will and Dot Robinson.

According to the account in the *New York Times*, Warden Sage had suspended the usual rules, permitting the men to make all the noise they wanted at the performance, and when he introduced The Great Herrmann, turning over the program to the devilish wizard, the convicts hollered their approval.

Herrmann was in perfect form. When he stepped forward to inquire, "Could I borrow four or five watches?" the convicts responded with a shout of laughter. The magician used his guests to supply the expected watches. They were broken up and the pieces were loaded into a pistol. "Is there someone in the audience accustomed to handling a gun?" he asked innocently, soliciting even louder screams from the crowd. The gun was fired and all but one of the watches reappeared dangling from the rungs of a chair. The final timepiece was suspended from the back of a convict.

Herrmann then performed with silver dollars and cards. At the conclusion of his show, he picked up individual playing cards, scaling them over the crowd, and drawing increasing cheers as the cards were propelled farther and farther into the auditorium. "From the stage to the rear of the hall is 150 feet," according to the *Washington Post*. "The magician shot card after card over the audience, finally landing one on the shirt bosom of a smiling crook in the back row. It was done by the most simple looking turn of the wrist, yet was applauded as a marvel."

Will and Dot were transfixed by the spectacle. Herrmann performed instinctively and effortlessly. He concentrated on his simplest feats of sleight of hand, knowing they would delight the crowd. He twisted every punchline to draw the greatest impact from his captive audience. "Murderers laughed until tears rolled down their cheeks," according to the *Post*. "Second story men guffawed as 'The Great' gave them new points on their profession. Habitual criminals put on new faces for an hour. No stranger audience was ever assembled."

Alexander Herrmann, The Great, at the
end of his career.

At the end of 1896, as the holiday season approached, the Herrmann show was busy in upstate New York. On Thursday, December 10, the company arrived in Rochester, New York, and went to the State Industrial School, where Herrmann treated the boys and girls to a free demonstration of his magic. At the conclusion of the show, he invited all the children, the inmates of the reform school, to be his guests at the following Wednesday matinee. On December 16, the matinee at the Lyceum Theater hosted the children of the Industrial School, and Herrmann graciously extended the program, including extra tricks and jokes to entertain the boys and girls.

After the performance, he heard of a troupe of actors from a failed production of "Our American Cousin," stranded in Rochester. Herrmann was sympathetic with any theater professionals; he unselfishly came to their rescue, paying the hotel bills, supplying train fares home and pocket money for dinner, and, according to one writer, "sent the actors on their way rejoicing."

That evening was his last performance of the week in Rochester. As the Robinsons and the crew packed the show and transported it to the rail station, the Herrmanns were guests at a banquet in their honor at the Genesee Valley Club. Herrmann was in good spirits. He surprised the party with a number of impromptu tricks and anecdotes. Just before he left, he stopped to perform one last bit of card magic, his favorite, called The Egyptian Pocket. This was the trick where a spectator reached in the coat pocket of another and magically located the selected card.

After midnight, a group of friends accompanied the magician back to his rail car, and watched as the train took him toward his next day's engagement in Bradford, Pennsylvania. The Herrmanns rested in their elegantly appointed private rail car. It had been built originally for the actress Lily Langtry. Behind Herrmann's car were a sleeper car with the Robinsons and the cast and crew, and a baggage car with the illusions and draperies carefully packed in crates and hampers.

The next morning, as the train neared Ellicottville, New York, Herrmann was found stricken in his stateroom. An attendant wired ahead for a doctor and the magician gave instructions to his wife as he gasped for breath. "I guess I'm not going to get over this. Take the company back to New York. Be sure about that." By the time the train reached Salamanca and a doctor rushed aboard, Herrmann the Great was dead at the age of 52.

According to a newspaper account, "The small retinue of people who traveled with Herrmann, including his wife and assistants, were horror stricken at the sudden attack." Will and Dot Robinson were numbed by the terrible surprise, and sick with the loss of their friend. But they quickly resumed their duties as loyal assistants. Will sent telegrams from Salamanca announcing the great magician's death. He notified his father, the Martinkas in New York (whom he trusted to share the news with the world of magicians), and Harry Kellar. Kellar was then performing in Johnstown, Pennsylvania, and the same day sent a return message to his former stage manager. "The sad message announcing Mr. Herrmann's death came as a great shock to all of us. Please convey my heartfelt sympathy to Mrs. Herrmann. Harry Kellar."

There's no question that Herrmann's death quickly led to a remarkable boost in Kellar's career. It elevated him to the status of America's favorite magician, and opened doors to the best theaters. But there was no gloating for Harry Kellar. He was genuinely chastened by the news of Herrmann's death and saddened to lose his rival. A magician's journal had summarized the competition the previous year, concluding, "Herrmann and Kellar, on account of their neck and neck race to outdo each other, on account of the continued high character of their entertainment . . . stand today as favorites." Once Herrmann had died, Kellar realized that he'd been flattered to have such an adversary. Their battles had served to make him a better magician.

—⁓—

Herrmann's friends mourned his loss. He had a mysterious, attractive quality that was difficult to define and impossible to match. It was more than his dramatic appearance. "There was a strange fascination in the personality of Herrmann," one writer concluded, "a certain magnetism that impressed not only his audiences but those with whom he came in contact socially."

The funeral was held on December 20 at the Munn Masonic Lodge on Sixth Avenue at Twenty-third Street in New York City. Charles Heyzer conducted the Masonic rites, and Rabbi Joseph Silverman of Temple Emanu-El conducted the services. "He leaves the heritage of a beautiful character," Rabbi Silverman told the crowd. "Every man he believed to be his friend, and when those who loved him best chided him for it, he shook his head and said he had faith in human nature. . . . His work is finished, but his art will live and flourish."

Listening at the Munn Lodge was an impressive array of theater owners, actors, managers, and producers. Tony Pastor, the vaudeville impresario, was in the audience, as was Fanny Davenport, the actress who played Cleopatra the evening Herrmann's Theater was almost burned down. George W. Lederer, Herrmann's former manager who had suffered through several lawsuits with the magician, had forgiven his old friend. He served as a pallbearer.

Thousands waited on the steps of the Lodge, watching as the casket and mourners were led to a private train car. The magician's body was taken to Woodlawn Cemetery in the Bronx.

It was a cold, overcast day. As the sun was setting late in the afternoon, Will pulled a leaf from the wreath atop the coffin, slipping it into his pocket as a remembrance. As he and Olive Robinson walked down the gray paths at Woodlawn, they discussed their future in show business. The Robinsons realized that they'd spent too long assisting other magicians. It had been easy work and they'd received comfortable salaries, but they now had little to show for their success. As they spent their seasons working for Herrmann or Kellar, they'd seen old associates become successes in vaudeville.

It was time to put their long years of training to use.

Chapter 13

CHING LING FOO

Adelaide Herrmann didn't have a choice. Her husband's death had left her deep in debt. He had borrowed on his life insurance for creditors. She stopped the lease on Herrmann's yacht. She sold the train car, and held an auction of treasures from the Herrmann home at Whitestone, the countless knickknacks, medals, gold watches, framed proclamations, and souvenirs from the magician's long career. Most important, she scrambled to keep the show going, and to keep the name Herrmann in front of the audience. She explained to the press, "I am trying my best to bear up under my affliction, as it is my duty to continue the tour in order to act honorably by his creditors."

William Robinson had his doubts. He had always felt that her husband's good humor made up for her haughtiness, but Will and Adelaide barely endured each other backstage. Years later he confessed to a friend, "The old man [Herrmann] was all right. He made friends and his wife made them into enemies for him. She used everyone for a sucker." Now, he and Dot were the suckers, as she attempted to cajole them into staying with the show.

Robinson would only be tempted if there were a sizeable promotion. He'd spent years working with the Herrmanns and supervising their shows. He had even impersonated Herrmann onstage—and the performance was good enough to earn Herrmann's praise. When Adelaide explained that she needed to keep the show going, Will hinted that they could form a partnership; he would take over Herrmann the Great's role, performing the magic in the show. Madame responded with a lack of interest; she told Will she had no idea he was a performer.

The remark was typical of her insults, but it also stung because Robinson knew it was true: he'd spent over a decade as an expert in magic, but he'd never been successful on his own. Ironically, Alexander Herrmann had been one of his best roles. But to Adelaide Herrmann, the impersonation had been merely an amusement.

—⁂—

Will and Dot were initially determined to resume their vaudeville careers. In May 1897 they worked a week at the St. Nicholas Music Hall, on West Sixty-sixth Street in Manhattan. The St. Nicholas had recently been converted from an ice rink to a theater. It was not a prestigious booking, but the Robinsons invested a great deal in the engagement and clearly intended the week as a tryout—not only for return bookings at the St. Nicholas, but to bring in New York vaudeville agents and managers to show off their act.

For the engagement, Robinson returned to his billing as "Man of Mystery," appearing in the first half of the show with a number of classic,

William Robinson, after his years assisting
Kellar and Herrmann.

Herrmann-inspired mysteries. He had perfected the hat production—the trick that had sent tables crashing to the stage in Boston—and included it in his show. The Robinsons were determined to exploit their success with Herrmann. Dot, Will's assistant in the act, was listed on the playbill as Mlle. Florine—her billing from the Herrmann show—and the program explained, "Mr. Robinson was for ten years assistant to Herrmann the Great." Ten years was an exaggeration that erased his many seasons with Kellar.

In the second half of the show, Mlle. Florine returned for her own feature, The Maid of the Moon. The levitation was accompanied on the viola by Monsieur René Stretti, Alexander Herrmann's former musical director.

Florine's wonderful levitation should have been a showstopper. The Robinsons had fine-tuned Astarte during their many seasons of touring, but that also meant that the illusion had been seen by audiences for almost a decade in the Kellar and Herrmann shows. It was already old-fashioned: cumbersome, dark, and slow. The best vaudeville bills were organized around the latest sensations.

Not unexpectedly, Robinson's magic had been perfectly rehearsed. But Will made little impression as a magician. He avoided smiling, concealing his discolored teeth from the audience. He avoided speaking, uncomfortable using his own voice or projecting his own personality over the footlights. His years with Kellar and Herrmann gave him confidence as an actor in an illusion—playing a confused Irish servant, a belligerent Chinese immigrant, or a swaggering Russian spy. But his long experience as an assistant had ruined him as a magician. According to one associate, "Robinson had been such a superb assistant that he made a poor performer. An assistant must act so that he does not attract attention towards himself—must be, in fact, almost the invisible man. A magician, on the other hand, must be able to keep the attention of his audience completely in control, mostly on himself." Much of his work as an assistant had been silent, and "when he tried to be a magician in dress clothes he could not speak in an interesting manner." The great French magician Jean Robert-Houdin had insisted that a magician was actually "an actor playing the part of a magician." But Will had lost the ability to play himself.

The Robinsons reluctantly decided to accept Madame Herrmann's offer. They returned to the Herrmann show, supervising backstage and working as assistants.

—⚊—

Shortly after Alexander Herrmann's death, Adelaide had wired Alexander's nephew, Leon Herrmann, insisting that he stop his studies, come to America, and star in the touring show. Leon arrived on January 2, 1897, on the ship *St. Louis* from France. As he sauntered down the gangplank, Adelaide was stunned by his resemblance to her husband. Leon had the same wistful, coal-black eyes, the long waxed moustache and goatee, and the coarse black hair parted in the middle. He was a bit shorter and stockier—not quite the tall, angular Mephistopheles of Alexander. Adelaide Herrmann hastily arranged a special performance introducing Leon to the press at Hoyt's Theatre on Broadway, January 10, 1897.

There is no question that Leon was a talented magician. He had mastered excellent sleight of hand with billiard balls and coins. He was graceful and skillful at misdirection. But his specialty was small sleight of hand, and he had difficulty translating this to a large stage. He also couldn't match Alexander's famous bonhomie; Leon spoke very bad English and audiences found his personality chilly.

As the new Herrmann tour began, Adelaide guaranteed its success by including her husband's most sensational feature, the Bullet Catching Illusion. Despite her trepidations over this trick, in January 1897, she stood on stage at the Metropolitan Opera House in New York with a plate in her own hands and stopped the bullets fired from six rifles. She was familiar with her husband's secret and knew that the trick would make headlines and draw audiences to the theater.

She performed the trick the following month in Hartford, Connecticut. After the Hartford performance, she told a frightening story. The publicity for the trick had evidently sparked a debate between two local men, who remained unsure if the lady could really catch bullets. A newspaper reported, "a bet was made which resulted in one man going to the performance with a loaded revolver prepared to shoot Madame Herrmann at the same time that the guardsmen discharged their guns." Fortunately, the man's courage failed and he paid the bet rather than take his shot. Adelaide was informed of the near-accident after the show. "If he had shot and shot straight, he probably would have killed me," she told a reporter.

If the story is true—she may have invented it for publicity—it didn't prevent her from performing the Bullet Catching Illusion again, in September 1897, at the Grand Opera House in Chicago. Adelaide was desperate to keep the name Herrmann in front of the public and was relieved when the Robinsons agreed to rejoin the show and supervise the illusions.

Leon understood that he needed to include several of his uncle's larger tricks in the show. Will and Dot taught him the magician's part in The Artist's Dream and the decapitation illusion. But they also found Leon difficult. Onstage, his bad English left him unable to properly gauge the reactions of the audiences. Backstage, Leon preferred French, and was understood only by Adelaide and by his wife, Marie. He seldom included Will, Dot, or any of the other members of his company in his conversations. Leon had been a café performer in Paris; he arrived never having seen his uncle's show, or really understanding his uncle's performance style—he was filling a role that everyone in America knew better than he did. One associate later wrote, "He didn't know that the only reason he succeeded Herrmann was that his name was Herrmann."

To the people in his company, the magician compensated with an exasperating, high-handed mix of sanctimony and arrogance—the way someone young and inexperienced would try to elbow his way to the front. He was 29 years old, two years younger than William Robinson. Robinson hated teaching Leon the tricks, and Leon despised receiving lectures from his new assistant.

One of Alexander's favorite tricks had been called The Flags of All Nations. The trick began with a large empty metal vase. One by one,

Alexander produced silk flags from around the world. The flags were then tied together, wrapped into a bundle, and transformed into a flag of the United States. Alexander Herrmann would pause to comment, "And zis is zee greatest country on earth, America!" Invariably, the line received a burst of applause.

Leon learned how to operate the trick vase and produce each flag. But he couldn't understand the sensibilities of his audience. When the French flag was pulled from the vase, his eyes lit up and he would wave his hands up and down, carrying the flag forward to tell the audience, "France, France! Zis is my country! Zis is my flag!" When the American flag was produced at the finale of the trick, he managed to mumble, "And zis is a great country."

Adelaide upbraided him in numerous rehearsals. "Leon, when in Rome, you must do as the Romans." "But France is a great country," he insisted, hurt. At every show, he paused to fuss over the French flag. Standing in the wings, Will, Dot, and Madame Herrmann shook their heads.

Robinson brought back Astarte, the Maid in the Moon, teaching Leon how to perform the effect with Dot. He also arranged an elaborate sequence of Oriental magic—lavish productions of silk, lanterns, and vases—for Adelaide and Leon to perform together. This was the finale of the show and it was billed A Night in Japan. But for two full seasons with Leon Herrmann, Robinson considered his job hopeless. He told a fellow magician that Leon was "one of the dumbest fellows I ever saw."

Worst of all, Leon confused his audiences. He looked like Alexander Herrmann and performed many of the same tricks. He was often called Herrmann III and Adelaide billed their show "The Herrmann the Great Company," with advertising that placed Carl's, Alexander's, and Leon's portraits side by side. But if the crowds fondly remembered the devilish magician of a previous season, they were disappointed by Leon's careful, bloodless performances.

The newspapers had spent decades writing about Herrmann the Great's bubbling personality and his impromptu sleight of hand. After the show, when crowds greeted Leon Herrmann and his aunt Adelaide at the stage door—clamoring for an autograph and insisting on one more little trick—Leon held up a hand and snarled in response, "Je ne fais pas la magie dans la rue." He told his public: I don't do magic in the street.

—⁂—

After several years with B. F. Keith's theaters, Jim Campbell Robinson toured with Dr. Lothrop's stock company out of Providence, Rhode Island. In the early 1890s, he was diagnosed with Bright's disease, an inflammation of the kidneys. He returned to the Bronx, but Campbell continued to look for work at nearby theaters. He developed a short act for vaudeville, a comedy sketch with Annie A. Robinson, Will's teenage daughter, who was still living with the Robinson family. Grandfather and granddaughter included a few jokes and a song; the act was called "Grandpa's Darling."

By the late 1890s, Campbell's recurring health problems prevented him from performing; he was sometimes short of breath and found it difficult to walk, making travel impossible. Will decided to open a second-hand bookstore with his father, establishing a stable business for the old showman. The bookstore was called Campbell's and it was located at 50 East 88th Street, on the East Side of Manhattan. The entire family had been avid readers—Jim had performed an early Lyceum lecture as a "literary vagabond," and Will had been collecting crates of books throughout his travels, studying anything related to magic and Spiritualism. Robinson was enthusiastic about the new enterprise and sent all his magic books to Campbell's shop. Some books, intended for Will's personal library, were to be stored in the back room; others, extra copies, were to be sold by his father. When Will was off the road, he worked behind the counter at Campbell's with his younger brother Edward. New York magicians became regular customers at Campbell's, arriving to spend time with Robinson or browse the shelves for the books on magic.

Will had been contributing articles to a new journal for magicians called *Mahatma*. Robinson's columns were filled with general advice for performers: "If you go on the stage feeling downhearted and gloomy, don't expect your audience to be otherwise. . . . Make your patter short and to the point. The public, you will find, are better pleased than if you went too long story telling. Leave that to the lecturer or public speaker. . . . In learning or practicing a new trick, have a disinterested friend watch you and comment upon your work. . . . Whether in a private or public performance, have this one idea before you: brightness in costume scenery, apparatus, etc. Have it so when the curtain rises, the stage presents a brilliant light ethereal effect, instead of a dull one." *Mahatma* included a profile of Mr. and Mrs. W. E. Robinson that accentuated their skills as performers and slightly exaggerated these credits—Will added several weeks to the run of the Black Art act in Providence and Boston, and claimed to have toured the country with his act of "magic, spiritualism, mind-reading . . . being a good all-around performer." The magazine concluded, "Those who know Robinson personally find him a bright and interesting man to talk to, and one who is as well or better acquainted with magic and its followers than any other man in his profession. He is an extensive reader and has a valuable library of over two hundred works on magic, in all languages and ages, and is considered a good authority on all things in magic generally. He certainly has had a long and varied experience, and it will not be a surprise to some day see a new bright star in the magical sky."

Robinson's articles in *Mahatma* included some ironic statements. "Fame and fortune cannot be made in a season," Will advised his readers. "It takes years of hard struggling and determination to get there, and it is accomplished gradually, not suddenly. It has taken a prominent performer, now before the public, fifteen years to gain his present successful foothold." This might have been a pep talk he intended for himself. After fifteen years in magic, Robinson was best known as the assistant to Kellar and Herrmann; he was still attempting to carve out his solid foothold as a performer.

Even odder was his next bit of advice. "Secure a method and style of your own; adopt a name that is not similar to any other person, so as to avoid all suspicion of trading on another man's success." Of course, Will had achieved considerable success by copying illusions like Astarte, The Cocoon, and Black Art. Even his first stage name, Achmed Ben Ali, had been embarrassingly similar to the originator of Black Art, Ben Ali Bey.

—m—

While magicians studied Robinson's advice in *Mahatma*, they were unaware of his other, clandestine literary efforts. During the 1890s, *Scientific American* magazine and the *Scientific American Supplement* published elaborate explanations of magic illusions. They were positioned as popular science, the same way that new products or inventions were also explained within the pages of the magazine. Each explanation accentuated the optical illusion or ingenious mechanical devices responsible for the tricks. Many descriptions were accompanied by beautiful engravings, which managed to expose the secrets succinctly. Magicians were dumbfounded to open *Scientific American* issue after issue to find state-of-the-art magic from Europe or popular illusions from the Herrmann or Kellar shows.

Robinson wasn't responsible for writing the descriptions or selecting all of the illusions for the magazines. But he certainly helped the editors with his professional insights, guiding them to the best material and then explaining secrets. He had spent years studying magic literature, building illusions and searching out patents for new tricks. In the magazine, there were explanations of the Black Art Act, Robinson's Out of Sight Illusion, and Herrmann effects like the Trunk Trick and Stroubeika, the escape from a board with shackles. Harry Kellar was particularly disgusted to find descriptions of half a dozen of his most popular illusions, including the rope tie that formed the basis of his Spirit Cabinet routine and Cassadaga Propaganda, the little cabinet on the sheet of glass that Dot Robinson operated in the Kellar show.

For several years, the identity of *Scientific American*'s spy remained a genuine mystery in the world of magicians. But Robinson's name was slowly linked to the magazine, and his role became apparent.

In the spring of 1897, *Scientific American* ran a long obituary and tribute to Alexander Herrmann. Will Robinson penned it under his own name and included incidents from his life and heartfelt praise of his former boss, ending with the mention that Leon Herrmann was now performing in America.

Then, at the end of that same year, Munn and Company, the publisher of *Scientific American,* collected the tricks under one cover, with much additional material, including descriptions of theatrical special effects. The result was an impressive book titled *Magic, Stage Illusions, and Scientific Diversions, including Trick Photography.* Albert A. Hopkins was listed as compiler and editor. The magic authors Henry Ridgely Evans and H. J. Burlingame were thanked for contributions to the bibliography of magic literature, included at the end of the volume. But observant readers noticed special thanks tucked away in the preface: "Acknowledgments are due to Mr. William E. Robinson, the well-known prestidigitateur, for many suggestions and favors." Even the wording of the credit had Will's fingerprints. He no longer wanted to be known as an assistant, but now positioned himself as a "well-known" performer.

Studying the volume, Harry Kellar realized Robinson's part. Years later, in a letter to a fellow magician, Kellar explained that his former assistant had betrayed him. "I know that Robinson gave all my tricks away to Hopkins."

—⁂—

In the summer of 1898, the Trans Mississippi Exposition, a grand world's fair, opened in Omaha, Nebraska. The fair was devoted to the half of the United States west of the Mississippi, and exhibit halls were arranged within a grand court of white temples. The buildings were actually made of green wood and plaster, but they gave the effect of classical palaces devoted to invention, agriculture, or manufacturing. There was also the usual collection of state buildings, concessions, and a midway of rides and shows. A large section

Ching Ling Foo, the great Chinese magician, who appeared in Omaha.

of the fairgrounds was devoted to an Indian Congress, a showcase of
Native American tribes.

One of the highlights of the Exposition was the Chinese pavilion.
In the Chinese auditorium, the "Ching Ling Foo Troupe of Oriental
Wonder Workers" performed several times every day. The show was
advertised as being imported through special arrangements with the
Empress of China. The troupe was an extended family of enter-
tainers, a sort of authentic Chinese vaudeville, including acrobats,
jugglers, and musicians. The star was a tall, lanky wizard named
Ching Ling Foo.

Foo performed only a few tricks onstage, but each was strikingly
foreign to American audiences, brilliantly executed, and perfectly
amazing. His specialty was walking to the middle of the stage and
stepping onto a wide floor cloth—the cloth demonstrated that no
trapdoors were used. Foo wore a dark Chinese robe with long
sleeves, and a small pillbox cap on his head. He held a large piece of
embroidered fabric in his hands, about four feet square. The magician tossed the fabric in the air, watched it fall to the ground, picked

it up, stroked it, and twirled it. As he reached beneath the fabric with both hands, a round shape appeared. Foo drew away the cloth and discovered a wide flat glass bowl, about a foot across, filled with walnuts. He handed the bowl to an assistant. He twirled the cloth in the air one final time. As it settled down onto the stage in front of his feet, he lifted the cloth slightly and another circular shape appeared. Foo adjusted the fabric and pulled it away dramatically. On the stage was an enormous porcelain basin, over eighteen inches across and nearly as tall. It was filled to the brim with sloshing water and floating red apples. As Foo took his bow, two assistants stepped onto the stage, dipping ladles into the water and emptying it into wooden pails. One held up a sign that read, "85 lbs.," indicating that this was the weight of the bowl of water.

—⁂—

The Chinese wizard was born in 1854 outside Peking. His real name was Chee Ling Qua. Ching Ling Foo was selected as a stage name when he came to the United States, suggesting the tinkling Chinese syllables that sounded authentic to Americans—something they would find on a menu in a Cantonese restaurant. Foo had worked for many years in the mercantile business, connected to a firm that had a branch office in San Francisco. When he was thirty, he began to learn magic as a pastime and to amuse his friends. He found he was proficient at the art, and was soon entertaining Chinese officials and prominent Europeans visiting his country.

Ching Ling Foo was a natural performer, with a swarthy, bony face and a bright smile that glowed from one perfectly placed gold tooth. In China, he typically chattered through his tricks, relying on his remarks to misdirect or amuse the audience. But as he spoke no English, he learned to present his magic silently. His technique to engage the audience and keep them off guard was a strange modulation of pace. One observer wrote that he was "deliberate, exasperatingly so at times." Foo would slow down his movements and pause over tiny details—adjusting the fold of a piece of fabric or showing his hands empty in a particular way. Through his leisurely pantomime, he caught the eye of the audience, smiled broadly, and teased them into watching closely. Then he would suddenly explode with movement: "When he was ready to act, he was as near to chain lightning in his movements. For a big man he was exceptionally graceful in swift movements." It is not true that the hand is quicker than the eye, and Ching Ling Foo's magic did not depend on the speed of his movements. But his odd bursts of energy were disarming and exciting; they served as the punctuation for his flawless, precise technique.

He presented the repertoire of traditional Chinese tricks, which had been studied and handed down from generation to generation. In fact, troupes of Chinese jugglers had performed the bowl of water trick in London in the early 1820s and in the United States in the 1850s. But Foo's performance was new to his audiences in America, and the trick became his trademark.

The story about the Empress of China arranging Foo's trip to America was the work of a press agent. Ching Ling Foo had been performing magic professionally since 1896, and was working in San Francisco at the time of the opening of the Trans Mississippi Exposition. His family joined a group of Chinese performers who were headed to the fair. Once there, he became a star. His tricks made headlines and drew crowds to the Chinese pavilion.

Ching Ling Foo was grateful for his reception in America, but the fair actually proved to be an exhausting, tragic summer for the magician. On August 1, 1898, his ten-year-old son died suddenly while the family was in Omaha. Foo found it impossible to cancel his shows, and performed that day with tears in his eyes. He was a proud, stubborn man. When some magicians went backstage to meet him, they found the Chinese wizard brittle and impatient. From most descriptions, he was quick to infer an insult or a rivalry. But Foo was cheerful and accommodating when he perceived an expert. Ching Ling Foo overcame the language barrier through his magic, forming lifelong professional relationships through his wonderful sleight of hand.

—∞—

Late that summer, the Boyd Theatre in Omaha, Nebraska, hosted the Herrmann show—including Leon, Adelaide, Will, and Dot. The public was aware that they had two masters of magic in their city— one from the East and one from the West—and they watched with interest as Foo and his family arrived for Leon Herrmann's show, taking their seats in a prominent box near the stage. Ching Ling Foo leaned over the railing to study the performance of western magic.

Before the show began, Leon was told of his special guests. One of Leon Herrmann's specialties was the Chinese Linking Ring Trick: linking eight large metal rings into a chain. For twenty years the Linking Rings had been the West's idea of an authentic Chinese trick, and it was included in the programs of many magicians. Ching Ling Foo did not perform it at the Exposition.

Leon foolishly pointed the trick directly at his guest. He stepped to the edge of the stage and presented each of his neat, crisp movements —linking the rings and assembling them into various shapes—for his fellow magician. Leon performed the trick well, but his deliberate grandstanding was in terrible taste—a soldier polishing his medals in front of the general. The crowd noticed that Foo watched the trick coldly, without expression, and failed to applaud.

Several nights later, when the Herrmanns were finished with the engagement, Ching Ling Foo's company hired the Boyd Theatre and gave a demonstration of their skills. This time it was the Herrmann party that watched with interest from the box.

Ching Ling Foo entered with a set of eight Linking Rings on his arm. He slowly counted all the rings, and then began linking and unlinking them, combining his moves with expert juggling. "He tossed a ring high into the air, linking it on the fly as it fell," according to an expert magician who watched that night with his mouth open. Foo rolled another ring on the stage, giving it backspin so it skidded to a halt and returned to him. "This ring he linked while it was in motion. He then followed with an exhibition of Linking Rings beyond description. Some in the air, some thrown from him and returning, some springing about the stage, all being linked and unlinked rapidly in the most marvelous manner." Halfway through the demonstration, he stopped suddenly and uttered a single syllable: "Bah!" He tossed the rings backstage, demonstrating his disgust for the trick, and then proceeded with his famous effects.

Will Robinson watched with interest as Ching Ling Foo performed his paper-tearing trick. Foo held both hands high, spreading his fingers and turning his hands at the wrists to slowly display the fronts and backs. He made a show of interlacing his hands, pointing out the open spaces between the fingers, the empty palms, the extended thumbs—nothing was hidden or concealed in his hands. Then he was handed a long, thin strip of tissue paper, about half an inch wide and nine feet long. He slowly tore the strip into short bits, about an inch and a half long, until he had a small bundle of pieces. He squeezed these between his fingers and then drew out the end of one small fragment, which slowly seemed to grow and grow. The audience realized that he bits of paper had fused together again into one long strip. Violating a basic rule of magic, that tricks should not be repeated for an audience, or they may begin to watch for the secret, Ching Ling Foo deliberately repeated the trick several times, apparently with the same strip of paper. It was a masterpiece.

The Chinese magician concluded the show with his fire-eating trick. He slowly ate bits of burning paper, and followed this by drinking from a can of water. Stepping to a table, he picked up large plate of bran and took handfuls of it, greedily scooping it into his mouth as if he had been handed a delicacy. After filling his mouth with dry bran, his cheeks bulged.

Foo picked up a fan and nervously fanned his mouth, his arms, his chest, pretending that things were getting warmer inside. He rolled his eyes, he seemed to chew and swallow. Foo now began blowing burning ashes from his lips, sending clouds of black smoke curling to the ceiling. The lights were lowered and the magician opened his lips wide, showing a glowing inferno of red embers.

He gobbled more and more bran, and finally put his fingers to his lips, withdrawing long colored ribbons—and then more and more ribbons until he had a pile of streamers at his feet. An assistant reached into his mouth, slowly pulling out a striped barber pole, six or eight feet long. The audience burst into applause.

But there was more to come. With mighty puffs, Ching Ling Foo spit balls of fire from his mouth; they exploded across the stage and ignited the paper ribbons. Concealed fireworks in the ribbons began sizzling, sparkling, and popping. It was a sensational, fiery finale to the show. Ching Ling Foo nodded, acknowledging the cheers from the Omaha public with a gold-toothed grin.

There's no record of the Herrmann and Ching Ling Foo parties meeting after the performance. Leon Herrmann must have felt the sting of the Chinese magician's insult. But if events had been just slightly different—if the stars had realigned on that particular day in 1898—Ching Ling Foo and William E. Robinson would have formed a close friendship. Robinson was something of a scientist with magic. He loved to discover new techniques, and admired experienced performers. He'd analyzed tricks of the Indian mystics for *Mahatma* magazine and would have been flattered by Ching Ling Foo's private demonstrations of genuine Chinese magic. But unfortunately, when they first met, Will was part of Leon Herrmann's entourage.

Ching Ling Foo never became a friend to William and Dot Robinson. He became something much more important, a formidable enemy.

Chapter 14

KEITH'S UNION SQUARE

The Herrmann show was playing at the Tabor Grand Opera House in Denver, Colorado, at the end of October 1898. Across town, a young magician named Howard Thurston was performing his card tricks at the Alcazar, a beer hall and variety theater. Thurston had several good effects in his act. He deftly plucked individual cards from the air and made them disappear again at his fingertips. It involved a secret bit of sleight of hand that had been shared among a small group of East Coast magicians. Thurston's version of the Rising Cards consisted of cards that levitated out of the deck, soaring through the air and into his hand. Thurston and his wife, Grace, had spent months experimenting with the trick, slowly perfecting each detail, and the Rising Cards always received a good response from his audiences. But Thurston felt trapped at the lowest rung of the ladder, as his act bounced from beer halls to honky-tonks. When he noticed that Herrmann was coming to town, he resolved to see the great magician, to sell his trick or obtain an endorsement.

Thurston and his wife boldly marched into the lobby of the Tabor Grand, demonstrating his sleight of hand as patrons assembled for the show. He was hoping to attract some attention, or maybe even force a showdown—he was desperate for any kind of publicity.

The Herrmanns and the theater managers wisely ignored Thurston, but Billy Robinson, standing quietly in a corner of the lobby, acknowledged the young magician and agreed to meet with him the next day at the Tabor Grand. Thurston was overjoyed. "Billy Robinson!" he told his wife. "He's supposed to know more about magic than any man living. They call him the magician maker. He's been Herrmann's stage manager for years."

The next day, in the quiet of Robinson's backstage workshop, Thurston boasted of his Rising Card illusion and explained his plan to perform it for Herrmann. Robinson asked him, "Can you describe this trick of yours?" Thurston responded with a glowing account of the marvel he was presenting at the Alcazar—cards that flew through the air and into the magician's hand. Will wasn't fooled. "Yep. I know it. You'll find it in Roterberg's book done with a horizontal thread and a hook card." The previous year, in a neat technical book called *New Era Card Tricks*, August Roterberg had described a similar trick with illustrations. Robinson not only knew the book, he had contributed a card trick of his own for his friend Gus Roterberg's book.

Thurston smiled. He'd actually added a number of improvements to the trick. He'd simplified the way the cards were selected, and could move to different positions on the stage to make the cards rise up. "I'm sure you know the trick," he told Will, "but if I can show it to Herrmann and sell it, you won't spoil my game, will you? I'm very hard up. My wife is sick and I am working in a dive. We've got to get some money." Robinson agreed to help. He urged Thurston to contact Leon Herrmann at the Palace Theater. Will told Thurston that he could set it up on Herrmann's stage before an evening show.

—⁊⁊—

Thurston was right when he told Will that he was performing in a dive. But Thurston's wife wasn't sick. Howard Thurston was not only a talented magician but also a con man. He had a dozen sob stories that he used to skip out on a hotel bill, avoid a sheriff, or pawn a worthless watch.

Howard Franklin Thurston was eight years younger than Robinson. He was born in 1869 in Columbus, Ohio, had little formal education, and grew up selling newspapers on the streets, or racing programs at the tracks.

Thurston was well known as a "run 'em in and run 'em out" man at carnivals and circus sideshows, the spieler in front of the tent who boasted of the wonders inside. Thurston had a beautiful, melodious baritone voice, which gave him prestige on the stage and concealed his scruffy background; he had actually spent several years training for the ministry at Dwight Moody's Mount Hermon School. He dressed impeccably and had the placid features of a leading man.

Thurston had a fondness for magic and sleight of hand—unfortunately, these skills were generally used by him to switch a piece of jewelry or exchange a folded bill for a piece of tissue paper. He'd been inspired by Alexander Herrmann's show and, the story was told, hopped on a train one day to follow Herrmann instead of resuming his education.

In the 1890s, Thurston learned a simple maneuver with a playing card, a way of pinching it behind his fingers so his palm was empty. Magicians called it the Back Palm. The sleight seemed to appear mysteriously at Otto Maurer's magic shop in New York, and Maurer claimed that a Mexican magician had walked into the shop one day and demonstrated it. The maneuver was prized by a small group of magicians, including William Robinson. But it was Thurston who made the most of it, gracefully making cards disappear and reappear at his fingertips.

Thurston met young Grace Texola, who performed an energetic buck dance—an early tap dance that was a vaudeville favorite—when he was the manager of a carnival troupe of hootchy-kootchy dancers, "The DeKreko Brothers Congress of Eastern Nations." He quickly proposed marriage and vaudeville at the same time. They set off to make their fortune in show business.

Thurston's card act was ingenious and mysterious, but the magician needed a break to have vaudeville managers take notice of his skills. In a beer hall, ten minutes of card tricks—no matter how artistic—seemed cheap and ordinary. Thurston had considered Alexander Herrmann's show his early inspiration. Now he was hoping that Leon Herrmann would provide a necessary boost to his career.

Leon Herrmann told Howard and Grace Thurston that he would be
delighted to see their Rising Card trick. He asked if they could perform it right there, in his hotel room. Grace Thurston felt her
stomach tighten. The trick required a good deal of preparation, and
it was impossible to walk into a room and present it. At the same
time, if they admitted this, they would be giving away an important
part of the secret. Howard pretended to consider the request, but
concluded that it really should be seen on a stage. He suggested setting it up on Herrmann's own stage that afternoon, and presenting
it behind the curtain. At first Herrmann demurred. He didn't want
anyone backstage with his apparatus. But Thurston assured him
that they would work closely with Robinson and wouldn't disturb
any of Herrmann's apparatus.

Thurston and his wife dashed out of the hotel, picked up a small
toolkit with a tack hammer, brads, special playing cards, and spools
of fine black silk thread. They went backstage at the Tabor Grand,
found Robinson, and explained their plan. In order to guarantee success for the young magician, Will flew in a black velvet background;
based on his experience from his Black Art act, he knew that this
would conceal Thurston's threads.

Grace pounded small nails into the wooden flats at the sides of
the stage, stretching horizontal threads so they were just above head
height. The Thurstons' system was to attach small counterweights
on the ends of the threads, so they were always under tension. Grace
installed several horizontal threads, at slightly different heights, so
her husband could move about the stage, rather than performing the
trick in only one position.

Thurston found the house electrician and pressed a ten-dollar gold
piece into his palm. He then described a simple deception. He would
ask the electrician to turn up all the lights on the stage. He would continue asking for more and more light, but as soon as Thurston put
his hand into his pocket, the electrician was to refuse him any
more light. Thurston instinctively knew how much light could be
on the stage without exposing the presence of the fine silk threads.
The electrician shook his hand and agreed to the ruse.

Thurston then indulged in one final bit of treachery. He had told Robinson that he wanted to sell the card trick to Herrmann. But sensing that he was about to have a big fish on the end of his hook, he knew that this performance might be worthy of headlines. Thurston dashed to the *Denver Post* and found the city editor's desk.

"I'm Howard Thurston, and I'm going to do a trick for Herrmann on his stage before he goes on tonight." The editor told him that this hardly rated as a news story. "But here's what makes it great," Thurston breathlessly continued. "What if he's mystified, by a practically unknown American magician? Isn't that a great story, if I can fool Herrmann?" The editor argued that Herrmann would never admit to being fooled. Thurston insisted that he'd get Herrmann to say it. He convinced the editor to have a reporter ready to hear it.

Thurston brought the reporter back to the theater and hid him in a dark corner backstage to witness the performance.

Thurston paced off the performance space, reaching up with his hands, using his delicate, dramatic gestures to contact the threads that his wife had stretched across the stage. He was ready.

Leon and his wife, Marie, were late returning from dinner that evening, and by the time they sauntered onto the stage, there was barely time for them to change and apply their makeup before the show. Thurston and his wife had been waiting patiently, but Edward Thurnaer, the company manager, was surprised to find the young couple on the stage, and insisted that they leave immediately.

Leon interrupted, telling Thurston, "I shall be pleased now, to see zee treek." Adelaide Herrmann stormed at her nephew, pointing out that the show would be delayed. Leon overruled his aunt. "Yes, we hold zee curtain. I shall see zis treek."

There was a dull roar on the other side of the curtain as the audience settled into their seats in expectation of the show. The Herrmanns took their place, standing next to the curtain and facing the back of the stage. The carpenters, managers, and assistants stood alongside them, awaiting this special demonstration. Will and Dot also took their place to watch Thurston's trick.

Howard Thurston took a deep breath and tried to appear every bit as calm and collected as Leon Herrmann. "Thank you, Mr. Herrmann. This will only take a few minutes." He realized that his career was on the line. "Lights, please!" he called to the electrician. "I need plenty of light for this trick." The lights glowed, brighter and brighter as Thurston watched closely. He put his hand in his pocket. "More lights!" he asked again, and stood calmly, as if he hadn't a care in the world. "Sorry, young fellow. That's all the power I can give you," the electrician called from the wings. The stage was well lit, but not as brightly lit as it could have been. Thurston's first deception had worked perfectly.

"You will understand that all objects may be animate, although they seem inanimate . . ." He paused and then repeated the line, a bit louder, so he could be heard above the clatter of the crowd in the auditorium.

Thurston pulled a deck from his pocket and asked five spectators to select playing cards, including Madame Herrmann, Will Robinson, and Leon Herrmann.

It seemed as if the cards were freely selected, but Thurston had actually forced all five cards—using a careful bit of sleight of hand to ensure that each card went to the right person. After the five cards were returned to the deck, he shuffled the cards casually. During the course of his shuffles, he brought the five selected cards to the top of the deck. He dipped his hand into his pocket and palmed five additional cards, secretly adding these to the deck. These five cards were duplicates of the chosen cards, but each had a small triangular flap of cardboard glued to its back.

Thurston stepped back a few paces, directly beneath one of the invisible threads. He held the deck in front of his chest in his left hand. With his right hand, Thurston made a few mysterious passes over the cards. His fingers located the thread and pulled it down, the same way a clothesline is pulled down to receive a garment. His hands came together to square the cards. Working from a sense of

The drawing from the *Denver Post*: Thurston mystifying Leon Herrmann.

touch, he caught the thread beneath the little cardboard flap on the back card.

Thurston raised his right hand over the cards again and paused dramatically. When he loosened his left hand's grip on the cards, the thread pulled the first card, a duplicate of Madame Herrmann's selection, into the air. The card soared straight up out of the deck, smoothly ascending through eighteen inches of space and landing in Thurston's raised right hand.

Leon Herrmann clapped his gloved hands in approval.

Thurston lifted the card from the thread, placing it on the face of he deck. Because Grace had positioned several threads around the stage, he could move closer or farther from the Herrmann company and still accomplish the trick. One by one, each card flew from the deck and was shown to the person who had selected it. The last card, Leon Herrmann's selection, was boldly revealed just several feet from the magician. Thurston was confident that the lighting and scenery on the stage would conceal the threads perfectly.

Thurston finished by switching the five tricked cards for the five unprepared duplicates—the cards with their little flaps ended up palmed in his hand. He offered the deck to the magician and made a slight bow. Meanwhile, Grace was hiding in the wings. She reached up and yanked down all of the threads.

Leon probably suspected the secret, for Grace noticed that as he walked towards Thurston, he raised his hand in the air—a casual gesture designed to snag a thread that might be over the stage. Luckily, Grace had just reeled in the invisible silk threads, and Leon's hand missed them.

Thurston's trick was a good one, but his performance for Leon Herrmann was a particularly deceptive one. It was the array of little touches—calling for the lights, moving from one place to another as different cards floated, and then quickly pulling down the threads— that proved especially mystifying to another magician. Herrmann never suspected that his stage and his crew could have been sub- verted to work against him. He also never expected to be ambushed for his reaction. As he finished the trick, Thurston dashed over to Herrmann and the hidden reporter stepped out from the wings to hear the conversation. "Did it mystify you?" Thurston asked. Herrmann shrugged. "Yes, M'sieur. Très bien." Thurston teased the magician by explaining part of his secret and earning another compliment, "Ah, yes, very clever." Herrmann was pushed toward his dressing room and Will Robinson set the props for the opening of the show.

As the stage door slammed, the reporter told Howard and Grace Thurston that he'd heard all he needed. He dashed back to the news- paper office and the next morning, the *Denver Post* ran a two- column article titled, "Herrmann, the Magician, Mystified by Another Magician." A drawing portrayed Herrmann and his party watching young Thurston performing his marvel. The article wasn't exactly what Thurston had wanted. His name didn't even make the headline. But he and Grace were happy with the recognition, buying extra copies of the paper, clipping the article and sending it off to agents back east. In his own publicity, Thurston rephrased the head- line, becoming, "The Man who Mystified Herrmann."

Over the next year, Thurston worked better and better engagements.

Early in 1900, he was booked at the Bijou Theater in Boston, and later that year obtained an engagement at the prestigious Palace Theater in London, where his card routine became a sensational hit. Ironically, the act that earned cheers at the Bijou and the Palace was almost the same act that had entertained the drunks at the Alcazar, starting with card manipulations and proceeding to his famous Rising Card routine.

—⁓—

Leon, Madame Herrmann, and their manager Edward Thurnaer were embarrassed by the newspaper story, but even more enraged to realize that their stage manager had played a part in the deception. Ironically, Thurnaer was the man who had first tried to lure Robinson away from Kellar for Alexander Herrmann. In a letter to a colleague, Robinson admitted that he'd done it all "against Herrmann's wishes, also our manager's. They raised hell to think I would do such a thing. Well, I had hell every day for months, and all on account of doing a good turn for a dirty loafer." Robinson might well have been jealous of Thurston's success, categorizing him as a loafer because he had only invested several years in the profession before becoming successful.

William Robinson never regained the trust of the Herrmanns. He and Dot continued with the show for another couple of months and left by the beginning of 1899. Their long careers as magic assistants were finally over.

—⁓—

Several years later, when Robinson complained in a letter about Thurston's conduct, it was because Thurston had implied he fooled Robinson with the trick. "I gave him a black velvet set so the thread could not be seen. Ask him if he remembers that, and then he will change his mind about fooling me," Will wrote. He was also offended that Thurston had implied he fooled "The Great Herrmann" (Alexander) instead of Leon Herrmann. Will was still fiercely loyal to his old boss. "The Great Herrmann was then dead. There is no excuse of any kind for him to drag in the Great Herrmann's name." Curiously, Robinson didn't complain about Thurston sneaking a reporter into the theater, which suggests that he had known about the plan.

Thurston always took credit for his own tricks, but in a 1901 interview, during the height of his success with the card routine, he publicly credited William Robinson as helping him with his manipulation act. He knew that Robinson, working in the same city, would have seen this acknowledgment.

At the Tabor Grand Opera House, Robinson realized that threads were being used and that the lights and scenery were being adjusted to deliberately fool Leon Herrmann—on Herrmann's own stage. Despite his publicity, Thurston was not the man who mystified Herrmann. Robinson was. It was the ultimate betrayal by a magic assistant.

Perhaps that's exactly how Robinson intended it. He'd figuratively set fire to his bridges, riling Kellar by exposing his tricks in print; then he schemed so that Leon Herrmann was bested by a beer hall performer. Will and Dot were tired of working as assistants, but they had seemed unable to make the leap to their own act. Robinson was deliberately forcing the issue. There was no turning back now; both bridges were burning nicely.

—m—

At the end of 1898, Munn and Company, the publishers of *Scientific American*, produced an attractive and informative little book titled *Spirit Slate Writing and Kindred Phenomena*. The title page explained that the author was William E. Robinson, "Assistant to the late Herrmann." Robinson's preface explained that the book was the result of his own studies in magic after attending hundreds of séances in America and abroad. It was a fashion for mediums to produce messages on small school slates, and many ingenious methods had been created to accomplish this fraud. Robinson's book was a cold, hard look at various tricks from the séance room. An associate later claimed that Will's expertise in this subject was a result of his earlier, nearly criminal work in Chicago, and *Spirit Slate Writing* may have been an attempt to put the subject behind him. The book, advertised through Campbell's bookshop, also included explanations of tricks of the Davenport Brothers, mind-reading deceptions, and a few conjuring tricks in an appendix.

In addition to writing *Spirit Slate Writing*, Will also appealed to his fellow professional magicians, offering to build and sell illusions. One ad, from an 1898 trade journal, boasted, "Something New Under the Sun," and offered titles of Robinson's original ideas: "Envanishment, The Weight of Love, The Ladder of Fame, The Witch's Daughter, Cupid, Kyoto, Mumbo Jumbo, Satan's Bride, Scribe of Buddha, Birth of the Lily, The Smuggler, Life and Death, Creation, Youth and Old Age, The Woman of the Flames." They were attractive titles, but a few—like Kyoto—sound like copies of Herrmann or Kellar illusions. He also advertised, "Books on magic bought, sold and exchanged, Photographs of magic celebrities for Sale." He sold a small booklet of tricks to his fellow magicians, titled *Extraordinary Mystical Novelties*, and distributed a catalog of tricks for sale titled *A Few of Robinson's New Ideas*. The catalog offered short manuscripts for sale, his personal secrets for various tricks with cards, handkerchiefs, and other small apparatus.

But the Robinsons didn't intend to just sell tricks to other magicians. Will petitioned his old associate, B. F. Keith, for a tryout week at the most prestigious vaudeville theater in the country.

A decade earlier, Will Robinson had first met the theater owner, Benjamin Franklin Keith, and performed at his innovative vaudeville theaters in Providence and Boston. The Achmed Ben Ali act had been a big hit for Keith. Since that time, Keith and his partner, E. F. Albee, began assembling a prestigious string of theaters across the East Coast. By 1899, Keith-Albee was synonymous with vaudeville, and scoring a success under their management meant that a vaudevillian had reached the top of the profession—a guarantee of success in the field. Keith and Albee had became managers of the Union

Advertising art for the Robinsons' new act; Dot's name is misspelled.

Square Theater in New York, just one block west of Tony Pastor's famous theater, in September 1893.

For their Union Square tryout, Will and Dot chose their very strongest material. The Maid of the Moon had been perfected over the years with Kellar and Herrmann. The hat production act was in good shape, and Will smoothed over all the mechanical problems. He filled out the act with other bits of classical conjuring. Dot performed a few trick shooting specialties.

They premiered for Keith and Albee on March 20, 1899, and ran for exactly one week. Once again, the Robinsons demonstrated that they were capable of presenting a professional show and of filling out a bill, but their act failed to generate any interest with the Union Square managers. The *New York Clipper* recorded their appearance with the faintest of praise, "Professor W. E. Robinson in a good illusion."

There were no more bookings from Keith. After twenty years of frustrations in magic, and season after season with Kellar and Herrmann, it was a failure the Robinsons could not afford.

—m—

Exactly six weeks later, on a sunny spring day, William Robinson turned the corner at Broadway and looked across the street at Keith and Albee's Union Square Theater. Over the marquee hung an enormous bloodred banner, proclaiming the name of their latest star: Ching Ling Foo.

During his time in Omaha, the Ching Ling Foo troupe attracted the attention of a theatrical manager named Colonel Hopkins. Foo appreciated his reception in America, and wanted to stay and continue performing, but he found himself trapped in a legal battle. The engagement at the fair had been on an exclusive basis. The magician had agreed not to work in vaudeville and that his only American appearance would be at the Exposition. B. F. Keith told Hopkins that he was interested in the act, but he feared that the magician would be sent back to China under the Alien Labor Law. Colonel Hopkins successfully appealed to the courts, insisting that the troupe were artists, not laborers.

A permit was granted and the Ching Ling Foo troupe—magic, plate spinning, and juggling—was brought to the Union Square Theater on May 1, 1899.

After Foo's first week of performances, the *New York Clipper*—the same theatrical journal that had barely acknowledged Robinson—reported on the Oriental wizard: "The nearest thing to a sensation this house has known for many months." Two weeks later, the *Clipper* wrote, "Phenomenal business continued. Crowds filled all seats, overflowed standing room."

After six weeks, Foo's troupe began a triumphant march across Keith's circuit of theaters—Boston, Providence, Philadelphia. They then returned to the Union Square in the middle of August for "an indefinite duration," and generated "a jam for admissions almost unprecedented."

The theater unfurled an enormous banner above the street, proclaiming that the wonderful Chinese wizard had appeared "40 weeks with Keith Theaters!" The act headlined at the Union Square until November 11, 1899.

—〰—

We don't know how many times William Robinson stood at the back of the crowded theater, sullenly watching as the Chinese wizard drew loud cheers. It was the engagement he should have been given, and the response he'd always dreamed of receiving. But Robinson was a pragmatist. Just as Kellar had found a rival in Herrmann, and used the competition to focus his skills, Will was now preoccupied with the Chinese magician.

Hidden in the shadows of the auditorium, he watched Foo's precise movements, again and again—the deliberate pantomime, the broad gestures, the slow, delicate mysteries enhanced with brief flashes of personality. He studied it all, the same way he'd studied Ben Ali Bey's Black Art act.

Once he'd made his decision, he told Dot.

Chapter 15

THE FOLIES BERGÈRE

The Herrmann show was shattered by arguments and litigation. Adelaide Herrmann came to despise Leon, and she finally left in the autumn of 1899, taking her tricks and starring in her own vaudeville act. This included A Night in Japan, the sequence of Oriental magic tricks devised by Will Robinson.

Leon continued with the show and adopted the billing "Herrmann the Great." Adelaide objected, insisting that this was her husband's trademark; yes, she claimed, there had been a number of Herrmanns, but only one who was proclaimed Great. She sued her nephew to prevent him from using the title.

The judge was understandably confused. Even after Alexander's death, the show had been billed The Great Herrmann Company. Leon's real name was Herrmann. The judge ruled that it was Leon's discretion if he wanted to be called great.

One week, early in 1902, both Herrmanns happened to be playing in Newark, New Jersey. Leon presented an impressive two-and-a-half-hour show at the Empire Theater. When interviewed, he was asked about his famous aunt. Leon took the role of a continental gentleman. "She is a fine lady and a wonderful illusionist," he told the reporter.

Across town, at Proctor's Park Place, Madame Herrmann was included on the vaudeville bill. The same reporter asked her for a comment about her nephew. "He's a bum," she answered.

Leon continued touring with a shorter act for vaudeville. In 1907, he returned to France and worked in Europe, but contracted pneumonia while performing in Russia. He recuperated in the south of

Leon and Adelaide Herrmann in A Night
in Japan.

France and returned to his home in Paris, telling his wife that he was feeling much better. But the next day, May 16, 1909, he was stricken and died. He was forty-two years old.

Madame Adelaide Herrmann had a long, successful career in vaudeville with several different acts. Although there have been few woman magicians, audiences prized Madame Herrmann as one of the very best: an actress, sleight-of-hand artist, and entrepreneur.

—⚏—

When Ching Ling Foo returned to the Union Square Theater in the summer of 1899, the management indulged in various publicity stunts to promote their new star. A large Chinese flag, supposedly a gift from the Empress in recognition of the magician's achievements, was displayed between two lampposts in front of the theater. The week of August 20, Foo's porcelain bowl of water was displayed in the lobby of the theater. The bowl was heavy enough that few spectators could even lift it. A nearby sign boasted of Foo's impossible feat, and offered $1,000 to anyone who could duplicate his famous Bowl Production trick.

These bold wagers were common practice. The idea of the challenge was to gain publicity, and people in show business seldom took them seriously. On the few occasions when such a wager was accepted, invariably the fine print prevented anyone from winning. Several months after Foo's challenge, Robinson himself accepted a thousand-dollar slate-writing contest with a medium. After a short burst of publicity, the contest never occurred. But Ching Ling Foo was unfortunate enough to offer his challenge at the same time that magicians were scrambling to add his mysterious new tricks to their act. The Bowl of Water Production was the latest novelty, and it was making headlines. In July, *Mahatma* magazine, the magician's journal, had reproduced a full exposure of Foo's act that had been printed in the *New York World*. Included was a diagram explaining how the bowl was hidden. *Mahatma* was happy to repeat Foo's challenge, and goad its readers into claiming the money: "Ching Ling Foo offers $1000 to any man who will duplicate his bowl trick," the magazine wrote that autumn. "Two or three magicians have his outfit and claim they can do his act. Here is a chance for them to make money and call his bluff."

Unexpectedly, *Mahatma* linked William Robinson's name to the challenge. "Robinson offered to duplicate the trick, but very funny to state his offer was not accepted. [The challenge] was a Chinese game of bluff. . . . The wily Chinaman backed out and his challenge was taken out of the press. It is stated by those who have seen Robinson do the trick that he does it just as good as the Chinaman."

A thousand dollars was a lot of money, and a few magicians must have been tempted by the offer. But Will was neither naive nor arrogant enough to march down the aisle at the Union Square and try to engage in a duel. He had just played the theater for a week's run and considered himself a professional.

The *Mahatma* story is a glimpse at a behind-the-scenes drama that was being scripted and staged by William Robinson. Readers should have been able to guess at his plans.

First, Will had already built a version of Ching Ling Foo's Bowl of Water trick. It was completed by the time Foo made his challenge that summer.

Second, Robinson was anxious to publicize the fact that he was very good at performing it.

Third, he used the challenge to portray himself as the injured party. He was waiting to pick a fight with the Chinese magician.

—⁓—

The secret was that the bowl was concealed beneath the robes of the magician.

It was a real porcelain bowl, filled with water. A special waterproof cover was fitted tightly across the mouth of the bowl. No one has ever been sure of Ching Ling Foo's exact method. One magician suspected that he used an animal hide to cover the bowl. New York magicians utilized a disc of rubberized cloth with a stout cord in the outer hem.

The cover was several inches larger in diameter than the mouth of the bowl. It was placed atop the bowl. A clever bit of hardware, a ratcheted wheel, was attached to the cord. This allowed the cord to be gradually tightened around the side of the bowl until the cover was watertight. In this position, the bowl could be lifted and turned on its side.

Beneath his robe, the performer wore a heavy leather belt around his waist. Straps at the back of the belt hung behind the performer's legs and supported the bowl in a shallow sling.

When the Chinese magician stepped on stage, the heavy bowl was just behind his legs, hanging sideways in the sling. The wide Chinese robe concealed the bowl from the front.

Producing the bowl called for a specific sequence of actions. The magician stood on a small carpet in the center of the stage. He twisted the piece of fabric in his hands, showing it to be ordinary and laying it flat on the stage. As the magician picked up the back edge of the fabric, he spread his legs wide, leaned forward, and bent his knees so one side of the bowl contacted the stage. The heavy bowl made a quarter-somersault between the performer's legs, emerging from beneath his robe. The bowl was now upright beneath the cloth. The magician took half a step back, freeing his robe and ensuring that the bowl was in the center of the fabric. He then reached under the cloth and opened the ratchet. The cord went slack, freeing the rubberized cover. As the magician pulled away the fabric, the special cover was hidden beneath it.

It was a tough trick to perform. It even required rehearsal in walking—a sort of wide-legged swagger was necessary to compensate for the weight of the bowl. The costuming had to be perfect to conceal the bulge of the bowl from the front. The harness and rubberized cover had to be well made. Finally, the magician needed to be precise and confident in every movement.

Based on his experience with Oriental-looking tricks, such as the Herrmanns' Night in Japan act, Will looked for illusions that would complement the Bowl Production. He found it in Professor Mingus's Gold Fish Trick. Walter Mingus Hopler was a New Jersey magician who decided to assemble an act of only original illusions. In 1893, he created the Gold Fish Trick, which he presented in New Jersey and New York in vaudeville. The idea was startlingly simple and elegant. Mingus showed a long bamboo fish pole. He attached a small piece of bait to the hook, and swung it out over the audience. As the hook jiggled in the stage light, he gave the pole a gentle snap, and a live goldfish appeared dangling from the end of the hook. Mingus reached up to take the fish in his hand, and then dropped it in a small glass aquarium on his table. The fish swam around inside the tank.

He repeated this three times, materializing three goldfish in midair.

In 1895, Mingus performed the trick at Tony Pastor's 14th Street Theater. The following year, he fell heir to a small fortune and retired from the stage, becoming a successful merchant in Bloomfield, New Jersey. New York magicians scrambled for the secret. Robinson, an insider at Martinka's shop, was one of the first to hear about it. He knew it would suit an Oriental act perfectly.

Gradually, Will realized that he wouldn't be able to simply present an Oriental act. He needed to be Chinese. The robe was an essential part of the act, and it only looked right on a Chinese performer. Ching Ling Foo had demonstrated the advantage of a language barrier: a magician could work silently. Will would need to adopt a role—the same way he played parts in Herrmann's illusions—that would explain the costume, the props, and his inscrutable silence.

Will selected wardrobe from Mott Street in Chinatown, and Dot added extra panels of fullness to accommodate the bowl. Based on Will's experience playing a Chinese assistant, he bought a black wig and swarthy greasepaint. He trimmed back his hairline—his hair was already thinning—and shaved off his long waxed moustache. He remembered his boss Kellar shaving his moustache because he thought it would allow him to speak better. Ironically, Robinson was now shaving his moustache so that he could avoid speaking on stage.

Just as Ching Ling Foo was supported by a group of jugglers and acrobats, Will felt it was necessary to use an Oriental juggler to add authenticity to his troupe. He contacted a Chinese juggler who worked under the name Prince Fee Lung. Fee Lung had been one-half of a vaudeville team named The Bedlams. This was the act that followed Will and Dot on the bill at the St. Nicholas Music Hall; the Robinsons had stood in the wings and listened to the riotous response from the audience. Fee Lung's specialty was to be suspended by a hook braided into his thick black pigtail. Once dangling over the stage, he swung like a pendulum and juggled burning torches.

The final element of the Chinese impersonation would be Dot. Ching Ling Foo's magic was sedate and austere, but Robinson sought to improve on the Oriental tricks with added color and action. Dot, the renowned magic assistant, had been levitated, locked in trunks, turned into a ghost, or made to disappear. She had spent years onstage with the Black Art act, completely invisible to the audience. Now she would play an important and highly visible part as a delicate Chinese princess, draped in embroidered silks and padding about in felt slippers.

There was an unusual accident in Manhattan on October 28, 1899, an unexpected tragedy in the middle of a magic show.

It was a Saturday night, and Michael Hatal was performing at an Odd Fellows lodge on East Fourth Street in Manhattan. Hatal was 32 years old, a cabinetmaker by trade, but as an enthusiastic amateur magician he spent his free time at Martinka's magic shop or rehearsing new ideas for his program. Hatal billed himself as The Hungarian Herrmann.

Two hundred people watched his performance that night: fellow lodge members, and their wives and children. Mrs. Hatal assisted as her husband produced tissue flowers from a cone of paper and produced half-dollars from the air. Finally, Hatal introduced his feature trick, stepping forward to give a suitably dramatic introduction. "I hold in my hand an old fashioned rifle. I shall load it with two bullets."

Hatal showed a glass filled with large lead bullets. In another glass was black gunpowder. He handed the glass of bullets to someone in the front row for examination. He took a pinch of powder, sprinkled it on a plate and set fire to it, so the audience saw the flash of light and the puff of smoke that told them it was really gunpowder.

"I shall ask someone to shoot at my heart, and I will endeavor to catch the bullets." He asked for an experienced gunman from the audience. "It is necessary that I have for this trick a first-class marksman, a man who will shoot straight at my heart."

Reportedly, Hatal's wife approached him and whispered something in his ear: she warned him against going ahead with the feat, feeling her husband had not rehearsed it properly. But it was later said that this was not a new trick; Hatal had performed this version of the Bullet Catching Illusion on several occasions. He certainly didn't exhibit any concern, but waved away his wife and stepped forward with the rifle.

Frank Benjo, a 28-year-old member of the Lodge, was seated in the third row. When no one immediately volunteered to fire the gun, he stood. "I'll help you," he told the magician.

Benjo poured powder into the barrel of the rifle. Hatal handed him two bullets and these were also dropped inside. Benjo then loaded a paper wad and shouldered the rifle as The Hungarian Herrmann stepped to the opposite side of the stage.

A number of people in the small auditorium exchanged nervous glances. Several women stood and left the room, fearing the unpleasantness of the rifle shot. Hatal knew that he had the crowd on the edge of their seats.

The magician held a small silk flag in front of his chest, and urged Benjo to use this as a target and fire on the count of three. He counted slowly. There was a tremendous explosion and a cloud of smoke. Mrs. Hatal shouted, "He's shot." As the smoke cleared, the audience saw Michael Hatal lying on his back on the stage. His face was white. Blood spurted from his chest.

Women screamed. Men ran for help. A few members of the lodge rushed to the platform and regained order. The magician was taken to Bellevue Hospital, but doctors quickly realized that his injuries would be fatal. One bullet had entered three inches above his heart and the other penetrated his left lung.

Frank Benjo was arrested and taken to the hospital for identification. Fortunately, Hatal was still conscious, and absolved Benjo of all blame.

We don't know Hatal's intended secret. The magician explained to the police that he was responsible for selecting two composition bullets—just wax and lampblack—that were among the lead bullets in the glass. Perhaps Hatal was distracted, or excited, or had not properly rehearsed this part of the deception. The injury, Hatal admitted on his deathbed, was solely the result of his own clumsiness.

Frank Benjo was jailed overnight and released the next day. Michael Hatal died Sunday evening, October 29, from his injuries.

It was a weird accident that occupied the minds of New York magicians for weeks; it would have fascinated William Robinson if he hadn't been so busy working on his new Chinese act.

—m—

Before Will and Dot finished all their rehearsals, Robinson realized that he might be too late; there were already too many "Chinese" magicians vying for position in America. *Mahatma* reported on a magician in Cleveland who was rumored to perform Foo's act, and a New York wizard, Frank Hewes, who had mastered the bowl trick. At least two other professionals were rumored to be working on imitations of Ching Ling Foo's act.

Robinson knew that no one in America could catch up. Ching Ling Foo had the name, the reputation, and the publicity. He had the management of B. F. Keith, which guaranteed a circuit of theaters, and would open doors to additional vaudeville houses across the country.

But as Ching Ling Foo sought to fulfill those lucrative contracts, it would prevent him from conquering new territories. Will decided that he didn't want to stop and fight. He wanted a new battlefield, all to himself. It was the best decision of his career.

He contacted a New York manager named Ike Rose, who was then working in Paris. Starting in 1899, there was a fashion for American variety acts in Europe and Ike Rose was responsible for the trend.

In the late 1890s, Rose married a can-can girl who worked under the name Sarahet. She was heading a troupe of dancers at Koster and Bial's Music Hall in New York. The next morning, Rose arrived at the theater to demand an increase in his wife's salary. He wanted $100 per week for her services. The new bride remained home that morning, reduced to tears. She was convinced that her husband's demands would end her contract.

He not only got the raise at Koster and Bial's, but he went on to successfully manage her solo act. In 1898, he took her to Europe and made Saharet a star. Although few European managers would agree to Ike Rose's salary demands, he agreed to a percentage deal, and then arranged a series of publicity stunts to draw crowds to see her. Saharet was a pretty showgirl and a competent dancer, but by the time Ike Rose was finished marketing her charms, she was one of Europe's classical beauties and a favorite of German society.

His experience quickly put Rose in a position to import acts to Europe, and return European acts to American vaudeville. He'd heard of Ching Ling Foo's phenomenal success and thought that Robinson's plan was perfect. Rose wired Robinson's troupe to come to France immediately. He had a contract with the Parisiana Theater.

Will and Dot sold the Astarte illusion to Leon Herrmann, who had always loved the trick and was determined to use it with his wife, Marie. Will's sixteen-year-old daughter, Annie, was living with Jim and Sarah Robinson. Jim and Edward Robinson, Will's brother, continued operating Campbell's.

Robinson also sold his prized library of books, hidden in the back room of Campbell's bookshop, to a New York physician and enthusiastic collector of magic, Saram Ellison. To his friends, it seemed as if Will was trying to dismiss all the old elements of his career.

In April 1900, *Mahatma* published a brief note from its Paris correspondent: "It is rumored that W. E. Robinson, the late Herrmann's assistant, is coming over to present the Ching Ling Foo act."

—m—

The Parisiana Theater was a disappointment. In his enthusiasm, Rose had managed to oversell the act to the Isola Brothers, promising miracles from the mysterious Chinese magician, and received a wonderful contract for 8,000 francs per week. When Will, Dot, and Fee Lung performed the trial show, manager Isola just shrugged. The show was interesting, but it was still a bit rough and didn't offer the sensations he'd expected. He told Ike Rose that he'd give him 4,000 francs for the act. The reduced salary was a common ploy for managers; once the act traveled across the ocean, the performers were at the mercy of the theater and found it difficult to negotiate. But Ike Rose had confidence in the act and was enraged at the Parisiana's manager. He grabbed Isola by the collar and screamed into his ear, "Contract cancelled!"

Will and Dot had never worked with anyone like Ike Rose, who refused to be discouraged, and kept the couple's spirits high as he continued to move forward. Rose negotiated a new contract at the Folies Bergère. Because this was a much larger stage, Will turned to a friend, Charles DeVere, for help. DeVere was a British magic dealer and prop maker who had a shop in the Passage Saulnier, just opposite the stage door at the Folies Bergère. His wife had performed an Oriental act as Okita, and he offered Okita's painted backdrops to Will to fill the stage. He also encouraged him to add the Linking Rings to his show, and gave him suggestions about recreating the fire-eating trick of Ching Ling Foo.

After haggling, Rose agreed to accept 4,000 francs per week from Forbee, an impresario at the Folies Bergère. It was much less money than he wanted, but he was happy to have his magician performing at the famous Folies Bergère. On March 15, 1900, William Robinson—as Hop Sing Loo—stepped on the stage for the first time.

—⁓—

All the last-minute changes, additions, and adjustments took their toll. Prince Fee Lung was a definite hit. Hop Sing Loo's tricks were disappointingly slow and unsteady. But when the new Chinese magician took the stage for his finale—the famous Bowl of Water Trick—the act collapsed into an embarrassing fiasco.

It was the usual formula: a simple mechanical failure, the raw, numbed nerves of an opening performance, and a poisonous dose of adrenaline. Will stepped forward, flourishing the fabric and tossing it to the ground. He exhaled, picked up the back edge of the fabric, took a half step toward the audience, bent his knees, and dropped the concealed bowl to the stage. It tumbled into place perfectly. But when he reached beneath the cloth to release the cover, his fingers caught on the ratchet. Will grabbed the cloth, and pulled it dramatically. It was his final gesture of the act, and it should have been the trick that started the audience cheering. Instead, the back edge of the bowl was lifted off the stage, sending a gush of water and apples spilling across the hardwood floor of the Folies Bergère.

The musicians stopped short of their final chord. They dropped their instruments, overturned their chairs, and ran from the pit as they were doused by streams of water cascading over the front of the stage. Will took an awkward bow as the audience snickered and stagehands appeared with mops. The curtain fell.

Backstage, the stage manager of the Folies delivered the bad news. The water had dripped through a small trapdoor in the center of the stage, soaking Loie Fuller's special lighting. These were the fixtures, beneath the stage, that illuminated her white silk robe during the Fire Dance. Fortunately, Fuller was not working in the Folies at that time, but her equipment was stored under the stage, awaiting her next appearance.

In later years, when Will told the story of his spilled bowl at the Folies, he included an amusing twist on his new identity. The impresario Forbee stormed back to the dressing room and threatened Ike Rose. "I should fire your Chinese act on the spot! I am told there is another fine magician in town, ready to take your place. It is a very talented American named Robinson!"

Ike Rose stepped in, dismissed the accident as a mere technicality, and negotiated a compromise. Hop Sing Loo's salary would be reduced to pay for the damage, but the Chinese magician would remain in the show.

Several days later, Ike Rose was proven right. Hop Sing Loo's spilled bowl of water was quickly forgotten when the management faced a real disaster. The closing number of the Folies Bergère, the hit of the show, had been a spectacular pantomime titled "La Flamenca." On stage were a crowd of flamenco dancers, a procession of matadors, sixty actors, and 25 live bulls. The production cost a reported 100,000 francs. The climax was an actual bullfight on stage; the stage crew erected a heavy metal fence across the front of the proscenium to protect the patrons. But during the performance on March 21, a snorting, galloping bull charged the railing. The audience was unsure if the fence would hold, and dashed for the exits. There was a stampede, with spectators screaming, shoving, and tumbling out of the way. The police came in to investigate, temporarily closing the show and then banning the bulls from the stage.

Will and Dot were secretly grateful for the scandal, which had made headlines in Paris and overshadowed their wobbly performances. They worked diligently on the act, rehearsing each day and making steady improvements each evening. Ike Rose loved the result. He contacted London and secured their next engagement.

With Rose's help, Hop Sing Loo managed to stay one jump ahead of the competition. Several months after his Folies engagement, when the Exposition Universelle opened in Paris, the Chinese Pavilion on the Exposition grounds hosted a group of Chinese magicians who "produced large bowls of water, a la Ching Ling Foo" and also performed the Fishing Trick, copying Will's success at the Folies Bergère.

—⁓—

A Paris magician sent back the first review for *Mahatma*:

> Hop Sing Loo, otherwise Mr. Wm. E. Robinson, as well and favorably known in the United States, opened at the Folies Bergère, and assisted by Miss Dot Robinson and a clever Chinese equilibrist gave a very good imitation of Ching Ling Foo. For want of rehearsals, it went somewhat slow at first, but has improved greatly since. Still, your correspondent who knows Robinson's capabilities, feels assured he would have made a greater success had he given an evening dress performance and exhibited some of his admirable hand and mechanical illusions, as he is out of his element in Chinese business and the French people are difficult to please.

Will and Dot knew that the reviewer was wrong. Despite the false starts at the Folies, Robinson had never been as good a performer as Hop Sing Loo. He was most comfortable on a stage hiding behind the impersonation of a Chinese wizard—the deliberately quiet, cold, mysterious master of the art.

His portrayal was based in part on Ching Ling Foo, and in part on the stereotypes of the day. In 1870, the American poet and playwright Bret Harte published "Plain Language from Truthful James," a tale of a euchre game played opposite Ah Sin, a Chinese card sharp. Ah Sin took the cards with a deceptively innocent smile, "childlike and bland," but was soon revealed to be a proficient cheat, with cards stacked on the deck and aces concealed in his sleeve.

> Which is why I remark,
> And my language is plain,

That for ways that are dark
And tricks that are vain,
The heathen Chinee is peculiar,
Which the same I am free to maintain.

A similar character from Harte's 1876 play, *Two Men of Sandy Bar*, was an inscrutable, nefarious Chinaman named Hop Sing. This character was probably the inspiration for Robinson's stage name.

Ike Rose didn't like the name. When he sent back a report to the *New York Clipper*, he omitted the name Hop Sing Loo, writing, "W. E. Robinson made a big hit at the Folies Bergère. He has Prince Fee Lung, Chinese acrobat with him." When the show was ready to move to London the following month, Rose demanded that the magician find a more impressive name.

Will and Dot rearranged syllables on a page and suggested new combinations to Ike Rose, but the manager insisted on something as appealing as Ching Ling Foo. Later, T. Nelson Downs, an American coin manipulator working in Paris, claimed that he solved the problem for his friend Robinson. His suggestion was Chung Ling Soo.

Of course, it was a ridiculously derivative idea, hardly one that Downs should have boasted about. Ching Ling Foo . . . Chung Ling Soo. But Ike Rose liked it. The real Ching Ling Foo had been getting publicity, and as his name became known in Europe, any confusion by managers wouldn't hurt the Robinsons' new act. As they said in England, "In for a penny, in for a pound." If they were going to capitalize on Foo's success, there was no reason to hold back.

Later, Robinson retold the story, claiming that Fee Lung, the Chinese member of the troupe, suggested their stage names. He thought Will should be Chung Ling Soo, which translated to Extra Good Luck. Dot should be called Suee Seen, which meant Water Lily.

In fact, the name Suee Seen is an approximation of Water Lily in Chinese. But Chung Ling Soo does not translate to Extra Good Luck, or anything else for that matter. It is three syllables of gobbledygook designed to sound like Ching Ling Foo. In that sense, the name did prove to be very good luck.

Chung Ling Soo; an odd costume, including
slippers with turned-up toes.

On April 16, 1900, the London *Evening Standard* advertised a special feature at the Alhambra Theater in the West End. "Chung Ling Soo. Tonight. The Great Chinese magician will make his first appearance in Europe tonight. He will perform his remarkable bowl trick, containing three pails of water and live ducks, his fire juggling, angling for and catching live goldfish in mid-air, and a group of new feats never before seen in this country."

That evening, at ten o'clock, Chung Ling Soo, the Marvelous Chinese Magician, swaggered onto the stage and into the spotlight. And with the very first cheers—with the assurance that Chung Ling Soo was a music hall sensation—William Robinson began his most incredible deception.

Chapter 16

THE ALHAMBRA THEATER

C hung Ling Soo stood in the bright oval of blue-white lime-light at the Alhambra in Leicester Square and grinned. He greeted the audience by clasping his hands together in front of his chest and then energetically bobbing his wrists up and down—westerners called the gesture a Chinese handshake. Suee Seen met him in the center of the stage and handed him two porcelain soup plates.

Soo held the plates high, showing them to be ordinary. Stepping to a table that held a wooden box filled with bran, he dipped one plate inside, scooping up the grain. When the dish was heaped with bran, he handed it back to Suee Seen, and then turned the second plate upside down and used it to cover the bran. Soo picked up a Chinese fan, opened it, and gently fanned the plates while he smiled at the audience. Uncovering the plates, every bit of the bran had disappeared. Instead, two white doves fluttered their wings and perched on the edges of the soup plate.

As the dainty Suee Seen took the doves offstage, Soo stepped over to a long table that held five metal tubes. The tubes were about a foot tall and of graduated diameters, a setup that gave the trick its name, the Organ Pipes. The largest tube was about six inches across. Soo rapidly showed that each tube was empty by using a routine of passing the tubes through one another—nesting and separating them in succession. Finally, he reached into the tubes, producing dozens of long silk streamers, handfuls of toy balls, bouquets of flowers, and a small pyramid of glass wine bottles.

By now, the Marvelous Chinese Conjurer had reached a comfortable pace. He moved to another small table and picked up a bright metal vase with straight sides. He turned it over in his hands, showing it empty to the audience. Suee Seen stepped onstage with a pitcher of water. She tipped it into the vase, filling it. Soo swirled the vase between his hands, then peered down into the water. He reached inside and withdrew a silk flag, miraculously dry. This was followed by another flag, and then another. The Chinese magician ended up with an enormous bundle of silk—flags from dozens of different countries. He finished by twirling the flags between his hands and transforming them into a gigantic Union Jack, which drew cheers from his London audience.

Chung Ling Soo then performed the fire-eating trick—it was an abbreviated version of Ching Ling Foo's version, which had been presented at the Omaha fair and in vaudeville. Soo showed several squares of paper, set fire to them using a candle, and pushed the burning bits of paper into his mouth. He then ate the burning candle, followed by mouthfuls of paper shavings. He blew sparks from his mouth, produced ribbons and a long, narrow pole painted like a barber's pole. Finally he reached beneath the ribbons and produced a large Chinese sunshade. The umbrella sprang open in his hands and Soo spun it back over his shoulder, jauntily twirling it as he walked into the wings.

There was another burst of applause as he stepped back to the center of the stage. Suee Seen met him there with a fishing pole and a small table that held a globular glass bowl filled with water. The Aerial Fishing Trick was next, and it created a minor sensation in London, as it was new to audiences and even other professional magicians there. Soo held a long bamboo fishing pole with four or five feet of string on the end. He reached into his pocket and withdrew a small piece of bait, attaching it to the hook on the end of the line—it looked like a short lead sinker—swinging the hook out over the heads of the audience.

He paused dramatically, as if he had focused on a shoal of invisible fish swimming over the heads of the audience, and maneuvered his hook delicately through space, looking for exactly the right spot. The spotlight tightened to the end of the fishing line and the crowd in the stalls gazed up at the string in expectation. With a snap of his wrist, the Chinese magician located the magical fish. Suddenly, a small goldfish, about three inches long, appeared, dangling from the end of the line. Soo pulled the fishing pole back to the stage, reaching out and unhooking the tiny fish. He reached over and dropped it in the round fishbowl, where it swam in circles. He followed this with two more pieces of bait, and caught two more goldfish. As Suee Seen carried the bowl to the wings and the spectators burst into applause once again, Chung Ling Soo clasped his hands and bobbed them up and down, acknowledging the audience.

Now it was Fee Lung's turn. As Soo exited, Fee Lung tumbled on from the wings, carrying a long chain with a metalwork bowl suspended from each end. Inside the bowls were cotton batting, soaked with fuel and set aflame. Twirling the chain over his head like an enormous baton, the bowls made a circle of flames over the juggler's head. For his second feat, a rope was lowered from the flies. Fee Lung attached a hook that had been woven into his thick pigtail. The hook raised him by his hair, lifting him high over the stage as he swung from side to side, juggling flaming torches.

As Fee Lung took his final bow, Chung Ling Soo stepped back onto the stage. Suee Seen unrolled a large flat floor cloth, demonstrating that no trapdoors were used. Soo took several deliberate steps to the center of the cloth. He held up a large embroidered square of fabric, flourished it from side to side, and then lowered it to the stage. Stepping back and lifting away the cloth, the audience saw an enormous earthenware bowl, filled with water and containing two floating ducks. The ducks were lifted from the bowl and shooed off the stage; they quacked and waddled as the water ladled out into wooden buckets and Soo stepped forward for his final bow.

The act was fifteen minutes long, and it was packed with unusual sensations.

Actually, there was very little in Chung Ling Soo's act that was Chinese. The music was a medley of western "Oriental" songs, tinkling melodies and minor chords. The dove trick, flag trick, and metal tubes were not only European inventions, but well-known

The mysterious Chinese magician, star at
the Alhambra Theater.

ones at that. "I would rather see an old trick well done than a new
one which is devoid of ingenuity," he had advised his fellow magicians several years earlier in *Mahatma* magazine. Now he filled out
his exotic new act with comfortable, tried-and-true mysteries. The
flag trick was the same one he had struggled to teach Leon Herrmann.
Professor Mingus's Fishing trick, first seen just several years earlier,
was an American invention.

The only two Chinese tricks were the fire-eating effect and the
famous Bowl Production. Even these tricks were pale imitations of
Ching Ling Foo's originals. Soo performed a quick version of the fire
trick, eliminating some of the ribbons, the embers, and firecrackers
to simplify the trick. The Bowl Production was expertly done but
had none of the preliminary buildup—the small bowls of walnuts—
that were part of the authentic Chinese routine. Chung Ling Soo's
clothing was a conglomeration of caps and robes, hurriedly assembled from Mott Street in New York's Chinatown or from theatrical
costume shops. Mac Fee Lung gave suggestions about authentic bits
of wardrobe or gestures, but in fact the Robinsons weren't concerned

with being authentic. They sought to make the act flashy and sensational. When it came to the costumes, they had little regard for whether they had purchased men's or women's clothing, or even if they were wearing them backward.

In April 1900, the London audiences couldn't discern a real Chinese act, but they could appreciate a talented performer. The hallmark of Chung Ling Soo's act was not the Oriental trappings, but the magician. The Alhambra audiences could sense that they were watching a magician of great experience: a knowing, mysterious presence. It was apparent that he'd spent many years studying magic in a faraway land before coming to London, and was qualified to perform these wonders. The fifteen minutes with the Marvelous Chinese Conjurer gave the reassuring feeling that they were in the hands of a master.

—⁓—

Chung Ling Soo's success benefited from a broad popular taste for exotic Eastern cultures that had simmered through the last years of the Victorian era. The fashion was called Orientalism, evidenced in faux-bamboo furniture, Japanese or Chinese patterns on vases, textiles and prints, and flamboyant, pagoda-inspired architecture.

Many elements of Orientalism were tied to British imperialism, attempting to incorporate into English taste the most romantic and alluring elements of India or the Middle East, areas included in the swelling empire. As the British pushed to increase trade with China, they were both fascinated and confounded by the beautiful, mysterious culture. "China is simply old, very old—that is, remote and strange," in the words of Max Muller, a scholar of Indian culture and a promoter of Victorian Orientalism. Muller insisted that there were no intellectual bonds between the cultures, "no electric contact between the white and the yellow race." China was a vast, perplexing land of designs, colors, shapes, and objects, which could be rearranged and reassembled to form Western fantasies of the East.

Orientalism was not a cultural movement so much as a bit of

Suee Seen, as she appeared in the
Chung Ling Soo act.

frosting applied to the gingerbread of Victorian design. In an effort to
be especially colorful, fanciful, and exotic, these Oriental designs
were seldom authentic and often preposterous. *The Mikado*, Gilbert
and Sullivan's 1885 "Japanese" comic opera, was a good example. The
orchestrations were lush and the costumes were bright montages of
Japanese robes, tunics, pants, and slippers. To the London public, *The
Mikado* seemed more Japanese than real Japanese culture—which
prized understated, elegant designs, and tasteful moderation.

Similarly, Chung Ling Soo's magic act was a late Victorian
caprice, perfectly fashionable. If Soo had really been Chinese, if his
act had been authentic and not exaggerated, his tricks and costumes
would not have pleased his overeager public. As an impersonator, he
was better than Chinese—he was free to match the public's fantasies
of old China.

—⁂—

The Alhambra audiences loved Chung Ling Soo, and the management extended the booking. Will and Dot's initial engagement continued for a remarkable twelve weeks. The magician and author Will

Dexter later explained the importance of Chung Ling Soo's first appearance. Not only did the magician make headlines in London, at the most prestigious variety theater, but the steady, relaxed engagement gave William Robinson a unique opportunity to refine every detail of the act. "Those three months were the making of Chung Ling Soo," wrote Dexter. "Had he been booked round the Provinces, a week at a time, the probability is that the constant moving around would have given him little time to perfect the show." The grueling policy of Continuous Entertainment—Keith's vaudeville innovation—hadn't reached England. At the Alhambra, there was only one evening performance on weeknights.

After years of experience on stage and many false starts in their careers, the Robinsons didn't take anything for granted and never lowered their guard. They were cautious and smart. They listened to the subtle reactions of their audiences, not simply the bursts of applause, but the small murmurs and gasps that hinted at the audience's feelings about each trick. Building on the initial success, they worked to eliminate the act's weaknesses and magnify its successes. Will and Dot rehearsed changes during the day and Will continuously experimented with new effects.

Magicians generally treated their performances as a sort of concert, skillfully arranging one trick after another to create an overall impression. A large effect might be followed by a small one in a deliberate change of pace, or to pause before working up to a new crescendo. These peaks, valleys, and changes of direction were a careful part of the performance formula, the specific order of an act a sort of calculus, designed to create the very best impression on an audience. But after his many years in show business, Will had developed his own philosophy, a stunningly simple formula for Chung Ling Soo. "Every trick was arranged on an ascending scale of effect," an associate later explained. "He went from one marvel to a greater." In other words, Chung Ling Soo's fifteen minutes was arranged along a simple stair-step progression, leading the audience in one straight path upward. The second trick was better than the first. The third received even more reaction; the fourth was better still. The Marvelous Chinese Conjurer was a success, and William Robinson was taking no chances.

—⁂—

Shortly after the Alhambra premiere, Robinson stopped using the trick with the nested tubes. It was slow and ordinary. He substituted a trick in which a number of cloth balls disappeared from a cylindrical metal container and reappeared in a glass box. At the conclusion, there was a final surprise when he opened the metal container and withdrew a round cage with a bird inside. The trick was no more Oriental than others in the act. He'd actually gotten the apparatus from his friend DeVere in Paris, and it was identical to the prop used by the French magician Robert-Houdin forty years earlier. But it was faster and flashier than the Organ Pipes.

The vase of flags gave him another opportunity to refine his presentation. In early 1900, the British public began reading about the Boxer Rebellion in China, a disorganized and violent uprising against Westerners. The Boxers had begun several years earlier as a mysterious cult from the province of Shantung, China. Rebelling against foreigners and foreign influences in their country, the Boxers fought with primitive weapons like knives and poles; they were convinced that their magical powers would resist foreign bullets.

In the last decade of the nineteenth century, China suffered a series of natural disasters and was faced with pressure to trade with America and Europe. The Boxers emerged in response, determined to bring down the Ch'ing government and drive out the "foreign devils" that were ruining the country. The empress attempted to subvert the threat of violence by tacitly endorsing the Boxers as they moved toward Peking.

Despite the Empress's appeasement, the Boxers became known for their horrific warlike charges—accompanied by the clang of gongs and drums, the warriors stomping on the ground and waving their swords to invoke the "spirit soldiers" that would support their cause. They slaughtered missionaries, tore up railroad tracks, and burned churches.

As stories of the Boxers reached London newspapers, Chung Ling Soo was appearing at the Alhambra. At first, the magician benefited from the publicity. Audiences were intrigued by the accounts of the Boxers' magical abilities, and curious about the Chinese wizard who had just come to their city. But the flag trick forced the audience to take sides. Following Alexander Herrmann's formula, Soo reached inside to produce the new Chinese flag, a dragon against a yellow background. The magician was surprised to hear boos from the audience. Rather than avoid the problem, he played it up to appeal to the crowd. When he held the flag high and heard the first hiss of disapproval, he stopped to frown at the audience, crestfallen. His eyebrows rose and fell as he pointed to the flag, and then out at the crowd again, soliciting more and more response from the eager audience. Finally, he seemed to get the message. Scowling, he threw the flag to the floor and stomped upon it. He quickly bundled together the remainder of the flags, attached them to two cords that had been lowered from the flies, and transformed them into the gigantic Union Jack. The quick succession of boos, laughs, gasps, and cheers provided the perfect climax to the trick and left no doubt of Chung Ling Soo's loyalties. The necessary gestures and feints were also useful for the trick; stopping to perform the little comedy with the Chinese flag gave the magician the perfect pause to switch the bundle of flags, ready for the finale with the British flag.

—⁊⁊⁊—

Once he was settled in London, Will took the first steps to patent his tricks. It was an effort to ward off imitations of his act. He filed two patent papers in 1900.

Presumably his patents applied to the novelties of the act, the Fishing Trick and Bowl Production. Despite their stated purpose, patents for illusions only advertise secrets by making details of the invention public knowledge. Rather than protect the tricks, the paperwork would only explain them for potential copyists. Robinson, of course, could only attempt to chase down the imitators and bring them to trial, a time-consuming and difficult enterprise.

It was a system that Robinson knew well and had abused many times; he had duplicated The Cocoon Illusion by obtaining a copy of the patent for the invention. Realizing that he had made a mistake, Robinson stopped his applications for the patents before the process had been completed; the claims were never completed.

Will's misguided attempt to protect his act was hugely ironic. Chung Ling Soo was completely an imitation, and his tricks had been cobbled together from other men's inventions. Robinson's career had always depended on this free and easy trade of ideas and a cavalier attitude about intellectual property. He had built the latest illusions from Europe for Herrmann or Kellar. He had then carried secrets back and forth from one magician to another. Finally, he had explained some of the best material in *Scientific American*, disclosing magicians' trade secrets to the public. Robinson knew how easily an idea could be stolen. When he stopped his British patents, he resigned himself to imitators and shrugged off any damage. In a letter to the magician Ernest Wightwick, Robinson noted that a juggler named Mapleton was performing his Fishing Trick—really Walter Mingus's trick—at a South London music hall. "I don't think I will bother with any of them," he admitted. "Only time and money loss and [it] advertises the other party." His solution was to move forward, performing new tricks and better tricks, forcing the competition to try to keep up.

Robinson saw Chung Ling Soo as not merely a role, but an ideal persona—the quiet, all-knowing wizard, anxious to please his audience. A talented enough actor to avoid the obvious clichés, onstage Robinson didn't squint, grimace, or grunt, the way a typical "Chinee" was portrayed in a West End comedy. He stopped wearing garishly yellow makeup, simply using dark greasepaint to give the suggestion of a healthy complexion. Robinson gave Soo a natural grace and dignity, and in each performance the character made a connection with his audience despite the apparent language barrier. Chung Ling Soo was more than a stereotype; he became a part of William Ellsworth Robinson. "The moment I step upon the stage, I lose my identity and become Chung Ling Soo," Robinson told a friend.

A photo shows Robinson out of makeup.

A 1900 photographic portrait, inscribed to his friend the London magician David Devant, seems to dramatize the transition. It shows Robinson in a traditional business suit, his hairline shaved back to accommodate the Chinese wig that he wore during the act. He signed the photo, "Robinson, Man of Mystery," preserving the billing from his old act. It shows a man who is half Robinson, half Soo.

During the triumphant three months at the Alhambra, the contracts arrived in a thick stack. The Marvelous Chinese Conjurer was booked for months in advance throughout Great Britain, with additional offers from Germany and France. Chung Ling Soo became the role of a lifetime, and the magician never worked again under his real name. He signed his letters Chung Ling Soo, or Soo. To his friends and associates in England and America he was known as Rob.

~m~

Part of the legend of Chung Ling Soo is that Rob, the quiet American, hid completely within the character—he denied his American ancestry, dressed the part on the street, and jabbered convincingly in something that sounded like authentic Chinese. But the story is only partly true. The British public's interest in this new magician naturally attracted the press, and Chung Ling Soo found that he was invited to discuss his background, Chinese culture, and his training in magic. Robinson was delighted with the publicity, and was reluctant to disappoint his audiences by destroying the illusion. Journalists for the *Weekly Reporter* and *Chums* magazine visited backstage and found the magician in his robes. "His skin is yellow, his eyes are black and oblique, and his teeth are absolutely inky as those of all true celestials of rank should be," according to the *Weekly Reporter*. Curiously, Robinson's dark, stained teeth were taken as authentically Chinese, although the writer managed to ignore the magician's gray-blue eyes.

Chung Ling Soo did not speak a word of English, the reporters were told. Questions were directed at Fee Lung, who, in turn, rephrased the question in perfect Chinese. Rob considered the question with a pensive expression, then let loose with a long string of mock-Chinese gibberish. Fee Lung, well acquainted with how the obvious press questions should be answered, "translated" it all into English. The backstage performance was tedious and the result was never very satisfying. The *Weekly Reporter* quoted the magician with a series of boasts and pronouncements that could have been taken from a pulp novel: "I, Chung Ling Soo, of the Brotherhood of the Shining Stars, who am known throughout the Celestial Empire as 'He of the One Button' . . . shall perform real marvels which will astound the wise and cause the magicians to tremble."

Robinson only engaged in this game on rare occasions. After most shows, he and Dot went back to their dressing room, changed into their street clothes, and slipped out of the theater, unnoticed. Professionally, journals like *Mahatma* or the *New York Clipper* reported that William Robinson was playing successfully in London with a Chinese act, or listed his real name in conjunction with reviews of Chung Ling Soo. British music hall artists and magicians, who had met Rob on his previous visits or knew him by reputation, were aware that he was playing a role onstage.

But even offstage, Robinson couldn't resist a bit of deception. In conversation, he used a clever trick to find a connection with new acquaintances. He told his British colleagues that his father was Scottish. It's true that James Campbell Robinson was of Scottish heritage, but official records show that he was born in New York. Rob found that this little exaggeration made a quick bond, and he gradually expanded the lie. Yes, he told visitors backstage, he had also been born in Scotland . . . or in England. Or, to form a particular affinity, he asked the visitor's hometown. Upon hearing it, Robinson raised his eyebrows and let out a surprised whistle, explaining that he had been born in exactly the same town. Based on his skills with dialects, he learned to soften the twangs of his American accent, sounding convincingly English. Rob intended it all as a friendly gesture, but it added another confusing layer of deception. Chung Ling Soo was a theatrical fake; William Robinson was a personal fraud.

One day during the Alhambra engagement, two British magicians, Frederic Culpitt and Ernest Wightwick, met on Agar Street in the West End of London. As they walked and discussed their profession, Culpitt asked Wightwick, "Well, Ernest, after all, just what is a magician?" He was referencing Robert-Houdin's famous definition: "A magician is an actor playing the part of a magician." But Wightwick, like many others, was jealous of the success of their friend Robinson. After a long, thoughtful pause, he answered. "I suppose, Fred, that a magician is a Scotchman playing the part of a Chinaman." Wightwick had been fooled. It was an American playing a Scotchman playing a Chinaman.

A fellow entertainer sent a letter to *The Encore*, a theatrical journal, confused about Soo's identity, but sniffy about his ordinary, mechanical tricks. "It does not matter what rot it is, if it only has a foreign aspect. . . . I am not against the artiste, but I am against him putting on old mechanical work, [for] which an Englishman, Irish, Scotchman or Welsh, could not get one pound a week!"

In fact, English variety theaters seemed very appreciative of magicians. The term vaudeville was strictly an Americanism; the British called this particular mix of novelties music hall. Since the 1870s there had been a long tradition of innovative British magic, and many of these performers found success in the music halls. But in the last years of the nineteenth century, there was a sudden interest in American specialty acts, magicians who exhibited a particular artistic flair. Thomas Nelson Downs, a one-time telegraph operator from Marshalltown, Iowa, had learned coin manipulations during the long, tedious hours in the telegraph office. In 1899 he took London by storm as the King of Koins. His entire act was coin tricks, and his feature was the old coin-catching routine that Downs rechristened The Miser's Dream.

Howard Thurston, the young card magician whom Rob had helped in Denver, Colorado, was another import. After mystifying Leon Herrmann backstage at his theater, Thurston worked steadily through the next season. Late in 1900, he received a contract for the Palace Theatre in London, where his simple, sophisticated sleight of hand was a hit with the public. "Mr. Thurston has developed quite a new form of card entertainment, one which not only amuses, but absolutely mystifies the audience," wrote the *Daily Mail*. "He has brought to a pitch of perfection the art of palming a pack of cards."

One warm summer day in 1900, Will and Dot Robinson were riding up the Strand in the top level of an omnibus. They were hunched over the latest copy of the *New York Clipper*, studying the fine print to see where their friends were working back in America, when they heard a voice alongside them. "Excuse me, isn't your name Robinson?" They were surprised by a distinctly New York accent, and looked up to find a short, muscular young man with curly black hair, balancing himself as the bus lurched around a corner. He held out his hand. "Nice to meet you, Mr. Robinson. I'm Harry Houdini."

—⁂—

It seems amazing that the performers had not met earlier. Houdini was thirteen years younger than Robinson, and they had both grown up in New York and learned magic by leaning over the counter at Martinka's shop on Sixth Avenue. They crisscrossed through dime museums, vaudeville theaters, and even the Columbian Exposition in Chicago, where Houdini performed on the midway. Houdini had seen Robinson onstage with Kellar and Herrmann. Robinson had read about Houdini's early engagements in *Mahatma*, which occasionally ran a small photographic portrait of the escape artist.

Harry Houdini was born Ehrich Weiss in Budapest in 1874, the son of a rabbi, Mayer Samuel Weiss. His family emigrated shortly after he was born, first settling in Appleton, Wisconsin, then Milwaukee, and finally on the East Side of Manhattan.

The young magician took the name Houdini from the great French magician of the previous generation, Robert-Houdin. Years later Houdini insisted that the name was intended as a reverent homage to his idol in magic, but of course it was common practice in show business to copy names and try to benefit from the reputation of another performer—just as William Robinson had done. Houdini worked the usual dime museums, circuses, and variety shows with an act of standard tricks. But he made little impression on his audiences. Houdini had boundless energy and admirable drive, but he couldn't feign the elegance and sophistication needed for gentle tricks with handkerchiefs and flowers. For a short time, he billed himself as the King of Cards, performing energetic flourishes and sleight of hand with playing cards. Houdini muscled his way through the maneuvers, but his brash, rough-around-the-edges personality turned the act into a demonstration of juggling rather than magic.

His early success was with an escape trick. He purchased an old trick trunk and developed an ingenious, split-second presentation. Working with a partner—his younger brother Theo—the act was billed as The Brothers Houdini and the trick was called Metamorphosis. Harry Houdini's hands were tied behind his back. He was placed in a large cloth sack, the mouth of which was tied shut with rope. Houdini was then lifted and locked into a large trunk.

The trunk was surrounded by a framework of curtains. Theo stood next to the trunk and pulled the curtains shut, concealing himself and the trunk from the audience. He clapped his hands three times. The curtain was whisked open by Harry. He was completely free, but the trunk was locked tightly and Theo was nowhere to be seen. The trunk was opened, the bag untied, and the missing brother emerged from inside.

Metamorphosis was a hit, and became an even better trick when Harry replaced his brother with his new bride, a pretty, diminutive brunette who was performing in a dime museum act called The Floral Sisters. Her name was Wilhelmina Beatrice Rahner. Harry called her Bess.

In 1899, during an engagement in Minnesota, the Houdinis met Martin Beck, the manager of the Orpheum vaudeville circuit. Beck liked the magician, but felt that the act was holding him back. He urged Houdini to give up the ordinary conjuring tricks and concentrate on the escapes. Within months Houdini was a headliner on the Orpheum circuit. The magician worked hard for Beck, developing dramatic publicity stunts in every city to attract crowds to the theater. He boldly dared local police, insisting that he could escape from their jails. He stepped to the front of his stage, challenging the gentlemen in the audience to bind him with rope, chain, or handcuffs.

Houdini became the world's first escape artist. He was fiercely proud of the new act and loudly proclaimed his innovation, but the idea was not strictly original. Bernard Marius Cazeneuve, a French magician, and John Nevil Maskelyne, the London illusionist, had both performed the trunk escape. Herrmann had featured it for years with Dot Robinson locked in the trunk. Spiritualists had long been secretly escaping from ropes in the dark of a séance room; Robinson himself had described these tricks in his book *Spirit Slate Writing*. Houdini's real innovation was a bold honesty about his escapes and a swaggering challenge to his presentations.

His success in America had just ignited when he rushed to Europe in the spring of 1900. It was a bold career move. Houdini and Beck calculated that the timing was perfect for a European premiere. Houdini opened at the Alhambra, his first engagement, just as Chung

Ling Soo had closed and moved on to the provinces. He was an instant hit in London. Audiences appreciated his heroic pride, his athletic prowes, and his clear, crisp enunciation. His act seemed to embody the David and Goliath myth—one man taking on the world—as well as the typical Yankee pluck that had become a cliché throughout Europe.

The Houdinis and the Robinsons quickly became good friends: four experienced performers and expatriates who had taken London by storm. Dot and Bess were like sisters: tiny and delicate, but toughened show business professionals. Their husbands called the duo the peanut sisters. They visited each other backstage, shared late-night meals and swapped show-business gossip. Over the next months, the Houdinis' and Robinsons' paths continued to cross. At the end of 1900, they were surprised to find themselves working together at the Wintergarden Theater in Berlin, where both American acts were greeted with loud cheers. Rob and Harry kept in touch by forwarding letters to the next engagements. "If I ain't mistaken, I think you come here next week," Rob wrote to Houdini from Halifax, England. "Well, if so, I have paved the way for you. Knocked their eye out last night and made 'em hungry for magic."

—m—

Both Soo and Houdini had been unlikely stars. William Robinson had been a poor speaker and a reticent performer. His fault had been that he was too deliberate, never impulsive or exciting enough to become a great magician. Young Ehrich Weiss could project his voice from the stage, but was unrefined, too aggressive and impatient to be performing classical magic.

Both became successful by finding the perfect, deceptive roles. In the music halls, they each donned their character before stepping onto the stage. Chung Ling Soo was a subtle, mysterious foreign master, the Marvelous Chinese Conjurer. Harry Houdini was a mythic figure, boasting his challenges from the footlights, the man who could not be restrained.

At the end of 1900, just as Chung Ling Soo and Houdini were established as music hall stars, they were surprised to discover the latest import from America. It was a bold, flamboyant, operatic magician who managed to mix every bit of Houdini's bluster with Chung Ling Soo's fake Oriental grandeur. It might have been the strangest act in show business. Its star was certainly one of the world's most enigmatic performers. He called himself The Great Lafayette.

Chapter 17

THE GREAT LAFAYETTE

H. Edward Moss was an enterprising British theater manager. By the early 1890s, he had assembled a string of prestigious variety theaters in Scotland and the north of England that became known as the Moss Circuit. Moss was an important force in the reform of music hall, eliminating the smutty comedians and lascivious dancing girls of old and featuring circus acts, magicians, jugglers, and military bands—entertainment for the entire family. While he wanted his theaters to be palaces of good taste, he also wanted them to form landmarks in their respective cities. Beginning in 1892, Moss and highly regarded theater architect Frank Matcham would collaborate on a series of beautiful theaters throughout England.

To fill his fantastic theaters, Moss sought the most sensational music hall acts. Shortly after Chung Ling Soo's opening at the Alhambra, he asked to meet the Chinese wizard. He was surprised when a quiet Yank in a dark suit arrived for the appointment. Robinson politely considered Moss's offer, but the manager wouldn't meet the magician's price or work around his other engagements.

When he realized that he couldn't have Soo, Moss searched for a competing act and settled on The Great Lafayette, a German-born magician, protean artist, travesty performer, and spectacle producer, who had been creating a sensation in American vaudeville. One of Lafayette's great features was an imitation of Ching Ling Foo, including the Chinese bowl of water trick.

The last week of August 1900, the Hippodrome bill featured a number of sensations, including Gautier's Great Equestrian Act, The Plunging Horses. As a special attraction, Moss featured The Great

Lafayette. His billing read, "The Most Wonderful Magician, Musician, Mimic and Wizard of Modern Days."

—⚏—

The lights inside the Hippodrome dimmed and a mauve Mercedes touring car pulled onto the round circus track at the end of the auditorium. The program boasted that this was Lafayette's "locomobile, a car which has beaten the world's record and can travel a mile a minute." The locomobile described two or three wide, deliberate circles. Two acetylene gas lamps mounted on the side of the car provided the illumination, casting strange shadows that swept across the balcony and walls of the theater. Finally, the limousine stopped dramatically. The driver's door opened and a liveried black chauffeur stepped out, wearing polished boots and a dark tunic with shiny brass buttons. With military precision, the driver stepped to the rear of the car, turned the handle, and snapped open the door.

The man who emerged was wearing a long black velvet riding coat, white gauntlet gloves, and a jaunty cap and goggles. He tossed the cap and goggles to the driver and took three forceful steps up the stage, turned, and bowed to the audience.

The Great Lafayette was small and Napoleonic, with a square jaw, straight back, and tight features better suited to a bank manager than an entertainer. His light brown hair was parted severely in the middle and pulled back across his forehead. But on stage, he was magnetic, moving with the self-assurance of a general and the delicate grace of a ballet dancer.

After his sensational entrance, he stepped to a thin table. Atop it was a glowing oil lamp, about a foot tall. Lafayette picked up a fabric banner, about three feet square, holding it between his two hands. He swept the banner in front of the lamp, covering it from view, and then teasingly pulled the banner away again. The lamp was still there. Staring down the audience, he repeated this flourish with the banner several times, as the audience leaned forward in their seats, anticipating his first miracle. Finally, he swept the cloth across the

The Great Lafayette, the magician, travesty, and quick-change artist.

tabletop, showing that the lamp was gone. He circled the table and
turned the cloth over in his hands, showing the audience that the
lamp was nowhere to be seen.

Then he took several steps toward the table again, held up the
banner for several seconds, and pulled it away again with a flourish.
The lamp had returned.

Lafayette followed this with a bewildering array of features. He
donned a wig, glasses, and a cloak, picked up a baton, and impersonated a "Hebrew conducting an orchestra." These costume impersonations, called travesty acts, were favorites of vaudeville and
music hall audiences. At the climax of the demonstration, the
orchestra suddenly stopped playing and Lafayette dashed offstage. The
stagehand, who had been standing on the opposite side of the stage,
turned to face the audience, slowly removed his disguise, and revealed
that he was actually The Great Lafayette.

The feature of his performance was a "Travesty on the greatest conjurer that ever lived, Ching Ling Foo, a Chinaman." Lafayette came onstage in a Chinese wig and a long, full black robe trimmed in crimson. He shook out a square embroidered cloth and waddled to the center of the stage. He crouched, lowered the cloth to the stage, and unveiled a large bowl containing several pigeons, a turkey, and a gray "Tennessee Hound." The stage was cleared and he returned, still in his Chinese costume, to produce two tiny black children. The program called them "Piccaninnies." As Lafayette stepped offstage, the two little children demonstrated a Cake Walk in time to some lively ragtime music.

Finally Lafayette returned to the stage, out of Chinese makeup, brandishing a large cloth sewn with a pattern of brilliant electric lights. He dashed from one side of the stage to the other, waving the cloth. Finally he lifted it away to reveal a large bowl filled with flames and belching red smoke. Lafayette flipped the cloth over his head, covering himself from view, and then pulled the cloth away again. He was now dressed as a lady dancer in a long glittering gown and a full wig of golden tresses. Lafayette twirled around the stage and took his bow.

—⁂—

Today it's impossible to appreciate the appeal of the strange hodge-podge that constituted the act of The Great Lafayette. It was pretentious, energetic, and dazzling, in spite of the fact that there wasn't much magic. Written accounts seem to suggest that the best part of the act was Lafayette himself, in particular his dramatic entrances. But once he arrived, he did very little. The *Daily Telegraph* wrote, "All London should see his production. His feat with the two little piccaninnies is full of surprise and charm." The reviewer from the *Morning Advertiser* seemed both awed and perplexed by the act. "It is impossible to describe his performance. One sees it and one wonders."

One of Lafayette's acquaintances later insisted that the flamboyant showman was the most hated man in magic. Visitors backstage found him imperious, rude, and secretive. He demanded fierce loyalty and military precision from his stage assistants and personal servants. He seldom socialized with other magicians or music-hall artists. He fussed over his pets to the exclusion of other people. One of his favorite sayings, delivered without any apparent humor, was, "The more I see of men, the more I love my dog."

Lafayette was born Siegmund Ignatius Neuburger to a Jewish family in Munich, Germany, in 1871. His father was a silk importer. Young Siegmund left home and emigrated to America in the late 1880s. He quickly looked for an opportunity to combine his artistic flair with his interest in the theater. He painted scenery in New York and then traveled to the west coast. In Seattle, he worked for the theatrical producer John Cort.

When it came to performing, whatever Neuburger lacked in skills he made up for in ambition. In 1892 he was appearing in a New Haven dime museum with a standard magic act: "Lafayette, the Man of Mystery, in Necromantic Conjuring." For several years, Lafayette also exhibited a freak named Clarence Dale, a pretty, curly-haired six-year-old "Big Headed Boy" with a skull, according to his billing, "48 inches in circumference . . . scientists amazed, ethnologists puzzled, the public astounded. His head is the largest in the world. Sings sweetly."

In 1892 Lafayette went to Europe with a bow-and-arrow act consisting of trick shots—he struck a strip of tissue paper, edgewise to his arrow, as it dangled from the fingertips of his assistant, and then knocked a straw from between her lips. Despite Lafayette's outsized showmanship, the act consisted of small tricks and seemed ordinary. After a failure in Berlin, he came to London and tracked down Edward Moss, insinuating himself into the great man's office. Before Moss could throw him out, Lafayette planted his feet and boomed his challenge to the theater manager: "What would you think of a man who could do with a bow and arrow everything that a crack shot can do with a rifle?" Moss glowered. "If it is the show that I saw peremptorily closed down at Berlin a few weeks ago, I could do nothing but politely decline it."

Having failed with Moss's theaters, Lafayette managed to secure a

Lafayette in costume, with his dog, Beauty.

week's engagement at the Alhambra before returning to the United States and resuming the tour with the Big Headed Boy. He began building on the act, adding new costume changes and features. He imitated John Philip Sousa, the famous March King, with his distinctive pince-nez glasses and sharp goatee. Lafayette gave a humorous impression of Sousa leading the band, complete with the composer's trademark flourishes. Later he added imitations of Strauss and Offenbach.

In 1899 Lafayette shared a bill with Harry Houdini at the Grand Theatre in Nashville, Tennessee, and the two struggling magicians became friends. According to one account, Lafayette's pet dog had just died. In an effort to cheer him up, Houdini went to the local pound and found a cute puppy, a spaniel with a soft gray coat, and presented it to his fellow performer. Lafayette fell in love with the dog. He named her Beauty, traveled with her everywhere, and incorporated her into his act.

Beauty was actually a mongrel, but Lafayette would never consider such a slur on his pet. He invented a sophisticated pedigree for his dog, calling her a Tennessee hound or a gheckhund, supposedly a rare breed from the nonexistent island of Gheck in the Azores.

In 1900 Lafayette, like William Robinson, recognized the impact of Ching Ling Foo's act and copied the famous bowl of water production. In March of that year, Ching Ling Foo played at the Empire Theater in Cleveland while Lafayette presented his impersonation of Foo just down the street at the Star Theater. Months later, he was engaged by the Keith circuit, presenting his copy of Ching Ling Foo at the Union Square, the very same theater where Robinson had failed his audition and Foo had become a star. "The Great Lafayette," his billing announced two years later, "The First to Produce Travesties of John Philip Sousa and Ching Ling Foo." It was an odd distinction, aimed at his rival, Chung Ling Soo.

—⁓—

Moss was happy to forget about Lafayette's disappointing bow-and-arrow act, hiring Lafayette in 1900 to star in his new Hippodrome in competition with the latest London sensation, Chung Ling Soo. Robinson wasn't bothered. When Houdini wrote to him, complaining about the unfair managers who were booking other escape artists in their theaters, Rob took on the role of older brother to Houdini, offering advice and calming his friend's temper.

> Old chap, these managers are all alike, every one of them: English, German, American or French. They are not running their houses for pleasure. They are in it to make money. They are not fighting the artist; [they are fighting] the other house. When in London, Moss sent for me. I refused his offer. What did he do? Brought over Lafayette. What for? To do [damage to] me? No, it was to hurt the house I was working in. It's a game of chess, and the cleverest man wins, not the shit heel. . . . Now, old chap, you must not feel sore at my blunt way of putting things. I believe you would rather scrap than eat.

The Great Lafayette played for three weeks at the Hippodrome. He returned to the United States to fulfill his engagements with Keith, steadily building the size of his show, filling the stage with new wonders, elaborate new scenes, costumes, and dozens of assistants.

Lafayette demanded a high salary and surrounded himself with luxuries. He seemed to have few friends, refused drink, and, according to his own interviews, didn't seek female companionship. Many years later, a magician recalled seeing the Lafayette show. "I recall going with my father and uncle. The adults said what a queer sort of bloke he was, and there were a lot of nods and winks, but as a child I was unable to understand their double meanings."

Today it is difficult to judge how many of Lafayette's flamboyant eccentricities were deliberately cultivated to attract attention. He was a master of publicity and made headlines—one way or another—wherever he went.

There's no question that Lafayette was his most obsessive when it came to his beloved dog. Beauty slept in her own bed in his automobile, traveled in his train car, contractually stayed in each hotel with her master, and had the run of each theater. Her silver collar was engraved with the names of the first-class hotels that had accommodated the renowned gheckhund. For dinner, Beauty sat at the table with Lafayette and shared a cordon bleu, multicourse meal, served by a white-gloved servant, eating off a gold plate.

When one acquaintance took a liking to the dog, he innocently inquired if Lafayette was willing to sell her. For several moments, Lafayette was speechless, gasping, and red-faced with anger. Finally he hissed his response: "Would you sell your wife?"

—◊—

Will and Dot Robinson worked hard to expand the Chung Ling Soo show. Rob improved his fire-eating trick, adding more ribbons, more fire, and more smoke, until he had reached Ching Ling Foo's level of expertise. Soo's new finish for the trick involved a cascade of flags and fireworks suspended over the stage, which gave him a spectacular

An early Soo poster, showing his four feature tricks.

exit. The new version was so good that—holding fast to his formula of building surprises—he moved it to the end of the act, and presented the slow, methodical bowl of water production in the center of the performance.

He also added several old tricks, redressed and restyled to look authentically Chinese. One of Kellar's favorite tricks was the growth of two rose bushes in two pots of earth. It was a beautiful and poetic effect. Two small rose sprouts were pushed into two plain flowerpots. Kellar picked up a large, conical tube of cardboard, showing it to be empty, and using it to cover one of the pots. Lifting the tube seconds later, the sprout seemed to be a bit larger. He re-covered the pot, pulled the tube away, and showed a large rose bush in full flower, blooming with white roses. Stepping across the stage, he covered a second pot, revealing a second rose bush of pink roses.

A British magician named Stodare had first performed the rose trick decades before Kellar, but the American magician had learned it carefully, turning it into a masterpiece of misdirection. The secret was simple. The rose bushes were hidden in nesting tubes behind a set of tables on stage, and at perfectly timed moments, Kellar lowered the cardboard, surreptitiously picking them up, ready to deposit the plants in the pot. But each gesture and small surprise was designed to throw the audience off guard. Robinson had seen Kellar perform the trick hundreds of times, and had studied the gestures. For Chung Ling Soo's act, he decorated the tables as short Chinese screens and used two chrysanthemum plants, one with white flowers and one with yellow. When the flowers were revealed, little Suee Seen stepped onstage with a wicker basket. Soo clipped the fresh flowers from the bushes, dropping them in the basket, and Suee Seen carried them up the aisle to present them to ladies in the audience.

Robinson's second new trick was the Chinese Linking Rings, actually an old trick, genuinely Oriental in origin, but a longtime favorite of Victorian magicians. Robinson had performed it as a boy, watched Alexander and Leon Herrmann's versions, and seen the one-time-only performance of the rings by Ching Ling Foo in Omaha. It was hackneyed by 1900. But Robinson knew that he could turn it into a miracle.

Rob's term was that he gave a "happy show." He took enormous pride in these old warhorses, the favorite tricks from his youth. When all the music-hall magicians were searching for new tricks, he was perfectly happy reviving the classics. "If you remember right, my show contained mostly old tricks nobody was doing," he wrote to a friend in England. "They'd not been done for years, and not [done to their] best." Rob felt that including the classics guaranteed that his tricks would please the audience, and not just please the magician. He was always amused to see these old tricks, treated with disdain by his fellow magicians, become popular again after Soo's performances.

—⁂—

"When will conjurers learn they can make more money doing what the other chap does not do?" Rob wrote in a letter to a fellow magician. "Other magicians are now giving my show, trick for trick. Now all this is good for me and detrimental to the copyist. I am always working for a large salary. Every other conjurer doing the show of

Chung Ling Soo is an advertisement for Chung Ling Soo." Of course, Rob's views on originality were always ironic, and his pragmatism never justified his own thefts. Rob concluded his letter with surprising sanctimony, "The principle I work on . . . keep away from another man's show as much as I can."

Rob always recognized that his job involved salesmanship—onstage and off. He kept in touch with theater managers, offering notes and gifts to remind them of his success. He also encouraged them to have him back, season after season. In 1901, as Chung Ling Soo, he published a little booklet called *Fairy Tales from China*, with his portrait on the front cover. The translated stories were gleaned from other books, and the pages also included sketches and photos of the magician. He knew it was a good idea to send music-hall managers "some little token every now and again, just to keep him green in their memory."

During his touring, Rob visited antique stores, dressed in a dark suit and his wide-brimmed fedora. He quietly collected any Chinese costumes, bits of furniture, carved jade, embroidered cloths, or swords. These curios were packed in cases and carried with the show. He offered theater managers an opportunity to display his collection—mementos of the recent Boxer Rebellion—as a special attraction. This included an elaborate ebony palanquin, a chair with handles, supposedly built for the Dowager Empress of China. The entire collection was insured for four thousand pounds. On a weekday afternoon, the stage would be cleared and turned into an improvised museum. Spectators were invited to enter through the stage door and view the colorful array of Chinese artifacts. Newspaper advertisements promoted the exhibition, which brought housewives and schoolchildren to the theater. Many returned in the evening to see Chung Ling Soo wearing those same costumes in his performance. It was a nice bit of advertising for the local theater manager, and served to convince the public of Soo's authenticity.

Chung Ling Soo was rewarded with contracts years in advance, and managers throughout Europe clamored for his time. At the end of 1901 he worked a long tour throughout Germany, remaining through the holidays and performing in Berlin in March 1902. He returned to Great Britain in the spring, working his first engagements for Moss. His Bolton contract at the end of March indicated that he was receiving 45 pounds sterling per week for his company ($225); the contract called for one performance every evening. It was a hefty fee for music-hall work, indicating his headliner status. "I am not doing so bad for an old Chinaman," he wrote to his friend Houdini. "I have plenty to eat, plenty to wear, a place to sleep and a few coppers put away for a rainy day."

In 1902, Soo began a three-month contract in Manchester, working for a company called Hamilton's Excursions. Part of the show consisted of a travelogue accompanied by glass slides of exotic locations. He resumed his tour of English cities throughout the holiday season, noting "phenomenal business," and then returned to Hamilton's Excursions for a long engagement in Birmingham.

Touring was difficult, however. Audiences differed from town to town, and a success one week could be followed by indifference the next. A particular theater manager or stage manager could make the job difficult. Even the venue's previous week's acts made a mysterious difference. "I followed here after Hilbert," he reported to Houdini from Hull, telling what he'd heard about one of Houdini's imitators with an escape act. "He was an awful frost, and the house did rotten business." But in Sheffield he scored a triumph from a rival. "Oh me, oh my, but I knocked 'em high. Biggest thing in magic ever been in this town, and they had them all. French [an imitator who performed the bowl of water trick] was the last one. But they never knew he was here, after Monday night. Well, I guess I have said enough about myself."

—m—

On March 22, 1903, Rob opened a letter from his brother and read that his father, James Campbell Robinson, had died on March 10 in Philadelphia.

"I am completely broken up. I am canceling all work until

August," he wrote Houdini. But his success as Chung Ling Soo trapped him for another full month in England before he could sail for the United States. "I cannot get away from these people sooner. I have been coaxing them all along to let me go home to see my dad, but they would not. Now it's too late."

Jim Campbell had suffered with Bright's disease for a decade and was forced to stop performing. With his son Edward, he had run Campbell's bookshop—with much of the stock supplied by Rob—on the Upper East side of Manhattan. In 1900, at the time when Chung Ling Soo was first appearing in England, Jim Campbell briefly edited and published a monthly journal about Spiritualism and the occult, called *The Open Door*. Despite his son's long experience with Spiritualism—setting up the tricks in the Chicago medium's parlor in Chicago and even writing a book about séance frauds—*The Open Door* remained sympathetic to the cause, and its editor, James Campbell Robinson, was also listed as the founder of "The Brotherhood of Immortals in the Flesh."

When his health failed, he stayed with his daughter in Philadelphia; he was a patient at the Hahnemann Hospital, undergoing surgery when he died. He was 70 years old. The body was sent back to his son Edward's home in Manhattan, and then buried in a plot at Woodlawn Cemetery on Friday, March 13. It was more than a week later before William E. Robinson even heard the news.

Rob and Dot sailed on the White Star Line's *Oceanic*, arriving in New York on April 29. On the ship's log, William Robinson's age was given as 42 and his occupation as "showman." Dot, who was still fair-skinned and delicate, took the opportunity to remove six years from her age, claiming she was 34.

When Rob and Dot visited Woodlawn, they found that James Robinson's grave was just down a short path from Alexander Herrmann's. They'd both been inspirations to the couple, providing their educations and opportunities in show business. It was James Campbell Robinson who first taught his son magic, and introduced him to the saloons, dime museums, and vaudeville theaters of New York. Jim Robinson also took custody of Annie, freeing his son to continue his career. Jim secured Will and Dot their most important engagement, at Keith's Providence theater; as the stage manager, he supervised Achmed Ben Ali's new Black Art act. He consoled the couple during their decades on the road with Kellar and Herrmann and their failed attempts at stardom. But he lived long enough to hear of Chung Ling Soo's amazing success in England. Unfortunately, he never saw his son's Chinese act.

In entertainment, Jim Campbell was a jack-of-all-trades, but he'd lived through some of the most tumultuous changes in show business. Throughout his career, he'd scrambled as one trend in variety entertainment was surpassed by another. This had been the most important lesson for his son Will—entertainers were lucky to reach the top of the ladder, but it took constant effort and ingenuity to remain at the top.

Rob and Dot stayed in Manhattan with Rob's brother Edward and his wife, Helena. All three of James Campbell Robinson's children, William, Edward, and Maud, had been in show business for a short time. But Edward was now working as a clerk in the bookstore and also giving lessons in elocution. Annie Robinson, Will's daughter, was now nineteen years old and living on her own. In Philadelphia, Rob and Dot saw William's mother, Sarah Titus Robinson, and his sister Maud, who had married Joseph E. Buch.

—m—

When the Robinsons visited Philadelphia, Harry Kellar was playing in town that week. Rob and Dot attended his show at the Park Theater and visited with the Kellars backstage. Kellar's show was filled with a number of new effects with coins, bells, and a large globe that rolled up a plank. One of his features was still Out of Sight, William Robinson's invention, in which a lady disappeared while dangling in a chair over the stage.

On May 2, Rob attended a meeting of the newly founded Society of American Magicians in the back room of Martinka's shop, where he met the French magician Buatier deKolta. DeKolta was renowned for his inventions—he had created The Cocoon that Robinson copied early in his career—and was appearing in American vaudeville for the first time in his career, at the Orpheum Theater in Brooklyn.

Robinson couldn't resist seeing the latest acts and studying the latest American magic. In the three years since he'd left, there had grown a new trend. Acts were faster, flashier, and filled with sensations. The American magician Horace Goldin filled his vaudeville act with dozens of tricks, which he performed at a blistering pace and without speaking a word. Assistants on stage tossed Goldin the props or quickly set tables and trays in place, so he could dash from one mystery to another.

Howard Thurston had returned to the United States with an elaborate illusion act. Now he did not simply manipulate playing cards. He appeared onstage dressed as an Asian prince, complete with riding boots and a silk turban. He produced a lady from a tank of water, made a gold ball float around the stage, and produced inflated balloons from an empty hat. One of his assistants, dressed in the silk gown of an Eastern princess, levitated high above the stage and revolved in space as Thurston passed an unbroken hoop over her.

Lafayette's new vaudeville act no longer included the Chinese tricks. Instead, he starred in a magical melodrama called The Lion's Bride. He devised an exotic melodrama featuring a live lion onstage. The pacing, snarling, roaring beast would be the latest addition to Lafayette's collection of wonders—a danger designed to lure the audience into the theater.

Rob and Dot returned to England at the end of the summer of 1903 and continued their tour. But the competition looming in America was apparent and Rob felt the pressure to take the next step. If the Chinese magician Chung Ling Soo was to stay in front of the public, he would need new tricks, bigger tricks, and more spectacular tricks.

Chapter 18

DEFYING THE BOXERS

Chung Ling Soo appeared for three months at Edward Moss's London Hippodrome, working through the holiday season at the end of 1903. During his finale, the fire-eating trick, he produced hundreds of ribbon streamers. Many of these were secretly taken from pockets in his costume and concealed in his hands. The ribbons had short weights sewn into their ends, and were then tightly coiled into little round bundles. By gripping the free ends of the ribbons, then giving the coils a toss, a cascade of ribbons seemed to shoot from his hands and tumble over the heads of the audience before he drew them back to the stage. The effect was colorful and led the fireworks in the finale.

One night at the Hippodrome, Robinson invited a prominent British agent to come to the theater to see the show; the magician was courting the agent for a string of engagements and was intent on impressing him. He had his guest seated in the royal box, closest to the stage.

During the fire-eating trick, he paused to look up at his guest, and then took a deliberate step closer to the box. With a mighty toss, he shot a coil of ribbons over the heads of the audience and in the direction of the agent.

Either Soo was standing a bit too close to the box or the ribbons were a bit too long. The ribbons cascaded open and the tiny weight snapped like a whip against the agent's jaw. Wide-eyed, the man drew back in pain and then flushed with rage. The audience laughed. Soo's finale was ruined and the planned tour never materialized.

—m—

Frank Kametaro: assistant, juggler, stage manager, translator.

There was an important change in Chung Ling Soo's cast. Mac Fee Lung had left the show to tour with his own juggling act in music halls. Shortly after the beginning of 1904, he was replaced by a tall, distinguished Asian gentleman named Fukado Kametaro. His associates knew him as Frank.

Kametaro was a wonderful addition to the show, a juggler and magician. His specialty on Soo's program was the ladder of swords. He displayed a dozen sharp swords, demonstrating their ability to slice through apples. The swords were arranged in an upright A-frame, forming the horizontal rungs of a ladder with the sharp edges pointing upward. Kametaro then kicked off his slippers and carefully walked up the ladder, step by step. It was a perilous journey; each foot was pressed straight down onto the blade. If he dared to slide his foot a fraction of an inch as he adjusted his balance, he would have been severely cut.

A seasoned professional, Frank Kametaro also worked as the stage manager for Soo's show, unpacking the props and installing the scenery every week during the tours. Mabel Kametaro, his Yorkshire wife, also traveled with the show, arranging Dot's costumes and helping with the wardrobe changes. In addition to his features, Frank was seen throughout Soo's act, taking part in the illusions. He spoke the necessary introductions in pidgin English and always looked elegant and convincing in a Chinese cap and a silk robe, adding further authenticity to the act. It was another fraud. He was actually Japanese.

Although he didn't speak Chinese, offstage he was occasionally required to do the "translation" routine with visiting reporters so that Chung Ling Soo could appear suitably, inscrutably Chinese. Now the procedure was surreal in its complexity. The reporters spoke English, which was instantly understood by Kametaro and Soo. Kametaro repeated it in his own version of fake Chinese. Soo responded in a different fake Chinese. Kametaro nodded and answered the original question in English.

Soo continued with the Stoll circuit of theaters, returning to the London Empire in the spring of 1904. A trade journal reported that he was now traveling with 14 in his company—assistants and backstage technicians—and received 1,075 pounds a week, the equivalent of almost $5,400. Although he paid his troupe out of this salary, two pounds per week was a respectable wage, leaving plenty of profit for the magician.

—⁓—

American vaudeville theaters were often designed with shallow stages. Most vaudeville acts traveled light and worked with few props or scenery; a performer might enter from the wings with a hat and cane, move directly to the footlights in an effort to get as close as possible to the spectators and the pit orchestra, perform, take a bow, and dash back into the wings. Few acts demanded much room on the stage, so the stage area was meager and the backstage cramped.

Such venues could be tough theaters for a magic act. Some tricks might depend on distance from the audience to help disguise Black Art, wires, or trapdoors that were necessary for the illusion. The props for the act—tables, boxes, or heavy cabinets—were often fighting for space backstage, where they were pushed from one wing to another to clear the way for other acts on the bill. A dozen years

Percy Ritherdon, the mechanic behind
Soo's greatest illusions.

earlier, William and Dot Robinson's illusion, The Cocoon, relied on wires and a trap in the stage floor. As Jim Campbell had advised his son, it was an impractical trick for vaudeville.

But the new British music halls were luxurious, particularly Matcham's Empires and Hippodromes. Stages were deep and spacious, built to accommodate trained animal acts or circus performers as well as magicians. There was plenty of room in the wings, big loading doors that led to an alley, and floors that could be easily equipped with trapdoors. Rob realized that the music halls were perfectly suited to big magic. The expansive oak floors and wide backstage were like a blank canvas, an invitation to the magician's creativity.

By 1902, Rob had found a collaborator in Percy Ritherdon, a twenty-nine-year-old electroplater who owned a factory and metal-working shop in Northbridge Mill in Bolton. The local theaters called on Ritherdon to make special props and equipment. Gradually, the reputation of his firm grew among theater professionals. Ritherdon and Company could produce beautiful wood and sheet metal props, and were capable of machining, turning, and casting. Most important, Percy had an interest in conjuring and a good understanding of magic apparatus. Rob arrived with pencil sketches of what he was trying to accomplish, and during his tours returned to Bolton to check the progress of each idea. Each prop was tested and rehearsed before taking the illusions on the road. Ritherdon himself supervised Chung Ling Soo's projects in the shop; workers were entrusted only with individual parts, and the finished product was assembled in a locked room under Ritherdon's watch—secrecy was always paramount. "Each trick is perfected, [worked] a dozen times or more, and then probably put on one side for a time until [an even] more effective way of working it has been thought out," Ritherdon explained to a reporter. "You see, Mr. Soo can afford to wait. He always has half a dozen new illusions in the making."

In August 1904, Soo and his company took a brief vacation from touring so he could finish some of the new material for his act. The latest tricks were designed to make the audience sit up and take notice, colorful costume spectacles with more than a hint of danger.

—m—

A wide, low table was brought to the center of the stage. Overhead, a tall metal tube was lowered on a rope. The tube was slightly conical in shape, with sloping sides. It was about six feet long and two feet in diameter at its bottom edge. As it was lowered, Soo and an assistant took the lower edge of the tube and swung it forward, allowing the audience to peer inside and see that it was completely empty. The tube was lifted again so that it was suspended high over the table.

Suee Seen entered and hopped up onto the table. Soo raised his hand, giving a signal to the crew offstage. The tube was rapidly lowered, covering Suee Seen. Soo clapped his hands and a moment later the tube was raised. Suee Seen was gone, and in her place was an enormous orange tree in a pot. As the metal tube was pulled up, the branches seemed to bloom, widening in an impressive display of green leaves and colorful ripe oranges.

Soo and his assistant reached up and picked many of the oranges, placing them in a basket. The magician stepped forward with the basket in his hand, tossing oranges into the crowd. At the finale, he pointed to the side of the stage and Suee Seen entered from the wings to take her bow.

Soo's Orange Tree was a beautiful piece of apparatus. In the center of the tree was a conical tube, slightly smaller in diameter than the large tube that the audience saw. The smaller tube was painted green and covered with foliage. Dozens of branches were attached to the tube. Each was hinged, so it tended to flop down, like the ribs on an upside-down umbrella.

The leaves of the tree were fabric and the oranges were made of soft rubber.

The inner tube was inserted in the outer tube and locked inside with catches. The branches and foliage were trapped between the walls of the tubes. When Dot reached up and released the catches, the outer tube was pulled away, leaving the tree around her.

As Soo and his assistant stepped in to pluck the oranges off the tree, their robes masked the area beneath the low table. Dot slipped through a trap in the tabletop and a trapdoor in the stage. Meanwhile, the trick basket switched the rubber oranges for real oranges—each one had a small paper tag with a portrait of the magician attached. As Soo tossed the oranges to the spectators in the balcony, Suee Seen ran up the stairs from the basement, and dashed back onto the stage to take her bow.

—⚬—

Even more spectacular was the Cannon Illusion. For this illusion, Soo's assistants were dressed as soldiers, pushing onto the stage an enormous cannon with a wide barrel. Little Suee Seen then stood at the mouth of the cannon. Soo and Kametaro lifted her and twisted her body so that she was horizontal. She was slid into the barrel of the cannon feet first. There followed a large black cannonball, taken from a stack of similar projectiles.

Soo loading Dot into the Cannon Illusion. Kametaro at left.

The ball was rammed inside and the cannon wheeled forward and turned to face the audience. Soo wheeled it from side to side, playfully trying to find the best path through the crowd. He finally took careful aim at the balcony. There was a loud explosion, a puff of smoke, and the cannonball flew over the heads of the audience, describing a long, smooth arc. The audience screamed; many ducked or scattered out of the way. But the cannonball landed in the back of the stalls with a light thud, then bounced high in the air, tumbling from one seat to another. It was just a large rubber ball. The auditorium erupted in laughter as Soo grinned with satisfaction. He pointed up to the dress circle and the spotlights turned to find Suee Seen, now standing in the center aisle. As she ran along the front of the balcony, she distributed postcard souvenirs to lucky members of the audience.

The rubber cannonball was a bit of comedy borrowed from Alexander Herrmann's show. Herrmann had borrowed a hat from the audience, crushed it in his hands, and loaded it into a small cannon with a cannonball. The ball bounced through the auditorium and the hat was discovered, restored, in a box hanging from the ceiling of the theater.

Soo's giant cannon was similar to a cannon used by the American magician Horace Goldin in his vaudeville act. One side of the cannon barrel had a trapdoor. As he loaded the ball into the cannon, Suee Seen twisted her body through the trap and a corresponding opening in the wheel of the cannon, finally sliding through a trapdoor in the stage. A shroud of fabric, tossed over the back of the cannon, momentarily concealed her exit. When the cannon was wheeled forward and aimed at the audience, she ran out the stage door and around to the front of the theater. In the darkness, she sneaked down the aisle to the front of the balcony, where she took her bow.

—⁂—

The cannon trick was deliberately overstated and comical, a burlesque of the old act of firing a lady out of a cannon. But another new trick was designed to be realistic, dramatic, and newsworthy. Defying the Bullets—billed on Chung Ling Soo's posters as Condemned to Death by the Boxers—was William Robinson's version of the famous Bullet Catching Trick from the Alexander Herrmann show.

Rob retained the military pomp from Herrmann's performances. Five of his assistants were dressed in Chinese armor: leather tunics with bronze plates. They entered to the dissonant drums of the Boxers, forming a line on the stage. Suee Seen took five lead bullets into the audience in a tin cup and asked that they be scratched with identifying marks. The bullets were brought back onstage as spectators from the audience supervised the loading of the rifles. Each soldier packed his rifle with a black powder charge, a marked bullet, and wadding. The spectators retired to the side of the stage. The gunmen stood on the audience's left.

Chung Ling Soo stood to the audience's right, holding up a porcelain plate at arm's length—this was the target for the bullets. The gunmen took aim at the magician. Kametaro took his position behind the line of fire and then gave the signal by lowering his sword. All five guns discharged at once, in imitation of a firing squad, and Chung Ling Soo jerked the plate back dramatically. The bullets were heard as they rattled against the porcelain plate. He showed the identifying scratches to the spectators and took his bow as the bullets were returned to the members of the audience who had marked them.

It was a great trick. It was filled with drama and allowed for plenty of production value. Soo enhanced it with costumes from his collection, and elaborate Chinese scenery. His early advertising for the trick showed six riflemen. Reviews describe between four and six. Soo carried six rifles and costumes with his touring show; the number of riflemen depended on the size of his cast that week. When he played in London, five or six gunmen were used in the trick.

Following Herrmann's philosophy that the trick should be a special feature, Condemned to Death by the Boxers was presented sporadically. Rob seemed to cycle it in and out of his performances according to his own tastes, whenever he felt he needed a change of program. Because of this, he seldom advertised it, and avoided promising it to the audience for any given week. Although a large quantity of beautiful Chung Ling Soo lithographs were produced, advertising a great many of his tricks, today very few posters for the Bullet Catching Trick have survived. There were probably very few ever printed.

Like all of his illusions, Chung Ling Soo's bullet trick was a masterpiece of magic. It had been carefully designed to be practical for two shows an evening in a music hall, yet mystifying if spectators came back to see it again and again. For his Bullet Catching Trick, Herrmann had relied on bluff and bluster, depending upon the soldiers to work as his confederates and conceal the fact that blanks were being loaded into their rifles. That method was fine for Herrmann's occasional charity performances. But the spectators who stepped onto Chung Ling Soo's stage, watching the powder and bullets loaded into each rifle, were genuinely mystified by the procedure.

On special occasions, Soo used members of the audience as gunmen. For a 1906 Bolton appearance he advertised that members of the Sunderland Football Club would load and fire the rifles. But he soon stopped this procedure, realizing that it was unwise to trust the volunteers. He had occasional difficulties with the spectators.

"Those damn jealous conjurers are mischief makers," he wrote his friend Houdini from Dublin. "I had on stage Sinclair, and he did his best to spoil the bullet-catching trick. [Two nights later] he sent his assistant up, and this guy got so fresh, I [pushed] him off the stage and kicked his ass in the bargain." Because the trick involved Rob's safety, he wouldn't tolerate such disturbances. Spectators who thought they were watching a placid Chinese wizard were surprised to suddenly encounter a tough scrapper—Rob had a strong grip and an explosive temper. His victims were also surprised to hear his whispered profanities, in perfect English, as he grabbed them by the scruff of their necks.

—⁓—

The most ingenious part of Chung Ling Soo's Bullet Catching Trick was the presentation. In fact, the controversy over the Boxer Rebellion had made it very difficult to be a Chinese magician in Edwardian England. Rob had found that it was even difficult to be an imitation Chinese magician.

The rebellion was ended by 1901, but the stories of the Boxers' violence against Americans and Europeans filled the newspapers and had fostered a definite prejudice against the Chinese. Even worse, the Boxers' strange belief in occult powers had made the sect, in many people's minds, a group of wild, violent Chinese magicians. Despite his fame and success, Chung Ling Soo encountered audience members who were inclined to believe the worst about the music-hall wizard, grumbling when he appeared onstage or hissing his act.

Condemned to Death by the Boxers was a melodramatic scene to demonstrate his loyalties. Kametaro introduced the trick by explaining that the audience would now see how the great Soo "was condemned to death by the Boxers during the rebellion, and executed by firing squad." His assistants entered beating drums and ringing gongs, the famous Boxer clamor that began every battle. Over their metal plate armor, the gunmen wore tied red sashes, another trademark of the Boxers.

Chung Ling Soo's wonderful Bullet Catching Trick was more than just an illusion, it was an appeal to his audiences. Like the English, he had also been terrorized by the Boxers. His magic was not only more powerful, but a mark of solidarity with his audience.

—∽∿∽—

Chung Ling Soo was more than four years into his reign as the music hall's "Marvelous Chinese Conjurer" when he faced a real Chinese enemy. It wasn't an imaginary battle with the Boxers, or a melodramatic trick for his audiences. It was a bizarre challenge from Ching Ling Foo—the real Chinese magician.

William E. Robinson suddenly realized that he had everything to lose.

Chapter 19

THE LONDON HIPPODROME

William Robinson had managed to create a Chinese magician who mostly performed European or American tricks. The Chinese elements had been used for decoration—a costume, a prop painted with a dragon, a table covered with embroidered fabric. Although he had managed to fool his audiences, at the end of 1904 this deception was on the verge of collapsing.

Starting on the day after Christmas, 1904, Chung Ling Soo was booked for three months at Moss's London Hippodrome. But before he arrived in London, he'd heard the news. "Ching Ling Foo with ten Chinese opens at the Empire Theater," he wrote to a friend, "and also another troupe of six Chinese at the Alhambra. Both of these theaters are within one block of the Hippodrome. So you see, I have plenty of work cut out for me."

Ching Ling Foo, the authentic Chinese magician, had been a success in American vaudeville through 1900. He then returned to China. Rumors traveled to the United States that the old wizard had been killed during the Boxer troubles, but he and his family were living in Shanghai, where he had invested in a Chinese theater. He was booked for London on the Moss and Thornton circuit and arrived with a new American manager, Leon Mooser, at the end of 1904. The magician told reporters that he would have come to England earlier, "had he been able to find a manager to pay him the 250 pounds a week he demands."

Ching Ling Foo hinted to the British reporters that his lack of bookings was, in part, due to his competition in London. Before he arrived, Foo realized that Soo was the enemy. (The Chinese family

Ching Ling Foo at the time he came to the
London Empire Theatre.

names were actually Ching and Chung, but the British press differ-
entiated the two performers as Foo and Soo.) Ching Ling Foo's
friends in vaudeville informed him that the famous Chung Ling Soo
was actually William Robinson, the American who had served as
Leon Herrmann's assistant. By the time Foo and Mooser arrived,
they were ready for a battle, and hoping to gain some publicity.

On Chung Ling Soo's opening night at the Hippodrome, Foo and
Mooser bought seats in the front row and snickered through the performance, pointing and whispering to each other. The next day, Foo
told a reporter from the *Weekly Dispatch* that he was now convinced that Chung Ling Soo was not Chinese, but actually a "foreign
devil." He insisted that he could actually smell that he was a Westerner as the magician passed him in the theater. "Shall not one Chinaman know another?" Foo asked the reporter.

Ching Ling Foo became more and more agitated as he discussed
his rival, gesticulating wildly and speaking faster and faster; his
pidgin English required careful translation from Mooser. "He's not a

Chinaman at all, but a Scotch-American named Robinson," he gushed. Even more outlandish, Soo was wearing robes that would have earned a death sentence for any Chinaman short of one of royal rank. "Him have head chop if he go to China," Foo succinctly explained. "All Englishmen alike. All wear pretty clothes if they want. But Chinaman, no. Chinaman wear only what he allowed." Ching Ling Foo explained how Soo's show included many foolish choices: "He wears woman's dress. Him one big fool."

The next day, Mooser offered an official challenge on behalf of his artist: "I, Ching Ling Foo, am the original Chinese magician. There is no other native-born Chinese sorcerer in London at the present time. I offer one thousand pounds [five thousand dollars] if Chung Ling Soo, now appearing at the Hippodrome, can do ten out of twenty of my tricks, or if I fail to do any one of his feats."

A reporter from the *Express* raced across the street to the Hippodrome and found Chung Ling Soo in the middle of a performance. The reporter was impressed by the magic and noted that the audience cheered when the magician caught six bullets on a porcelain plate. "In appearance, Chung Ling Soo is very Chinese," the reporter wrote. "His skin is yellow, his eyes are black and oblique, and his teeth are inky as though he has devoted a long life to chewing opium." But the magician would not grant an interview. "It was useless, his secretary explained, because he spoke no English." Finally Kametaro, speaking on behalf of the magician, responded with the kind of grandiloquence he had perfected during their translation games. "Chung Ling Soo is wroth with the street sorcerer who has slandered him, but his rank as a Mandarin of the One Button precludes him from entering into any controversy with one of an inferior class." He strongly hinted that Ching Ling Foo had stolen Chung Ling Soo's tricks. Soo's authentic history, Kametaro told reporters, was "brilliant as a spring morning, when the zephyrs' idle play and fleecy flecks float o'er the azure sky." Supposedly, Chung Ling Soo had every right to wear the royal robes. He had been honored by the Empress Dowager, commanded to court, and promoted to "celestial honors," achieving the rank of Mandarin.

The notion of a commoner promoted to a Mandarin was a story designed to make Foo's blood boil. Foo had actually performed before the Empress of China. "The dignity of Chung Ling Soo," Kametaro calmly concluded as reporters scribbled their notes, "is too sublime to permit him to enter into any discussion with a slave who has sat at street corners, juggling for cash."

—⁂—

Kametaro's bold pronouncement successfully stalled the reporters for a day, but it did nothing to calm Ching Ling Foo's wrath. On December 28, the reporter for the *Weekly Dispatch* arrived at the Hippodrome with a copy of the challenge. Rob, Dot, and Frank Kametaro huddled in the dressing room and studied it carefully. Surprisingly, it seemed like a good bet. Rob was unsure if he could really perform ten out of twenty tricks, but the last clause of the challenge, "or if [Foo] fail[s] to do any one of [Soo's] feats," seemed to guarantee success. If Rob and Dot could fool Ching Ling Foo with even one trick, they would win the challenge and gain the publicity of having bested their accuser.

The reporter sat outside the stage door at the Hippodrome for three days and nights, waiting for an answer. Finally, he was granted an audience with Chung Ling Soo's secretary. "Negotiations were conducted by means of an interpreter," he reported. Yes, Chung Ling Soo would agree to the duel of magic:

"We, the undersigned, guarantee to put in an appearance at the *Weekly Dispatch* office next Saturday morning (January 7, 1905, at 11 a.m.) to meet Ching Ling Foo, who has issued a challenge to Chung Ling Soo to perform ten of [Foo's] twenty tricks. Chung Ling Soo has been informed of Ching Ling Foo's performances up to this date, although he has not had an opportunity of personally witnessing them." This was untrue. As William Robinson, he had studied the entire act very carefully. But he cleverly tried to point out that he was at a disadvantage. "Ching Ling Foo has had an advantage in seeing Chung Ling Soo's demonstration. Up to the present, Ching Ling Foo has performed only five feats of magic, all of which Chung Ling Soo is prepared to duplicate in effect at the *Weekly Dispatch* office." Rob signed the agreement using his autograph of Chinese characters.

There was one additional clause, agreed on a handshake but not written into the agreement. Robinson's secret fear was that when they met, Ching Ling Foo would lunge for him, ripping off his braided queue and exposing him as a fraud. He made the newspaper office agree to a glass partition between the magicians, so there could be no personal contact.

Mooser first agreed cheerily to the contest, saying they would be happy to meet Chung Ling Soo anywhere. But the manager of the Empire Theatre—where Foo was appearing—wanted no part in the competition. When Mooser finally responded on behalf of his client, he suggested a subtle change in rules:

"They stipulate first, that Chung Ling Soo prove before members of the Chinese legation that he is a Chinaman. Second, that Ching Ling Foo will perform any ten Chinese tricks performed by Chung Ling Soo, and third, that Chung Ling Soo cannot perform ten out of twenty tricks performed by Ching Ling Foo."

The new challenge would have devastated Soo, but fortunately the *Weekly Dispatch*, happy with the publicity and anxious to move the duel of magic forward, blithely ignored the changes. They sent a

Foo's troupe of Chinese performers, with manager Leon Mooser.

response to Mooser protesting the latest additions: "I trust you will not place obstacles in the way of the meeting, on the terms already submitted." To their readers, they explained, "It has been sought in some quarters to change the issue into one of the nationality of the rivals. This is a mistake. The public is not interested in the ancestry of Soo or Foo, it is interested in their conjuring, and this is the question the *Weekly Dispatch* wished to solve." Once again, the event swung in Chung Ling Soo's favor. The London newspapers followed each twist and turn of the story, gleefully speculating, "Did Foo Fool Soo?" or "Can Soo Sue Foo?"

—⁓—

The Robinsons had only a few days to prepare, and they anticipated the very worst. Everything about the performance seemed to be an uphill struggle—a performance in a newspaper office in the morning, an attempt to impress reporters and also mystify a fellow magician. Realizing that the future of Chung Ling Soo's act might be at stake, they prepared for every contingency and staged an elaborate publicity showdown. Rob trained his assistants for the special performance and engaged a genuine Chinese secretary, Chai Ping, who could understand what was being said and interpret correctly. Meanwhile, they prepared an act of ten tricks that could be performed at the *Weekly Dispatch* offices, not authentic Chinese miracles but impressive examples of conjuring. To be sure he was prepared with extra miracles, Rob wired his friend Houdini, who was appearing in Chatham that week. "Send your method needles or can you see me Friday morning? R."

Houdini's Needle Trick was based on an old sideshow stunt, but Houdini had turned it into a miniature masterpiece. He performed it in impromptu shows or under difficult conditions to impress an audience—just the sort of show Rob was planning at the newspaper office.

Houdini would show several packages of sewing needles, having them examined. The individual needles were removed from the packages and placed on his tongue. Closing his mouth and swallowing, Houdini seemed to devour the needles. He asked members of the audience to examine his mouth. They looked beneath his tongue or alongside his gums, but agreed that needles were gone. Houdini then picked up a spool of white cotton thread, reeled off several yards, and rolled it into a bundle. He swallowed the thread. He finally winced, coughed, and cleared his throat, throwing back his head. A small end of white cotton thread appeared at his lips. He pulled it slowly, revealing a sparkling needle perfectly threaded on the cotton. As he pulled, he revealed another needle, and then another. He finished with the thread stretched between his hands, bristling with the missing needles.

"Robinson asked for my method of doing the Needle Trick," Houdini later wrote, "knowing that Foo, if he did the needle experiment, could not stand the examination which my method allows. I jumped to London and taught Robinson the trick." Houdini volunteered to be a judge for the contest. Robinson was nervous about the performance, and wary of his excitable friend. He didn't really want another magician present, and he discouraged Houdini from attending. But Houdini was anxious to be at the center of any controversy and knew his way around publicity stunts. Against the wishes of his friend, Houdini appealed directly to the managing editor of the newspaper, securing a seat in the London office for the showdown between the Chinese magicians.

—m—

On the morning of Saturday, January 7, a long red Panhard touring car slowly rolled down the Strand and turned onto Fleet Street, leading a procession of automobiles. Chung Ling Soo and Suee Seen, dressed in their oriental finery, sat in the back seat, smiling confidently and waving to crowds on the sidewalk that stopped to gape. It was a spectacular entrance, worthy of The Great Lafayette. Soo and Suee Seen arrived at the *Weekly Dispatch* offices at precisely 10:30, stepping out of the car as Kametaro held a bright parasol over

Soo's company traveling in an open car, which always drew crowds.

their heads. A retinue of secretaries, translators, and assistants followed closely, carrying the necessary magic apparatus into the offices.

"He was immediately escorted into the great room that had been specially fitted up for the trial," according to the newspaper's account. "Little Miss Soo accompanied him, and his secretary, Chai Ping, followed his master like a shadow." Rob raised his eyebrows when he saw Houdini, but he wasn't surprised by his friend's tenacity. He gave a subtle wink. In the adjacent room with Houdini was a crowd of observers who would serve as judges for the challenge: managers from the Palace and Hippodrome theaters, a representative of the Savage Club, and reporters from seven other newspapers. Chung Ling Soo removed his black silk cap and adjusted his robes. He took a stance in the middle of the empty office, behind the glass partition. The Marvelous Chinese Conjurer folded his arms, took a deep breath, and smiled "a smile full of meaning and mystery," according to one viewer. Soo didn't speak a word. He waited for the arrival of his challenger.

The minutes ticked by in silence.

At eleven o'clock, the hour of the challenge, the crowd waited breathlessly, expecting the door to swing open and Ching Ling Foo's company to arrive. But the challenger wasn't coming. By eleven-thirty, a flurry of telephone calls had been placed, attempting to locate Mooser or Foo. No messages had been returned. "Yes, I get it," one newsman interrupted the silence. "Perhaps Foo is here, but Chung Ling Soo's made him invisible!" Laughter echoed around the room, breaking the tension. Robinson's tight grin relaxed as he realized that he had won by default.

"Perhaps Mr. Soo feels that he should start," the editor suggested. The message was relayed through the translator, and the Chinese magician nodded enthusiastically. "Chung Ling Soo would be honored to perform for this illustrious group." Soo tore up a strip of tissue paper, crumpled the pieces into a small bundle, and then restored them to a single strip again. He showed a large tablecloth, whirling it between his hands and lowering it to the ground before revealing a basin on the floor. For this special performance, the bowl wasn't filled with water but with fruit pies and joints of meat for the reporters' lunch.

The assembled crowd applauded warmly as Soo quickened his pace. After preparing for days, he realized that this was no longer a dare; it was merely a performance for a group of appreciative news-papermen. He knew he'd won. Now he needed only to win them over. He produced a bowl of goldfish. He swallowed burning embers and bowls of cotton wool, producing ribbons from his mouth. He finished with the linking rings.

After he'd performed ten Chinese tricks, Chung Ling Soo paused, looked around the room, and broke into laughter. As the audience offered a burst of applause, the magician released a loud yelp of triumph that echoed through the offices. It was twelve noon. Soo's secretary thanked reporters on behalf of the magician. The newspaper recorded that Soo received "a royal send-off when he saluted the *Weekly Dispatch* staff and drove off, for a multitude had assembled to see his departure." The red automobile rolled down the street, leading the procession back to the hotel. The duel was over.

Robinson never even got to Houdini's needle trick. He didn't need it. That evening, still woozy with his success, he sent his friend a telegram: "Houdini, God bless you, all I can say. R."

—m—

Mooser later insisted that Ching Ling Foo had never actually agreed to come to the newspaper office, and that the magician had spent that morning at a dentist's appointment. Yes, Mooser insisted, he had tried to arrange a challenge. But when Soo insisted on a glass barrier, "it was obvious Chung Ling Soo did not want to be addressed in Chinese," and the conditions were not met. The notion that Ching Ling Foo had been rendered invisible, which Mooser had read in the press, was simply ridiculous.

The evening of the challenge, the *Weekly Dispatch* received a note from Leon Mooser. "Yours received. Can only meet 'Robinson' under conditions mentioned in my previous letter. Have no object to gain by meeting under other conditions." But by then, it was too late. The articles were written, the winner had been declared, and the story was finished. Later that night, the Hippodrome was filled to capacity; the public was anxious to see the Wonderful Chinese Conjurer, now proclaimed the victor in the London press.

The orchestra leader planned a surprise that night. At Chung Ling Soo's spot in the program, instead of the magician's regular entrance music of Oriental minor chords, the conductor raised his baton and led the horns through a stirring rendition of Handel's "See, the Conqu'ring Hero Comes." Chung Ling Soo stepped onstage and momentarily froze. When he realized what had happened, his placid features shattered into a broad grin and the audience roared their approval. Soo stepped to the footlights and the audience stopped the show with their applause.

The Encore, a theatrical journal, boasted of Soo's success: "Chung Ling Soo repeats here, for the benefit of his would be antagonist, an old Chinese saying, 'Don't throw mud at your neighbor, or your hands will ever remain dirty.'"

Two weeks later, Chung Ling Soo ran his own ad in *The Encore*. "He said I Couldn't, But I Did! The Original Chung Ling Soo, who has been mystifying British audiences for the past five years, was challenged by Ching Ling Foo from the Empire Theatre. Chung Ling Soo most successfully accomplished [his challenger's] tricks. The challenger and his money failed to put in an appearance and have not since been heard of. Chung Ling Soo, the Original Chinese Conjurer, at the London Hippodrome."

—⁂—

At the Empire Theatre, the verdict cast Ching Ling Foo in the role of the loser. To the public, it seemed as if he were the imitator; and the name Ching Ling Foo had been deliberately chosen to capitalize on the success of Chung Ling Soo. In fact, Ching Ling Foo's wonderful program now seemed a bit of a disappointment. It was really a sort of Chinese vaudeville show, with a troupe of performers offering different acts. Foo stepped onstage and produced a plate of oranges, followed by a small bowl of water. Another member of the company performed some juggling, spinning a porcelain basin atop a stick. His daughter, Chee Toy, stepped onstage to sing two western songs very sweetly, and without a trace of an accent, "Because I Love You" and "Just One Girl." There were more acrobatics and juggling tricks before the magician reappeared to perform the famous production of the basin of water. He followed this with the production of another small bowl of water, and then a demonstration of a top spinning on a string. "There is not much conjuring in the program, but it is nevertheless very interesting, amusing and clever," one review concluded. In fact, these authentic, austere Chinese acts were no comparison for Chung Ling Soo's royal robes, colorful scenery, and elaborate illusions. After five seasons before the British public, Soo had developed a good sense of exactly what they wanted. Ironically, he had also spent five seasons indoctrinating them in what was "Chinese." And he'd convinced them.

Ching Ling Foo played for one month in London. He followed this with short engagements in Europe before going home to China. He never returned to England.

—⁓—

Years later Houdini wrote, "Mooser personally told me that Ching Ling Foo never knew what was going on since Robinson craftily took advantage of every issue." But Houdini exaggerated the situation. Rob played his cards carefully and was probably behind many details of the contest. But he was also very lucky that morning at the *Weekly Dispatch* offices. Mooser and his client made a serious mistake by allowing their challenge to be commandeered by the newspaper. If Ching Ling Foo had only arrived that morning, the newspapermen might have found a new hero. There are many reports of Ching Ling Foo's skills with sleight-of-hand magic in just these kinds of impromptu performances. His Chinese tricks were unusual and particularly puzzling to professional magicians. There's little question that he could have dazzled the reporters and fooled even an expert like Robinson.

Houdini, like many of the day's magicians in England and the United States, was embarrassed by the Foo-versus-Soo fiasco. Robinson was well known and admired by his friends in show business, but the battle with Ching Ling Foo—Rob's high-handed response, his gloating ads, and box office successes after the contest —was part of an especially uncomfortable game of hardball. It seemed unnecessary in the world of music-hall performers, where there should have been work for everyone.

In a later manuscript, Houdini praised Ching Ling Foo. "He told me that I was the best American magician he had ever witnessed, and I informed him that he was the best Chinese magician I had ever seen." But Houdini noted a weariness in the great Foo's manner.

In 1904 in London, he seemed to be bowed down with the weight of his years. Bad handling [by the management] finished Ching in Europe. At the time of their so-called duel, Foo not turning up, the thing was written up for the benefit of the London Hippodrome at the expense of poor Ching Ling Foo. Robinson, who never was a success in evening dress, is to all intents and appearances on the stage a full-fledged Chinee. The British public accepted him as a genuine Chinaman, but all managers knew that Soo was an American. He does a very clever performance, but I think it was a mean advantage that was taken over Ching Ling Foo.

Maurice Raymond, a fellow magician who befriended both Ching Ling Foo and William Robinson, thought that Soo's triumph was "one of the cruelest things ever perpetuated in show business." The American critic and magic writer John Northern Hilliard remembered Robinson from his days with the Herrmann show. Hilliard was especially blunt about the famous duel:

> There is an ethical aspect to this case that invites discussion. In commenting disparagingly on the professional abilities of the Chinese conjurer, in belittling his originality and his achievements in the magic arts, Mr. Robinson (Chung Ling Soo) is really throwing stones at his own crystal dwelling place. So far as the Western hemisphere is concerned, Ching Ling Foo is indisputably the originator of this peculiar act, and Robinson is merely an imitator. Robinson is shrewd and has a head for business. In the dress suit of a modern magician, he would not be successful, despite his knowledge of the art. It is ridiculous for Robinson to pose as the "Original Chinese Magician" and to say that Ching Ling Foo is a "performer of the streets." This may be good showmanship, but it is not fair play.

Hilliard pointedly included Robinson in a list of originators in magic—"Alexander Herrmann owed much to the genius of Mr. Robinson"—and also in a list of imitators. "Clever and original as he is, he has appropriated the most striking features of Ching Ling Foo's program, and I believe that he has not lost any money by his sacrifice of originality."

The famous duel in London made spectacular newspaper copy and occupied the British theatrical press for several weeks. But it made magicians uncomfortable, particularly those who knew the combatants. Many magicians admired Ching Ling Foo. He was a talented artist, an exacting performer, and a wonderful ambassador of Chinese magic. They were shocked to see just how ruthless—or desperate— their friend Billy Robinson had become.

—⁂—

The Tschin Mao troupe of Chinese jugglers toured Manchester later that year—a group of genuine Chinese following on the coattails of Ching Ling Foo. The conjurer with the troupe performed the fire-eating trick and produced fish bowls from beneath shawls, but the public remained indifferent. "The comments of the audience were very funny; they were united in their opinion that he was not so good as the other Chinaman, Chung Ling Soo," a reviewer for a magic journal noted. "Chung Ling Soo came first, gives them a good value for their money, but now every other Chinese magician who comes along is a living advertisement for he of the One Button, who has the nerve to take tricks that many of his brother magicians would not touch with a twelve foot pole."

Riding his wave of publicity, Chung Ling Soo offered his exhibitions of Chinese artifacts and granted more interviews—he was discovered sitting in his dressing room wearing silk robes, surrounded by burning incense and sipping tea while Kametaro played the translation game. The *Weekly Reporter* quoted the magician, "My marvels, up to now have been witnessed by the Imperial Sister of the Sun, the Chinese Dowager Empress. In China, my country, there is a proverb which says, 'Tell the envious the secret of thy success and lo! They will be dumbfounded.'" He offered completely ridiculous explanations of his tricks. For example, the cannon trick was accomplished when little Suee Seen "was exchanged for a paper figure," loaded into the cannon and blown to pieces in the explosion. Such explanations were designed to intrigue the audience and lure them into the theater, where they would be doubly fooled when they saw the real illusion.

—⁂—

But just as certain singers prefer ballads, or certain painters spend their careers representing landscapes, great magicians fall in love with certain kinds of tricks. They invariably collect secrets, feel possessive about particular techniques, and hoard little maneuvers or subtle touches. Often they rely on familiar secrets to guarantee a deception. There's logic to this, but also a certain amount of superstition.

Writing about his friend Chung Ling Soo, Houdini felt that he "certainly [produced] some good things now and then, even better than the new stuff of other illusionists." But as a rule, his friend Rob preferred to "pin his faith to the old, presenting the same to the audience in a new guise."

One new trick in Chung Ling Soo's program was a good example, even though it received little notice from his audience. Suee Seen went into the audience and collected four finger rings from obliging spectators. She brought them back to the stage on a chopstick. Soo delicately picked the rings from the chopstick and attempted to load them into a small pistol. Of course, the rings were too large. The magician looked puzzled, and then signaled to one of his assistants to bring a larger gun. A large-barreled pistol was delivered, but Soo was forced to hammer the rings into misshapen bits of metal before he rammed them into the pistol—the procedure drew laughter from the audience.

He fired the pistol at a small wooden box that was hanging over the stage. Inside, he found three small, pretty bouquets of flowers. Tied to each bouquet was a ribbon with a ring. These were quickly returned to the audience as an expression of consternation played across the magician's face; counting on his fingers, he realized that he had lost one ring. Another small box was brought onstage, filled with chocolates. These were distributed to the spectators so the box was empty. It was closed, then quickly opened again to show a rabbit inside. Around the rabbit's neck was a bright satin ribbon, knotted with the fourth ring.

Of course, it wasn't really a new trick, but just a version of the old nest of boxes that had been featured by Kellar. A journal for magicians gave an account of the trick and speculated on Soo's secrets, noting that the gun was probably "the old fashioned conjuring pistol with a large upper barrel to receive the objects and a small [concealed] barrel underneath for the charge." This was the same sort of pistol that Kellar had used in his show, the pistol that had mysteriously and dangerously misfired during one performance. Robinson had heard of Kellar's accident, and it is odd that he would have used a similar gun in his own performance.

Perhaps Rob innocently forgot about Kellar's problem. He remembered it fondly from his days as an assistant. He knew it could be deceptive and practical. Perhaps he was proud enough to think that he could design a trick pistol that would be perfectly safe, knowing that his machinists at Ritherdon's company could deliver a quality product.

"I am not foolish enough or conceited enough to think I am a great conjurer," he confessed to a friend in England. "I am content with being a good showman. At the same time, a sensible one. I try to make my show contain tricks not in other magicians' programs. But I have a hard time keeping it Soo."

—∞—

At the height of Chung Ling Soo's success, his career depended upon many ingenious, small secrets and one enormous deception. His close associates thought that they knew the secret of Chung Ling Soo—his identity, William Robinson. But Robinson's personal life was filled with even more secrets—about his marriage, his background, and his relationships. "Billy made many friends and a few enemies," the magician Maurice Raymond recalled. "He was always rather fond of the ladies, and that led to some unpleasantness."

Chapter 20

TAVISTOCK SQUARE

The Lion's Bride was the name of The Great Lafayette's new vaudeville feature. Like many of his entertainments, it defied definition. It was a melodramatic spectacle, a romantic fairy tale set within a Persian harem—precisely the sort of story that was popularized, a decade later, in silent film serials. Most of all, The Lion's Bride was a testament to Lafayette's skills as a designer and producer. It was a sensational draw across the United States.

Like many illusions, it seemed to evolve over several seasons. When he started performing it in 1901, The Lion's Bride was given a pretty circus setting, and the story concerned a bride who was determined to make a mystical sacrifice, offering herself to the king of the beasts. Lafayette's first version of the trick was "a cheap affair," according to *Mahatma* magazine, but the magician quickly turned it into a lavish extravaganza. "Lafayette is an erratic performer in many ways, but he is a showman. He will spend money to make an act, and he will spend money not alone for costumes but for stage dressing and properties." Lafayette was committed to the success of The Lion's Bride.

The following season, the scene was renamed Majesté, The Lion's Bride. "Words fail to convey the deep impression caused by this startling production," gushed one review. "Picture the interior of a modern circus, including a well conducted menagerie, freaks, brass bands, strong men, gymnasts, et cetera, and standing conspicuously at the center of a tent, a beautiful red and gold cage, containing a colossal untamed lion."

The performance was an enormous success and the theaters were "crowded at every performance," but Lafayette wasn't satisfied with the result. He enlarged the production, moving the action to a Persian harem, allowing him to indulge in elaborate oriental scenery. He also included the illusion in a new production called Hiawatha Song, giving it a Wild West setting. A season later, he incorporated several additional quick-change illusions and lengthened the play into two acts. He now envisioned a lush jungle setting. The scene was titled The Bride of Thibet, or Krishna the Divine. After seasons of continually tinkering and adjusting—adding new lighting effects, dramatic music, and additional costumes—Lafayette had his perfect spectacle.

According to the script, the beautiful Tibetan princess was in love with a young miracle man named Krishna the Divine—the dashing Krishna was Lafayette's part. Krishna was idolized by the local natives for his mastery of magic and his powers over nature. But the couple's plans were thwarted when the King of Bengal was told of the beauty and wealth of the princess. The King decided impulsively that she would be the perfect wife for his son, the Prince.

In the second act of The Bride of Thibet, the princess was stolen from her home by the King's servants and taken to a clearing in the jungle. As she was chained in place in the middle of the stage, a group of hunters and slaves arrived, pulling a live lion that had just been captured on a hunt. The lion was placed in a large iron cage in the middle of the clearing. It paced up and back throughout the action of the play, twisting in the cage and snarling at the actors.

A rattle of swords and a trumpet fanfare announced the entrance of the King, his son the Prince, and a procession of servants. They announced their plans for the marriage and insisted that it take place at once, in the jungle clearing. The Princess was unchained and brought forward. She proudly rejected the Prince, insisting that she would rather face death than marriage.

Upon her dramatic refusal, the music built to a crescendo, and the audience noticed the staccato clamor of a horse's hooves from offstage. The hoofbeats grew louder and louder as the cast turned to face the hero. Astride a snorting white stallion, Lafayette galloped onto the stage, his sword drawn and his burnoose flying, calling for the slaves to unhand his beloved. It was a spectacular entrance for The Great Lafayette.

The King and Prince leapt into action. They ordered Krishna to be captured. As Lafayette jumped from his horse, he was seized and held fast by the King's servants—standing with his back to the audience at one side of the stage.

The King ordered the marriage to proceed. The Prince and Princess—she was now resigned to her terrible fate—listened to the mystical Tibetan ceremony. As they were pronounced husband and wife, Krishna could take no more. "Stop!" he cried out. "Stop at once!"

The King turned on his heel, ordering Krishna killed. The slaves hesitated, fearing Krishna's legendary powers. Enraged, the King drew his own sword and rushed to the prisoner, stabbing him savagely. As Krishna collapsed into a heap, he cried out, "Father, you have killed me!"

The King stepped back, disbelieving his own eyes. He turned over the body of Krishna and pulled away the burnoose. Instead of Lafayette, the audience gasped when they saw the actor who had been playing the Prince.

The King rushed to the Prince, standing next to the Princess. He grabbed him by the shoulders, turning him so he could see his face. Instead of his son, he was shocked to see that the bridegroom was actually Krishna. The two young men had miraculously changed places.

Enraged, the King held Krishna at the point of his sword. "You've managed to bewitch my household, but you shall not triumph. Yes! I shall have the Princess as my own bride! I order it!" The princess recoiled in horror. She wriggled free of her captors and dashed offstage. A chase ensued, with a crowd of servants and slaves rushing after her.

She was captured and brought back to the clearing. Surrounded by a bristle of bright sword blades, the beautiful Princess was delivered to the King. She refused him. He threatened her with a fate worse than death—she would be delivered to the king of beasts and become the lion's bride. The Princess begged for mercy but refused the King once again.

Now the music built to a sweeping march as the Princess was led to the lion. A door in the side of the cage was opened. Suddenly, Krishna escaped from his captors, dashing offstage. Presumably, the sight of his beloved's sacrifice was too much for the sensitive young magician to endure.

The King turned his attention back to the Princess. She was pushed into the cage and collapsed in a corner, sobbing. The lion paced, approaching the Princess. Suddenly a bolt of lightning shatterred the front of the cage so that it fell open. The lion roared and leapt toward the audience, landing on the King and driving him to the ground. The Princess screamed. The servants onstage drew back in horror. The spectators held their breath.

Another roar, a snarl, and then several seconds of eerie silence. The lion drew back and stood up. It was not a lion, but a man dressed in a lion skin. He snapped his head upward as the lion's head fell away from his shoulders. It was Lafayette.

The Princess ran to embrace her magical Krishna as the orchestra reached its final chord. The curtain fell for several seconds. When the curtain rose again, spotlights swept across the stage as Lafayette stepped from the wings to take his final bow. The audience noticed that the lion's cage was together again and the beast had magically returned for the curtain call. He was once again snarling and pacing in his cage.

—— ∭ ——

The Bride of Thibet was a typical pastiche of costumes and scenery and a strange, mixed bag of Oriental intrigue. Lafayette had managed to combine Tibet, Krishna, the jungle, a lion, and a phalanx of black slaves. It really had nothing to do with any culture on earth, nor even any mythology. But it was brilliant vaudeville entertainment and a sensational finale to Lafayette's show. Critics swooned. His salary rose and contracts arrived for years in advance.

If there were any criticisms of Lafayette's show, it was of the slapdash quality to the magic. "Lafayette as a magician strikes one as rather crude," wrote a magician's journal. "We do not know if the public are really deceived by any item of our subject's conjuring, but they like it and pay to see it." Other critics were leery of a show that was too spectacular, with a stage jammed full of people, costumes, and scenery. "Lafayette is undoubtedly an entertaining illusionist, and one also with imagination," concluded a music-hall publication, "but he is certainly inclined to be over-elaborate in his acts, and also, candidly speaking, there is altogether too much noise in the show."

Lafayette demanded expertise from the stage crews and couldn't abide any carelessness. Part of this precision was necessary, owing to the sheer size of the production. Lafayette employed over sixty people in his company, including musicians, supernumeraries, and technicians. He also brought his own horse and the star of the show, the lion named Prince.

By most accounts, Prince was a mature and agreeable beast. Shortly after Lafayette began performing The Lion's Bride, officials in Pittsburgh fined the magician twenty dollars. It was discovered that Lafayette was using an electric battery and metal plate in the cage to deliver a shock to poor Prince, ensuring that the lion snarled and roared on cue. This was a secret that the audience never knew.

—⁓—

Offstage, Lafayette indulged in different melodramas.

In September 1902, at a New Jersey theater, Lafayette and Beauty, the famous gray gheckhund, were standing in the lobby. The magician was tending to that week's box office receipts. The manager asked him to take his dog out of the theater, followed by a casual remark, under his breath, about fleas.

Lafayette responded with a flurry of epithets, delivered in louder and louder tones. A policeman was summoned, and Lafayette was arrested. On his court day, he arrived in a limousine. The magician was dressed grandly, with gray spats, a soft homburg, and a bright red silk tie studded with a diamond stickpin, and swinging a gold-topped walking stick. He sauntered into the courtroom and promptly called several witnesses who could testify as to Beauty's health and general condition. "My dog," the magician told the judge, "has been slandered."

The case was dismissed, but it quickly worked its way into the newspapers, attracting audiences to see the flamboyant magician.

That same year, during a brief tour of Great Britain, Lafayette purchased a house in London at 55 Tavistock Square—just above Russell Square, on the south side of a pretty, wooded park.

It was an imposing three-story home. The front door was painted in royal purple, Lafayette's favorite color, with a wooden plaque of gilt letters, "The Home of The Great Lafayette and Beauty." The interior was filled with elegant antiques and valuable paintings. Lafayette devoted an entire room to models of his theatrical sets, displaying scenes that he enacted onstage. The models were equipped with tiny electric lamps so that he could demonstrate the effects of different colored lights.

The magician's bedroom was draped with lavender and mauve curtains, and fitted with facilities for Beauty—including her own dog-sized settee, a porcelain bathtub, and a private toilet. A note in the foyer was posted for the benefit of all his guests: "You may drink my wine, you may eat my food, you may command my servants, but you must respect my dog."

During an American tour, Lafayette legally changed his name in a New York court. He was no longer Siegmund Neuburger, but was now officially The Great Lafayette. His business associates called him, simply, Lafayette. Certain female members of his company lovingly referred to their boss as Laffie. He signed contracts and checks T. G. Lafayette.

None of his fellow performers, including Chung Ling Soo and Houdini, ever felt they knew him. He was quiet and secretive offstage, grand without being pompous, warm without being friendly. It was impossible to understand how many of his extravagances were deliberately cultivated for the sake of publicity—where he drew the line between onstage and offstage. Or perhaps there was no line, and T. G. Lafayette lived a genuinely theatrical existence.

—∭—

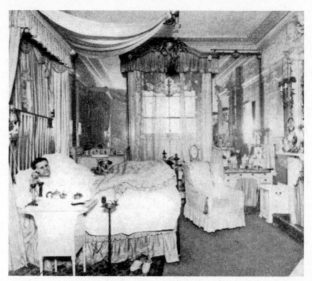

Lafayette and his dog, Beauty, in the bedroom at his house in Tavistock Square.

Mr. and Mrs. William E. Robinson were now, to many in the profession, Mr. and Mrs. Chung Ling Soo. Will relied on his wife's expertise onstage and her skills supervising the show backstage. Dot was devoted to her husband, sharing his plans for the Chung Ling Soo program.

When she wasn't wearing makeup, friends thought Dot looked older than her years, but this was easily explained, as she was never honest about her age. When she was out of the theater, she was quiet and industrious. On stage, Suee Seen was sweet and delicate. But backstage she was tough, surprising many stagehands who expected a demure little lady. For years she'd overcome her size by standing up to any challenge.

Soo once told a reporter about a new illusion in which Dot was required to crawl through a trapdoor and into a prop. As usual, she practiced her role carefully, working out the timing. When Soo finally decided that the trick was ready, it was introduced into the first show of the evening. But a small sliver of wood, the result of the rehearsal, jammed in the trapdoor. Dot heard her cue, pushed against

Dainty Suee Seen, as she appeared
onstage.

the door, and realized that she was locked out. Using her nails and fingers, she ripped away at the obstruction in an effort to save the performance. When the orchestra reached its final chord, she was ready with a sweet smile, her fingers torn and bleeding.

The integrity of the illusions was Dot's first concern. A young man named T. G. H. Wiley was working as a spotlight operator during one of Chung Ling Soo's visits to the Lancaster Hippodrome. Wiley was also an amateur magician. He watched the show one Monday night from his perch in the upper balcony, marveling at the illusions. The next night he came in early and walked around the stage, peeking at the beautiful apparatus.

He felt a vise-like grip on his arm. He'd been caught by Suee Seen. She dragged him over to the manager—her bursts of strength were always a surprise—and shrilly demanded that the boy be fired, at that very moment. The manager agreed. There was nothing he could do, as Chung Ling Soo was the star that week. As Wiley slunk out the stage door, the manager whispered, "Come back next week when this lot is done."

On another occasion, the tricks were being set up and rehearsed on a Monday morning as Dot supervised. A young man from the railway station arrived to take the bookings for the next weekend's travel. After filling out his forms, he was drawn to the colorful action on the stage. Soo's assistants, who knew of their boss's obsessive secrecy, quietly advised the bloke to leave. He nodded absentmindedly, but wouldn't step off the stage. When Suee Seen saw him, she turned on her heel and delivered a mighty punch, right "in the breadbasket" as one assistant remembered. He tumbled over backward and fell through an open trapdoor in the stage, with his arms and legs sticking straight up out of the hole. The boys in the Chung Ling Soo show pulled him out. Scraped and gasping for air, he stumbled out of the theater. He never knew what hit him.

In fact, Dot was good at keeping all kinds of secrets. "Little Suee Seen, otherwise Mrs. W. E. Robinson, is as successful as her husband in the art of make-up and acting," according to a profile in *Mahatma* magazine. "She certainly makes a bright and cunning Chinese maid and her valuable assistance has been one of the mainstays and success of Chung Ling Soo's act. Robinson is proud of his better half and says that she, instead of himself, deserves the most merit. They are certainly a well mated couple for deceiving the public."

They had been deceiving the public, and their friends, for twenty years. They had never married. Few acquaintances knew of Rob's first marriage and the complications behind Will and Dot's long relationship. It wasn't until the twenty-first of March, 1906—the year of their twentieth anniversary together—while they were touring in Manchester, that they went into a civil office in Chorlton. Will and Dot were married.

Will was 44. Dot was 42, but she took the opportunity to lie on her marriage certificate, claiming to be 30. Both were identified as "music hall artistes." Will added that he had been previously married to Bessie Smith, but was now "divorced." Presumably this exaggeration was for Dot's benefit, officially declaring an end to his previous marriage.

Unfortunately, it now seems that the Robinsons' official marriage in 1906 was not an act of love so much as an attempt at a fresh start, Will's effort to convince himself of his devotion. While Dot didn't understand how much their relationship had been gradually rattling apart, Will's friends knew of his numerous affairs over the years—careless, convenient assignations with local lasses or music-hall girls while on tour. Will may have justified the affairs by reminding himself that he and Dot were not actually married. Dot chose to ignore the rumors that rang through the dressing-room halls, busying herself with the trays of small props, the embroidered cloths, ribbons, and silk robes that needed to be ready before Will arrived at the theater.

—☙—

At a music hall in South Shields, as Chung Ling Soo and Suee Seen walked from the dressing room to the stage, they encountered a knot of performers in the wings, whispering excitedly. It was the habit of this music hall to keep the auditorium lights illuminated during the performance, and a man seated in the front row of the stalls had sat through the entire performance thus far reading a newspaper. A girl singer, a beginner in the business, had stumbled into the wings in tears, insulted that the man never looked up at her during her performance. A comedian had been the next act and had taken every opportunity to poke fun at the man. "Funny, a man paying five shillings for a seat to read a newspaper." The audience giggled, but the man continued reading.

Soo winked at his fellow music-hall performers and stepped onto the stage. As Soo was the star of the show, he was happy to see the man fold the paper and look up at his first two tricks. But evidently the patron wasn't impressed. He returned to the newspaper, ignoring the remainder of the act. Chung Ling Soo began to seethe. Like the previous performers, he became obsessed with getting the man's attention.

When he came to the Cannon Illusion, Soo turned the barrel and took aim at the raised newspaper, gesturing broadly his intentions. The audience roared their approval. The cannon boomed and the rubber cannon ball exploded against the newspaper, pushing it into the man's face. Not even knowing there was a cannon onstage, he assumed that the man sitting next to him had begun the assault. A free-for-all started in the audience, and the man was led outside.

The theater manager quickly intervened and after the show brought the man backstage so he could receive a proper apology from Chung Ling Soo. But once the man came backstage, the Chinese magician was suddenly unable to speak English, so he could only shrug and smile blandly, offering a signed photograph.

Of course, Soo rarely had such difficulties with the patrons. But his assistants were another matter. It was difficult to find reliable boys to take part in the show. They tired from the work, got drunk, showed up late in the morning, missed trains, broke props, or flirted with the girls on that week's show. Most perilous of all were the assistants who were interested in magic. Soo watched carefully if they seemed a little too curious about the props. He remembered his own days as an assistant working for Kellar and Herrmann, and how shamelessly he'd carried secrets from one magician to the other. He naturally feared a spy deliberately sent from another music-hall magician and hated trusting his secrets to his assistants. Despite his Chinese insouciance onstage, Soo was a hard taskmaster and displayed flashes of temper backstage.

In 1904, while touring in the west of England, Soo felt that one of his assistants had become lazy and negligent. Chung Ling Soo told him off with his favorite American slang, and finished by curtly informing the boy that he was fired at the end of the week. He knew that he should have barred him from the theater at that instant, but he needed the assistant to finish the engagement.

The next day the boy showed up, looking suspicious. He sullenly avoided any eye contact with the magician, and Chung Ling Soo expected the worst. During the performance of the Orange Tree Illusion, Suee Seen jumped onto the table and the tube was lowered, changing her into the tree. But as she attempted to push her way through the trapdoor in the tabletop, she found that it had been blocked by a piece of wood. It was a repeat of her previous accident, but this time she was actually prevented from finishing the trick. As Suee Seen pounded against the interior of the tube, Soo realized what had happened and turned just in time to see the assistant dash out the stage door of the theater.

The next day was Sunday and the Soo show was traveling to their next engagement. Many trains stopped at Chinley Junction, which became a busy thoroughfare every Sunday afternoon as the music-hall artists made their transfers. William Robinson was out of makeup, dressed in his dark suit and Stetson hat. As he stepped off the train to stretch his legs, the magician looked across the platform and saw the missing assistant, struggling with his luggage. The assistant looked up and their eyes met. Rob let out a yell and took chase, pushing other passengers out of the way and hurdling the tracks. As his fellow performers watched, he grabbed the boy by the collar, threw him to the ground, and offered "a good hiding." When he was finished, he dusted his hands, picked up his felt hat, smoothed his coat, and smiled broadly at the assembled crowd. Self-satisfied that he could still hold his own, Rob sauntered back onto the train.

—m—

Through the summer of 1906, Chung Ling Soo toured in Germany with his new act. At the end of the year, his company returned to London for another long holiday engagement at the Hippodrome. In January 1907, the show moved to Hull, opening at the Palace on the twenty-first.

When Rob arrived in Hull, he went down to Alexandria Docks. He was expecting some scenery from Germany that had been sent directly to Hull. As usual, he was dressed inconspicuously, in a suit and hat. "Just before gaining entrance to the docks," he later told the police, "I saw twelve or fourteen men standing in the road. They all gazed hard at me, but I thought little of it at the time." But as he proceeded down the docks, he heard a voice call out, "That's him." Two rough-looking fellows rushed out at him, and before Robinson could defend himself he felt two sharp blows, one against his head and the other against his arm.

As he tumbled to the ground, the men took flight. He was dazed by the injuries and it took him some time to come to his senses and stand up. By that time, the men were gone. There was no robbery, and no apparent reason for the assault.

Robinson in a typical offstage pose, with his favorite hat.

The magician seemed slightly embarrassed by it all. Reporters wrote that the famous Chung Ling Soo had been assaulted, but Soo told them that he was certain that the whole incident was a case of mistaken identity. He was not in his makeup or costume. "No Englishman would attack me, for I know your people. They are the best and most appreciative I have ever played before," he concluded. He returned to the hotel and had his scrapes and bruises treated. Despite the incident, he went on with the first performance.

Soo made a joke of the publicity, sending out pictures of himself wearing bandages. But the incident in Hull sounds suspicious in many details—his trip to the docks by himself and his casual dismissal of his injuries. Perhaps it was the residue of the British public's feelings toward the Boxers; a few sailors had recognized the famous Chinese magician and responded with a chauvinistic flurry of fists.

But it is more likely that the assault on the docks may have been evidence of his dangerous personal relationships. "During his Don Juanish moods, Billy had a few adventures and two blackmail attempts that I know of," according to Maurice Raymond, one of

Robinson's friends. "Not finding the 'easy mark' they expected, [his attackers] quit on the run."

If one of Rob's dalliances had involved a local girl, an angry father or brother may have summoned the star for a showdown. He was certainly in a "Don Juanish" mood. Shortly after this incident, Rob began an illicit affair while he was touring in England.

Her name was Janet Louise Mary Blatchford. She was born in the English town of Plymouth in 1885. When she met the man who played Chung Ling Soo, she was less than half his age, twenty-one years old, pretty and petite, with dark eyes and a wave of chestnut hair. Her friends called her Lou.

Her father, Henry Blatchford, was deceased; he had been a soldier. The family later recorded that Lou's mother, Mrs. Emma Blatchford, managed a theatrical boarding house. This would have explained how Lou and Rob first met. But the family home was in Mutley, some distance from the music halls of Plymouth, and was not listed in city directories as a boarding house. It seems that the Blatchfords had some ties to show business, perhaps through Plymouth friends or relatives.

Lou fell in love with Rob, who was exotically mysterious when he was in costume and sweetly mysterious in person. We don't know the details of their affair. Like Rob's other relationships, it might have been brief and easily forgotten; but in May 1907, Lou discovered that she was pregnant.

Meanwhile, the Soo company had continual, annoying problems with the Bullet Catching Trick. While performing in Birmingham, a local gunsmith came onto the stage and thought he detected the secret of the trick, reasoning that the bullets had been secretly withdrawn from the gun. He stopped the show and announced to the audience that he suspected there was a trick to the guns. Soo fixed a bland smile, nodded, and proceeded with his finale.

After the performance, the gunsmith felt flushed with success and came to Soo's dressing room to argue the point. Rob, now out of costume, was waiting for a squabble, and stopped the man at the door. "Do you really think anyone is so damned stupid as to think I can catch bullets shot from guns? For God sakes, laddie, I never claimed it was anything but a trick! I'm a magician!"

But the seeming danger of the trick was an invitation for mischievous thrill-seekers. The magician was aware he was tempting fate. At the London Hippodrome, Soo was performing the trick with five riflemen. He held up the plate and gave the signal to fire. As the five rifles cracked loudly, the magician was shocked when the plate in his hand shattered into small shards of porcelain and his fingers were badly cut.

The broken plate mystified him, although Soo had contemplated many possible accidents with the trick. "There was always the danger that some stupid person, thinking to catch me, would manage to put something into the one of the guns after we had withdrawn the bullets," he later explained to a reporter from *The Football Post*. He admitted that he had all five bullets palmed in his hand, ready to reveal them on the plate. "There was no reason for the plate to break." Soo calculated that a button or a small bit of metal had been dropped into the barrel. He questioned his assistants and tried to discover what had gone wrong, but there was no good explanation. Knowing the precautions he'd taken with his routine, he was confused. "I worked for weeks with my fingers taped up," he shrugged.

In January 1906, a magician named Professor Blumenfeld was performing at the restaurant of the Hotel Cigogne in Basel, Switzerland. He grandly announced the Bullet Catching Trick, having a bullet marked and dropped into a pistol before handing the gun to a spectator and urging him to shoot.

The spectator took aim and shot, killing Blumenfeld on the spot. Somehow, the magician had failed to withdraw the bullet.

Soo was aware of Blumenfeld's fate and concluded that the magician had been using the old method with the metal tube hidden inside the barrel of the gun. But once again, there was never a proper explanation for the accident. "There is a danger in the trick, and I can tell you, as a matter of absolute fact, that every conjurer who has stuck to it has ended up being killed or seriously injured," Soo told the reporter. He'd decided to stop performing the illusion before much longer. "I like the trick myself as a spectacular production, but I have come to the conclusion that life is worth living."

Chapter 21

LONSDALE ROAD

In June 1907, the London *Daily News* ran a brief story. "Chung Ling Soo is a humorist as well as a conjurer," it noted. Soo had recently advertised in a theatrical journal, and the *Daily News* couldn't resist repeating the ad. "Wanted by Chung Ling Soo, a first class wardrobe mistress for a long tour. To one able to mind her own business, and not Chung Ling Soo's, a comfortable enjoyment is assured."

The newspaper assumed that a magician had plenty of professional secrets, and so Soo would naturally shun a potentially nosy employee. But the ad wasn't as funny as the *Daily News* assumed. Chung Ling Soo's many private secrets were now causing tempers to sizzle and angry sparks to fly between the dressing rooms of Suee Seen and The Marvelous Chinese Conjurer.

A wardrobe mistress going in and out of the dressing rooms would have to deal with slammed doors, arguments, and bursts of tears. Soo needed someone who was willing to ignore all of it.

—⁂—

Dot was enraged. When Will told her about Louise Blatchford's pregnancy, she stormed and cried, realizing this might be the end of their relationship and the collapse of the career they had constructed together. Dot naturally blamed her husband for his indiscretions, but she also blamed him for capitulating to the girl.

Will's previous children had conveniently been spirited away, raised quietly by other families. Dot knew that her husband's careless attitude had been morally wrong, but she was selfishly grateful that his previous children hadn't interfered with his career or his life with her. Lou's hold over Dot's husband was different—Lou insisted on having a father for her child and wanted the stability that could be provided by a wealthy music-hall star. Dot was shocked to find that Will was no longer careless or dismissive of his indiscretions but was willing to take on the role of father.

His surfacing guilt over the dismal relationships with his previous children was behind Robinson's decision. He never really knew Annie and Elmore. They were born at a time when he was starting his career and viewed a family as a hindrance. Now that he had money and fame, they were fully grown and living somewhere in America—lost to him forever. After twenty years it was apparent that Dot would not bear him children, so Lou's pregnancy gave him his last chance to establish a real family. Through his mistress, he was unexpectedly offered a chance to atone for his previous mistakes as a father.

Dot, his loyal wife, found herself ensnared by the secrets she had concealed for twenty years. Few people knew that she had been the original other woman in William Robinson's life. Dot was the one who pulled him away from his first wife and children. Now that Will and Dot had finally married, she found that the roles were reversed. It was now Lou, as the other woman, who commandeered the husband's attentions.

Will moved his pregnant mistress up to Barnes, a fashionable area just west of London, where he had purchased a new house. It was a large, whitewashed three-story brick mansion that comprised two addresses at 48 and 50 Lonsdale Road. He named the house Kia Ora, a Maori term meaning good luck.

On February 3, 1908, Lou gave birth to a son. The child was given the name Ellsworth James—his father's middle name and his grandfather's first name.

Ellsworth's birth signaled a change in Robinson's life and career, an honest attempt to become a responsible father, simplify his relationships, and create a home that would be good luck for his family.

—∽—

Will and Dot called a truce and formalized their relationship as a simple business proposition. They would remain married. Dot would continue working with the show and would receive a good salary, £25 ($125) per week, for playing the role of Suee Seen and assuming her backstage responsibilities. The cast of the show referred to them as Mr. Soo and Mrs. Soo.

In every city, Will took his own room in theatrical lodgings or a hotel. Dot roomed with Frank and Mabel Kametaro and their young daughter, Nina.

Lou remained in Barnes, generally ignored by the touring company and unseen by Dot. When she occasionally visited Will on tour, or sent messages, the company referred to her as Mrs. Robinson. Most weeks on tour, Will would board a train on Saturday evening after the last show and return to Barnes for a leisurely Sunday with Lou and baby Ellsworth. Meanwhile, Dot and the Kametaros supervised moving the show and setting it up in the next city. Will arrived on Monday afternoon, sometimes perilously late for the first show, applying his makeup and changing into his robes as he dashed into the theater.

There was one more complication, an ironic bit of playacting included in the Chung Ling Soo show. Nina Kametaro was a toddler. She was half Japanese, with pretty oriental features and dark hair. She was introduced onstage as Bamboo Flower, Chung Ling Soo's child. Many portraits featured Soo, Suee Seen, and Bamboo Flower, standing together as a proud family.

In the act, Chung Ling Soo now made his entrance with tiny Bamboo Flower by his side. They walked to the footlights hand in hand and she was given the first bow before scampering into the wings. Several minutes later, Bamboo Flower came onstage with a "lucky coin," an antique Chinese coin threaded on a ribbon. She grandly stepped forward to award it to the patron in the stalls who had purchased the first ticket at that evening's performance. The publicity stunt was described in newspapers, and brought crowds hoping to win one of the lucky coins.

The Soo "family" with Nina, and
(standing) cast member Suee Chung and
Frank Kametaro.

Like many of the secrets woven through Robinson's life, Chung Ling Soo's "child" seemed to confuse the onstage fantasy with the offstage deceptions. It was a strange dramatization of the magician's private life.

There's evidence that William Robinson was attempting to eliminate some of these deceptions. To other theater professionals, he had been generally accepted as a westerner; he introduced himself to friends as being from Great Britain. Members of the press kept his secrets and avoided mentioning his ancestry, allowing readers to conclude that he was Chinese. But the pointed duel with Ching Ling Foo had forced him to formalize his Chinese credentials. In interviews he felt a need to remain silent or conduct the translation game. Rob was uncomfortably trapped.

In 1907, Robinson made a conscious effort to simplify his role offstage, wearing western clothes, speaking English in interviews, and detailing his background. An article in *Entr'acte* magazine explained his new story for his character.

> Chung Ling Soo is a combination of East and West. His father was Scotch and his mother Chinese, and although born in China, he has spent a good part of his life in Western countries. His father, a missionary named Campbell, married a native girl in Canton. These mixed marriages are said to be not at all uncommon, for missionaries are human after all, and the girls of Canton are said to be the prettiest in all China. The name Chung Ling Soo meant extra good luck, and it was given to him because he happened to be the first boy born into the family after a run of four girls. Chung was a young medical student in Canton when one day he was attracted by a conjurer at a street corner....

A pretty lithographic poster, used to advertise the Chung Ling Soo Show, dramatized this story. The poster showed Chung Ling Soo seated on an oriental throne in front of Scottish and Chinese flags. A small portrait showed "his father," a red-whiskered, tartan-wearing Scotchman. Another portrait showed "his mother," a demure Chinese maiden.

Soo's poster, advertising his Scottish and Chinese parents.

It was another jumble of fact and fiction. In an effort to tell the truth, Robinson had managed to create a story that was only slightly more truthful than the last one. But it explained why he dressed and spoke like a Westerner offstage.

He still quietly confided that he had been born in England or Scotland. It was a little secret that he shared to make a quick connection with a new acquaintance. Rob told the magician Ellis Stanyon and his wife that he was from Chester; it was an especially convincing story, as Rob recalled the areas around town where he had played as a boy. He told others that he was from Barnes, Bolton, Wigan, Lancashire, Yorkshire, and the East End of London. Many heard that he was an Aberdeen boy. Others were told that he was from Glasgow. When he played in Glasgow, he told friends that his father was from Dumfries, Scotland.

Despite the angry duel with Ching Ling Foo, the Chinese community seemed always to admire Chung Ling Soo. Soo attended lavish Chinese meals in London's Denman Street, often honored as a guest and treated to rare delicacies. "The first course consisted of unfired China green tea," according to an account of one of Soo's parties, "and was followed by sets of dishes which included yin wah tong (bird's nest soup), leung yee (a freshwater fish), chow mein (a biscuit-like basis over which is spread a mixture of pork, Chinese mushrooms, et cetera). These were all carried down with drafts of Chinese wine. Chopsticks were also provided." In Cardiff, the Chinese community purchased rows of seats for his performances. At the Queen's Theatre in Poplar, in the East End of London, Chinese immigrants cheered the performances and sent gift baskets of food backstage. Witnessing this reception, some of his friends assumed that the Chinese were fooled into thinking he was also Chinese.

They were not fooled, but they were satisfied with his characterization. There were very few authentic Chinese performers, and even fewer honorable impersonations. Chung Ling Soo was proud and artistic on stage. He did not color his skin yellow, indulge in pidgin English, or make stereotypical gestures. Offstage, he did not try to deceive them into thinking he was Chinese, but treated them with respect. Chung Ling Soo may not have been authentic, but he was a grand imitation, and the Chinese community pragmatically appreciated the prestige he brought to his role.

—⁓—

Houdini's attitude toward Rob changed subtly. He and Bess were surprised to discover that Rob was suddenly part of a family, and were uncomfortable meeting Lou and little Ellsworth. It made them think of the peanut sister, Dot, who was no longer included in their visits with Robinson. They'd always enjoyed her company and admired her as a professional.

The hard-hearted duel with Ching Ling Foo had also served to sour Houdini's opinion of his friend. Rob and Houdini maintained amicable relations, but the old camaraderie, the brotherly relationship they'd once shared, was over.

In 1906, Houdini began putting out his own publication for magicians, called *The Conjurer's Monthly Magazine*. Houdini couldn't resist using the journal for his own crusades, attacking his rivals, praising his own appearances, and subtly rewriting history to favor his view of magic. He also enjoyed printing gossip about his fellow performers. Comments about Chung Ling Soo often had a flinty edge to them, as if he were anxious to settle a score.

There were professional comments, hinting that Robinson depended on others for his success: "Abraham Blitz is the nephew of [the magician] Signor Blitz and a true friend of Chung Ling Soo," *The Conjurer's Monthly* reported. "It is whispered [he] helped put Robinson's new act together." Or: "Ike Rose has not been connected with Chung Ling Soo for several seasons. Ike is the man who made Chung Ling Soo (W. E. Robinson) a success, and let us hope that Robinson will not forget it." There were also personal jibes about his appearance: "Chung Ling Robinson: How are your teeth and let us know if that newly discovered 'tooth-grower' you have is worthy of publication." And Houdini hinted that Robinson had neglected his family in New York: "If W. E. Robinson reads this paragraph, or any

of our readers should know of his address, kindly advise him to communicate with [Edward W. Robinson]. The folks are anxious."

—◊—

Houdini's *Conjurer's Monthly Magazine* also took his friend to task
for being a strikebreaker. As music halls became owned by a small
number of powerful producers, there was less competition for the
performing artists. In 1907, a group of performers formed the Variety
Artists Federation, in an attempt to standardize salaries and sched-
ules. The variety artists struck in 1907 over a disagreement about
matinees. Up until that time, management could request an extra
matinee show, without extra pay. During the strike, managers
scrambled to fill their theaters with acts. Oswald Stoll wired Soo,
asking him if he would be willing to work. Chung Ling Soo promptly
responded that he was not only available for work, but also willing
to put together a special two-and-a-half-hour program—all his own
magic—if needed. Unfortunately, Soo's letter was made public.
"William Robinson, known as Chung Ling Soo, offered to give a two-
hour show to Mr. Stoll at any of his houses. What has Robinson to
say about this?" Houdini's *Conjurer's Monthly* reported. "Mr. Stoll
did not even ask [for this special show] from Robinson, but then I
presume [Rob] never thought that his letter would become public
property. I am sorry that it is an American that is held up to us men
of mystery as a good strikebreaker." To hammer home the point,
Houdini's next issue reported, "Chung Ling Soo's name does not
appear among the candidates [for the Variety Artists Federation]. A
lot of conjurers would like to see Soo in the V.A.F. So go ahead, Rob,
and become a fellow artist." Several months later the magazine
mentioned, "our friend Chung Ling Soo has finally fallen into the
ways of the V.A.F., having paid his company for all extra matinees at
Gloucester."

In fact, William Robinson was leery of anything, or anyone, who
interfered with his ability to play a theater. He was happiest on
stage, and took almost as much pleasure working on new illusions

in a workshop. The fantasy of Chung Ling Soo kept him busy and preoccupied; his work kept his mind off his personal problems. In 1908, his music-hall act was over thirty minutes long, filled with a number of astonishing new illusions. There were even more miracles in the works, and no end in sight. Ritherdon, the man who ran the Bolton workshop, told a reporter in 1908 that if Soo continued "inventing at the rate he has done in the last twelve months, he will never live to wear [out] his mysteries."

—⁓—

Donald Stevenson was an amateur conjurer and machinist who became a friend of the magician. He was always impressed by Rob's boy-like fascination with magic, and the peculiar way he was struck with inspiration. Once day, during one of Soo's engagements at the London Hippodrome, he and Stevenson were walking on the street when they were interrupted by brewer's draymen. They were unloading crates of beer to a nearby pub. Robinson stopped suddenly, hypnotized by the actions of the deliverymen. He grabbed Stevenson's arm. "There's an illusion in those crates! See the moves those men make as they're stacking them. Quick, back to the dressing room." They dashed to the theater and filled pages with notes and drawings, sending out for sandwiches so they could work through the idea. When Rob had figured out the process, he put Stevenson to work building the finished illusion. It was called The Magic Bottle. Five wooden crates were filled with bottles of stout. The crates were stacked, and the entire stack screened by a fabric canopy. Seconds later, the crates had been transformed into a gigantic bottle of stout. When it was opened, Suee Seen emerged from inside.

"His all absorbing interest was the study of magic and the planning of new illusions," Stevenson remembered. "He hardly ever thought or talked about anything else, and counted upon spending about two-thirds of his earnings in keeping his show the finest magical performance ever produced." Robinson often presented Stevenson with wonderful puzzles—some idea for an illusion or a small device that he needed for part of a trick. "Think it out, laddie, think it out," he told the young engineer. Later, Stevenson recalled, "Many a headache that short sentence has given me."

Another of Soo's new tricks, a creation of Ritherdon's, was called The Living Target. Soo showed an arrow attached to a long rope, loading both into a rifle. Suee Seen stood on the opposite side of the stage in front of a large round target. Soo took aim and fired. The rope was propelled across the stage, through the lady and into the target. The trick was a difficult one to stage, but the image of the rope passing through the lady's body was breathtaking and drew fulsome applause from the audience. Like all of Soo's illusions, it was months in development. By a strange coincidence, The Living Target, Suee Seen's mock execution, was introduced at the same time the Robinsons' backstage melodrama was unfolding.

One remarkable illusion was billed as The Crystal Lamp of Enchantment, or The Slave of the Lamp. Soo introduced it early in 1908, although a friend reported that it took over a year of development and four separate prototypes before Robinson was satisfied with the results. The magician spent £400 ($2,000) on the illusion. The finished product was a magnificent piece of workmanship from the Ritherdon shop.

The curtains swept open on a tall crystal lantern, standing on the stage floor. It was actually a six-sided glass cabinet, about six feet tall and two and a half feet wide. Each side was a thick piece of glass set within a bright nickel-plated metal frame. On the roof of the lantern was a large metal ring. Assistants turned the lantern on its small casters, showing every side.

Chung Ling Soo took a flaming torch from an assistant and walked up to the crystal lantern. He opened the front door—one of six panels—showing the interior and then pushing the torch inside so the audience could see that the glass container was empty. He then slowly circled the lantern with the torch, so that each transparent panel was displayed.

The torch was tossed to an assistant as the front door was closed. Two cables were lowered from the flies, and these were attached to

The Crystal Lantern; Suee Seen magically
appeared inside.

the ring on top of the lantern. Soo gave the signal and the lantern
was lifted three or four feet into the air.

As it swung gently, Soo reached up, grabbed an edge, and gave it
mighty spin. The lantern revolved rapidly, twinkling as each panel of
glass reflected the stage light. The magician took a step to one side
and pulled a small pistol from his belt. He raised the pistol in the air
and fired three times. Suddenly the dark interior of the lantern
seemed to fill with color. As the lantern began to lose momentum and
the spinning slowed, the audience doubted their senses. The patch of
color became recognizable as the hands and face of Suee Seen. When
she first appeared, she seemed to be stationary as the lantern revolved
around her. But a second later she was seen turning inside with the
lantern, revolving in and out of the light.

Soo dashed toward the lantern as it was lowered to the stage
again. He reached forward to steady it. As it touched the floor, the
front door swung open and Suee Seen stepped out for her bow.

Few stage illusions have ever mixed the delicate finesse and mechanical expertise of Rob's beloved Crystal Lantern. It was accomplished by an innovative application of the Black Art principle.

As the curtain opened on the illusion, Dot was concealed beneath the stage, standing on a special elevator trap. After the lantern was shown, it was positioned over the trap. Soo showed it was empty by using the torch, and then closed the front door. That was the signal for the trap to move. Dot was pushed straight up into the back half of the lantern.

The audience didn't see her entrance because she was hidden behind a piece of dark fabric attached to a spring-roller blind. As she came through the floor, the fabric unrolled in front of her. It matched the color of the curtains hanging at the back of the stage.

The lantern was specially constructed with an inner compartment. The six walls of the lantern spun freely, but the inner compartment did not turn. This meant that Dot, behind her fabric camouflage, was not seen as the lantern turned.

The gunshots were the cue to release the roller blind. It quickly opened, like an iris, revealing Dot standing at the back of the lantern. A special door inside the lantern allowed her to lock up the inner and outer parts of the lantern, which meant that she spun inside it during the last graceful revolutions.

By the time the lantern reached the stage, she was ready to open the door and take her bow.

The visual illusion depended on a number of subtle touches. Each pane of glass was actually two thicknesses, with a thin layer of gray-blue mosquito netting sandwiched in the middle. This gave the lantern a slightly hazy, smoky look that concealed the interior as it spun. Rob experimented with different colors of fabric for the roller blind to create a precise match; he found that a dark gray, seen through the mosquito netting, perfectly duplicated the background.

Each week, when they unpacked the show at the theater, Soo's boys needed to install the special elevator in the stage. This required cutting a hole in the floor and dropping their mechanism into the basement. They also needed to suspend the rigging that would lift the lantern in the air. The prop was large and heavy, almost a thousand pounds when it was assembled. The weight gave it momentum and kept it spinning smoothly during the performance. But lifting the crate of glass required four men.

Worst of all, the lantern was delicate. If another prop were wheeled into it backstage, the glass sides of the lantern could shatter. For this reason, the company carried crates with extra panes of glass, ready for an emergency.

During an early performance, as the lamp was set whirling, one of the large, double-thick panels of glass—almost two feet by six feet—slid out of its frame like a guillotine blade. It shattered, and a large, jagged shard was embedded, upright, in the oak flooring of the stage.

The accident startled Soo, standing just several feet away, inspiring a string of expletives muttered under his breath. After that, Soo and Kametaro took responsibility for the prop each week, checking and double-checking each bolt and hinge. The Crystal Lamp of Enchantment was a pretty trick, but no one in the audience realized how perilous it was to operate.

—⁓—

The Mystic Cauldron was Soo's new finale for the show in 1908. A small, round, iron cauldron, about two feet across, was carried on the stage and tipped forward. Soo plunged a torch inside, so the audience could see that the pot was completely empty. It was suspended from chains that hung from a tripod, like a witch's cauldron. Beneath it, the magician slipped a ring of gas jets. When the jets were ignited, the flames licked the circumference of the pot.

Buckets of water were poured inside by the assistants as Soo paced around the roaring flames. Soon, steam began boiling from the top of the cauldron. He opened a tap on the side and poured out a bucket of steaming water. Satisfied that he was ready to cast his spell, he signaled to his assistants, who marched onto the stage bearing baskets of dead animals. Each animal was a slightly comic, dilapidated stuffed skin. The Chinese magician picked up a moth-eaten rabbit skin by his fingertips, registering obvious distaste, and then dropped it inside the cauldron. This was followed by several more furry rabbits. Then he showed a number of floppy ducks—cloth bodies with feathers—and these were scooped into the steaming cauldron. He followed with doves and chickens.

Soo stirred it all with a large stick and dipped his hand into the hot brew. He emerged with a live rabbit, and then a second and third. Bright white ducks popped up from the cauldron and the assistants lifted them out. The ducks waddled around the stage and were led into the wings. Then Soo scooped out a handful of doves that took flight, followed by the chickens, who jumped from the cauldron and scampered around the stage.

There was another burst of steam. The assistants poured more cold water into the cauldron and the fire was extinguished. Soo reached inside one final time and pulled out a hand. Suee Seen immediately stood up within the Mystic Cauldron. She was perfectly dry, adorned in bright Chinese silk. Soo lifted her from the iron pot as the audience burst into applause. It was as if she had been conjured by a magical recipe.

Like most of Robinson's favorite illusions, the cauldron was based on an old idea, a trick found on playbills in the early 1800s. He enlarged it and added to the routine.

It was all operated from beneath the stage. Within the gas ring was another cylinder of metal. This was hidden behind the flames. A round trapdoor in the bottom of the cauldron allowed Suee Seen to be pushed up through a trapdoor in the stage floor, through the metal ring, and into the cauldron.

The appearance of the steam called for another ingenious secret. The walls of the cauldron were of double thickness. Water poured into the pot was directed into the walls and trickled off beneath the stage. The steam was generated from a boiler in the basement. Assistants attached a hose to the cauldron, sending the steam up so that it seemed to boil over the edge of the pot on stage.

It was Suee Seen, standing halfway through the floor and half in the cauldron, who handed up each rabbit, duck, and chicken. At the climax of the trick, she was pushed straight up on the elevator trap so she could make her entrance.

Dot was regularly burned by the blasts of steam, leaving her with ugly scars on her hands and arms. One night during a performance, a new assistant picked up a bucket of water and poured it into the cauldron. Although he'd been rehearsed in this careful procedure, stage nerves got the best of him and he missed the inner lining. Instead, he spilled the bucket of water on Mrs. Soo's head as she was pushed up on the elevator.

Dot didn't miss a cue, but handed up each waterlogged rabbit and bird, then took her own bow dripping wet but smiling sweetly, the perfect Chinese princess.

—m—

"Chung Ling Soo must, by now, have a bank book as long as his Chinese pedigree," according to a 1907 article in a magicians' journal. "He says he will not take any more contracts at a certain salary; it must be on shares or not at all. He assures us that he is playing to an average of seven-hundred to nine-hundred pounds per week gross." One contract from the end of that year showed that Soo was carrying a company of 11 people. For his weekly salary, he was guaranteed 55 percent of the gross up to £200 ($1,000), and then 60 percent of the next £100, and 65 percent of everything over the next £300. It wasn't unusual for him to earn £360 per week ($1,800). One day another magician noticed Robinson's pocket bulging with bank notes. Rob shrugged, saying that was simply his petty cash. But his friend urged him to take the petty cash from his pocket and count it out. It totaled more than £1000 ($5,000).

Soo's contracts called for the magician to supply advertising posters that could be pasted up around town to draw crowds to the theater. Chung Ling Soo's colorful lithographs became famous throughout the industry. Most magicians focused on two or three different styles of posters, but Chung Ling Soo produced a dazzling array of images to advertise his show. Most of his posters were the size of small paintings; in the printing trade they were called half-sheets. Some posters portrayed individual illusions: Dot rising from the Cauldron; Dot impaled on the rope in The Living Target; or Soo posed with the Linking Rings. Other bright posters focused on artistic images of the magician: holding a lamp, the caption proclaimed him "The Light of the World"; standing atop the crest of a mountain, he "Has Reached the Highest Pinnacle of Fame"; or posed to show twelve separate grins and grimaces: "A Few Facial Expressions during The Fire Trick." Many of the posters are strikingly artistic, superimposing the magician's image on a pretty mosaic, a Willow Pattern plate, an artist's palette, a peacock feather, or a Chinese fan. Some scenes were designed to portray him as a profound man of mystery: gazing at a Chinese landscape or entering a sacred cave. One poster showed Soo standing atop a gigantic hand as he was lowered from the clouds—the caption explained, "A Gift from the Gods to Mortals on Earth to Amuse and Mystify."

The range of his posters is indeed mystifying. For many years it was thought that he had invited an art school to produce images for his show; this explained the various styles and the painterly images. But the design of a multicolored lithograph is not a job for an art student, and Soo's posters show the masterly touch of professional lithographers; most were printed by the British printing houses James Upton or Horrocks.

"Chung Ling Soo is a great believer in paper advertising," according to one article. "He can probably put up more different sheets than any other show at present in England. He has no less than three thousand pounds worth of printing lying in stock at his lithographers, all of which we are told is paid for." A photo taken in Bristol shows a high wooden fence festooned with Soo advertisements of every size, shape, and color. Thirty-one separate posters are pictured. Over the course of his career, he may have had as many as one hundred.

In early 1908, when Soo played the Olympia Theatre in Liverpool, Charles Hand, a theatrical agent and a friend of several years, approached him with a strange proposition. Hand was just starting a new publication called the *Liverpool Theatrical News*, and was searching for a sensational story.

The agent wanted to publish the fact that the public's favorite Chinese magician was not Chinese at all, but actually a clever Lancashire lad who had been fooling the public. He laid out his plan for Robinson, pointing out that this would endear him to the British public and put an end to the tinge of racism that still haunted him from the 1900 Boxer Rebellion. The article would be written to suggest no cooperation from Soo; this would allow the magician to deny the allegations, should he choose.

Hand was surprised when Robinson nodded in agreement. It was a chance to set the record straight and also help Hand's new publication.

When Robinson signed the agreement, he did so with the anticipation that he'd just lit a fuse. He hoped that this article would help untangle some of the longtime offstage deceptions—the problems with Suee Seen and the Kametaros, and the hidden family in Barnes. At first, it seemed to be a big gamble. He would be trusting in the public's goodwill for the Marvelous Chinese Conjurer.

The article was planned with the title, "Chung Ling Soo, The Fraud." As usual with William Robinson, the truth in the *Liverpool Theatrical News* was to include a prominent lie: Hand actually believed that Robinson was from Lancashire. Robinson and Hand drew up an agreement and collaborated on the article.

The experiment wasn't put to the test. There's no evidence that the article was ever published. After only a few issues, *The Liverpool Theatrical News* went out of business.

—⁓—

Robinson's success had convinced him of Chung Ling Soo's durability, and he realized that no mere newspaper story could have ended his career. Decades earlier, he had analyzed the secrets of mediums in spiritual parlors. He knew that their séances consisted of crude tricks. But he also knew that exposing those tricks, as Kellar had often done from the stage, was a frustrating battle. The audience wanted to believe in the mediums and was willing to overlook any fraud.

Chung Ling Soo offered wonderful value to his audiences. For a few shillings, he transported them to a faraway land and showed them fantasies that seemed enchantments of everyday life: creating coffee from a pile of beans by magic, or flowers from seeds in a split second. After several years in the music halls, he had become a bankable star and a popular brand name. The public didn't require honesty from their magicians, simply magic. He realized that they wanted to believe in Chung Ling Soo.

Chapter 22

AUSTRALIA

With the continuing success of Chung Ling Soo's tours through England, many of his friends anticipated that the magician would return to the United States. There was little question that the Marvelous Chinese Conjurer would be a hit in American vaudeville. At the end of 1907, there were rumors that he had been signed to appear at the New York Hippodrome, an immense theater on Sixth Avenue in Manhattan that had opened in 1905, and that Soo would be appearing under the management of Marc Klaw and Abe Erlanger. There were also regular reports that E. F. Albee was negotiating for Soo's appearance. Albee was the partner of Robinson's old associate, B. F. Keith, and the two men managed the most prestigious vaudeville circuit in America.

But the American tour never materialized. A friend of Rob's darkly hinted that he was avoiding the United States because of the messy personal relationships he had left behind. It seems more likely that he was simply waiting for the best deal, one that would match his English salary. Rob had been seduced by the conditions in England, including the convenience of nearby workshops and large modern stages that would accommodate his illusions. When one magician asked him why he wasn't seeking a contract for America, Rob shrugged. "You know the old proverb. A prophet is never appreciated in his own land."

But Chung Ling Soo did sign a profitable contract to tour Australia and New Zealand under the management of Harry Rickards, a successful Australian impresario. Rickards arranged for the tour to begin early in 1909.

The Soo company onstage with their scenery and props.

Robinson was determined to assemble a good staff of assistants for the Australian tour. He was always searching for reliable mechanics he could trust to repair and operate the illusions. The Chung Ling Soo show was now a large, intricate production, requiring intense backstage labor. In any new theater, there was a carefully choreographed sequence as the props were removed from their crates, assembled, checked, and repaired. Small props and costumes were moved to the dressing rooms. Backdrops and pieces of special equipment were hung on battens. Trap doors were cut in the stage and elevators were installed in the basement.

Many theaters had raked stages—floors on a gentle slope to help the audience see a performance—and this added to the complications. Each week required a custom installation, adjusted to the theater floor. A common "rake" was 1 to 12, which meant that the floor rose 1 inch for every 12 inches back from the footlights. But these dimensions weren't standardized. A music hall may have a soft slope of half this much. A steeper slope made it impossible to use props with wheels, and difficult to walk and hit precise marks while presenting the illusions; it felt like performing on the side of a hill.

The Chung Ling Soo show carried special hardwood wedges anticipating the angles of a stage. These were screwed onto the bottoms of tables and illusions so that they would sit level on the stage. Without these adjustments, props might tip over or spill their contents. Other blocks were slipped under the elevator traps so that they operated smoothly up and down.

Soo depended on the Ritherdon shop in Bolton for repairs or replacement parts. He could wire his needs from anywhere in Great Britain and have pieces sent on a train the next day. But on an Australian tour, he wouldn't have this luxury. With no time to establish working relationships with Australian shops, his assistants needed to be ready for any emergency.

For several years Soo had tried to hire an artist and craftsman named Harry Leat, who built small tricks for an English magic shop named Ornum's. But Leat had no desire to go on tour and politely refused. Another metalworker from Ornum's accepted. Phil Davies was a tall, smooth-faced 27-year-old. He had been born in Calcutta, India, to a colonel in the British Army. Davies was a college graduate, overqualified to be soldering tin pans and metal canisters for magicians. But he enjoyed the work and quickly learned the techniques of magicians, coming up with a number of good innovations. His friends described him as a meticulous craftsman. He was also serious and thoughtful. He had a strange, slow way of speaking that gave the impression he was constantly deep in thought.

Davies was a good draftsman and carried a portable drawing board with him everywhere. When Rob and Davies discussed a mechanism for a trick, the young draftsman pulled out his board and a piece of paper, making a careful blueprint of the idea. Rob had always worked out his tricks the hard way, in his shirtsleeves, pacing around the shop, cutting, soldering, and adjusting to see if the trick would work. Davies's ability to visualize an idea and draw a plan was a new luxury for the magician.

Ernest Aldred, 27, was also hired for the tour. Aldred was a tall handsome Lancashire lad with curly dark hair and an upturned moustache. His family was from Bolton, and Aldred worked as a metalworker besides being an amateur conjurer. He may have been an employee at the Ritherdon shop before Chung Ling Soo took him on the road.

Soo and Aldred developed a warm father-and-son relationship. They discussed the details behind tricks, how they were best built or performed. Aldred was impressed with his boss's encyclopedic knowledge of magic. As a mark of honor, Soo took no delight in being mystified. Once, when he had puzzled over a rival's trick for many weeks without success, he went to Aldred for help. "Go and watch the show," he told his employee, putting an arm around his shoulder. "Tell me how it is done." Aldred reported back the next day, pulling out a pencil and making a little sketch of the secret. "Well done, laddie. That's all I wanted to know," Soo told him with a satisfied grin. According to Aldred, Soo did not use the illusion himself. But he couldn't bear being fooled.

Another assistant was a young Chinese boy named Suee Chung who was included in many of the publicity photographs for the show. Standing next to Soo, Suee Seen, Kametaro, and Bamboo Flower, he made a convincing addition to the Chung Ling Soo "family." Offstage, the company adopted Suee Chung, helping him learn English.

The new employees joined the show in the autumn of 1908, for a tour of Europe. Chung Ling Soo played for the month of September at the Alhambra in Paris, and through October at the Alhambra in Brussels. He then returned for dates in England, appearing in London during the Christmas holidays and back through the provinces at the beginning of 1909.

—m—

During the preparations for Australia, there was another important addition to the offstage cast. A friend of Rob's new family moved into the house on Lonsdale Road with Lou and little Ellsworth. Jurgen Neil Carlton was seven years older than Rob, born in 1854. Friends remember him as a dapper, burly gentleman with full ruddy cheeks and a neat pointed beard—he resembled Edward VII, the king of England.

Neil Carlton's background is unclear. He was a bachelor all his life, a show-business professional who had worked as a theater manager in Brighton in the early 1890s. In 1901, when he was 46 years old, he'd suffered a mental breakdown and was an inmate at Cane Hill lunatic asylum in Coulsdon. Records there listed him as a former theatrical manager and a "pauper." The following year, *The Era*, a British theatrical journal, advertised a fund for the benefit of Neil Carlton and collected donations on his behalf. The charity must have been successful. By 1908 Neil Carlton was working again as the assistant manager of the Palace Theatre—a music hall—in Plymouth. This was just down the road from Lou Blatchford's home in Mutley. Later that year, Carlton came to Barnes to live with Rob, Lou, and Ellsworth.

As a man of the theater, Carlton may have been an acquaintance of Rob's. But he never worked for the Chung Ling Soo show. Instead, he lived at the house as a companion and guardian to Lou and Ellsworth. Evidence suggests that he was Lou's friend; she had known Neil Carlton from Plymouth, and she was the one who suggested he come to live at Lonsdale Road. Soo's mistress may have insisted on having a man living in the house during the long stretches when Chung Ling Soo was on tour—his tour of Australia would mean that he was going to be away from home for most of 1909.

Neil Carlton's presence may have satisfied Lou, but it was an uncomfortable compromise for William Robinson. If he had not been so busy with the plans for the tour, or so anxious to calm the waters of his personal affairs, he would have thought twice before agreeing to the arrangement.

—⁊⁊⁊—

In January 1909, the Soo company took the show to Portsmouth, giving evening performances at the Hippodrome Theatre. The Soo show was now forty minutes long. During the days, his staff prepared the equipment for the long voyage to Australia—illusions were repaired and finished with a new coat of varnish. Before being packed in their crates for Australia, petroleum jelly was spread across the intricate metal mechanisms to prevent possible damage caused by weeks of exposure to salt air. Rob sent frantic notes to Percy Ritherdon asking him to deliver the latest illusion, a spectacular piece of equipment called The Birth of a Pearl. The trick was Soo's most complicated yet, an assemblage of sculpted wood, metal, and fabric, all powered by electric motors and adorned with lights and fountains. Ritherdon shared the magician's obsession for detail, and at his Bolton shop he had been fussing with the equipment for months to create the perfect effect. The crate for The Birth of a Pearl arrived just in time. The entire show was taken to Southampton and loaded onto HMS *Moldavia*.

On board were Rob, Dot, Frank and Mabel Kametaro and their daughter Nina, Phil Davies, Ernest Aldred, Suee Chung, and three additional staff members.

They traveled through the Suez Canal, with ports of call in India. In February the *Moldavia* arrived in Melbourne, and the magician's staff installed the show at the Opera House. In spite of his precautions, Rob was disappointed to find that many of the illusions required extensive repairs. Some of the metal parts had rusted shut and wooden panels had split during the voyage. Fortunately, his energetic new staff was well rested and anxious to get to work.

In Australia, Soo added additional assistants to fill the stage, plus a man named Caleb Cheong as his secretary. The company knew him as Kay; he was a young Chinese man who could write fluently in both English and Chinese. His principal duty was answering correspondence. This was an art in itself, as Soo's memorandum paper was printed in five colors, with a portrait of the magician and intertwined dragons surrounding the wide gold border. There was very little room left on the page for a message of any length. Because of his background, Kay Cheong was also Soo's link to the Chinese community in Australia.

Harry Rickards had done a magnificent job of papering the city with posters and filling the newspapers with tempting stories about the Chinese wizard. The Melbourne public had been gaping at the mysterious colored lithographs for many weeks, anticipating the wonders they would see, queuing for tickets. Chung Ling Soo arrived in Melbourne to find that he was already a star.

—⋙—

On Saturday night, February 27, 1909, an immense crowd at the Opera House was hushed with expectation as the curtains opened on Chung Ling Soo. He took leisurely steps to the front of the stage, pausing as assistants on his right and left bowed their reverent greeting. One assistant stepped forward to take Soo's conical mandarin's hat. Another removed the long yellow silk robe embroidered with bat wings, revealing a simple short black coat, and silk pants tied at the ankles. The marked simplicity of his costume contrasted with the dress of his assistants, who wore brightly embroidered silk robes throughout the act. It quickly focused all of the attention on the magician, casting him as an elegant, understated artist who

Soo's professional portrait used for the
Australian tour.

required no flamboyance. "There Soo stands, with bland, inscrutable smile, daintily coiling his pigtail around his neck," the Australian magician Charles Waller recorded. He teased his audience with his slow, pretty gestures. "This done, he suddenly smacks his hands as though to say, 'Ah, I am now ready.'"

He changed a large decanter of ink into a glass of clear water. Stepping to the opposite side of the stage, he then showed a decanter of water that became a decanter of ink. A bright purple silk handkerchief was tucked into a glass vase and instantly disappeared. In a flash, it reappeared, tied between two yellow handkerchiefs that were dangling from a lyre-shaped stand.

At this point—even with these minor marvels—the Australian audience had seen enough to realize that they were in the presence of a virtuoso, and they bubbled over with excitement. "The silence is broken by a loud exclamation, presumably of commendation, issued by a well-dressed Chinaman. Other Chinese take up the cry, so that for a time Soo can do naught but stand, hands tucked in sleeves, acknowledging the plaudits of the Celestials and Australians alike."

He showed four immense dice, about a foot square, and stacked them on a low table. They were covered momentarily. The dice disappeared and in their place was the delicate Suee Seen. He did the Fire Eating Trick—glowing embers, smoke and sparks—ending with cascade after cascade of silk ribbons, and then paper lanterns, flags, and fireworks filling the stage. Then he performed the Chinese Rings, a magnificent bit of pantomime with an ancient trick. He produced Suee Seen from the Crystal Lantern. He discovered handfuls of colorful Chinese toys, fans, and flags in a previously empty drum, followed by a large dish filled with water and goldfish. He fired the arrow through Suee Seen. He produced hot coffee from a vase filled with coffee beans. He cut a circle out of the center of a white handkerchief and then repeated the operation with a red handkerchief. When the pieces were magically restored, they had somehow become mixed. The white handkerchief had a red center and the red had been restored with a white center. Soo seemed genuinely puzzled by the mistake as the audience laughed.

Finally the curtains opened on his last illusion, the Mystic Cauldron. As the steam gushed from the top of the cauldron and Suee Seen rose into view, the audience roared their approval.

"The applause was terrific. With Soo smiling blandly at the center, the company lined up for the final curtain." The audience was besotted with the wonderful Chinese wizard, and wouldn't let him leave the stage. "I wish I could put the scene properly before you," Waller wrote. Finally, in an effort to bring the show to a conclusion, Frank Kametaro stepped forward, his cap between his fingers. "Ladies and gentlemen," he started with a pinched Asian accent, "my father, he not speak English very good." The audience giggled in response. Frank Kametaro looked every bit as old as Soo. "He say, thank you very much." Kametaro stepped back in line. There were loud shouts of "Bravo," as little Bamboo Flower ran onstage from the wings and jumped into Soo's arms.

"It is doubtful that Soo had been sufficiently praised for the great artist he really was," according to Charles Waller, who had seen the greatest magicians of his generation. "Soo's artistry was supreme. Magic has never known a greater than he. His impersonation of a Chinaman was in itself a thing beyond praise. He presented not only a high caste Chinaman, but what is not necessarily the same thing, an actual Chinese magician."

—m—

Soo's success was compounded by the fact that Australia was then in the midst of the White Australia Policy. After years of using Chinese labor during the Australian gold rush, and black slaves from Melanesia to work the Queensland sugar plantations, the government was fearful that it would be overrun by outsiders—in particular, nonwhites. By 1888, new Chinese immigrants were barred from Australian colonies. In 1901, the new Federal Parliament passed, as its first piece of legislation, the Immigration Restriction Act, "to place restrictions on, and for the removal of, prohibited immigrants." It created a "racial filter" in the form of a 50-word diction test.

Chung Ling Soo portrayed the embodiment of the problem—an outsider coming to Australia, steeped in native culture and unable to speak English. Rickards arranged a press luncheon one afternoon after the magician's premiere. Robinson arrived in a suit and his favorite flat-brimmed sombrero, determined to defuse the controversy. It took thirty seconds for the issue to be raised. As the magician entered the room and nodded his greetings to the reporters, one newspaperman quickly stepped up to challenge him. "Take your hat off," the newspaperman demanded. Rob's eyes twinkled as he whispered in a soft drawl, "Oh, you want to see if I have a pigtail, huh? Well, it'll be there tonight, and that's all we need to worry about. Let's eat."

For other interviews, Soo used the Chinese routine, with Kametaro or Kay Cheong playing the translation game. More than likely, members of the fourth estate played along. An article in the *Illustrated Sporting and Dramatic News* quoted a number of his remarks about his career and illusions. "The following remarks have been translated into common English," the newspaper explained—no doubt with tongue in cheek. Soo's remarks were filled with puns that were quite inexplicable as translations. "Tell you how the arrow is shot through the lady's body. She is well drilled for her work, that's all. Any number of girls get struck by cupid's arrow. Instead of sending the arrow just as far as the heart, we go right through with it."

The Chinese population in Australia had found a champion. Once again, friends were convinced that Soo's portrayal had been good enough to mystify the real Chinese. Perhaps some—like the man who shouted his approval on opening night in Melbourne—were deceived, but most politely overlooked the impersonation. During a time of overt discrimination, the white Australians were honoring him as a Chinese artist. It was flattering to the Chinese community, and if they understood the joke, they also must have appreciated the irony. After their performances, Soo and his wife, with Kay Cheong and other magicians in tow, often went for a late Chinese meal. He performed impromptu tricks for the restaurant staff. "The Chinese made a big fuss over Soo," one of his friends reported, "and were forever presenting him with something or other: a silk flag, or a teapot, or perhaps a bunch of flowers." During the Australian engagements, Soo and Suee Seen toured the cities in Chinese clothing, raised money for the sick and needy in the Chinese community, and were honored at a banquet hosted by the Chinese consul.

The show moved to the Tivoli Theater in Sydney on April 10, playing for six weeks. The response there was even greater than it had been in Melbourne. The critics at the *Illustrated Sporting and Dramatic News* seemed woozy with delight, desperate for new superlatives:

> Chung Ling Soo, with his gorgeous stage setting and appointments, is the shining star at the Tivoli. While Chung Ling Soo is appearing the other artists might be left off on a long holiday. He is a conjurer, illusionist and gentle humorist without words. The audience roared its wonderment, admiration and delight.... Soo is the biggest attraction the Tivoli has billed for some time. People who don't usually favor the Tivoli class of entertainment are hustling for seats to sample the new magician.... He is acknowledged, even by the management, to be quite the biggest draw that this house has ever had.... Chung Ling Soo continues to hold the stage at the Tivoli. All other performers are as cabbage after caviar.... Chung Ling Soo is in his last week at the Tivoli, and it will be a sorrowful city that will witness the magician's departure.

Another magician reported on the performances with similar astonishment:

> The engagement of this famous Chinese conjurer is the greatest and most profitable that Mr. Harry Rickards has ever secured for his patrons. Certainly, no magician has ever created such a sensation, caused so much talk, or given so much satisfaction to his audience. The great charm of his performance is that (as Charles Lamb says of roast pig) "the strong man may fatten on it and the weakly refuseth not its tender juices." While it affords substance for the thought and admiration of an adult, it is food for the amusement and wonder of

the child. And after the time spent in feasting on it overnight we do not rise in the morning and think what fools we have made of ourselves for wasting our time on such things.

It was hard to believe he was writing about a magic act.

—𝔪—

At the Tivoli in Sydney, Soo shared the bill with another magician, an English comedian named Fredric Culpitt. He had first met Billy Robinson years before, when Rob visited London during his employment with Herrmann. In music-hall programs, it was common to arrange several short, quick acts after the star, and Culpitt was given the unfortunate position of closing the show, appearing two turns after Soo. Realizing that he couldn't compete with Soo's star power, Culpitt presented an act called "A Chinese Travesty." It was a parody of the Marvelous Chinese Conjurer the audience had just seen.

Rob insisted on seeing the comedian's act the first night; he dashed off the stage and sneaked into a box so he could watch it from out front. One of Culpitt's gags involved his table, draped with beautiful Chinese silk so that it looked like an exquisite antique. When the tablecloth was accidentally pulled away, it revealed a dirty, broken wooden packing box.

Rob rushed back as Culpitt came offstage, shaking his hand and still grinning from the act. He'd loved it. "But look here, laddie," he told Culpitt, "I can give you a table cover for your soap box that will make your present drape look like ten cents." From his crates of treasures, Soo located a beautiful Chinese banner, festooned with elaborate characters and sewn with gold thread. Culpitt was very proud of the gift, and the embroidered cloth made the contrast with the table even funnier.

"When I returned to England, I showed the banner to a friend who was a professor at a school of Oriental languages," Culpitt later reported. "Pointing to the signs on the silk, I said, 'What do these things mean?' Without batting an eyelid, my learned friend replied,

'They indicate that you are a fully paid-up member of the Foochow Undertaker's Union.'"

—⁓—

In New Zealand, a reporter from the *Otago Times* arrived at the Grand Hotel to interview the great Chinese magician. "His mind was troubled, for Soo's facetious manager had told him that he would require an interpreter, that Soo could not speak a word of English. In a cane chair there reclined an unobtrusive gentleman, distinguished only by a pleasant smile, pink cheeks, a Scotch mouth and chin, sharp observant eyes, and a brown felt hat, unusual in size and Oriental in shape. 'Can you tell me,' said the reporter, 'where I may find Chung Ling Soo?' 'Yes,' replied the individual, 'I am he.'"

Somehow, Soo's manager gave the wrong instructions for the interview. But Rob was unflappable and well versed in his deceptions.

"'Why,' said the pressman, floundering unhappily, 'he told me you couldn't speak English!'

"'A little way he's got. I speak English fluently now.'"

Rob smoothly steered the conversation to the fiction of his early life, explaining how his father was a Scotch engineer named Campbell. His mother was Chinese, a member of he Chung family. He explained the customs of the Chinese, and how he had been imitated by a number of Chinese magicians, including one who used the name "Ching Ling Hee." Presumably this was Robinson's latest way of shrugging off the Ching Ling Foo controversy and the many imitators that it inspired.

The reporter was beguiled by the stories and flattered to be taken into the magician's confidence. When Soo held out his "big brown hand," the reporter shook it as "tears rose to his eyes. It was certainly a very, very strong hand." Soo pointed out that his grip was the result of hard work, long hours at the bench developing his illusions.

The show circled back to Sydney for another three-week engagement, and then returned to Melbourne before finishing in Adelaide in September. Rob was cagey enough to hold back many of his best illusions for these return visits, so he could offer new wonders for his audience.

The new Birth of a Pearl was an especially poetic effect. In the center of the stage was an enormous oyster shell, about four feet across. It was resting flat on a raised stand, like a closed book on a table. The shell was supported by three beautiful, carved dolphins. Soo and his assistant opened the large shell, showing that it was empty; it was lined with iridescent pink and gray silk. The shell was closed again. Colored lights played on the shell and a delicate water-fall descended from the edge of the stand, creating a pretty effect. The second time the shell was opened, the audience saw a large white pearl. The shell was closed and opened a final time. Inside Suee Seen was reclining dreamily, dressed in a pretty pink silk costume.

On his second trip through Sidney and Melbourne, Soo also per-formed the Cocoon Illusion, the Orange Tree, and Defying the Boxers—his famous Bullet Catching Trick.

Charles Waller told Soo that Defying the Boxers was actually too elaborate a trick. "To secure his effect he relied not on cleverness of method, but on lavish display," Waller wrote. "For this small trick he used a special setting and a host of supernumeraries. He was stub-born on this point, but I always claimed that the effect was over-dressed and overstaged. There were boxers, soldiers, chair-bearers and populace. But when all was ended, Soo had merely caught two marked bullets on a plate. I thought the small magical feat was drowned in an ocean of spectacularism."

—∞—

The Australian trip was redemptive for Rob. His company of assis-tants was fresh and energetic and the new illusion was successful. He was making money, earned rave reviews, and was treated as a star wherever he went. In Sydney, Culpitt and Robinson spent hours together, and Culpitt remembered their meetings fondly. "The asso-ciation was one of the happiest things of that never-to-be-forgotten tour. We lived in each other's dressing rooms, ate together in the chop suey joints at Randwick, mooned around the harbor, and spent glorious afternoons at Manley Beach. There was only one thing that Rob would discuss, magic!"

In Melbourne, Waller was also delighted to spend time with the magician. "He was a Bohemian, mixing with many different classes. A quaint little pie and coffee den in a street near the theater, knew him as one of its late patrons. There, or in one of the continental cafes, he would sit talking magic unendingly."

Dot noticed the difference. In recent years, Rob's personal life had been a continual source of worry. He had grown distant and irritable. But during his months in Australia, he regained the energy and enthusiasm from the beginning of his career. When Rob was lost in thought, it was with only the most glorious projects—fretting about a new routine or trying to figure out a mechanism for a trick.

Dot was also rejuvenated by the warm sunshine and reception from the audiences and fans. The Robinsons' previous successes together had been the result of steady, diligent effort. It was hard to appreciate the triumph in the middle of the struggle. But their stardom in Australia seemed instantaneous, effortless, and celebratory. A fellow performer noted, "Mrs. Soo was constantly by her husband's side. She was always smiling. She had a beautiful smile and nothing was a trouble to her." Dot felt as if she had her husband back again. Their personal problems had, quite literally, been left behind in England.

But before they left Melbourne, Waller suddenly sensed a chilliness in Soo's personality that was difficult to describe. "Though exceedingly kind and generous, he was nevertheless a very strange man." A dark cloud of worries seemed to shadow the Marvelous Chinese Conjurer. Waller wrote, "I knew that troubles were already gathering around him."

—⁕—

Near the end of the tour through Australia, Rob received a note from Lou. She was pregnant with a second child.

William Robinson was surprised, then angered, and finally rattled by the news. Why had Lou had been so secretive and waited so long to inform him of the news? Was the child actually his? Was Neil Carlton, the man living with Lou at Lonsdale Road, the real father?

Dot was enraged. It was a reminder that she'd lost her husband forever—to a woman who should never have been trusted.

"One day I hope to write the details of that trip Soo made to Australia," the magic builder Harry Leat explained years later. "I am the only man who knows all the facts from every source. It would be a story of humor, tears, entreaty, treachery and tragedy." Leat never explained the details that he had gleaned from the staff of the show. But the news of Lou's pregnancy was the obvious catalyst for the backstage problems that shook the company. Soo decided to hurry back to England.

Ernest Aldred had met a pretty soprano named Elizabeth Neville at the Opera House in Melbourne. He decided to remain in Australia with Elizabeth and told Soo of his decision when the company reached Adelaide. Soo's eyes filled with tears as he embraced the young man. "Oh, what will we do without you, laddie?" he murmured. He later presented Aldred with a watch, in gratitude for his service.

Mr. Rayson, one of Robinson's secretaries who traveled from England, also remained behind; he took a job with Rickards's Opera House in Melbourne. Finally, Phil Davies, the quirky draftsman from London, decided not return with the magician. "Soo had considerable domestic trouble," a friend of Davies's later wrote, "so much so that his mechanic, Phil Davies, left him and started building apparatus for magicians." Inevitably, Davies's business decision involved a certain amount of professional treachery—the kind of disloyalty that saddened Rob. After Davies set up shop in Sydney, some of his first projects were building copies of tricks he'd learned from Chung Ling Soo, the Birth of the Pearl and the Crystal Lamp of Enchantment.

—⁓—

Soo, Dot, and the Kametaros returned to England on the RMS *Mora* in September. In October, according to a report in a magician's journal,

Soo was "resting in the metropolis." But there wasn't much time for resting, as the magician was forced to hire a new group of assistants to resume his tour through Great Britain.

On December 17, 1909, Hector Robinson was born to Lou Blatchford. Hector was a cute boy with soft dark eyes and his mother's pretty chestnut hair. Although Rob might have doubted Lou or wondered about their relationship, he now resolved to make the best of the situation.

On January 21, exactly five weeks after Hector was born, both Rob and Lou stepped into the register office at South Hammersmith and recorded the birth. William Ellsworth Robinson, "showman," was the father. Janet Louise Mary Blatchford, "of no occupation," was the mother. On the birth certificate, they gave the child's full name as Hector Robinson Robinson. It was a curious mistake, especially as there was some doubt whether the boy would even be given the name Robinson. Perhaps it was an oversight, a slip of the pen from a nervous father, or a man determined to prove himself a father.

Neil Carlton, the mysterious, avuncular boarder, continued to live with the family at Lonsdale Road. By the beginning of 1910, the Marvelous Chinese Conjurer was back on tour.

Chapter 23

EDINBURGH

After Chung Ling Soo's return to England at the end of 1909, he was engaged on the Gibbons circuit, a collection of music halls throughout the English provinces managed by Sir Walter Gibbons, the former manager of the London Theatre of Varieties. But Soo was surprised by his competition; his long season in Australia had allowed his rivals to dig in their heels. Lafayette was now the star of the Gibbons circuit, and his headline-making show was grandly rolled out to open every new music hall.

The following year, both performers were back on the Stoll tour, playing Britain's finest theaters. "I see Lafayette is at Cardiff last week and I believe tremendous business," Rob wrote to a friend. "Set them crazy. I can't make it out." Music-hall performers found it almost impossible to see other acts unless they happened to be on the same bill for a week; Lafayette and Soo would never be booked together. Like most performers, Rob was both intrigued and bewildered by the reports he received about Lafayette's weird, spectacular production.

In 1906, while he was appearing in New York, Lafayette had added an important new cast member, Lalla Selbini. Lalla was 27 years old, a renowned beauty of the stage, with fair skin, red lips, and curly auburn hair. As a child she had appeared as a contortionist and later she performed acrobatics as she pedaled a bicycle in perfect figure eights across the vaudeville stage—the chief attraction was her skintight leotard, which showed off every curve. She was billed as "The Bathing Belle on the Bicycle." Reportedly her beauty attracted Oscar Hammerstein, the New York impresario; she posed for the murals that decorated his Opera House.

Lalla befriended Lafayette when they worked together. She asked his advice about joining a burlesque company. He invited her to dinner and for a ride in his motorcar. Lalla insisted that the relationship "was platonic," but Lalla's husband, Willie Pantzer, was offended to hear that the magician was spending time with his wife, and angrily ran to the *New York Morning Telegraph*, accusing Lafayette of alienating her affections. Willie Pantzer and his wife had been married for four years, but they did not work together. He had his own act as a head balancer—balancing objects or other people on the top of his head.

The story raged through the newspapers for several days in September of 1906 as Pantzer challenged the magician to fisticuffs. Lafayette boldly accepted, sneering that he hoped Willie was now "balancing his head at a proper angle, [so] the belligerent brain will once more regain its equilibrium."

There never was a duel, just fulsome publicity for all three performers. Articles portrayed Pantzer as proud and muscular, Lalla as beautiful and bewitching, and Lafayette as fearless and manly. All three must have sold tickets. The magician pointed out that Lalla had been supporting herself with her own act; Pantzer could neither provide for her nor give her good career advice. "That is the kind of man he is," Lafayette sniffed. As for Lafayette and the pretty Lalla, "there was no affection between us," Lafayette told the newspapers, "only regard and esteem."

When Pantzer attempted to sue for alienation of affection, the case was quickly dismissed. Lalla went on to tour with Lafayette, becoming an important addition to his company. Besides her bicycle act, she took the role of the beautiful Princess Pari Banu, the captive maiden in The Lion's Bride.

—◊—

From season to season, Lafayette had been tinkering with The Lion's Bride, and finally decided to set it in a mythical Persian harem. Lalla Selbini was a Christian maiden, captured by the evil Pasha and

Lafayette, on horse at left, in The Lion's Bride.

doomed to be his wife. Lafayette played Hasim Ne Barl, the maiden's lover and the Persian envoy. He added one more twist to the plot— an odd bit of female impersonation just before the finale. As the maiden was about to be sacrificed to the lion, Lafayette sneaked into the harem and released her. He then sent the lady away on his horse as he dressed in a gown and veil, taking her place.

When the Pasha's soldiers arrived, the lovely maiden—actually Lafayette in his disguise—was thrown to the lion. The lion paced the cage, reared up, and pounced on the helpless victim. Suddenly, the lion threw back its fur to reveal Lafayette, who stepped out of the cage. To wild applause, the maiden dashed onstage to be reunited with her hero and the curtain fell.

Early in 1909, when Lafayette was working for the Gibbons circuit at the Burnley Palace Hippodrome, there was another unexpected accident with the lion. It was the end of the act and Lafayette had just entered the lion's cage when he noticed that two sliding bars had not dropped into place. Prince, the lion, had realized that he was free. He slid between the bars and padded onto the stage. "The lion's loose," Lafayette whispered to his staff. The fireproof curtain was quickly dropped on the scene as the cast scrambled for the exits and stagehands climbed ladders into the flies of the theater.

The lion snarled and pawed at Lafayette, who was armed with a pistol loaded with one blank shell. The performer circled the stage, shouting commands and beating the lion back into its den; when it was finished, Lafayette had endured scores of small scratches on his thigh and calf. His leg was washed with an antiseptic and bound tightly. He dismissed his company and cancelled the next six weeks of engagements.

—⁓—

Chung Ling Soo decided to stop performing his own big, spectacular, colorful, death-defying illusion. In the spring of 1910, Soo told the press that he would eliminate Defying the Boxers. During a recent performance of the trick, the magician had suffered from another "trifling accident"; the nature of the injury wasn't clear, but it caused him to reconsider the trick. Chung Ling Soo told the press, "Every conjurer who has performed this trick for any length of time has been shot dead." A published account concluded, "We cannot afford to let this clever Chinaman be killed."

Dot was pleased to hear the news. For years, she had wished her husband would eliminate the illusion from the show. Dot told friends that it made her uneasy.

—⁓—

Robinson took enormous pleasure in building his own workshop behind his home on Lonsdale Road. Although he still used Ritherdon's shop in Bolton, the opportunity to have his own fully equipped shop was the fulfillment of a dream, a connection with his days at the Martinka factory in New York. The structure was three stories tall, equipped with a trapdoor so he could test illusions. He installed motorized drills and saws, a four-and-a-half-inch lathe, wood and metal benches, and a wide assortment of hand tools. Shelves held spare parts for his show, boxes of materials that he thought might prove useful, extra illusions that he had purchased, half-finished ideas, and favorite pieces of apparatus that he had picked up over the years—any tricks he liked and wanted to work into his show.

Soo contacted his friend, the magician and engineer Donald Stevenson, urging him to help run the shop. Stevenson worked at Lonsdale Road, sharing the expenses. It was a well-equipped shop for all of his projects. When Soo wanted help with his magic effects, Stevenson billed him for his time.

Soo commonly dashed off notes from his dressing rooms in various theaters, sketching a small device that Stevenson was to make and send to the next city. Sometimes he gave particular instructions. He sent Stevenson meticulous instructions for how to cut and solder small metal "glitters," polished decorations that looked like prisms of glass on stage. "Your humble servant made them about twenty years ago for a set of tables," he wrote to Stevenson. These were the decorations on William Robinson's glass tables that overturned during his hat trick.

Stevenson described Soo as "a quiet, modest, retiring man, never happier than when working away at models with his own hands." Stevenson knew that Soo was on the verge of a brainstorm when he would absentmindedly pose an idea to Stevenson: "I've got a ken o' crazy idea . . . ," he would invariably start, his American drawl coming to the surface.

He was meticulous with all his projects. He used plywood—a new product and considered a luxury—for many of his tricks. When he couldn't find the plywood he needed, he would glue and press layers of veneer, making his own so it was just right. Stevenson always recalled the efficiency of Soo's shop—neat and clean with everything at hand. Soo used glass jars with screw lids to hold small nails and hinges; the lids were screwed to the undersides of his shelves. With one hand, the magician could reach up and—with a half twist—have the jar of parts in his hand.

This perfectionism carried through to the finished product. When he was satisfied with his results, he would gush to Stevenson, "That'll get them guessing, laddie!" His goal was always to mystify not only the public but his professional colleagues as well. But if he was unsatisfied, he would quickly scrap a project, even if he'd spent months on it.

Stevenson had long had an interest in airplanes, and Soo came to share his research and experiments. Together they built a number of model planes. In 1911, a British company approached them about developing and building new models. These were sophisticated designs, built of plywood and made to fold up and transport. One made by Stevenson and Soo was six feet across with a 15-inch propeller, powered by long rubber bands. Soon Lonsdale Road became one of the first model-airplane factories in the country. Soo suggested a number of interesting improvements in his models, such as the use of propellers in the rear of the plane. In a letter to Houdini, who was learning to fly his own airplane on the continent, Soo wrote, "So you are having a go at aeroplanes. Well, perhaps I will surprise you when you get back. This old Chinaman says but little."

The model-airplane business ended in 1914, with the outbreak of the world war; a safety concern led to government controls on model planes.

—⁓—

On March 10, 1911, a girl was born to Louise Blatchford at Lonsdale Road—William and Lou's third child. The new baby should have inspired celebration. Instead the little girl was greeted with doubts and uncertainty. Six weeks after the event, when the birth was registered in London, there was still no name chosen for the child. She was later given the name Mary.

Billy and Bessie Robinson's first child, Elmore, had similarly remained nameless for several weeks in 1885. Since then, the birth of every one of his children forced Rob into a dark, distressing reexamination of his affairs.

Sadly, little Mary's birth hinted that the Robinson family had reached an uneasy truce. For six days a week, Louise was in charge of the family, and Neil Carlton, Lou's friend and the boarder at Lonsdale Road, served as the father figure. The little boys even called him Papa.

Every Sunday, Soo's habit was to return to Lonsdale Road. But now he seemed to spend most of his time at the workshop in the back garden, quietly occupied with new ideas or models. "It was

Will and Lou, with (left to right) Hector,
Mary, and Ellsworth.

extraordinary the amount of time Soo found possible to spend in the
workshop," remembered Donald Stevenson. "When he was performing in the Provinces, he would travel up during Saturday night,
after his show was over, spend Sunday in the workshop and journey
back to the Provinces during Sunday night."

Following Chung Ling Soo's success in Australia, Lafayette was
booked to take his show there the following year; according to the
contract, Lafayette would be guaranteed no quarantine on his dog,
Beauty, and assured of a record profit. He was commonly rumored to
be earning the highest salary in music halls, £1,000 per week ($5,000)
and £40,000 during the previous season. Lafayette's new program was
titled "A Carnival of Conjuring," and his billing proclaimed him
"The Man of Mystery," which had been W. E. Robinson's old title in
the United States.

The Lion's Bride was no longer a standard part of his act; Lafayette reserved it for special matinee shows or extra-long engagements. When he appeared in Edinburgh on April 30, 1911, for a two-week run, the public was delighted to read posters announcing this popular feature. Lafayette was booked at the Empire Palace, Stoll and Matcham's beautiful music hall in Nicolson Square.

But when Lafayette arrived in Edinburgh he was facing a terrifying personal tragedy. Beauty, his beloved gray "gheckhund," was sick. She had been pampered luxuriously for fifteen years, but a lifetime of soft living and rich foods had taken a toll. She had been operated upon several weeks before, when Lafayette appeared at Southsea. Now the performer engaged a surgeon and two nurses to stand by on 24-hour duty at the Caledonian Hotel in Edinburgh. Despite their care, Beauty died of apoplexy, succumbing in her sleep on May 4, 1911.

Lafayette was inconsolable in his grief. In his hotel room, he propped up the dog's body on a silk cushion and surrounded it with flowers. Over the years, his associates had heard Lafayette sadly lament, "If my dog dies, I shall die too within a few days"; now they feared for his state of mind or even his safety. Lafayette always believed the dog brought him luck, and he now explained that his luck had ended. It seemed to be a heartening sign when he insisted on performing every night. Although reduced to tears offstage, he soldiered through his shows, using Mabel, a dalmatian and another of his dogs, for Beauty's various tricks. During the days, he occupied his time by making arrangements for Beauty's burial in Edinburgh.

—m—

Dunbar and Sons, the Edinburgh funeral directors, had difficulty in purchasing land at the local cemeteries, which refused the use of consecrated ground for a dog's burial. Finally, a compromise was reached. Lafayette purchased a pretty plot for Beauty just inside the entrance at Piershill Cemetery, promising that it would also serve as his own final resting place.

Beauty was embalmed and placed in a small oak casket with a

glass lid. She reposed on her right side. Her head rested on a satin pillow, with her engraved silver collar on a separate pillow. Lafayette arranged for the funeral to take place on May 10. Every day he traveled to the undertakers in visitation, mourning his beloved pet.

On May 9, Lafayette was finishing the second show of the evening. Business that week had been good and the auditorium was filled. It was 10:45, and the magician was onstage in the melodramatic extravaganza The Lion's Bride. The scene was reaching a climax; Lafayette had just donned the gown and veil in anticipation of being thrown into the lion's cage.

An Oriental lantern was hanging high over the action; it consisted of seven electric bulbs in a hexagonal lamp decorated with bits of colored gelatin. The lantern sparked and sputtered, bursting into flame. As the audience's attention was drawn up to the lamp, the cable holding it snapped and it suddenly crashed to the floor. The small ball of orange fire tumbled onto the cushions and props that decorated the stage—the carpets, plush drapes, fringe and swags that simulated the gaudy splendor of the Rajah's harem. In a moment, fire surrounded the cast. It curled up the edges of painted canvas as the entire proscenium danced with flames.

The stage manager cut the rope that suspended the metal fire curtain. The curtain quickly rumbled down its track, cutting off the auditorium from the flames on stage. But behind the scenes, a door to the alley had just been opened as the performers rushed outside. The sudden blast of air pushed against the fire curtain like wind against a sail. The runner at the bottom edge of the curtain jammed in its track and the fire curtain stopped moving, just several feet above the stage.

Another blast of air sent sparks and tongues of flame out from under the curtain, singeing members of the orchestra and spectators in the first few rows.

—✺—

Later there was suspicion that the lamp had been made with colored celluloid, which would have been highly flammable. But E. Ward

Russell, a member of Lafayette's company, insisted to authorities that he had used gelatin. He believed that a short in the electric wires had ignited the lamp. One of Lafayette's black assistants, portraying a slave, threw himself onto the flaming lamp in an effort to extinguish it, but the flames had already spread. Lafayette's scenery had not been fireproofed, and the many backdrops of canvas and muslin, filling the stage and dangling overhead on battens, fueled the fire.

The lights backstage flickered and went out, plunging the performers and technicians into darkness. One of the harem girls thought she saw Lafayette in the lion's cage, wearing the lion skin and unaware of the problem. There were shouts of "Run for your lives," and Lalla Selbini circled the stage, which was filled with thick, sooty smoke. She called out, "Are you all right, Laffy?" before she was forced to exit the theater. Witnesses heard the lion roaring in the confusion, and the horse Arizona's hooves stomping as it pulled against its tether.

The pass door on the off-prompt side of the theater—the door to the audience's left side that went backstage—might have served as an exit for some of the cast. But it had been locked. Crew members later claimed that the magician insisted on the door being locked to prevent the public or theater crew from sneaking backstage and studying his secrets. Other reports suggested that the door had been locked to protect the audience from the lion.

Eighteen minutes after the fire started, the theater's fire curtain broke loose and crashed to the stage. As it did, it folded and collapsed through the floor in a dangerous jumble of metal, cables, and burned splinters.

—◊—

The night of the Edinburgh Empire fire, the crowd was fortunate. There were screams and shoves, but in general the audience responded calmly and exited the building efficiently. The flames that lunged from beneath the curtain were confined to the front section of the orchestra, and there were few injuries. The auditorium became dangerously smoky, but the electric lights remained illuminated and exits were obvious. There were almost three thousand people in the audience that evening, but every spectator survived the fire. C. B. Fountaine, the theater manager who had been watching the tragedy from the back of the balcony, was relieved to see that the crowd "behaved magnificently."

There was surprisingly little damage to the auditorium. The walls and drapes had been stained by soot and some of the seats in the front rows burned. But sheet music in the orchestra had remained intact, hardly singed.

Before it collapsed, the fire curtain largely accomplished its job. The heat and flames were confined to the stage, which was completely destroyed by the flames.

Many of the performers escaped, dashing from the dressing rooms into the alley. Lafayette was still in his Persian costume from The Lion's Bride. According to one witness, he remained outside the stage door for several minutes, watching as his cast assembled, taking mental note of who was left inside. But he was distressed when he realized that his animals, Prince the Lion and Arizona, his black stallion, were still trapped on the stage. At about 10:50, a man overheard Lafayette say, "I'll have to go in and get my horse." Then he disappeared into the flames.

—⁂—

The magician's famous mauve limousine waited near the back of the theater. It had arrived at the end of the performance to take Lafayette to the funeral parlor to see Beauty for the last time. Lafayette's German chauffeur was standing at attention, awaiting his next instructions.

In the darkness of the alley, the cast noticed that Lafayette was missing. Just before midnight, two members of the fire brigade pushed their way into the theater and noted a number of bodies. They reached Lafayette's dressing room, but it was empty.

In the following hours, the fire's toll became apparent. Prince, Lafayette's lion, perished. One eyewitness recalled seeing the lion burst out of its burning cage with its mane on fire. Arizona, the horse, was also killed by the flames.

Two victims were the midgets in Lafayette's company. Alice Dale was the little lady in the mechanical teddy bear costume, drawing laughs and applause during her pantomime with Lafayette. Joseph Coats was a young dwarf who was Alice's understudy, and also appeared as part of the Rajah's court. Several of Lafayette's bandsmen and stagehands also lost their lives.

Early the next day—on the morning that had been scheduled for Beauty's burial—Lafayette's charred body was found backstage. He was identified by his costume, the shoes he wore onstage, and the nearby sword that he had brandished during The Lion's Bride. The workmen at Piershill Cemetery had prepared Beauty's grave by eleven o'clock that morning, and were awaiting Lafayette's arrival when they were informed of his death.

—*m*—

The showman's remains were sent to Glasgow for cremation. Walter Maskell, Lafayette's London attorney, immediately wired William Grossman, a New York lawyer and a longtime intimate friend of Lafayette: "The G.L. burned to death. Your presence needed here immediately." Alfred Nisbit, another of Lafayette's attorneys, was concerned when he heard that Lafayette's body was without his finger rings. It seemed odd to Nisbit that the valuable diamond ring and a distinctive heavy gold ring were not located, and he urged authorities to search the theater for the jewels.

On Friday afternoon workmen were still uncovering wreckage in the theater. A total of eight cast members and stagehands had been identified as victims, including Lafayette. But there was still one young man in Lafayette's company who was missing. J. W. Bell went under the professional name of C. E. Richards. He was listed in the program as a trumpet player in Lafayette's band.

Beneath the collapsed fire curtain, in the basement under the stage, investigators uncovered a badly burned body. It was lying on its back with its fists raised, as if to ward off falling debris. The men quickly assumed that they'd found Richards. When they looked closer, they noticed that the body was clothed in the costume of a Persian prince, and had elaborate, diamond-encrusted finger rings. It was The Great Lafayette.

The body was discovered just forty-five minutes after the supposed ashes of Lafayette had returned to Edinburgh.

—⁂—

Around the world, newspapers had reported the strange circumstances of Beauty's death and Lafayette's fate in the fire. But now the story became bewilderingly surreal. The secret for many of Lafayette's illusions was that he used a double. This double didn't need to be a perfect match with the performer—elaborate costumes, headpieces, and beards concealed much of the magician's face during his illusions. But he needed to be of the same size and build, able to duplicate the magician's gait and mannerisms for brief moments during the show. C. E. Richards had been Lafayette's double, but to conceal his role he was listed in the program as a member of the band.

Richards surreptitiously took Lafayette's place so that the transformation illusions could be accomplished. For example, during The Lion's Bride, Lafayette sent Lalla Selbini offstage on his horse, and then donned a gown and veil to take her place. But as he moved to the side of the lion cage, he stepped behind a piece of scenery and was exchanged for Richards, in the same costume. This allowed Lafayette to sneak to the back of the stage and don the lion skin, ready for the climax of the show.

True to his role as Lafayette's double, Richards had been mistakenly identified as Lafayette and cremated in his place. Lafayette's actual remains were hurriedly cremated so that the planned funeral could proceed on Sunday, May 14.

—⁂—

It was by most accounts the strangest funeral ever seen in Edinburgh. It certainly made headlines around the world. It was "a weird spectacle, recalling rather some old pagan rite than anything within the domain of modern experience," wrote one reporter. "It was the greatest free show the Scottish capital has seen in many years," according to another. The crowd lining the route from Dunbar and Sons mortuary to Piershill Cemetery was estimated at two hundred thousand. The *Evening News* commented, "One felt a twinge of regret that Lafayette, a man who lived in an atmosphere of advertisement, was not there to see it."

According to *The Encore*, "It had been resolved that the casket with the remains of the dead should be placed in the same coffin as that of the dog, another of the eccentricities connected with this extraordinary funeral." Following Lafayette's wishes, the funeral director opened the small square coffin that contained Beauty, and carefully placed the square box—Lafayette's ashes—between the dog's paws, "leaving the creature to watch over the remains of its master." Ladies of the company wept uncontrollably. Mabel, the Dalmatian, poked her nose from the window of the limousine until the chauffeur opened the door so she could stand with the other members of the company.

Beauty's coffin was then sealed with its glass and oak lids and placed in the vault. This was carefully closed and locked. When

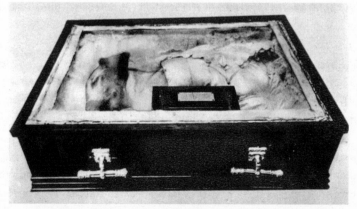

The glass coffin; Lafayette's ashes are between Beauty's paws.

music-hall artists and Lafayette's company were admitted to the grave, minutes later, they saw only the slate covering the coffin.

—⚬—

Lalla Selbini had sent a floral spray in the shape of a theater arch, with curtains of red roses drawn back to show a white curtain of lilies of the valley. Across the lilies were the words, "The Last Act."

Harry Houdini was unable to attend the funeral, but he sent a spectacular floral tribute, a cushion of white flowers with a dog's head sculpted in forget-me-nots. The attached card read, "To the memory of my friend, The Great Lafayette, from his friend who gave him his best friend, Beauty."

Lafayette's sad fate had an irresistible appeal to Houdini, combining his fascinations for the morbid, the maudlin, and cold, hard publicity. "I envy him," Houdini said of Lafayette. "He fooled them in life and he fooled them in death."

—⚬—

Chung Ling Soo was also busy touring, about to begin a week of performances in Hull. But like many of his fellow showmen, he had been glued to the newspapers, following the strange news from Edinburgh. He sent a floral wreath to Piershill Cemetery with his sincere condolences.

Soo remembered Lafayette as the ambitious young German showman in New York. He had been Billy Robinson's competition as they both scrambled to put the latest Chinese tricks into their acts. Both young men proved to be instinctive showmen and skillful innovators. But Soo never felt he really knew Lafayette.

Like Billy Robinson, Siegmund Neuburger owed his success to becoming someone else—a character that was bigger than life and guaranteed to intrigue an audience. On stage, they had both been the "Man of Mystery." Offstage, they had perfected their daily mysteries to a fine art.

After the Edinburgh fire, Scottish officials reacted by tightening the fire regulations in each theater. Chung Ling Soo's staff noticed the difference. If the stagehand were smoking onstage, Scottish firemen would knock the cigarette out of his mouth, and then toss the man into the alley. Although all of Soo's scenery had been fireproofed when it was manufactured, when the show played in Scotland, firemen required Chung Ling Soo's staff to reapply the fireproof chemicals. On a Tuesday morning a fireman arrived at the theater to supervise the operation. Each painted backdrop was lowered and stretched flat on the stage, and then soaked and scrubbed with a special liquid. The chemical saturated the backdrops and made the dyes run together, ruining much of the expensive scenery. But the magician couldn't object to the procedure, or the sudden interest in theater safety.

Chapter 24

ASLEEP IN THE AIR

Lafayette's lawyers, Grossman, Maskell, and Nisbit, were puzzled by the magician's estate. Lafayette had once been billed as the "Millionaire Conjurer," but when he died there was surprisingly little money, less than £2,300 ($11,500). J. C. Matthews, a former manager of Lafayette, couldn't explain the discrepancy. Lafayette was actually "not a great spender, unless entertaining," Matthews told the *New York Morning Telegraph*. Offstage, the magician had few pretensions, often wearing inexpensive clothes. He drank moderately, but he occasionally "took risks at cards."

Adding to the confusion, there was no will. According to one report, Lafayette had torn up his will just days before his death, when Beauty died. Although Lafayette had not been on good terms with his brother, Alfred Neuburger was his only heir. But Alfred refused to pay for the elaborate funerals of Lafayette, Beauty, and Richards, the double. In 1913, he was sued in court by the undertakers and forced to pay the costs of £411 (over $2,000). Lalla Selbini claimed to have inherited Lafayette's properties. More than likely, she made an arrangement with Alfred Neuburger to continue performing the show. She salvaged any remaining costumes and props, and rebuilt others. Traveling with 30 performers, she presented the Travesty Band and The Lion's Bride, touring through Britain and America.

Selbini was attractive, talented, and diligent. She worked hard on stage, but the show now seemed to be a collection of confusing, hollow spectacles. In fact, it became apparent to audiences that it had never been much of a show. "Selbini tried to make a go of it," wrote the magician Guy Jarrett, "but it didn't go at all. The vehicle, the material wasn't there. The show had been The Great Laf himself, mostly ballyhoo."

—⁓—

Chung Ling Soo's latest illusion was titled A Dream of Wealth. It was a spectacular, complicated effect. Ritherdon had started work on it before Soo left for Australia, working for well over a year before Soo was satisfied with the results.

The curtain opened on a small stand holding a spirit lamp. Above the lamp was a pretty casket, about the size of a metal cash box.

Soo picked up a pitcher of water and poured it inside the casket, filling it nearly to the brim. He then slammed the lid of the box and warmed the contents over the lamp.

The audience was intrigued by this odd experiment. Soo stopped to peer inside the casket several times, looking up at the audience with a grin.

Moments later he decided that he was ready to reveal the surprise. When the casket was tipped over, the water had disappeared. In its place, the magician discovered a cascade of bright gold coins. Soo spilled the coins onto a tray, but held one up to his eye, examining it as a jeweler looks over a fine gem. He winked at the audience.

Poking his fingertip back into the casket, he was surprised to find a paper note. He turned it over in his hands. It was a white five-pound note—a rectangle of white tissue printed with copperplate script. When he reached back into the casket, he discovered a flurry of white five-pound notes, gushing from the casket and tumbling onto the stage floor.

Soo and his assistants greedily scooped them up, attempting to catch them. Two boys entered with low tables. The tabletops were surrounded with wire mesh, forming shallow boxes to contain the bills. But the notes seemed to multiply, filling the tables with small mountains of white paper. The notes fluttered off the stage like butterflies, falling into the orchestra pit and wafting into the first few rows: the audience was surprised to discover that they were clever

A contemporary sketch of Soo and The
Dream of Wealth.

counterfeits, with the magician's picture in place of the great seal of
the Bank of England.

As Soo gathered a bundle of white notes in his hand, they were
suddenly transformed. They seemed to swell and grow, morphing
into a gigantic rectangle of white silk, 25 feet across. It was decorated as a one-thousand-pound note. Fine cords quickly pulled up the
top corners so that the note was suspended over the magician's head.
He gazed up at it longingly, licking his lips with cartoon glee as the
audience burst into applause.

But that was just the first surprise. Soo picked up a pistol and fired
a blank shot into the air. The oversized silk note suddenly collapsed.
It seemed to be sucked into a massive gold metal coin that appeared
magically, hanging over the stage. As the corners of the white silk
disappeared inside the coin—invariably the audience gasped to see it
being pulled in this way—Soo fired a second shot. The center of the
twinkling, seven-foot coin opened like an iris, transforming it into a
golden star. At the same time, gold coins began cascading down from
the points of the star. The coins clattered onto the stage, bounced
into the audience, and flickered in the stage light. Now the star
opened a second time, revealing a Chinese goddess of good fortune.

It was Suee Seen, in a sparkling silk robe. She poured coins from a cornucopia in her outstretched hands. The coins tumbled out over the stage—literally a sparkling dream of wealth—as Soo stepped forward to take his bow.

The Dream of Wealth was not really a trick, but an act in itself, teasing the audience with a small mystery before the pace quickened and the magic grew into a dazzling full-stage spectacle.

It was a lot of trouble. Soo's assistants spent hours each week, in the darkness backstage, folding paper banknotes and stacking coins. The large golden coin that held Suee Seen was one of Ritherdon's mechanical marvels, filled with levers, pull cords, and concealed hinges. It took four of Soo's men to lift it and hang it over the stage when the show was set up at the beginning of the week. Releasing the giant note and then drawing it quickly into the coin required an intricate bit of timing; it was quickly wound onto a winch by an assistant high up in the grid.

Once she was concealed inside the giant coin, Dot's job was the usual mix of hazards. She was quickly swung out over the stage. As she caught her balance, she operated the various tricks—special cylinders that dropped the stream of coins, or levers that opened the triangular petals of the gold star. At the finale, as she was revealed to the audience, her job was to smile sweetly, looking perfectly relaxed.

It wasn't perfect. The golden coin started suspended from a track at the side of the stage. As the large silk bank note was pulled into the air, the coin was rapidly pulled in place. A strip of scenery, at the side of the stage, camouflaged its movement as it crossed behind the bank note. But on wide stages the audience seated at the side could see it moving. Percy Naldrett, a London magic manufacturer, pointed this out to Soo one day. Soo put his arm around Naldrett. "I know," he said. "It's not too good. It's the broad effect that matters, but I will be perfect if I possibly can. Tell me how to overcome it, and I am your friend for life."

Like many of Soo's best ideas, The Dream of Wealth was based on old tricks. The streams of coins were a variation on the old money-catching trick Robinson had performed as a boy. The thousands of white banknotes was a new version of deKolta's old trick of producing tissue flowers from a cone. Houdini was jealous of the illusion, later writing that his friend's new trick was "in my estimation, the greatest money producing mystery in the world."

—⁓—

Robinson developed a special matinee show, two full hours of magic, that he could present during his week-long music hall engagements. These Saturday matinees were appealing to the theater managers. They were advertised as a special feature and brought in families and children—audiences that might not ordinarily come to the music hall. Because Soo presented the entire show himself, it meant that the managers didn't need to negotiate with other variety acts for a matinee that week.

But the Chung Ling Soo matinees were much more than a commercial enterprise. They were the manifestation of Rob's dream to organize his own show—his version of Kellar's and Herrmann's productions. "The lengthy program performed entirely by himself and assistants demands more than an ordinary repertoire," reported one magazine. "There is more real magic in this single entertainment (worked entirely in silence on Chung Ling Soo's part) than in any dozen average programs now before the public."

Without the luxury of speaking, Chung Ling Soo's pantomime presentations required special acting skills so his audience could follow every step of the magic. His silence also meant that he could not indulge in any time-consuming banter with the audience. Because of this, the shows were packed with one trick after another to fill the two hours. Programs list at least forty separate tricks that he performed. The first half usually consisted of many small tricks, including favorites that Soo had performed when he was back in New York working as Robinson. For example, he performed the Mesmerized Cards, his version of the Rising Card Trick. Escape of a Penny was a borrowed coin appearing in the ball of yarn. The Surprise Omelet was the dove produced from a chafing dish. With a Piece of Paper was Soo's name for the torn and restored strip of tissue.

Other small tricks were some of his favorites that had been cycled in and out of his music-hall performances. Demon Smoke was a glass vase that filled with smoke as Soo puffed on a cigarette. How to Make Coffee was the coffee-vase trick—hot drinks made from dry beans. Flying Handkerchiefs was the silk square that disappeared on one side of the stage and appeared tied between two other handkerchiefs. The Unlucky Finger Rings consisted of borrowed finger rings fired into nested boxes—this was the trick with the special pistol, like the one Kellar had once used.

The second act consisted of larger tricks—like the Linking Rings or Kametaro's Sword Walk up a ladder of blades—mixed with a number of favorites from his evening show. Soo would often finish the matinee with the Crystal Lamp of Enchantment and the Mystic Cauldron.

Soo was often at his most relaxed when he was performing these long concerts of magic, reveling in the opportunity to present his favorite tricks. Sometimes, when Chung Ling Soo was working with members of the audience on stage, he whispered instructions to them. This could lead to some unexpected surprises for the volunteers.

When he was performing in Hull, a boy named Reg Pocklington stepped onstage to help with a trick. Soo was producing eggs from a hat and handing them to the boy. The magician noticed the boy's knowing glances, so he whispered, "Do you know how it's done?" Reg quickly responded, proudly, "I'm also a conjurer!" "Splendid," Soo replied.

Young Reg took his seat, and at the end of the show, as he reached into his pocket for his handkerchief, he discovered a hard-boiled egg that had been rubberstamped, "Compliments of Chung Ling Soo." He was completely bewildered by how Soo had sneaked the egg into his pocket; it impressed him more than any of the tricks he'd seen that day.

Rob loved the matinees. The assistants hated them. The show took hours of numbing preparation. Handkerchiefs were folded, cards were stacked, coins were counted, ribbons were rolled. During the show, dozens of tiny gifts worked their way into the audience; these had to be purchased before the show, tied with ribbons or special tags, and hidden in the various props. He gave away boxes of chocolates, signed photographs, oranges, flowers, toys, and a loaf of bread.

Because the magician insisted on secrecy backstage, he would not allow his assistants to prepare the apparatus in the wings or set the props on tables behind the curtains, where the stage crew could examine them. All of the small tricks were arranged in dressing rooms upstairs. Assistants were required to bring them down in time for their entrance onstage, and then return them to the dressing room again. Because of the number of tricks and the pace of the show, this meant a continual procession up and down the stairs.

For decades, Robinson had been successful in keeping secrets from the stagehands. But when he encountered a dangerously dishonest assistant, the Marvelous Chinese Conjurer was devastated.

—m—

In 1910, with three of his best men remaining in Australia, Soo had been anxious to find reliable assistants to help with his show. In London he met a man named Watson who seemed wonderfully qualified. He had just finished working with Charles Carter, an American magician, during his world tour. Carter carried tons of elaborate apparatus and performed many specialties copied from Harry Kellar. After his work with Carter, Watson was the assistant to Charles Aldrich, another American vaudevillian who had been successful in British music halls. Aldrich's specialties were magic, juggling, and quick change. His Protean Act consisted of a series of astonishing changes of costume—each executed in mere seconds.

When Watson left Aldrich, Will Goldston, London's leading magic dealer, employed him briefly to manufacture tricks and provide ideas for new products.

Goldston is a puzzling figure in the world of Edwardian magicians. He was born in Liverpool in 1877, the son of Maurice Goldstone, a Polish tailor. In 1905, when he was 27, he moved to London to operate the Theatrical and Entertainments department—

including costumes and conjuring tricks—at A. W. Gamage's department store in Holborn.

Chung Ling Soo was an early supporter of Goldston. According to one friend, Soo deliberately went to Gamage's one day, buying dozens of tricks that were useless to him—he later gave them away to schoolboys and amateurs—so that the new manager, Goldston, could start his business with a full cash register.

Goldston made his living by selling tricks and publishing books and magazines that exposed the most popular tricks—often the exclusive tricks featured by his professional clients. Will Goldston was particularly cold-blooded about rushing these secrets into print, and his professional colleagues treated him cautiously. Houdini considered Goldston a friend but had been often stung by his articles and books. Even Goldston's compliments could conceal a strange, sharp edge. In a Goldston publication, *The Magician Annual* for 1909–1910, there was a cartoon titled "New Lamps for Old." It showed Chung Ling Soo, his Oriental robes worn over an assortment of old clothes. The shadow cast by the magician was that of a tattered ragman, struggling with a bundle on his back. The shadow was labeled "Old Tricks."

Professionals had often laughed over Soo's fondness for old tricks, but this wasn't a flattering portrait of the profession's great star. In retrospect it seems that magicians often befriended Goldston because they were afraid of him—like offering food to a wild wolf so he wouldn't bite. If Goldston didn't like someone, he could inflict a great deal of damage.

When Soo hired Watson to work as an assistant in his show, he should have checked the man's references with Carter, Aldrich, or Goldston. Instead, Soo was anxious to employ him because Watson had promised Soo a precious secret. The offer was a nefarious bit of larceny, an illusion purloined from another man's show. Despite Chung Ling Soo's high-flown pronouncements about originality, he couldn't resist the temptation.

The Kellar Levitation was the crowning achievement of Harry Kellar's long career. It was a beautiful illusion. The lady, introduced as the Princess Karnac, reclined on a low couch in the middle of a brightly lit stage. As she was lying horizontally, she slowly ascended. Kellar circled the floating lady, making graceful, magical gestures with his hands. When she was suspended about six feet in the air, the couch was removed and Kellar passed a solid metal hoop around the lady—twice. The hoop was then examined by members of the audience. The lady descended to the couch and the magician took his bow.

When Kellar introduced the trick in 1904, it stunned the critics and his fellow American magicians. It seemed as if the wizened wizard had finally achieved the goal of a perfect mystery. Kellar introduced it with a convincing tale about his travels to India—how he tracked down a native fakir and purchased the precious secret on the banks of the Ganges.

But a few magicians, who had been to London, knew that it

A poster advertising Kellar's new levitation illusion.

looked familiar. John Nevil Maskelyne, the London magician, had perfected the invention in 1900, and produced it at Egyptian Hall, his small theater in Piccadilly. Kellar had arrived in London and tried to buy the illusion for his shows just after the premiere in 1900. Maskelyne wouldn't sell. So Kellar resorted to a time-honored technique. He found a spy.

Paul Valadon was a German magician and sleight-of-hand artist employed at Maskelyne's Egyptian Hall. Kellar hired Valadon to star in his American tours, and hinted to Valadon that he would make him his successor when Kellar retired several years later.

In return, Valadon supplied a drawing.

Valadon revealed that the basic principle of Maskelyne's levitation was based on deKolta's Cocoon, using dozens of fine wires and a complicated system of offstage counterweights. Under careful lighting, the wires were invisible to the audience.

Kellar took Valadon's sketches to Mr. Todd of the Otis Elevator Company in Yonkers, New York, developing apparatus that was suitable for Kellar's touring show.

Unfortunately, the Kellar-Valadon partnership was not as successful as the trick. Valadon toured with Kellar for three seasons, presenting his own segments in the show and supplying Kellar with additional ideas purloined from England. But Valadon and his wife didn't get along with Mr. and Mrs. Kellar—they were invariably trapped between Kellar's explosive temper and Eva's simmering arguments. It was the same dance through the minefields that Rob and Dot had faced twenty years earlier.

In 1907, Valadon left the Kellar show and Kellar surprised his associates by naming a new successor: Howard Thurston.

Since his success in London, the young card magician had built up an impressive act and toured the world with his illusions. When he heard that Kellar was planning on retiring, Thurston impulsively contacted the old magician, making an offer to buy his show. After Valadon left the show, Kellar agreed that Thurston would prove to be a worthy successor. Their contract called for Thurston to purchase the equipment and to take over Kellar's routes and advertising.

Most of all, he purchased the right to be named America's leading magician, and received Kellar's endorsement. They toured together for one season before Kellar retired in 1908 and moved to Los Angeles. Thurston made an initial payment for the show and paid a royalty to Kellar for several seasons.

In Thurston's hands, the Levitation of Princess Karnac became a masterpiece. The beautiful trick was perfectly suited to Thurston's lyrical baritone. During his introduction, when he told the audience that they were about to witness a ceremony from the Temples of Love in India, the audience watched breathless in anticipation. As the princess rose into the air, she was seemingly held aloft by Thurston's beautiful oratory. "By the power of my right hand I command you to rest and sleep. Rest, I say. Round your form I cast the mystic spell. Surakabaja. Surakabaja. Rise, rise, Fernanda."

By 1908, the famous Kellar Levitation had become a bit of pirate's plunder. The secret of the ingenious trick was voraciously sought by a number of leading magicians. They knew the backstage story of how Kellar had acquired the trick, and this naturally inspired further espionage, scheming, and thievery. Fritz and Carl Bucha, two of Kellar's assistants, were hired away by Charles Carter, another American magician. The Buchas brought the secret of the illusion to Carter, who had it duplicated in New York for his own show. Carter also hired Watson as an assistant.

Carter took the levitation illusion on a world tour, ending in Great Britain in 1910. When performed it in Manchester, one reviewer, who had seen Maskelyne's original levitation, praised Carter's, insisting, "It is magnificent—it is perfect."

During his many months with Carter, Watson took surreptitious notes on his boss's illusions. When he left the show in Great Britain, he had a very good drawing of the metal cradle, the wires, and the rollers responsible for the levitation.

Soo was interested. He had never witnessed Kellar's levitation—when he last saw Kellar's show in 1903, the trick was still being developed—but he had heard many accounts of it and he knew that it had been featured by a number of important American magicians.

Once when he met with Kellar in London, he offered to purchase it. Kellar said that he wouldn't sell it at any price. Kellar, in turn, offered $500 for Soo's Crystal Lantern illusion, but Soo refused, as he was then considering touring in America and didn't want the effect seen there.

Most of all, Kellar's wonderful levitation fascinated Soo as an invention and a piece of machinery. Many years earlier, he had experimented with steel wires when he built deKolta's Cocoon illusion, and he was anxious to have the latest developments.

But, greedy for the secret, Soo overlooked Watson's treachery, hiring him to assist in his own show. Soo had a copy of the Kellar Levitation built, and he put it into his show under the attractive title Asleep in the Air.

Because it was a complicated trick to set up, Soo only used it for several seasons. He later substituted a different device for the levitation, invented by his friend Servais LeRoy. But magicians fondly recalled the wonderful effect he achieved as tiny Suee Seen floated in the middle of the stage. Chung Ling Soo opened an oriental silk fan and gently fanned her body, as if the tiniest drafts of air were holding her in space. Circling her from side to side, twisting and undulating the fan to and fro, Soo's delicate gestures added to the magic.

—m—

Soo heard that Watson was untrustworthy. Houdini had worked with Carter in Australia the previous season, and Houdini warned Soo about the assistant.

Next, Soo heard from Will Goldston. Shortly after Goldston hired Watson, a quick-change artist and juggler named Charles Aldrich told Goldston that the assistant had stolen Aldrich's secrets during the time they had worked together.

But despite the warning, Goldston kept Watson on staff, and even published some of these purloined secrets in his magazine. It was only later—Goldston reported to Soo—that he found Watson to be dishonest and dismissed him.

Moving from magician to magician, the backstage thievery and the exchange of secrets must have reminded Rob of his early years with Kellar and Herrmann. He knew just how much dangerous and valuable information an ambitious, duplicitous assistant could acquire. He had been such an assistant himself.

"You were the first to warn me of him," Soo wrote to Houdini. "Unfortunately, I already had him in my employ and could only wait for an excuse to discharge him." By then it was too late.

Soo smelled a rat. He realized that there was something strange about Goldston's story—how he had continued to employ Watson, and even published the secrets Watson supplied. Soo went to Gamage's and asked for a private meeting in Goldston's office.

Chung Ling Soo told Goldston that he had been forced to fire Watson, and he was now concerned that Watson might have stolen some of his latest plans. If Watson came to Goldston with any new idea to sell him for his books, he asked Goldston not to take them. They would be stolen goods.

Goldston took the advice soberly and offered his hand, "as a man and a Mason." Soo was aware of the Masonic grip during their hand-shake—both Goldston and Soo had been initiated as Masons and this was a guarantee of Goldston's good intentions.

Soo returned the favor by supplying several small tricks for Goldston's publications. He even offered to author a book on Chinese magic, to be published by Goldston. Soo's *Chinese Magic* book was advertised "in preparation" in 1911. He was attempting to feed the wolf.

—⁂—

Chung Ling Soo had been badly deceived by the magic dealer. Will Goldston's business was not keeping secrets, but selling secrets. And Goldston realized any secrets that caused so much concern from Chung Ling Soo must be especially interesting.

Throughout 1911 and 1912, Goldston advertised an ostentatious, leather-bound book titled *Exclusive Magical Secrets*. The book's publication was imminent, and the publisher offered it on a subscription basis. Goldston promised his readers important, innovative secrets from magic's most important artists. The cost was 25 shillings ($6.25), an astonishing price for a magic book. The binding was made with a lock on its outer edge, to seal the covers. Presumably this implied the priceless value of its contents.

When Soo saw his friend Goldston's new book, his blood boiled.

The two small tricks he offered had been included—a trick with a bowl of rice and a trick with a stick of hard candy—and grandly credited, "Invented by Chung Ling Soo."

There were separate chapters on "Quick Changes" and "Juggling," filled with Charles Aldrich's secrets, not credited and, presumably, without Aldrich's permission.

Under the chapters "Chinese Magic" and "Stage Illusions," Goldston had included full descriptions of three of Soo's most popular effects, the production of silk handkerchiefs and toys from an empty drum, The Mystic Cauldron, and The Living Target—the rope that was shot through Suee Seen.

There were also four effects that Soo had been secretly planning. They were taken from preliminary sketches and prototypes in Soo's shop. There was no credit given in Goldston's book, but Soo knew how he had acquired the ideas. Watson had seen the illusions and discussed them with Chung Ling Soo while he was employed as an assistant.

If Chung Ling Soo needed any further proof, *Exclusive Magical Secrets* also contained a full diagram of Kellar's Levitation—the same information Soo had acquired from Watson.

—⬥—

"Goldston is a born crook," Soo wrote to Houdini. "More so than Watson, as he is the one that entices men like Watson on." Of course, Soo was ignoring the fact that he had also enticed Watson with the promise of a good job. Now he wanted vengeance. "I have asked Goldston to correct this injustice to me and he says he has done me no injury either knowingly or unknowingly. So I am going to get to the bottom of it, not with the intention of dragging your name in."

The problem for Soo was his friend Houdini's relationship with Goldston. In the past, when he was editing his own magazine, Houdini had gleefully pointed out Goldston's indiscretions, writing, "G—, the errand boy clerk, posing as editor. Why a legitimate firm [Gamage's] should employ a man of this caliber to further their interests is hard to surmise." But Goldston and Houdini had since come to an understanding. Houdini was the president of The Magician's Club, the organization Goldston had founded. *Exclusive Magical Secrets* included a chapter of Harry Houdini's tricks, all sanctioned by Houdini. And the book was dedicated to Harry Houdini with effusive praise for his skills "as a performer and as a writer," offering glowing tribute to his friendship, his counsel, and his honor "as a great artiste and a great man." It was the sort of sugary praise lapped up by Houdini, and a cagey move by Goldston to secure his support.

"Don't say I brought your name in willingly," Soo now begged Houdini. "I hate to do it, but I am going to get justice. I shall show up his whole past errors and, of course, show all the performers he has so daringly betrayed by exposing their tricks."

—⁓—

By the beginning of 1913, Robinson's temper had cooled. He wrote to Houdini, "I am not a man that holds any malice. I have done my best with all my friends to respect and protect any and all of their interests, and would not go out of my way to injure Goldston. All I wish from him is a letter of regret and apology, and a written understanding not to repeat the injury in the future."

Another letter was sent to Goldston. "As requested by you during our last interview, I am putting in writing what I wish you to do," Soo wrote. "I am not trying to create any trouble for you. I am simply trying to protect my interest."

In Goldston's magazine, *The Magician Monthly*, he published the apology.

Chung Ling Soo, like all great magicians of the day, is a subscriber of *Exclusive Magical Secrets*. But unlike these others, he has a grievance in respect of the book. He states that some magical effects invented by himself have been explained in it without his permission. Accepting his statement, I feel that a public expression of regret on my part is due him, and I offer it in the form of this note.

Much of the material included in *Exclusive Magical Secrets* was the result of my own thought and work; some of it was generously given to me by Harry Houdini and other notable inventors; the rest I acquired by purchase. The magical effects to which Chung Ling Soo refers would seem to belong to the last category. They were brought to me by an apparently bona fide vendor and purchased by me as being worthy of a place in *Exclusive Magical Secrets*.

I am advised that in English law there is no copyright in magical effects. But, as a matter of honor among magicians, even if not a matter of law, I think there should be such copyright. Accordingly, I am very sorry that any magical effects invented by Chung Ling Soo should have been published in *Exclusive Magical Secrets* without his consent, and I trust that he will accept this expression of regret in the spirit in which it is offered.

The spirit of that apology was a colossal shrug. It was a fitting gesture from a careless scoundrel. Chung Ling Soo was finished with Goldston. He scrapped his plans for the exposed illusions and cancelled the book on Chinese magic.

But Will Goldston—always in search of new secrets—wasn't finished with Chung Ling Soo.

Chapter 25

THE EXPANDING DIE

A t the same time that Soo's disagreements with Will Goldston were surfacing, the Robinson household faced a sad loss. On November 16, 1912, while he was living at 50 Lonsdale Road, Neil Carlton died of cancer of the esophagus. Carlton was 58 years old.

Just six years earlier he'd been listed as a pauper, but he had somehow amassed a small fortune while living with the Robinson family. His estate was valued at over £5,600 ($28,000). In his will, he made provisions for Louise Blatchford ($500) and her three children ($1,500 each). There was neither money nor recognition for William Robinson.

Rob dutifully arranged a plot and a memorial stone at a nearby cemetery in East Sheen. The curbstone was engraved "Private Graves of Wm. E. Robinson." The plot was also large enough to accommodate Rob, Lou, and the three children.

The inscription on the stone hinted at the confusing role of Neil Carlton within the family. Along with Carlton's name and death date, the pedestal was engraved with an unexpected word in parentheses, the children's nickname for their boarder: "Sacred to the memory of our dear (papa)."

Goldston's public apology for explaining Chung Ling Soo's tricks in his book was followed by his very private apology to the magician.

The February 1911 issue of *The Magician Monthly*, Goldston's magazine, had included an article written by Professor Hoffmann.

Hoffmann was revered as magic's great literary figure; he was the author of *Modern Magic*, the book that had become the textbook for Billy Robinson and many others in the 1870s.

Hoffmann's article in *The Magician Monthly* was titled "A Magician's Dream." It was a intended as a harmless bit of fiction; his dream involved a humorous series of fantasies involving professional magicians. At one point in his dream, Hoffmann and an old wizard happened to meet a tall Chinese magician.

> "Chung Ling!" I exclaimed. "Soo it is!" said the elderly magician. Just then, Chung caught sight of Aga [a pretty young lady] who floated coquettishly towards him. "Yum, yum!" he remarked with a seraphic smile, at the same time tickling her under the chin with the tip of his fan. Just at that moment, however, a natty little Chinese lady appeared upon the scene. "Yum, yum, indeed; I'll yum yum you," she said, pulling a long pin out of her back hair. "Sue Seen!" cried Chung.

Hoffmann described the Chinese magician disappearing out of sight, with "Sue Seen" in hot pursuit. The section concluded, "What happened after that I can't say, but I was glad I was not Chung Ling Soo."

After the article was published, other magicians informed Hoffmann that his invented comedy was a little too true to be funny. Hoffmann wrote to Goldston, the magazine's editor, in December 1912.

> I am very sorry to hear, from a private source, that there is trouble in the Chung Ling Soo household. I need hardly say that, if I had known this, nothing would have induced me to write as I did about him. Please let him know this, if you have any opportunity of doing so. I take it for granted that you were not aware of it, or you would not have allowed me to make such a painful mistake.

Goldston couldn't have intended any offense with Hoffmann's article. But he'd been careless. Goldston, like every other professional magician in London, knew about Soo's mistress and his three children in Barnes.

—〰—

In 1913, a young man named Percy Mayhew became a member of the Chung Ling Soo cast. Mayhew had worked with other magicians and was an experienced stage electrician. On the afternoon Mayhew joined the show, Frank Kametaro quickly took him through the elements of that evening's performance, explaining his duties for each illusion. In the Orange Tree Trick, it was Mayhew's job to walk on stage with two real oranges palmed in his hand. Chung Ling Soo would reach for them, Kametaro told him. His job was to hand them to the magician.

Mayhew had never met Soo until that evening, onstage, during the performance. The magician had been spending the day at his workshop and flew through the stage door just minutes before the first show of the evening. His dresser quickly helped him into his costume as his props were being set onstage.

During the Orange Tree Trick, Mayhew did as he'd been told. He palmed the oranges and walked on from the wings. Because he was walking on from the prompt side—the audience's right, as they were looking at the stage—Mayhew's left side was toward the audience. To conceal the oranges, he held them in his right hand, hoping his body would cover them.

When he reached the tree, Soo was muttering under his breath. "Well, laddie, where are you, where are you?" Mayhew reached up to surreptitiously hand the magician the oranges, but their hands bumped uncomfortably and Percy realized he'd used the wrong hand. He awkwardly tried to shift the oranges into his left hand, and ended up dropping them onto the stage—by now the audience saw the entire operation. Soo exploded with whispered expletives as Percy picked up the oranges, put them in his left hand, and handed them to Soo. "See me in the dressing room afterwards, laddie," Soo snarled under his breath.

Between shows, Percy opened the dressing room door and found Rob, without his Chinese wig. His head was shaved, except for some tufts of hair on the side of his head. He was looking down, writing with

William Robinson at a desk backstage.

a quill pen. Percy quickly closed the door. He'd actually been convinced that his new boss was "half-caste Chinese," and was confused
by the bald man sitting at the desk. He wandered down the hall, and
finally realized his mistake, returning to Soo's dressing room. As he
opened the door, Rob was laughing.

"Haven't you been in here before?" he asked the young man.
Percy explained that he thought he had walked into the wrong room.

"Now, laddie, about those oranges. Who told you to come on that
way?" Soo continued. Mayhew explained that Frank Kametaro had
showed him how to do the trick. "No," he said, "those oranges have to
be in your left hand." Percy had made an amateur's mistake, trying to
keep the oranges away from the audience. He should have concealed
them by using the back of his hand. Soo's temper cooled and he laughed
about the boy's error, showing Mayhew how to perform the maneuver.

Percy Mayhew stayed with Soo's show for several seasons and was
responsible for various duties—packing the show, helping to move it,
setting it up in the new theater, preparing the small props for hours
before every performance, and appearing onstage as an assistant.

Sometimes, when the show played the Palladium in London, there were three shows a day, and Percy would arrive at the theater early in the morning to begin his preparations—rolling the ribbons, folding the thousands of banknotes, tying the oranges with their little tags, folding silk handkerchiefs. Percy was paid "35 bob" a week for his services ($7.50).

—๛—

Like Percy, there were many who were surprised by their first encounter with the Marvelous Chinese Conjurer. Soo was temperamental backstage. He spoke very little to his assistants, but cursed loudly when anything went wrong. During an engagement in a seaside music hall, Soo spent the afternoon in the empty theater rehearsing a new trick. The magician was secretive about all such rehearsals, but he was unaware that a fireman from the theater had wandered into the dark auditorium and was quietly watching from the back of the stalls. Soo was smiling innocently until the trick misfired. Then he exploded with his favorite "Yankee" expressions, "God damned cock sucking son of a bitch!" He stomped across the stage in his Chinese robes. Later the fireman found Soo's assistants. "I thought you buggers were Chinese!" he grinned. "Sure, we're Chinese," the assistants responded. "Bugger the Chinese. Your guv'nor isn't talking Chinese!"

During the weeks when Lou and the children visited the show, Soo became even more irritable.

For years, Dot had busied herself with the show. Every Saturday night, she was in charge of arranging the show's transportation to the next city. She ensured that everything was properly packed, arranged with the railway men, and arranged the company's train schedule. Mrs. Soo—as the members of the company called her—was the boss during the weekend.

After the last show on Saturday night, Soo would quickly run to a train and return to Barnes. He spent the weekends with his mistress, Mrs. Robinson—as Lou was known by members of the company.

On Monday, Dot and Kametaro supervised the Chung Ling Soo

company, twenty-five people, as they set up the show in the new theater. Soo would arrive in the evening, just before the first show. He'd dash from the train station to the theater, change his clothes, apply his makeup, and step onstage for the first show of the week.

Occasionally he was late, delayed by bad weather. "Very often, we would be lined up at the stage door to the dressing room, and strip his clothes off as he came in, otherwise he would not have been ready for the show," Percy remembered.

During the week, Soo lived at a hotel. Dot lived in a theatrical boarding house with Frank and Mabel Kametaro and their daughter Nina. Dot's affections were lavished on a ratty blond Pekinese dog that spent the shows on a cushion in her dressing room and was carried in and out of the theater in the crook of her arm. Dot received her weekly salary from Soo in a thick bundle of folded notes, tied with string—£25 plus expenses.

Lou—Mrs. Robinson—was seldom seen. She spent her time in Barnes with the children. But occasionally, at a resort town like Southsea, Lou would arrive with the children in tow, to spend the week and see the performances. During those weeks, Dot was livid. She was still jealous of her husband. She had learned to ignore Lou but was angered when she was forced to see her with Will.

Lou and the children watched the show from a box. If she dared to send a note backstage to her husband—handing it through the metal pass door at side of the stage—Dot tried to intercept it, tearing up the message before it reached Soo.

—⁂—

During the weeks when Lou was visiting, Robinson used his work as the excuse to avoid his personal problems. He managed to occupy his time, all day and every day, in the theater, supervising repairs on all the equipment.

His assistants learned to dread those weeks. They were required to come to the theater early in the morning and stay through the day, working on the equipment.

Robinson sat on a table in the middle of the stage, reading a book and directing the various jobs. One constant source of work for the crew was a little wooden stool, a solidly built prop that was used in the watch trick. During the show, Soo would borrow a pocket watch and wrap it in a piece of fabric. He would then place the bundle on top of a small wooden stool.

A man from the audience was handed a large mallet and told to smash the watch as Soo stood back and smiled serenely. The pieces of the watch disappeared and the restored timepiece was later discovered in the middle of a loaf of bread.

The trick was especially funny if a large, good-natured fellow—a soldier or a sailor—wielded the mallet. If he played along with the joke, he sometimes gave the watch a mighty wallop and smashed the stool to pieces as well. This made the trick even funnier. But the assistants were often forced to repair Soo's wooden stool.

When the job was finished, Rob would look it over and ask, "Is that the best you can do, laddie?" Sometimes, registering his displeasure, he broke the stool again and handed the pieces back to the assistant. "Ready for six o'clock tonight, or don't show yourself!" The assistants realized that these workdays weren't really about accomplishing anything in particular. Soo wanted to keep everyone busy, preoccupied, and a safe distance from Mrs. Soo and Mrs. Robinson.

—m—

If Soo could be impatient with his assistants, he was dangerously short-tempered with the theater staff. At one small music hall in Wales, there was no stage door. The theater had been constructed against another building, and the only entrance was through the front door and down the center aisle. All the crates of apparatus had to be carried across the seats, and before every performance the cast arrived early so they could be in their dressing rooms before the audience entered.

During the first show of one particular evening, the two flymen were drunk. Curtains were being raised and lowered throughout the show—sometimes showing the wrong backdrop or carelessly exposing a trick.

Soo stopped the show and ran backstage, climbing the metal ladder to the flymen's ropes and hollering at the stagehands. When he finally caught one of the men, he grabbed the stagehand's collar and belt, lifting him so his feet barely touched the ground, and marched him down the aisle of the theater. When Soo reached the exit, he threw the drunk stagehand into the street, slammed the door, and returned to the show.

It was an unexpected performance for the audience, who watched in stunned silence. For the second show of the evening, the rest of the crew walked out in protest, prompting a long argument between the magician and the theater's manager.

During a week when Soo was engaged at the Chiswick Empire, west of London, he had an argument with an oboe player in the orchestra. Before a matinee performance, the oboe player, named George Webb, was dashing up the dressing room stairs to the orchestra's office. He fell over a chair that had been carelessly left in the passageway. Webb looked up at the nearest dressing room—it was labeled "Mrs. Soo"—and pushed the chair inside, loudly explaining that the rules called for stairs and passages to be kept clear.

Mrs. Soo and her Pekinese dog were startled by the interruption and complained to Soo. The magician insisted that he would not start the matinee until the offending musician came forward, apologized, and was fired. Webb was brought to the magician's dressing room, but as soon as he heard Soo speak he said, pointedly, "Oh, so you're not a Chinaman after all!" This inspired another explosion from Soo, who threatened to punch the oboe player in the nose. The theater manager arrived and calmly explained that he could not fire the musician. The conductor was in charge of that department. The conductor was brought up to the magician's dressing room. He agreed to fire the man if the magician could instantly supply another qualified oboe player.

Meanwhile, the curtain was delayed and the audience was

beginning to whistle restlessly. The manager explained that Soo was perilously close to violating his contract. George Webb proudly went back to his seat in the orchestra and the show went on.

Unfortunately, George Webb was a good friend of Harry Leat, the London magic manufacturer. Leat had a devilish sense of humor, and one day engaged Soo in a conversation about musical instruments. "If there's one instrument I prefer, it's the oboe," Leat suggested, steering the conversation in a specific direction. "I don't like the oboe," Soo responded. "Oh, but you should, because it's so much fun to punch the oboe player's nose," Leat continued with a deadpan expression. Soo eyed him suspiciously, but was afraid to continue the conversation.

All his life, Billy Robinson had idolized Alexander Herrmann, the easy, graceful bon vivant of the magic world. But Chung Ling Soo found his success by following his other mentor, Harry Kellar. He was a perfectionist, a careful student of magic, and a connoisseur of fine mysteries and well-made apparatus. Unfortunately, he'd also inherited Kellar's ridiculous temper. He kept many acquaintances off-guard and—more conspicuously—at a safe distance.

—⁊⁊⁊—

Rob had also grown leery of his old friend Harry Houdini. Whereas he had once admired Houdini's straight talk and brash approach to show business, he was now annoyed by Houdini's arrogance. In 1913 Harry Houdini's mother died unexpectedly while the escape artist was touring in Europe. Houdini was fascinated by the idea of Spiritualism, and he was obsessed by the idea of contacting his mother's spirit. But he was quickly offended by the many frauds he discovered in séance rooms, and he began a crusade against these hoaxes.

One day shortly after his mother's death, Houdini and Soo happened to meet in Newcastle. Houdini had just arranged to see a medium at the home of a local bookseller, and he urged his friend Rob to come along for the evening. He knew that Robinson long had an interest in Spiritualism and was an expert in these deceptions.

During the séance, as a luminous ghost entered the room, Houdini boldly reached up with a knife and cut a bit of fabric from the spirit. When the lights were turned up, Houdini was simmering with excitement; he was ready to denounce the medium and bring the evening to a spectacular, melodramatic conclusion, but Rob begged his friend to settle down. Houdini reluctantly agreed to remain silent.

Remembering the many séances he had attended with his father, Robinson knew that many of the manifestations were crude deceptions, but he also respected the sincerity of their host and the sanctity of the evening—it was partly a religious service. "Now you old fighter," Rob had written Houdini a decade earlier, when they were first starting their careers in Europe, "I believe you would rather scrap than eat!"

Unfortunately, Houdini's next scrap was a professional argument with Soo.

In his search for useful tricks, Chung Ling Soo had long been fascinated by Buatier deKolta's last creation before his death, The Expanding Die. He saw deKolta perform it in America during his visit in 1903.

DeKolta walked onstage with a small valise, like a doctor's bag. He placed it carefully at the side of the stage, explaining that it contained his wife. At the end of his act, the magician reached inside the bag and removed a large black die—it was a fabric-covered cube about eight inches square with white dots painted on it. He placed it on a low, thin-topped table in the center of the stage. Suddenly, the die expanded, growing in three dimensions at the same time. It seemed to swell with an odd, lopsided hop. Within a fraction of a second, the die was nearly a yard square.

DeKolta stepped to the side of the die and lifted it straight up. Beneath it, his wife was sitting cross-legged on the table.

The trick was a mechanical wonder, a weird contraption that testified to deKolta's odd genius. The edges of the cube were made of telescopic tubing, surrounded by long expansion springs. The sides were covered with black silk. Closing the springs was a meticulous operation, an hour-long process involving special hooks and straps. When

Buatier deKolta with his famous Expanding Die trick.

the large cube had been pushed down into a small cube, it was locked tightly and covered with a black wrapper to resemble a spotted die.

When the die was released, it quickly sprang open in every direction; a mechanic later described deKolta's die as a "mechanical bomb." When it was fully open, deKolta's wife sneaked inside it—his trick table was a separate part of the deception—so that she could appear at the finale.

After deKolta's death in 1903, his widow sold the apparatus to Will Goldston, and Goldston's wife, an entertainer named Leah Laurie, presented it for a season in music halls in 1908. Among the world of magicians the trick became legendary—partly because it was the master's last invention and partly because his arrangement of brass, springs, and silk was so complicated and mysterious.

In 1906, Soo wrote to Houdini asking, "If you can get me a deKolta die, I should like it as soon as I get my new show ready." But Soo never got his die. In 1912, Goldston sold deKolta's original to his friend Houdini. Goldston offered his "word of honor" that he would not build another one. Houdini was planning to stop working as an escape artist and make his debut as a magician; he jealously wanted this sensational trick for his own show.

But Goldston had double-crossed Houdini. In his 1912 locked book, *Exclusive Magical Secrets,* Goldston couldn't resist plumping sales by devoting a chapter to the construction details behind The Expanding Die. Following these descriptions and the other information he had gleaned over the years, Chung Ling Soo quickly began building his own Expanding Die, putting Ritherdon's shop to work on the complicated effect.

When Houdini heard that Soo was performing the illusion, he fired off a letter, insisting that he had purchased the exclusive performance rights from Goldston. Houdini recalled a conversation in which Soo pledged he would not perform the trick.

Soo quickly wrote back from Wales, where he was performing, with a blistering response. Houdini was "laboring under a delusion." Soo had not promised to avoid the trick. He had told Houdini that he wanted to perform it as soon as possible.

Besides, he pointed out to his friend, the trick had been published in Goldston's book. It was ignorant of Houdini to "give up a big sum for sole right of a thing after it had been given to the public for a guinea." Although he avoided saying it, this was his revenge against Houdini for befriending Goldston. The idea of Goldston's word of honor was laughable.

For over a decade, Soo had watched Houdini's nasty attacks drive rival escape artists out of the business. "If you think you are going to browbeat or bully me or intimidate me into not continuing to do [The Expanding Die], you have made a big mistake," Soo wrote. "I am not jealous of you, neither do I fear you."

In fact, the trick was not practical for either performer. Houdini actually took lessons from Goldston so he could follow the complicated process of setting and operating the prop. In the spring of 1914, when Houdini finally premiered his magic show in the English provinces, the performance was not popular with the audience. "Houdini's Grand Magic Revue" ran for only about a dozen performances. The Expanding Die was even less successful. The trick was difficult to work, unreliable, and strangely disappointing, a cartoonish effect. Houdini used it only a few times.

Chung Ling Soo's modern version was more successful, but it required constant tuning and adjustments backstage. It became an inconvenience for the magician and his staff. Soo cycled it in and out of his shows for several seasons, but it was never a feature in his program.

—⁓—

Chung Ling Soo had been reluctant to return to American vaudeville. Ching Ling Foo, his rival, was not.

The brothers George and Leon Mooser brought Foo and his troupe back to New York, where he opened at the Moulin Rouge Theater in December 1912. Ching Ling Foo was engaged as a special attraction in the latest edition of the Ziegfeld Follies. The producer billed him as "The World's Greatest Magician and His Own Company of Fourteen Orientals." Ching Ling Foo actually performed very little in the show. His associates demonstrated bowl juggling, plate spinning, and acrobatics. Chee Toy, the magician's daughter, was now a pretty young lady. She was advertised as "The only Chinese Comedienne in the world who Sings Popular American Songs." Her specialty was "Row, Row, Row" (the hit from that year's Follies) and "Snooky Ookums"; she astonished audiences by singing them "without any trace of an accent," according to one reviewer.

Ching Ling Foo provided the finale of the show, producing his goldfish and his famous Marble Bowl from beneath a large shawl. He then demonstrated the Diabolo, his whirling top that danced up and down a string.

The Follies was the most prestigious variety engagement in America, and Foo toured with the show across the east coast. He then worked in vaudeville for Lowe, Hammerstein, and the United Booking Office, reportedly receiving $2,000 per week. His next engagements were with Lillian Russell and Anna Held, and then he traveled across the country on the Orpheum circuit, appearing at the country's finest vaudeville theaters.

In July 1913, Foo hosted a meal for Houdini, Howard Thurston, and a group of American magicians. He visited the New York magic shops and mystified the local conjurors with his sleight of hand. He met with Harry Kellar, long retired, and the two masters swapped secrets.

It was a glorious reception for the Chinese wizard, and it must have been a comfort to him that so many of Robinson's old friends and associates acknowledged his mastery and offered their congratulations.

That summer, Foo had a special magical sedan chair made by the Martinka Company of New York, Billy Robinson's old employers. It was a strange mixture of Eastern and Western cultures. Chung Ling Soo had exhibited an ebony sedan chair, a real Chinese artifact, in England. He used it for his entrance during his trick Defying the Boxers. But Ching Ling Foo wanted a magical sedan chair, one that performed a trick. Brought onstage, it was opened and the magician stepped out. The sedan chair was then shown empty, and it was closed and carried around the stage. When it was opened again several seconds later, a lady was found inside.

By the time of Irving Berlin's popular 1917 song, "From Here to Shanghai," the magician had become an icon of the mysterious Orient.

Harry Kellar and Ching Ling Foo meet in New York.

I'll soon be there
In a bamboo chair,
For I've got my fare,
From here to Shanghai
Just picture me,
Sipping Oo-long tea
Served by a Chinaman
Who speaks a-way up high. (Hock-a-my, Hock-a-my)
I'll eat the way they do,
With a pair of wooden sticks
And I'll have Ching Ling Foo,
Doing all his magic tricks.
I'll get my mail
From a pale pig-tail
For I mean to sail,
From here to Shanghai.

When he returned to China in March 1915, Ching Ling Foo's pockets bulged with dollars and his ears rang with the cheers of his audiences. It was not only a professional success, but, after the embarrassing London showdown, a gratifying bit of revenge against his rival.

—m—

Chung Ling Soo was comfortable touring the English provinces, returning home on weekends, working on his new ideas, and earning a handsome salary. It was a comfortable career. But one night, during an appearance at the Queen's Theatre in Burslem, there was a fire backstage.

The theater had been built just several years earlier, in 1911. In the wings there was a short flight of stairs with storage underneath—the treads built on an open metal framework. The staff of the theater had a habit of sweeping the aisles between shows, and throwing the trash—crumpled programs, candy wrappers, and cigarettes—beneath the stairs.

During the second show, as Soo was performing onstage, these

sweepings caught fire. The cause was probably a smoldering cigarette butt. It wasn't noticed until flames began licking up from the
steps. One of the stage crew, coming down the steps, jumped over
the flames and landed on the floor. This pushed a cloud of smoke
onto the stage, and the magician noticed the problem.

He walked into the wings, calling out, "What the hell is going on
back here?" His men were scrambling to douse the flames. Because
the Queen's Theatre staff had been dismissed from backstage during
Soo's act—to preserve the secrets of his magic—there was no one
available to fight the fire.

Percy Mayhew ran through the pass door to the front of the auditorium and found the stage manager. He told him that the staircase
was on fire. The stage manager shrugged, telling him that as far as
he was concerned, they could "let it burn." The new theater wasn't
paying, anyway. Mayhew yelled, "Bugger your theater. We've got all
that stuff on stage and we're not letting it burn!"

Meanwhile, the other assistants located a four-inch fire hose and
attached it to a hydrant. They quickly flooded the staircase. At that
moment, Mrs. Soo came rushing in with her Pekinese dog in her arm
to see what was wrong. As the assistants looked up, the gush of
water knocked her over, sending her head over heels.

With the hopes that the fire would soon be under control, Chung Ling
Soo returned to the stage and resumed the show, nervously looking into
the wings for a sign: should he start evacuating the audience?

Soo kept pacing back and forth—performing a bit of his trick and
then walking into the wings, asking if the fire was under control.
When the staircase had been washed with water and the papers
extinguished, the assistants resumed the show. The audience never
knew what happened. Except for the raised voices and the wet costumes, the show proceeded as usual.

The next day the newspapers erroneously announced that Chung
Ling Soo had accidentally set fire to the theater during one of this tricks.

"It was funny," Mayhew later recalled. "We had this great
hosepipe and no one to help us."

It was actually the perfect formula for a disaster. But that night in
Burslem, Chung Ling Soo was the recipient of extra good luck.

Chapter 26

THE WORLD AND ITS PEOPLE

In January 1915, Chung Ling Soo stood on the stage at the Edinburgh Empire, the famous Frank Matcham music hall where Lafayette had lost his life four years earlier. Silhouetted against the plush curtains, Soo concluded his fire-eating trick, The Human Volcano, with a flurry of streamers and the crackle of bright pyrotechnics. The audience responded with rounds of applause. Soo's gestures and misdirection had been sharpened over years of performance, and his famous fire trick had become a masterpiece of conjuring and pantomime. It could have served as a perfect finale.

But now Soo smiled innocently and held a hand to his ear, as if listening for a distant sound. The audience was hushed. The orchestra was beginning the soft tom-tom of a military march as the curtain was pulled open.

Arranged on the stage was a semicircle of tall flagstaffs on metal stands. In the center of them all was a large metal globe of the world, about three feet in diameter. It was raised several feet off the stage on metal legs, so that it resembled an enormous desk globe in its stand.

Soo stepped to the globe and circled it, apparently studying the various countries and contemplating his next surprise. He placed his hand on the sphere as if he were ready to spin it, and then glanced up at the audience. Pushing against the front, the globe split into quadrants, like two sliding doors. The front half was completely opened, with sections pivoting back inside the globe. The audience could see that the sphere was merely a metal shell, entirely empty.

He snapped the globe shut again, locking the two sections together. Soo spun the globe to the right, and then reconsidered,

Chung Ling Soo's poster for his famous
fire-eating trick.

turning it to the left. He finally settled on a spot. He pushed his
finger through a small hole in the globe and emerged with a silk flag,
several feet across. He spread it wide, showing the American Stars
and Stripes. The orchestra broke into several bars of "The Star Spangled Banner" as the magician tossed the flag to one of his assistants,
who was standing at his side. The assistant quickly snapped the flag
onto a cord attached to the first flagstaff. He then gave several quick
pulls, lifting the flag to the top of the pole.

Soo rotated the globe back and forth. He pulled out flags from
Egypt and Mexico, then twirled the globe to the opposite side of the
world, discovering a Chinese flag. The magician pointed to the flag
with an exaggerated grin, and then pointed to himself as the audience burst into applause. Suddenly, the music shifted to "Land of
Hope and Glory," a British patriotic song, as the magician reached
into the globe and discovered an oversized Union Jack. This, of
course, drew the largest ovation of all.

But the trick had only just begun. The orchestra began the military march, "Pack Up Your Troubles," as Soo discovered a Belgian flag. Suddenly, he pulled open the sections of the globe and found a Belgian soldier crouching inside. The soldier stepped out, gave a smart salute, and shouldered his rifle. The globe was closed. A French flag was produced, followed by a French soldier.

Soo proceeded through the allies, finding a British tommy, a member of a Scottish regiment, a member of ANZAC with his distinctive Australian slouch hat, and an Indian ghurka wearing a turban. He finished with a Japanese flag and a Japanese soldier, followed by the Russian flag and a tall Russian in a Cossack's uniform.

The magical battalion drew cheers and whistles from the public—throughout the Great War, the British were following the latest news from the front and celebrating the glory of the Allied victories.

Then there was a drum roll and the lights brightened on the stage. Soo swung open the globe one final time to reveal tiny Suee Seen, in a long robe and crown, carrying a shield and a trident—Britannia personified. The orchestra played "Rule Britannia" double forte as Soo and his troops stepped forward in a line. From the wings came a sudden rumble of marching boots. The curtains were pushed aside and fifty actors in various national costumes marched on, filling the stage and drowning out the orchestra with their footfalls.

The curtains dropped, then were quickly raised again on the spectacle —one bow followed by another, and then another. The Marvelous Chinese Conjurer swept his eyes over the audience with a placid, self-satisfied grin, his fingers locked together in his famous "Chinese handshake." He had just given them a miracle.

—m—

The World and its People was a brilliant creation. It was first produced in 1913, a full year before the start of the Great War, with the cast dressed in folk costumes from different countries. But in the summer of 1914, as British troops were sent to the front, Soo realized that the tribute to the soldiers would be a stirring finale. He re-costumed and re-directed the illusion so that his audience could cheer on the Allied troops.

It was, after all, an elaborate version of the old Flag Vase, the overtly patriotic trick that had so flummoxed Leon Herrmann many years earlier. Not surprisingly, Soo's wonderful metal globe was a magnificent piece of magic apparatus.

At the beginning of the trick, Chung Ling Soo walked around the apparatus, subtly pointing out that the audience could see behind the globe and beneath it—there were no connections to the scenery or through the stage. When the magician began his routine, the silk flags were hidden within double walls of the metal sphere; their corners were arranged so they could be plucked effortlessly from the globe.

The Union Jack was a larger flag than all the rest, and Soo could depend upon the audience cheering at this point in the routine. As he faced the audience and held the flag outstretched in his hands, it momentarily screened the bottom part of the globe and the arrangement of metal legs that supported it.

On cue, assistants beneath the stage pushed up a wedge of glass mirrors. The mirrors were on a sliding trap, and they filled in the area between the legs beneath the globe. The props on stage were carefully arranged so that the mirrors reflected the surrounding table legs, flagstaffs, and draperies.

The mirrors were raised in a fraction of a second, closing off the area beneath the sphere. But as Soo quickly stepped away from the prop, the reflections in the mirrors gave the audience the illusion that they were still able to see through the open space.

With the appearance of the Union Jack, the audience felt the trick had just finished. Ingeniously, it was now about to begin.

All the soldiers and Suee Seen began assembling beneath the stage. They stood in a line on a raised platform, awaiting their cues. As the globe was snapped shut, each soldier was raised up behind the mirrors. He would enter the bottom of the globe and quickly locate a small seat, and a ledge to rest his heels. With his body tucked inside, the globe opened. As the soldier stepped out, the next man was ready to be lifted into the illusion.

The fifty additional cast members were not always used. This was a special finale that Soo used for big cities or long engagements. They weren't part of his cast. They were local supernumeraries hired by the theater—the equivalents of the spear-carriers in operas—and paid pennies for each performance. Soo carried dozens of elaborate costumes to fit the supers.

The World and its People required careful rehearsal and split-second timing to coordinate the actions below and above the stage. The sliding mirrors needed to move quickly and safely. The assistants operating the trap needed to deliver each cast member on a precise cue.

With Britain's entry into the war, The World and its People became a popular success with the music hall patrons. Ironically, the war was also making Chung Ling Soo's business very difficult.

—⦚—

Chung Ling Soo had a fifty-five-minute act in music halls. There were twenty-four people in the company. In addition to his tricks and illusions, they carried costumes, scenery and backdrops, tools, all the additional effects that he might want to substitute in the program, or any new effects that had arrived from the shop and were still being rehearsed. The show also traveled with all the tricks needed for the matinee program, plus the personal effects of his staff: clothes, cooking utensils, and reading materials. Rob carried a case of magic books with him, and another case that constituted his office on the road.

Because they toured almost all year, most of the company's possessions traveled with them from theater to theater. All packed on a Saturday night, the Chung Ling Soo show amounted to twenty tons of crates, trunks, and hampers. There were thirty-five "lines of scenery" in the Soo show, meaning thirty-five separate backdrops, or drapes, tied on wooden battens over the stage. Each of these drops was lowered, folded, and packed into a hamper. Illusions were disassembled and packed in their cases. Wardrobe, small props, and personal effects were locked away in trunks. The show was loaded onto three horse-drawn wagons and transported to the train depot. That same night, all the equipment was put in two railway baggage cars.

On Saturday nights, it wasn't uncommon for the staff of young men to work until three in the morning. Often they never bothered to go to bed; by seven that morning, they were required to be at the station to join the train.

The company traveled in a seven-compartment car assigned to them. It was designated with little silhouettes of Chung Ling Soo that the company manager pasted in the windows of the compartments. This avoided any confusion when the cast stumbled aboard in the early morning. This car, with the two baggage cars, was attached to a train going in the direction of their next city. The train might stop and the cars be shifted from one line to another before reaching their final destination. Many in the cast played cards throughout the journey, wagering the last bits of their salaries.

If the show was traveling in Wales—where trains didn't run on Sunday—they paid an extra five pounds for an engine off a mining train to take them to their next engagement. Monday morning, the crates would be taken to the new theater—trunks were moved into dressing rooms, and Soo's office, costumes, and personal props were set up in the star's room. Trapdoors were cut in the stage and the elevators installed for the illusions. Tricks were uncrated and assembled. Drops were hung in the theater. Costumes were unpacked and the assistants were in their costumes, ready to step onstage. By the time Soo arrived at the theater on Monday evening, the entire show was ready for a week of engagements.

Every year, the show played for sixteen weeks in the London area, where dozens of music halls ringed the city. These weeks were a special luxury for the cast, as the props were moved from theater to theater by truck. If the weather was clear, Soo's men sat on top of the piles of crates and triumphantly rode the truck across the city, like Hannibal's troops on the backs of their elephants. If it was raining, the assistants walked, moving from coffee shop to sandwich shop as they crossed London to their next showplace.

Chung Ling Soo depended on a troupe of strong, hard-working young men. They were now the same young men being sought by the British government for the military. Many quickly enlisted, and

Soo rushed to find new recruits for his own army. In October 1914, when German bombs began to fall on London, nighttime blackouts curtailed much of the music-hall business. Soo's contracts were based on a percentage of the box office total, and he quickly felt the impact of the war.

By 1916, Soo's company staff consisted of only eight people, but the assistants still managed to transport the show and set it up in new theaters. Soo didn't stint on the show, but the process was now backbreaking work, and every new engagement an adventure. It became difficult to depend on the local stage crews for help; they were also reduced by enlistment, and stagehands were unprofessional and inexperienced.

Two printed programs from the Newcastle Empire in March 1916 show the problem. The theater printed two separate programs for that week. Soo was the early act on the first show and the last act on the second show. The extra time was required, between performances, for his assistants to reset all his tricks: fold thousands of paper banknotes, roll the ribbons, prepare the candies and toys, flowers and handkerchiefs. They barely had enough time to jump back into their Chinese costumes before it was time for the magician to walk back onstage.

One hot evening, Soo's assistants toiled in their workroom backstage. They were stripped to the waist, scurrying about the room to prepare all the small tricks for that evening's program. Suddenly they looked up and saw Chung Ling Soo, in his shirtsleeves, standing in the doorway. They were stunned to see him. He had always made it a habit to avoid the workroom and seldom spoke to assistants unless something was wrong. Soo looked around and sheepishly said, "I'll give you a hand." For several minutes he moved awkwardly from one table to another, folding paper notes and tying bundles of ribbons. He wasn't very good at it. The boys had become experts in pinning the bundles shut or tying the perfect slipknots around each bundle of banknotes. They'd been doing it for years, virtually in their sleep. Examining the hundreds of tiny jobs responsible for his performance, Soo mumbled his appreciation to a beleaguered staff: "I didn't know you had all this to do."

By the following Monday, after a day in Barnes, Soo returned with a small metal device with a roller and a crank. He had made it to speed up the process of rolling the hundreds of silk ribbons for the fire-eating trick, and handed it to his assistants, explaining that he thought it might help. But the assistants noticed that Soo never returned to the workroom, and never simplified any of the tricks to make their jobs easier.

—⁘—

Despite his concern about the danger of the Bullet Catching Trick, and his public statement that he would drop the illusion from his show, Chung Ling Soo never really stopped using it. He presented it infrequently in the years after 1910. Percy Mayhew traveled with Soo for several years, and recalled performing Defying the Boxers on only a few occasions. The magician never presented it on his special Saturday matinee programs; these appealed to families and children, and the dramatic Bullet Catching scene would have been out of place.

But it was a convenient feature, and could be included in the show as a change of pace. Soo must have felt that during wartime, the title Defying the Boxers reminded too many music-hall patrons of the unpleasant news from the front. When he appeared at the London Palladium in September 1915, the programs advertised the trick as The Charmed Bullets. This was the title Professor Hoffmann had used in his 1876 book *Modern Magic*.

Although some of the production value was lost with his smaller cast, Soo found that the trick was just as effective with just two gunmen and two rifles. With fewer bullets examined, selected, and marked, the routine moved faster. He also noticed that the trick was more interesting if soldiers were in the audience. They came onstage to examine and load the guns, giving the trick even more credibility.

Percy Ritherdon stored the extra rifles at the Bolton shop, and purchased the lead bullets and black powder for the trick, sending them on to Soo during his tours. "Things are very difficult with the war,"

Soo told a colleague. "Why, if I want to buy a little bit of wire, it's a job to get it, and it's becoming more and more difficult to get powder for the bullet catching." Coarse black powder was Soo's preference. It was easier to use. But during the war the magician was forced to use a fine powder.

In previous years, professional friends had occasionally helped Soo prepare the gun loads for the show. But he was now more secretive and cautious about all of his effects. The rifles for Defying the Boxers were locked in Soo's own trunk. He prepared the guns before each show, alone in his dressing room. That was the only way he could protect the secret and guarantee that the trick would be perfectly safe for the performance.

When he played in Cardiff, Wales, Chung Ling Soo visited with an old friend, an amateur magician named Charlie Williams. Williams was then devoting much of his time to going around to local hospitals and entertaining the wounded troops. One soldier he had met that week dabbled a bit in sleight of hand, and told Williams how upset he was that Chung Ling Soo would be playing in town but that he would be unable to see him.

When Williams relayed this story, Soo winked and said, "All right, Charlie, you can rely on me." The next day, wearing his suit and felt Stetson, Soo arrived at the hospital with Williams. The famous magician had stopped to purchase loads of cigarettes, pipe tobacco, and chocolates. The two men worked up and down the aisles of the hospital, performing impromptu card tricks. When they left, the soldiers found it hard to believe that the famous Chung Ling Soo had actually visited them.

On September 23, 1915, while performing at London's Palladium, Soo offered his glorious all-magic matinee for the benefit of wounded soldiers, "all at Soo's cost," according to a newspaper account. Seven hundred wounded men arrived for the show, clogging the sidewalks outside the theater with a "pathetic spectacle of motor cars, char-abancs, nurses, doctors and necessary attendants." With the wheel-chairs pushed into the aisles and the wounded men settled into their seats, the magician was at his very best, offering all his finest tricks from over the years, redoubling the chocolates, flowers, oranges, and souvenir gifts that were lavished on the audience. It was an unex-pected afternoon of fantasy for this particular audience.

As his tours continued, Soo took every opportunity to seek out hospitals and offer impromptu performances. A fellow magician, Arthur Ainslie, spent a Sunday afternoon with Chung Ling Soo on the train returning to London. With some satisfaction, Soo explained that he'd had a busy week, performing every day for "the boys." Ainslie asked how he managed with the Chinese makeup and wardrobe. "Oh, I don't care now. I go just as I am and give them card tricks and the [linking] rings and one or two other things," Soo explained. He found that officers often refused to believe that this gray-eyed man in the wide brown Stetson was actually Chung Ling Soo. "But they get the idea when I perform," he smiled. These low-key, unexpected performances were a special delight. They gave him a chance to use the pocket tricks and card sleights that he had been studying all his life, but which were too fussy and small for his stage act. The pleasant, social card tricks; the easy humor delivered in a soft whisper; the modest performances of wonderful magic: the soldiers never realized that they had been watching a rare perform-ance by Billy Robinson.

—⁂—

The long, wearying years of war had deteriorated the music-hall business. Staff was difficult to obtain, attendance was down at many theaters, and performers' salaries suffered. The magician determined that his show would find more success overseas.

On January 5, 1917, the show sailed on HMS *Medina* on the start of a world tour. Theatrical journals announced that first engage-ments were to be in India, followed by Africa, the Far East, a return to Australia, and Japan. *Encore* reported that the tour was projected to last five years, continuing on to South America, the United States, and Canada. After his success in 1909, Soo's return to Australia had been anticipated. His performances in American vaudeville had been negotiated and delayed for many years, but it seemed inevitable that he would return to the United States and receive the welcome of an international star.

The Performer published the surprising news that Soo's tour would also include China. It seems especially bold that Soo would have considered performing in a city like Shanghai, but his passport for that year included visas for India, Ceylon, China, and Japan, indicating his intentions. The *Magic Wand* magazine published the magician's itinerary: Malay States, Singapore, Hong Kong, Shanghai, Tientsin, Peking, Vladivostock, Japan, Manila, and Siam.

The show opened in Bombay, playing a long engagement. The press reported that he had beaten all attendance records in that city. For one show, Chung Ling Soo entertained the "five hundred wives" of a local potentate.

Leonard Williams—the son of Soo's friend in Cardiff—was then in the merchant navy and happened to be at anchor off Bombay when he heard Soo was playing in the city. He arrived between the early and late shows that evening and called backstage. The manager said that Chung Ling Soo saw no visitors, but the young man told the manager to deliver the message that he was "a Williams from Cardiff." Moments later Soo dashed around the corner, saying, "Come right in, my boy!" They chatted as Soo's assistants dashed about the stage, preparing the second show. When Suee Seen entered, Soo asked her, "Do you know who this is?" She looked at the boy closely and then burst into a smile. "It's Charlie Williams's boy!" she said. As he sat in the dressing room, applying his makeup, Soo promised Leonard Williams that he would write to his father. He picked up a grease pencil and scrawled the Cardiff address on the mirror.

Leonard Williams watched the show that evening. Years later, he recalled Soo's slow entrance, bowing to the center of the auditorium, and then to the left and the right. Soo's eyes traveled along the front row until they met the young man's eyes, and he stopped to make one extra bow. Someone behind Williams whispered, "He evidently knows someone here."

Chung Ling Soo's show then moved on to the Empire Theater in Calcutta, where it had another critical success and was extended for many weeks. But when the show reached Shanghai, China, the magician was prevented from playing at the large Lyceum Theater that was being used for Red Cross entertainments, and was forced to use a smaller motion-picture theater. Adding to the difficulty, Soo had become ill in India, and had not recovered; by late summer he was forced to end the tour. The journal *Australian Variety* later reported that the magician had suffered from "acute dysentery" and decided it best to return to England. The author Will Dexter speculated that a contributing factor might have been the difficulty and danger of travel during wartime.

Louise was glad to have Soo back. She was uncomfortable with the thought of Rob out of the country. The continuing war particularly unnerved her, and the occasional zeppelin raids of London terrified her. She feared that the family home in Barnes was too close to the center of the city to be completely safe. She rented another house—called Burrough Hay—in Taplow, south of the city on the Thames, moving the children and their nurse there for weeks at a time.

After Soo returned and recovered his health, he took steps to resume the tour; he wanted to start again in India and then continue west. The tour was intended for later in 1918, after he had fulfilled a number of engagements in Great Britain.

—᙮᙮—

The war had taken most of the reliable men from Britain's work force, and Soo was always searching for good assistants. Before going to India, he had hired a 17-year-old from Bradford, Jack Grossman, to tour with the show. During a long engagement in Aberdeen at the end of 1917, three of Soo's other assistants got into a drunken argument after the Saturday night shows. Soo was still not feeling his best, and he unwisely lost his temper and fired all three men. As soon as they walked out the stage door, the magician realized his mistake. He was forced to cancel the next day's matinee—which depended on dozens of small tricks—but managed to finish the week by depending on his new employees, like Grossman, and quickly recruiting additional help. Soo wrote a note of apology to the theater manager, making it all sound perfunctory. He was sorry to "disappoint them," but the magician insisted that his men were "drunk to the world, and I had to discharge them."

One of the new replacements was a 17-year-old from Salford, Dan Crowley. He quickly learned what was necessary backstage and onstage. But to Soo, Grossman and Crowley were simply two of his latest employees, to be pushed into costumes and marched through the rudiments of the act. After years of experience, Soo now invested very little in his assistants, fearing that they might soon be enlisted, or drunk, or running off to sell their secrets to another magician for a few shillings. The new men were trusted with just what they needed to know, and no more. They were given as few secrets as possible.

Twenty years earlier, when Will and Dot had worked with the Herrmanns, they used to enjoy standing in the wings and watching the boss. "He told me how he used to watch his chief night after night for months," recalled one of Soo's friends, "learning how to act the part of a magician, how to make well rehearsed jokes and effects appear to be impromptu, how to overcome any difficulties that might present themselves, and so on." Those hours with Herrmann had served as part of Will's education in magic. But Soo was reluctant to provide such an education to any of his own employees.

The incident with Watson, the assistant who sold secrets to Goldston, had inspired a new cloud of secrecy for Chung Ling Soo. Soo was temperamental about anyone—even his own assistants—watching from the wings. "There were a lot of tricks that I never had a chance to see," one assistant recalled years later. "I didn't dare go on the side of the stage. If he saw you standing there, looking, he would stop the trick he was doing and come off. If anyone was on the stage at all who shouldn't be there, he would want to know who you were, what you were doing."

The Wood Green Empire Theatre, north of London.

If there was a problem with a trick, Soo was reluctant to hand it off to an assistant. He would turn his back on the audience and reset the apparatus so he could proceed. His preference was always to handle these problems himself.

—m—

The week of March 18, 1918, Chung Ling Soo's company played at the Wood Green Empire, north of London. The printed program didn't supply a list of effects, only the information that "Chung Ling Soo will make selections from his repertoire." The program then listed nine of his favorites, "The Willow Pattern Plate [the opening sequence of small tricks], The Mystic Bottle, The Creation of a Butterfly, Home from the Market [his effect with the tennis balls and the bird cage], The Lady in the Case [a new title for the Crystal Lamp], The Living Target [Dot impaled against the target], A Dream of Wealth, The World and its People, The Girl and the Orange Tree, etc., etc."

Not listed on the program was Defying the Boxers, or The Charmed Bullets. As always, the trick was seldom promised, and seldom performed. Other magicians had used the bullet-catching trick for advertising purposes, to bring crowds into the show or to publicize a special show. But to Chung Ling Soo, it had just become another part of his repertoire—one of many tricks that were cycled in and out at the whim of the magician. There seems to be no special reason why it was included that week at the Wood Green Empire. Because of its dark drama and production value—with the entire cast in authentic Chinese costumes—Soo used the bullet-catching trick just before the end of the show, followed by fire eating and The World and its People. The new employees, Grossman and Crowley, were given the jobs as the two gunmen. For the assistants, the trick was an easy one, but they didn't like the heavy leather and bronze costumes.

—m—

On Saturday night, March 23, the last evening of shows that week, Soo had a visitor backstage. Cecil Lyle was a fellow professional magician, a well-known music-hall entertainer who became famous with an act of various hat tricks. He was billed as The Magical Milliner. During the war, Lyle was serving as a lance corporal in the army. Soo was scheduled to have a week off starting the next day, and he had invited Lyle to come to Taplow for a visit. But Lyle was unable to come, and instead visited the magician between performances at Wood Green.

As they chatted, Lyle sat in the upholstered chair in the dressing room. Soo told Lyle that he didn't feel well. He was suffering from indigestion and felt that it might be related to his bad spell in India. Suee Seen opened the door and delivered the three rifles that had been used in the first show, so that Soo could reload them. One was the rifle for The Living Target, and the other two were the guns from Defying the Boxers.

Soo set them on his dressing table and prepared several loads of powder wrapped in tissue paper. Lyle saw him tearing paper, and he saw him measuring powder in a metal tube. Lyle instinctively moved to the opposite side of the dressing room as they continued their conversation. He later explained that it was an act of professional courtesy. He knew that his friend was secretive about his illusions, and Lyle didn't want to appear too curious about Soo's procedure.

When Suee Seen returned several minutes later, Soo was still working at the table. She asked if he was finished and he said, "No, come back again." A moment later, Soo's carpenter called Soo out of the room; as he left, he handed Lyle a copy of *Variety* to read in his absence. Lyle was sitting in the chair and the guns were loaded, lying on the table. The powder and paper charges had been put away. Suee Seen stepped inside again, picked up the guns, and carried them from the room. As she was leaving, Soo met her at the door and saw that she had taken the rifles.

Realizing that the act would begin soon, Lyle stood up and excused himself to take his seat in the auditorium to watch the performance. He left at about 9:20.

Shortly before ten there was a knock on the dressing room door. "Places, Mr. Soo, places!" shouted the theater callboy, and the door immediately swung open. "I'm coming," Soo told the boy. The magician shuffled down the corridor in his embroidered robes and Chinese slippers, a step ahead of the callboy. He chatted idly, asking about the lad's accent. "My family's from King's Norton," the boy answered. "Well, well," responded Soo. "I thought I recognized that accent. You know, I'm not really from China. I'm from your area, a Birmingham chap myself." He gave the callboy a wink, and walked to the middle of the darkened stage, taking his pose in the center of his assistants.

From beyond the thick draperies there was a crashing chord; a gong rumbled and the sharp notes of the violins pulsed through the theater. Then, with the metallic rattle of ropes through pulleys, the curtain rose and the stage was washed in brilliant white light.

Chapter 27

THE CHARMED BULLET

E very magic trick has a flaw, a little inconsistency, a hiccup in the procedure that must pass unnoticed by the audience. If it didn't have a flaw, it wouldn't be a trick; it would be a principle of science.

The job of a magician is to disguise those flaws. A great magician understands group psychology and knows what an audience will be willing to overlook. He knows how to lead a group of people along. He knows what they'll be watching and thinking, and what they may be ready to ignore.

During The World and Its People, Chung Ling Soo could only walk around the giant globe at the beginning of the effect, before the mirrors were in place. And he needed to obscure the area beneath the globe for several seconds as the mirrors were shoved up into place. The use of the Union Jack was an ingenious bit of misdirection. It made sense to his British audiences that the Union Jack would be the largest flag of all, and that the performer would pause extra long to display it. It also gave the impression of a climax—the trick was over. It was at this precise moment, a kind of psychological "exhale," when the audience was relaxed, that Soo concealed the trick's flaw.

But just as no trick can be perfect, no flaw can be perfectly concealed. By working too hard to cover a flaw, with a suspiciously long pause or a flamboyant motion, the magician might inadvertently call attention to it. A great trick has a kind of simple elegance to these moments—a dance right up to the edge, without going over. The audience should have the feeling that the flag just happened to fall in front of the globe for a few seconds.

The psychology of a certain moment can be analyzed, the apparatus can be tested and rehearsed, but sooner or later the magician plays the laws of averages. Before a thousand people, or ten thousand or one hundred thousand, it may prove to be a miracle. But sooner or later the flaw will become apparent to someone.

At that point, any trick becomes obvious, or awkward. For someone in the audience, it goes over the edge. Or it fails completely.

—⁓—

At 10:45 p.m., Chung Ling Soo was nearing the end of his act. Crowley and Grossman dashed behind the curtains and pulled on their heavy Chinese armor. The costumes were exhaustingly authentic, made of leather and bronze plate, and they were hot under the stage lights. When the rest of the cast assembled offstage for Defying the Bullets, Crowley and Grossman walked over to Mrs. Soo's prop table in the wings, and each of them picked up a prepared rifle. They shouldered the guns and followed the procession onto the stage.

Kametaro stepped to the footlights, explaining how the audience would now witness Chung Ling Soo's escape from the Boxers. Kametaro solicited the help of two audience members to examine the equipment and supervise as the guns were loaded. Two British soldiers stepped forward, one in uniform and one in civilian clothes. They came up the stairs at the front of the stage and examined the guns proffered by Crowley and Grossman.

Defying the Boxers, with Kametaro and Suee Seen. Soo is at far right.

Two large lead bullets were selected and dropped into the tin cup that Suee Seen held in her hand. She carried the bullets down the aisle, finding two men to scratch identifying marks on the bullets.

Meanwhile, Kametaro showed the gunpowder and poured charges into the rifles, followed by paper wads. The soldiers tamped down the loads with the metal ramrods.

Suee Seen returned to the stage with the two marked bullets, handing one to each of the spectators. They examined the marks on the bullets so they could identify them, and dropped them into the barrels of the rifles. The soldiers followed with another paper wad, rammed in place. The ramrods were set on the table and percussion caps were placed on the guns.

Crowley and Grossman solemnly paced off fourteen strides from the magician, taking their positions on the left side of the stage (from the audience's viewpoint). Soo stood near the wings on the right side, with a porcelain plate gripped between his hands. Frank Kametaro led the two volunteers to a safe position, behind the gunmen. Kametaro then stepped to the center of the stage, where he would give the command to fire.

Suee Seen, having delivered the bullets to the assistants, had walked into the wings. She was adjusting the props for the fire-eating trick that would follow the bullet-catching illusion.

William Meader, an electrician at the Wood Green Empire, was standing in the wings when he heard a disturbance in the front row of the theater. Just as Soo was widening his stance and adjusting the plate in his hand, a man in the front row stood up and interrupted the trick. He may have had a bit too much to drink or been involved in an argument with someone else in the theater. No one onstage noticed what he was saying. Soo paused, waiting for the man to sit down before he proceeded.

Frank Moody, the stage manager, was standing on the prompt side of the stage—the audience's right side—just behind the magician.

Sergeant Spain, a member of the metropolitan police, was on duty that evening at the theater; he had watched the first show from the orchestra pit and was there again for the late performance.

Crowley and Grossman slowly raised their rifles and pointed them across the stage at the magician.

The orchestra fell silent.

Cecil Lyle, sitting in a box in the theater, leaned forward in anticipation. He'd never seen his friend Soo present this trick.

Frank Kametaro gave the command to fire.

—⁓—

Dan Crowley noticed that something was wrong a split second before anyone else.

He thought his rifle was extra loud, and he felt a distinctive recoil against his shoulder that he hadn't felt at previous shows.

But he'd performed the trick dozens of times before and knew his cue. Just after the rifles discharged, Dan Crowley and Jack Grossman

Chung Ling Soo in costume, about to catch
the bullet.

turned their backs on the action and walked into the wings, putting their guns on Mrs. Soo's prop table.

When Crowley heard the words, "Oh, my God," over his shoulder, his first thought was that the plate had accidentally broken and hurt Mr. Soo.

One of the soldiers who had volunteered that night, the man not in uniform, was Jack Jeppert. He had seen the show the previous night and thought it would be interesting to watch the bullet-catching trick from up close. He also thought that the report sounded strangely louder than it had been on the previous night.

Jack Grossman said that his gun had no recoil, but the powder charges were loud. Grossman was in the wings before he turned around to see Chung Ling Soo reel as his knees buckled.

The plate fell from Soo's hands and shattered on the stage.

Frank Moody looked up from his desk in the wings to see Chung Ling Soo take several tentative steps backward, toward him. As Soo twisted his body, Moody saw blood falling from him, brightly illuminated in the spotlight. He ran onto the stage and caught Soo's shoulders as he slumped backward. Moody lowered him to the ground.

"Oh my God. Something's happened. Lower the curtain!" Soo gasped. Moody called for the curtain, which rapidly cut off the scene from the audience.

From her position backstage, Suee Seen hadn't noticed anything different about the sound of the guns, but she did hear the plate hit the stage and shatter, and she immediately knew that something was wrong. She ran in from the wings just as her husband's body slumped to the stage.

—⁓—

There was an uncomfortable murmur through the audience as the white screen was lowered before the curtain, and the silent Bioscope newsreel began flickering. The audience wondered what they'd just seen. The magician's fall to the stage may have been intended as a dramatic conclusion to the trick, but there was something wrong with the strange hesitation of the actors and technicians running in from offstage. There was a jumble of bodies and a blur of voices that was not theatrical at all. The action had none of the elegance of Soo's performance, or the simple clear direction that made his magic so enjoyable to watch. It suggested a terrible mistake.

Backstage, as Dot kneeled at his side, Soo looked up at her. "Oh Dot, fetch a doctor, quick." Sergeant Spain had dashed around from the auditorium. Mr. James, the theater manager, was already phoning for local physicians, and located three who agreed to come. Kneeling, Kametaro asked Soo if he were in pain and received the reply, "Yes, a little."

As Dot supported her husband's head in her arms, he drifted in and out of consciousness. "I cannot stand it, I cannot stand it," Soo mumbled several times. She asked him, "Oh Will, whatever have you done?" But he was too weak to respond.

Cecil Lyle hurriedly left his box, dashed down the steps, and pushed through the metal pass door to the stage, where he found Soo surrounded by his assistants. Lyle paced nervously, trying to keep out of the way but circling the injured magician for any information about his injury. After seeing that Soo was being treated, Lyle finally decided that he could offer no help. He left the Wood Green Empire and waited for any news about his friend's condition.

Stagehands stanched the flow of blood. One pulled down a nearby strip of curtain and wrapped it around the magician in an attempt to keep him warm.

—m—

"The majority of the audience left the building without knowing what had occurred," according to *The Era*'s report of the incident. No one ever stepped onstage and explained the accident to the audience. The orchestra concluded with "God Save the King," the lights in the theater were illuminated, and the exit doors thrown open. The spectators stepped onto the sidewalk, questioning each other about what they had just seen. Some, still standing outside the entrance, noticed the clatter of doctors and ambulances arriving on Cheapside High Road and turning at Dovecote Avenue, a little alley that reached the stage door.

When Dr. Ernest Porter arrived at about 11:30, he found two other physicians, Dr. Mathison and Dr. Billson, as well as a trained nurse. The doctors examined the magician as he lay on the stage, semiconscious. Dr. Porter could barely detect a pulse. He found the wound in the front of the magician's chest on his right side. The bullet had entered two inches from the midline, fracturing the fifth rib. An exit wound on the magician's back was through the eleventh rib. The rib protruded about four inches to the right of the spine. The doctors dressed both wounds. Mr. Colter, a chemist from across the road, brought bottled oxygen; this was given to the victim and it seemed to ease his breathing.

Several hours after the accident, Lou Blatchford phoned the theater from the family's rented home in Taplow, worried because Rob had not arrived on the train after the performance. Mr. James, the manager, told her the terrible news.

At two-thirty, Chung Ling Soo was taken out of the theater on a stretcher and transported in an ambulance to Passmore Edwards Hospital in Wood Green. Dot stayed by his side. He regained consciousness a few times but could only complain about his hands and feet being "so cold." Dot removed his Chinese slippers and massaged his feet.

—◦◦◦—

Sergeant Spain asked Frank Kametaro for the rifles, and Soo's stage manager promptly brought them from the prop table and handed them to the police officer. Kametaro also reached down on the stage and picked up the two marked bullets. These had been palmed by Soo against the edge of the plate and should have been revealed at the end of the illusion, when the marks were confirmed.

Detective Inspector George Cornish arrived at the Wood Green Empire before Soo was taken away in the ambulance, and he began questioning the cast and crew about the shooting. Sergeant Spain turned over the rifles and bullets to Cornish for his investigation. Frank Moody, the stage manager, brought Detective Cornish to his desk at the prompt side of the stage to show him what he'd found. There was a tear in the canvas backdrop about four feet above the floor. A shelf several feet from Moody's desk held a small mirror that had been shattered. Among the shards of glass was a large lead bullet, flattened like a penny against the brick wall of the theater.

—⁓—

The doctors realized that the magician would not survive. Just two hours after reaching the hospital, at 4:55 a.m., Chung Ling Soo, the Marvelous Chinese Conjurer, was dead. A post-mortem examination revealed that the damage was caused by one enormous lead bullet fired from one of his rifles. It had entered the magician's chest, struck the right auricle of the heart, and grazed the upper edge of the liver before it caused the wound in his back. Considering the nature

Dot Robinson as Suee Seen.

of the injuries, doctors considered it miraculous that he had survived for so many hours. The official cause of death was listed as hemorrhage and shock.

As the sun was rising, little Suee Seen, the famous Chinese princess who had served as the object of Chung Ling Soo's magic, pulled her coat over her embroidered costume and wiped the tears from the greasepaint that now streaked and smudged her tiny, doll-like face. Still in her silk slippers, she tottered into the Kametaros' home on Courcy Road, stepped into the hallway, and collapsed into loud, sad sobs. She told Frank and Mabel Kametaro that it was finished.

At that moment, she was no longer Suee Seen. She had stopped being the assistant to the world's greatest magician, the former star of the Kellar and Herrmann shows, the invisible assistant to Nana Sahib. She suddenly became Dot Robinson once again—the former Olive Path, Olive Pfaff, Augusta Pfaff—a slightly plump, fifty-five-year-old former showgirl from Cleveland, Ohio, who had lived her life in the spotlight, but managed to keep so many profound secrets for three decades. Rob's life was ended. Her existence had suddenly stopped.

—⁓—

At the Wood Green Empire, as the theater's employees began to clear the stage, one lifted the blood-soaked curtain that had been used to cover the magician. "Don't throw that out!" one old stagehand called out. "Don't you know? The gore from a Chink is lucky." It was an old theatrical superstition. The next day, the stagehand hung the grisly artifact, a stained strip of fabric, in a dark corner at the back of the stage. It reportedly remained there for months, unnoticed by the music-hall artists.

Two weeks later, a magician named Billy O'Connor was playing at Wood Green and remarked to the stage manager about Soo's death. The stage manager led O'Connor into the cellar and pointed up at the stage flooring. Although the top of the stage had been cleaned, there was still an enormous brown stain that had saturated the boards. O'Connor was chilled to think that he was making the entrance for his act—performing tricks and drawing laughs—over the blood of his friend. The memory of the tragedy haunted performers at the Wood Green Empire for many decades.

—m—

From his first moments at the theater, Inspector Cornish realized that he was facing a mystery. In a different situation, it might have been a deliciously puzzling deception. But this was a tragedy, and Cornish wondered if the magician's death was an accident, or suicide, or even murder. The magician's mysterious identity and complicated private life added to the suspicion. Of course, Chung Ling Soo was a master of deception. Cornish had already picked up three bullets when there should have been two. He had heard accounts of the impossible feat of catching bullets on a porcelain plate—which Soo's employees were convinced could never fail, although no one seemed to understand how it had ever worked.

As proof of the inscrutability of the deception, Defying the Boxers had astonished hundreds of thousands of people, including Chung Ling Soo's colleagues within the world of professional magicians.

Now Cornish realized that he could only explain the death of Chung Ling Soo if he could explain his most wonderful deception.

Cornish took the bullets and rifles to a gun shop on Waterloo Road that had, according to Kametaro, repaired the rifles for Soo. But the inspector felt that he needed the services of a real gun expert. Robert Churchill had a shop on Agar Street in London. Churchill was a dapper man in his early thirties, with a small moustache and full cheeks. He was part of the famous Churchill family of gun makers and had become an expert in ballistics. This was still an early science, but Scotland Yard consulted him for many of their most difficult cases. Churchill had built the first comparison microscope in Great Britain, used to determine if a bullet were fired from a particular gun.

—m—

The newspapers broke the news with a mixture of sensationalism and puzzlement. Most reported that Soo's famous trick had failed, although no one could actually explain the trick or the failure. Monday morning's *Times* offered the headline, "Music Hall Magician's Death," with a brief account, suggesting that the magician was actually Chinese. "Chung Ling Soo Fatally Shot: A Trick that Went Wrong," wrote the *Manchester Guardian*; the article similarly gave the performer's name as simply Chung Ling Soo. Even in America, the *Washington Post* was unaware of the magician's real identity; the headline was, "Chinese Actor's Trick Fatal: Loaded Rifle Used by Magician in London Kills Him."

The *Daily Express* story was titled, "Shot on Stage: Mystery of the Death of Chung Ling Soo. Plate vs. Bullets." Their reporter actually interviewed people connected to the theater and revealed that the magician "was an American, aged fifty-nine, and was generally accepted as a genuine Chinaman." He was actually fifty-six. The American theatrical journal *Variety* knew William E. Robinson's name from his New York friends, and several days after the tragedy reported Robinson's ties to Kellar and Herrmann, and the fact that his act was copied from Ching Ling Foo.

But a lifetime of Rob's gentle lies inevitably worked their way into the obituaries. The *Daily Chronicle* wrote, "His name was Robinson, and he was born in Birmingham about fifty years ago." Many reporters from newspapers across Great Britain flattered their readers by finally parroting back the little secret Soo had once imparted: he was a local boy. He was not Chinese, but actually from Edinburgh, Aberdeen, Bolton, Liverpool, or Manchester. Some British theatrical journals even reported his place of birth as Philadelphia.

As his identity was revealed, there was another secret to be kept. As *Variety* wrote, "He is survived by a widow and three children." The sentence sounded simple, but only his friends realized how complicated that fact really was.

Dot remained at the house with the Kametaros, answering notes and making arrangements for the show and the cast. She didn't really have a home. Will Goldston mailed both Lou and Dot, sending Dot letters of condolence from other magicians. Dot wrote a note in return: "Will you kindly accept my sincere thanks for forwarding my mail to me. I esteem it a great favor. Yours respectfully, Dot Robinson, née Chung Ling Soo."

Louise had Marge Ward, the children's governess whom the family called Nurse Nana, respond to Goldston, inviting him to the funeral. "Mrs. Robinson wishes to thank you for your kind wire of sympathy to her in her terrible trouble."

Louise was devastated. She brought the children and Nurse Nana back to Barnes. "I thank you for your kind letter of sympathy," she wrote to a friend of Soo's, a fellow magician named Stanley Collins. "I don't know what I should have done, but everyone has been extremely kind to me. My poor darling was loved by everybody. The cross is very heavy but I just feel he is only waiting for me, and I hope that God will grant my wish and let me join him soon. We just lived for each other. I have my children, it is true, but they will never make up for his loss. He was a marvelous man in every way. I just feel I can't bear it. Lou Robinson."

—᙮—

Magicians were stunned. Those that knew of Rob's methodical techniques and legendary perfectionism were baffled by the accident. Adelaide Herrmann was still performing in vaudeville, and the press sought her opinion on Chung Ling Soo's death. She told them that the bullet-catching trick was always a dangerous one, even when her husband had performed it. But she was puzzled by the way Soo had died. It didn't seem to make any sense. He had been performing the trick for a long time. It was clear he had mastered it. Madame Herrmann had no theory about how the trick had failed.

Houdini was performing in New York at the Hippodrome Theater. When he heard the news, he dashed off a wire to Harry Kellar,

Robinson's old boss, who was retired in Los Angeles. Houdini then followed with a letter. "Regarding Soo, it appears that he was shot in the breast while doing the bullet catching trick. Have no details but read article in the Associated Press notices." Kellar responded, "Your note telling me of Chung Ling Soo's death came as a shock to me, like a flash from the clear sky. Please write me the details when you have time."

But as Houdini began to gather information, he became more and more puzzled. "From what cabled accounts I have read it seems as if there were something peculiar about the whole affair," he wrote Kellar. "There are only two ways it could have happened. One is failure of exchange in the plate [he meant Suee Seen's cup to hold the bullets], or mixture of bullets when handing them to the soldiers. It could not be possible that one of the men instead of loading the trick cartridge, would substitute one of his own, for that would be murder. You know the fake bullets look exactly like the genuine, but are made of a chalkish mixture." With his typical arrogance, Houdini was pronouncing how Rob must have done it, based on the historical methods of the past—the substitution for the bullets by composition bullets, like chalk, that would be smashed in the barrel and turn to powder in the explosion. But Houdini had been badly fooled by Robinson's method.

In the background of Houdini's speculation—"something peculiar about the whole affair"—were the nagging details of William Robinson's private life. Like Houdini and Kellar, all his professional friends wondered the same thing, whether his private problems had finally spilled into his performance.

—⁕—

Robert Churchill received the rifles and bullets the morning after Soo's death. Inspector Cornish took precautions to ensure that no one else had interfered with the weapons, so Churchill could properly examine the evidence.

Coincidentally, Churchill had seen a performance of Chung Ling Soo the previous year and was fortunate to see the magician catch the bullets on a plate. The trick held a special interest for him, as an expert in firearms. "I was as bewildered as everyone else as to how he did it," Churchill wrote. But during that performance, he had noticed a strange procedure. "They were 12-bore single-barreled muzzle-loading rifles with a small ramrod tube laid under each barrel," Churchill wrote.

> All muzzle-loading rifles have rods, which are used to ram the charges into the barrels. In the act, the ramrods were always put on one side as soon as the rifles had been loaded, and not returned, as one would normally have expected, to the tubes. I had remarked on this myself when I saw Chung Ling Soo's act. At the time, I thought that he must have dispensed with the business of putting back the ramrods because it would have meant a tedious delay at that exciting moment.

But the more Churchill had thought about it, the odder it seemed. He'd found the flaw.

Chapter 28

DEATH BY MISADVENTURE

On Thursday, March 28, just five days after her husband's death, Olive Robinson began revealing secrets.

On the first morning of the official coroner's inquest at the Wood Green Town Hall, the room was filled with curious spectators, newspapermen, witnesses, and friends of the magician. One notable absence was Louise Blatchford, although she was represented by a solicitor.

Alan MacKinnon Mayow Forbes, the Middlesex coroner conducting the inquest, looked up from his notes and called for the first witness, "Mrs. William Robinson." The assembled jury and observers held their breath as the tiny figure stood up and stepped to the front of the room, her high heels clicking sharply on the polished wooden floor. She was wearing a starched black dress and a heavy black veil that concealed her features. She paused to pull a tiny handkerchief from her handbag and settled into the chair with a low sigh. Many had seen the pretty Chinese princess, skipping across the stage during Chung Ling Soo's famous music-hall act. But the figure before them was a sad, tired lady.

Only when she began to speak did Olive turn back her veil, revealing a pale round face and red-rimmed eyes. She glanced over to nod at the jury, a group of local citizens who had been assembled to decide the cause of her husband's mysterious death. Reporters noted that she spoke with an American twang, answering Forbes's first questions with a polite, "Yes, sir."

The magician's real name, she reported, was William Ellsworth Robinson, and he would have been 57 years old the following month.

The reporters present began scribbling furiously. "Yes, sir," Dot responded, "I've assisted my husband in the States and all around the world. No one else had." She explained that they were married about twelve years ago at a registry office near Manchester. "We parted by mutual consent over domestic difficulties, as he became associated with another woman. Notwithstanding this, we have always worked together, for about twenty-five years." Olive explained that he was living at Lonsdale Road with Louise Blatchford. "He has been with her some ten or twelve years, and they have three children." She explained that her husband "left Louise Blatchford his sole executrix to his will." The reporters took careful notes, but few printed the details of their domestic affairs. In Edwardian England, the subject was avoided out of courtesy.

As Dot was asked about the incidents of Saturday night, she lost her composure and her eyes welled with tears.

Her part in Defying the Boxers was simple. She cleared her throat and explained the deception. She held the small tin cup that carried the bullets. When two lead slugs were selected onstage, they were dropped into this cup. She then carried them into the audience to be marked.

The bullets were marked by the audience and then dropped back into the cup. As she turned her back on the audience, returning the cup to the stage, she lifted out an inner lining in the cup. This removed the selected bullets, and revealed two other bullets that had been hidden in the bottom compartment. Chung Ling Soo had already marked these two bullets in distinctive ways—one had a large dot scratched onto it, and the other had an "x." Suee Seen concealed the lining of the cup in her costume. Her maneuver was achieved in a mere second; it was a simple exchange for an experienced magic assistant.

Onstage, the two men were given these bullets and they looked over the marks so they would recognize them again.

Dot paused. She was uncomfortable explaining these secrets. It was something she'd never done before, but she realized that the law required her to explain everything she knew. She took a breath and continued. Her husband had palmed two bullets with identical marks, a dot and an "x," so at the conclusion of the trick, the two volunteers on stage would look at these and believe that they were the same bullets they had been shown before the shots were fired. The bullets were not shown to the men who had marked them, however. At some shows, Soo gave the bullets to the men onstage, or presented them to guests. He boldly calculated that they would not work their way back to the spectators who had made the marks. So, there were not two bullets used. There were six—four prepared by Soo, and two marked by spectators in the audience.

Dot didn't mention it in her testimony, but when Defying the Boxers was first introduced, accounts suggested that Soo also switched the bullets as they were returned to the audience. After they had been identified onstage, they were dropped into Suee Seen's cup. As she came down the steps into the aisle, she switched the bullets for the spectators' marked bullets, and then returned them for verification. It was only in later years that he had simplified the routine, identifying the marks only onstage.

When she was questioned about the guns, the testimony abruptly stopped. Dot insisted that she knew "absolutely nothing." Soo himself always cleaned and loaded the guns. He would not allow anyone else to watch him do it. He always prepared the guns by himself so he was not distracted, for fear of making a mistake.

It seemed surprising to Forbes that Dot could be unaware of the details of the rifles. She had participated in the trick for twelve years, and had seen it performed hundreds of times. As his wife, she must have been concerned about the safety of this illusion. Dot had become complacent about the deception, and never had more than a rough understanding of the trick. During her testimony, Coroner Forbes helpfully explained that these were "not ordinary guns." Dot understood where he was leading, and she explained the little that she did know about the rifles.

"The bullets put into the guns were never intended to come out when the guns were fired," she said, nodding. They were removed when her husband cleaned the guns. She knew this was the case because she had seen dozens of marked bullets that had been removed from the rifles.

"There has never been an accident with this trick before. Never. There has never been any quarrel, and as far as I know, no one bears him any malice." Dot did admit, "My husband had a violent temper if anything went wrong, but it was soon over and he bore no malice. He was on good terms with the whole of his staff."

Dot mentioned that the "show has been broken up, no one else can run it." Reporters observed that during her testimony, others in the room had been weeping. She was a "pathetic figure," and a clear victim of the mysterious tragedy. Coroner Forbes thanked her and she left the room. The door slammed with a bang.

— m —

During his testimony, Fukado Kametaro, Soo's longtime assistant and stage manager, said simply, "I do not know the shooting trick." He could only report what he had told Sergeant Spain on the night of Soo's death, that two years ago the guns had been repaired by a man in Waterloo Road. Defying the Boxers was Soo's secret, Kametaro explained, and Soo was responsible for loading the guns.

Both Crowley and Grossman, the 17-year-old assistants who played the parts of Chinese gunmen, were frustratingly ignorant about the trick. They had been discouraged from thinking too much about the procedure or examining the rifles. Crowley explained how he was never given instructions about where to aim his gun, that he just pointed it in the general direction of the magician. At the fatal performance, Crowley's gun had kicked hard against his shoulder, but when he was asked if he still had the bullet in his gun, he responded that he couldn't say. "We're not allowed to look into the barrel."

Grossman had always made a point of aiming at the china plate, he told the coroner. On Saturday night, he thought that the guns seemed extra loud but believed that it might have been from "an overcharge of powder given to the committee by Mr. Kametaro" because a soldier had volunteered.

Forbes thought about this answer for a moment, and shook his head. "If you think the powder given to the committee ever exploded you are very simple," he told Grossman. "Simpler than I should have expected." Grossman responded, "The report must come from somewhere."

Despite shooting at a man night after night, both boys were perplexed about what was actually happening, or the potential danger. They'd been fooled by the trick.

—⁓—

The inquest invited some lurid speculation. Coroner Forbes announced that he had received an anonymous letter "in printed characters." Like all anonymous correspondence, it was not admissible as evidence. Dot had certainly been told about this letter. She later reported to a friend that the letter stated, "Rob was murdered and mentioned the party who was supposed to be the culprit."

Presumably, suspicion fell on Dot and Kametaro. She was, after all, the betrayed wife, and one rumor suggested that Kametaro knew the guns were faulty but was upset with how Soo had treated his wife. A reporter covering the inquest heard it said that Mrs. Soo and the stage manager had been "rather too friendly." Because of Soo's private affairs, it may have seemed significant that Dot was living with the stage manager. But she was actually living with the stage manager, his wife, and their child, and was a good friend of Mabel Kametaro. After her separation from Will, Dot never had a home of her own.

Forbes received another odd letter from Arthur Carlton, a well-known music-hall comedian and magician. Carlton was tall and slender, and he performed in clown makeup with an exaggerated egghead-shaped wig, adding to his height. He was billed as the "Human Hairpin." But Carlton was concerned with the rumors surrounding his friend Robinson. "Let magicians examine the guns," he pleaded with Forbes. Carlton knew that Robinson was an expert and would be able to deceive a gunsmith. Mrs. Robinson "only acted as an assistant for a number of years, and he happily lived with another lady, to whom he was very attached, and had a family." Carlton made no clear allegations, but offered hints about his private affairs. "Trusting you will accept this letter in absolute confidence and in the spirit in which it was written," Carlton concluded.

Forbes ignored the letter. By that time, Churchill, the gun expert, had done his job.

—⁓—

When the inquest resumed the following week, Robert Churchill took the stand. He was assertive and businesslike, carrying a sheaf of papers that contained his notes and observations. The two guns, he reported, were muzzle-loaders of an old style, at least twenty years old. Coroner Forbes was surprised that the guns could have been manufactured so recently, as they looked like antiques, but Churchill explained that they were inexpensive firearms made for "gun running to the Persian Gulf." The guns bore a Birmingham proof mark. Later it was reported that they may have been manufactured by the Snider Company.

Robert Churchill, the gun expert who discovered the secret.

Soo's two rifles had been machine stamped "3" and "4" on their barrels, with matching stamps on the breech plugs at the backs of the barrels. Presumably these were guns numbers 3 and 4 of Soo's arsenal; he had started performing the trick with six rifles.

When Churchill received the guns, the morning after the accident, he noticed that number 3 was fully loaded with a powder charge and a marked lead bullet. Number 4 was empty. This was the gun that had fired, killing the magician.

A normal percussion-fire muzzle-loader has a plug at the back of the barrel. This plug is fitted with a nipple, with a small opening leading to the barrel. On the end of the nipple, the gunman places a percussion cap.

When the trigger is pulled, the hammer strikes the cap and creates a spark. The spark travels down the small hole in the nipple and ignites the powder charge in the barrel, firing the bullet.

But Chung Ling Soo's rifles didn't work that way. In his guns, the hole that led from the nipple to the back of the barrel had been blocked. Another small hole had been drilled from the nipple to the back of the ramrod tubes—the narrow tubes beneath the barrels that were used to store the ramrods.

The barrel of the gun—which the audience had seen loaded with the duplicate bullets and powder—wouldn't fire. But a blank charge— just powder and wadding—had been hidden in the ramrod tube. As the trigger was pulled, the powder would explode, harmlessly.

The bullets were large and heavy. It was impossible to accidentally insert them in the small ramrod tube.

The reason that the ramrods were never returned to the ramrod tube was now obvious. The tube needed to remain open, as it was about to fire a blank charge.

That was Chung Ling Soo's wonderful secret. But on Saturday, March 23, the number 4 gun actually fired the bullet in its upper barrel, as well as the blank. When it double-fired this way, it killed the magician.

Churchill had made a careful examination of the gun. The threads on the breech plug, at the back of the barrel, were quite worn. Soo had evidently unloaded the guns after each performance by unscrewing the breech plug at the base of the barrel to remove the bullet and powder.

It was an unusual thing to do, as the breech plugs in most rifles were rarely unscrewed during the life of the gun. Churchill noticed two cuts across the threads from "constant use, loading and unloading." The result was that the threads of the breech plug were quite loose.

The final, tragic part of the formula was the fine gunpowder Soo was using during the war. It had worked its way along the threads of the plug, until the trail of grains had formed a tiny fuse. Eventually, the fine powder connected the spark with the upper barrel—and the bullet was fired.

Churchill was of the opinion that if Soo had been a bit less secretive and had sent the guns to a gunsmith, the fault would have been quickly noticed and corrected.

If the magician had removed the bullet loads the traditional way that one emptied a muzzle-loader—by using a worm screw and drawing out the charge from the muzzle end of the gun—he would have avoided the wear on the breech plug. Churchill explained that the worm screw would have left scars on the lead bullets, preventing Soo from using his carefully marked ammunition for another show.

Robert Churchill discovered the fault by pouring hot water into the barrel and observing that it worked its way along the threads of the breech plug. He then dried out the gun and began a series of experiments. He loaded it as Soo had done, and fired. He reported that he fired "about 20 shots," but was not successful in igniting the top charge. He observed, "I have burnt powder at the breech end of the plug, so proved to my satisfaction the correctness of my deductions."

There was no question that the accident had been a fluke. Churchill's testimony suggested that even small changes in the magician's procedure could have ensured the safety of the trick.

Churchill made one mistake in his testimony, which was corrected by Coroner Forbes. He said that the breech plug was easy to unscrew, and from this he assumed that Soo had been opening the breech plug for every performance. But Inspector Cornish revealed that he had taken the guns to the shop in Waterloo Road—Soo's gunsmith—before they were delivered to Churchill. It was in Waterloo Road where the breech plugs were opened, and they had been so tightly sealed—corroded shut—that Soo's gunsmith needed a screw hammer to open them, a special tool to pry open the screw.

The evidence suggests that Chung Ling Soo had regularly opened the breech plug to remove the ammunition for a period of time. This was how the threads became scratched and worn. But he had stopped using this procedure long before the accident and the breech plug had since corroded shut. Perhaps the magician was made aware that it would be safer to remove the ammunition from the barrel and use new, freshly marked bullets for every performance. The tragedy is that he realized the mistake too late, after the fine threads on the screw had been damaged.

In Coroner Forbes's summing-up to the jury, he pointed out "how simple it was," and how the trick should not have been a dangerous one.

The tightly sealed breech plug proved that there had been no foul play, as the back of the gun was corroded shut. Churchill's experiment, his inability to replicate the accident, had doubly proved that this was not a case of murder or suicide.

"Nor had there been any carelessness on the part of the magician," a newspaper later concluded. "The means he had taken to cut off the firing mechanism from the barrel was found to be perfect in both guns. It was only the effect of time and use on a part of the gun that ended his life so tragically. With every performance he was coming slowly, slowly nearer to his death, though he didn't know it."

Coroner Forbes could study the construction of the guns and listen to the testimony about their preparation. But he was wrong in offering an authoritative claim as to how simple and safe a trick could be. During a performance, night after night, year after year, the trick would have to endure newly trained assistants, or tired, experienced assistants, infusions of jangled stage nerves, or sheer monotony, laziness, fatigue, or illness. On a stage, everything became a bit more dangerous.

The jury had no difficulty reaching a verdict. They expressed their sincere sympathy to Mrs. Olive Robinson and ruled that her husband's case had been a tragic accident, officially "death by misadventure."

—⁕—

The inquest at Wood Green Town Hall was a model of rational evidence and experienced testimony. But when Dot testified, "there had never been an accident with this trick," she was mistaken. She had obviously been concerned, telling friends that she wished her husband would stop performing the trick. Chung Ling Soo reported at least two accidents in the press. On one occasion, something had been fired out of the lower barrel and broken the plate in his hand. This may have been a fragment that accidentally fell into the ramrod tube, or a small object secretly dropped into the tube by one of the volunteers from the audience. This injury inspired the magician's careful preparations of the guns.

Donald Stevenson recalled that Soo had also been struck in the face by the paper wads that were used to pack the blank charges. The flaming paper had been shot across the stage. Stevenson believed that, for this reason, Soo's earlier assistants had been instructed to aim over the magician's shoulder. This instruction wouldn't have been surprising. But neither Grossman nor Crowley had been told where to shoot. Unfortunately, they pointed their guns directly at the magician.

After Soo's death, a newspaper account revealed that there had been another near calamity several years before the magician's death. An assistant had accidentally replaced the ramrod in the rifle. Chung Ling Soo stopped the trick just in time, before the ramrod was fired across the stage.

—⁕—

The trick rifle, with the ramrod tube that fired a blank charge, was not a new idea. Like Chung Ling Soo's greatest tricks, Defying the Boxers had been created from a number of classic deceptions. He'd started with Herrmann's wonderful bullet-catching trick, with a line of military men shooting the marked bullets across the stage. But Herrmann's secret depended on the cooperation of the gunmen. It was a fine trick for special occasions, as Herrmann presented it. But it was too difficult to perform night after night.

Kellar's wonderful trick pistol, the gun used to fire the rings at the wooden chest, provided the perfect solution. It seemed reliable. The secret was buried within the body of the gun, away from curious eyes. Members of the audience could watch closely as the guns were loaded. The trick would mystify even the soldiers who fired the guns.

After the reports from the inquest, Soo's secret became obvious to Houdini. He wrote to Kellar in Los Angeles, "I wonder if he used a gun that fired blanks, and the real cartridge went into another part of the gun. That may have been why he was shot." Soon after that, Kellar received clippings from London papers explaining the secret, and he was stunned by the revelation. "It appears that Robinson used the double gun with false barrel," Kellar responded to Houdini. "This is a most dangerous practice as I found years ago when I used a similar arrangement for the ring pistol. When I [once] fired, all the rings were shot out of the top barrel. I could never account for the manner in which the upper chamber fired, unless there was a leak between the two, and when the lower barrel was fired the upper one was also ignited."

The old magician admitted, "I am astonished to learn that Robinson would be so reckless as to use that kind of gun, as he knew of my experience with the rings."

—⁓—

On Saturday March 30, 1918, William Ellsworth Robinson was buried in the family grave in the East Sheen Cemetery, next to Neil Carlton's coffin.

Sheets of cold rain descended on the funeral, but there were carloads of mourners, including many professional magicians, theater managers, friends, and assistants from the show. Will Goldston and his wife were there, as was Arthur Carlton, the music-hall magician who had sent a letter to the coroner. Donald Stevenson, the Kametaros, Suee Chung, and the boys from the Chung Ling Soo show paid their respects at the graveside. Dozens of professionals attended, including Nevil Maskelyne, of the famous family of London magicians, Oswald Williams, another music-hall illusionist, and Cecil Lyle, who had watched the last performance one week earlier. There were reportedly over one hundred floral tributes, including those from the Magician's Club of London, the Magic Circle, and the Wood Green Empire.

Dot paid for a sculpture for the top of the gravestone. The inscription was composed by Louise, and read, "In Everlasting Memory of William Ellsworth Robinson (Chung Ling Soo) / I miss thee when the morning dawns / I miss thee when the night returns / I miss thee here, I miss thee there / Dearest, I miss thee everywhere / Never forgotten by Lou and children / Ellsworth, Hector and Mary."

Dot Robinson and Louise Blatchford, Mrs. Soo and Mrs. Robinson, shared a carriage from Kia Ora, the house on Lonsdale Road, to the cemetery. At the side of the grave, they stood together in the rain, shielded by shiny black umbrellas, and joined in prayer.

As the minister spoke of the bereaved finding peace, Louise and Dot knew that Rob had finally found peace from his many secrets.

After they stepped away from the grave, Louise and Dot never met again.

—ᴍ—

Houdini always thought in superlatives, and he felt envy when other magicians obtained headlines. He was even jealous of obituaries. After the press reports of Chung Ling Soo's death and the speculation about the cursed bullet-catching trick, Houdini couldn't resist a chance to make headlines of his own.

In April 1918, he announced that he would perform the bullet-catching trick at a special benefit performance at the New York

Harry Houdini was tempted to try the
bullet-catching trick.

Hippodrome, a fund-raiser for the Society of American Magicians
and the Showman's League.

When he heard the news, Harry Kellar wrote from Los Angeles,
pleading with his young friend. "Now my dear boy, this is advice
from the heart. Don't try the damn bullet catching trick no matter
how sure you may feel of its success. There is always the biggest
kind of risk that some dog will 'job' you," he wrote, reminding Houdini of spectators who sometimes recklessly dropped pellets or buttons into the rifles. "Please, Harry, listen to your old friend Kellar
who loves you as his own son and don't do it."

Houdini was hardheaded and seldom ducked a challenge. But something about Kellar's appeal touched him. Perhaps he had been haunted
by Chung Ling Soo's perfect trick—seemingly so dependable—that
resulted in his death. Could Houdini really have devised anything
more ingenious?

He cancelled his plans to perform the bullet-catching trick. It was
the only trick Houdini had been afraid to attempt.

—⁓—

Kellar was concerned with Houdini's safety. But he also doubted whether the trick meant anything to the spectators. "It is a damn fool trick," he wrote Houdini. "The audience is never really impressed with the mystery, for they know it is a fake. So why risk one's life so foolishly?"

It was a strange distinction for Kellar, a man who had spent his entire career as a magician, performing before the public. It was a bit of armchair philosophy after too many years of retirement. Can a miracle be too impossible? Why perform any magic at all? Did anyone ever really believe that a woman really floated in the air, or that people could disappear in a fraction of a second? Did they ever think that Kellar communed with ghosts in his wooden spirit cabinet?

Did music hall audiences pay their shillings and really expect to see wonders?

Between 1900 and 1918, they did. When Chung Ling Soo came to town, they stood in line at the local Empire, took their seats, and listened to the overture. With the cost of a ticket, they became part of a pact, complicit in the agreement to create a fantasy.

When the curtains opened and the star stepped onstage, they never questioned if he were really a Chinese magician, or a New York theater professional, or a Lancashire lad. They didn't ask whether he was a loyal husband, or a good father, or an honest man.

Chung Ling Soo made magic. He could create thousands of five-pound notes, enormous white paper drifts of staggering wealth, from a pitcher of water. He caught fish in the air by swinging an ordinary fishing line over the heads of the audience. He discovered a pretty Chinese maiden in the center of a revolving glass lantern as it flashed and flickered in the bright lights of the stage. And, on special occasions, he caught bullets on a porcelain plate.

His audiences had agreed to believe in the Marvelous Chinese Conjurer. And, grateful for their trust, Chung Ling Soo had always shown them marvels.

EPILOGUE

I n April 1918, a Boston card magician named James Elliott, an old friend of Billy Robinson, wrote to the American sleight of hand performer T. Nelson Downs. "Robinson, I am sorry to say, was crooked. He had three wives at the time of his death," according to Elliott. "Carl Rosini knew two of them in Europe." Presumably Elliott referred to Bessie, Dot, and Lou. Rosini was an American vaudeville magician who performed in London and socialized with Soo.

But after Chung Ling Soo's death, few of his friends discussed the unusual situation of his wife and family. For most it was an embarrassment and best forgotten. Magician Harry Leat published a poem that hinted at the problem. Leat's "Farewell" began,

> By the side of the grave two women stood.
> It is not for us to condemn.
> Yet many I know thought they should;
> But we'll murmur a quiet requiem.

William Ellsworth Robinson's will was a simple document with sadly disappointing provisions for his wife. One-third of his life insurance policies were left to Dot. Two-thirds of the policies and the rest of his estate—his home and personal effects—were left to Lou and the three children.

Although the will did not leave her any of the props or costumes from the show, Dot produced an act to tour the music halls called The Chung Ling Soo Entertainments. Presumably she used some of her husband's effects that she and Frank Kametaro had secured after his death. A July 1918 magician's journal praised the show, writing, "The Chung Ling Soo atmosphere and tradition are being closely adhered to—wiser still, with no attempt at any imitation of the inimitable performer's personality." A later review commented, "It is magnificent, but it's not Chung Ling Soo." A magician named Royal Raceford presented the show. He paid Dot £20 a week in royalties during the tour. Bamboo Flower—Nina Kametaro—now took the role of the leading assistant, performing Dot's illusions. But Dot did not appear on stage.

Just months later, using the apparatus that she had inherited, Lou arranged for a rival show, first presented by a magician named Alfred Banks, who worked under the name Ching Wu, and later with magician A. W. Hartopp, from her home town of Plymouth. Hartopp had worked under the name Amasis in the English music halls. For the new Chinese act, he took the name Li Sing Foo.

Houdini wrote to Kellar in February 1919 with the latest gossip from London. "Met Ike Rose. He tells me that Dot Robinson is reported to have joined forces with Robinson's concubine. First time I ever had to use that word, but that's all the lady in question can be, for Dot is really married to Soo." But the rumor wasn't true. An advertisement in *The Peformer* in March 1919 announced, "Lou Robinson, sole owner of all the original effects, property, scenery, et cetera, of the late Chung Ling Soo."

In January 1920, Lou was involved in a minor scandal with a married man named Frank Halse St. Clair, who had managed the touring show and was then living with her in the house at Lonsdale Road. While she was on a trip to Brighton, visiting her sons in boarding school, St. Clair pawned some of her diamond jewelry. When she returned, she also discovered that her Daimler automobile and other property was missing.

St. Clair wrote Louise a long letter, begging for forgiveness. "I love you with every fiber of my very being. No man has ever loved you as much as I do." He asked that Lou accept his apology and wire a reply to the Charing Cross post office, where he would wait to hear from her. Instead of sending a telegram, she sent detectives and had him arrested. He was tried and sentenced to fifteen months in jail.

In a newspaper account of the arrest, there was an explanation that Louise "had the right to use the name Robinson, as she was associated with the late Mr. Robinson," even though "another lady was the legitimate Mrs. Robinson."

Dot was tired of the confusion. She placed an ad in *The Encore* explaining, "Mrs. W. E. Robinson, professionally known as Suee Seen, widow of the late William Ellsworth Robinson, popularly known on stage as Chung Ling Soo, is in no way connected to Lou Robinson who styles herself widow of Chung Ling Soo (St. Clair case)."

In February 1919, when Harry and Bess Houdini were in Bradford, they visited Dot. She had bought a house at 78 Tennyson Place in the smoky West Yorkshire mining town. "She seems to be in fairly good circumstances, looks better than when we last saw her," Houdini wrote to Kellar.

Houdini asked Dot about Rob's death. "I told her that there was a rumor that Rob had business troubles, and with his peculiar family affair, he may have sought death, but she says positively not. They had not lived together as man and wife for a number of years, and always traveled together really as partners."

Dot recounted how Rob's last words to her, "just before he closed his eyes," were, "Dot, forgive me!" "She has forgiven him everything," Houdini reported, "just like a woman."

But Dot had many complaints about the other woman. "They were going to go to India the week following," Houdini recounted her words, "and this was their last engagement in England. It appears that Miss Blanchard [Blatchford], who was Rob's mistress, made him make a will leaving everything to her, and Dot received only one-third of a life insurance policy that he had taken out some time before, for $1,000." Houdini concluded that the situation was "an awful tragedy," and mentioned, "he even willed Miss [Blatchford] his body, so the body was buried from her home. Imagine Dot having to go to this lady's home to bury her husband."

Will's death had publicized Dot's position as the wronged woman. It became obvious that he had been unfaithful, and she looked foolish. To old friends like Harry and Bess Houdini, she wished to blame Louise and defend Rob.

But Dot may have exaggerated this difficult situation. Signed contracts indicate that Soo would have been in England late in 1918, not on tour overseas. Perhaps he did ask for forgiveness just before he died. By all accounts, after being struck by the bullet, he said very little and was seldom conscious. By recounting the words "Forgive me," Dot could once again portray him as a hero, and by offering forgiveness she became a heroine.

—⁓—

The Chung Ling Soo magic acts only lasted several months in the music halls. Louise sold many Soo props and scenery in a public auction at the workshop on November 3, 1920. Associates who attended the sale were devastated to see the contents of his wonderful shop—tools, materials, crates of supplies, and treasured illusions—under the auctioneer's gavel. The Crystal Lantern illusion was sold for fifty pounds to a British performer named The Great Carmo. Fred Culpitt, the comedian who had worked with Soo in Australia, attended that afternoon and described the auction as "the last sad stab." Culpitt wrote, "Standing in a sink on the second floor was a large enameled bowl, full of dirty soapy water. The auctioneer's men had been removing the grime of many months from their hands. The bowl was marked 'Lot 58.' If it had not been for that bowl, many things might not have happened. It was the original water bowl with which Soo first won fame as a Chinese magician."

Lot 58, "Gas ring, three glue pots, tray, pail and a large enameled bowl," sold for fourteen shillings ($3.50).

Houdini claimed, "Had I been in London at the time of Soo's sale, it is my positive belief that I would have bought the major portion of his outfit." But many of Soo's illusions were still being used in theaters and weren't offered in the sale. These were later resold, destroyed, or lost. Today none of Chung Ling Soo's effects survive, but a few treasured artifacts—a plate from the bullet-catching trick and ribbons from the Human Volcano—survive in collections. His posters are still prized by magicians around the world.

—᠆ഝ—

In 1921, Louise married Tom Warnock, a music-hall comedian who worked under the name Warden. As part of the team Warden and West, he later became famous with a nightclub act called Biddy and Fanny. Both men dressed as old maids and their comedy consisted of off-color gossip. The family remembered Tom Warnock as a loving father to the three children. But for some unexplained reason, Louise never allowed the children to mention Chung Ling Soo or William Robinson in the household.

Louise Blatchford Warnock died in London in 1966.

—᠆ഝ—

Will Goldston continued to sell secrets. In the 1920s, he published the secrets of a number of Chung Ling Soo's illusions, including The Dream of Wealth and The Crystal Lantern. One of Soo's tricks described by Goldston, the production of a lady from a large balloon, had never been produced. Presumably this secret was part of the cache of illusions supplied by Watson, the assistant who had purloined Soo's best ideas.

When he ran out of secrets, Will Goldston sold stories.

In 1929, he published *Sensational Tales of Mystery Men*, as lurid and muckraking a collection as can be written about selling magic tricks in the West End of London. Goldston peppered the book with insights into his many famous friends, professional illusionists. One chapter was titled, "Was Chung Ling Soo Murdered?"

Will Goldston's actual suggestion was suicide. "The most ingenious and cold-blooded suicide that was ever planned! That is my theory. Already I can hear the mocking, deriding cries of the skeptics asking me for proof. Of course, I have no proof. But the facts are pregnant with suspicion."

Goldston then recalled the Thursday afternoon before Soo's death, when the magician arrived unexpectedly at the magic dealer's office. "Good morning, Will," he said. "How much money do I owe you?"

When Goldston answered, Soo explained, "It's like this. I'm paying off all my debts. I guess it's just about time I got all my affairs in order. The sooner I get things straightened out, the better I shall like it."

Goldston assembled eight observations.

1) Chung Ling Soo was worried by domestic troubles.

Goldston never specified the nature of his difficulties, or the fact that they had been resolved for many years, so readers would be forced to assume the worst. The rest of his evidence was a similar collection of overstatements or misinformation.

2) He cleared up all his business affairs before his death. 3) He was shot on his last performance on a Saturday night. 4) The gun that killed him had been tampered with. 5) Soo himself was seen handling the gun a few minutes before his performance. 6) The marked (real) bullets were never found. 7) The plate was not shattered by the bullets. This proved that Soo could not have held the plate before his chest according to his usual custom. 8) Soo himself loaded the rifle which fired the fatal shot.

Like any good conspiracy story, Goldston inspired a few new memories of the event, and these grew more poignant with each retelling. Typical was the recollection of Fred Bason, a bookseller who had been 11 years old when the magician died. He had obtained an autograph from the magician in the alley outside the stage door in Wood Green, the night before the shooting. Soo reportedly signed the autograph book and then returned it with tears in his eyes, saying, "That's the last autograph I shall ever give." Bason admitted recalling this story after reading *Sensational Tales of Mystery Men*.

Goldston's chapter inspired other versions of the story, and each took an exaggerated tone, ending in murder or suicide. The friends and family of Chung Ling Soo endured these strange tales for many decades.

—⁓—

Frank Kametaro, the Japanese stage manager and translator for Chung Ling Soo, spent the rest of his life as a barber and a decorator. He also performed the occasional magic show for special parties. He died in the 1940s.

The real Chinese magician, Ching Ling Foo, died in China in 1922. That same year, Harry Kellar died at his home in Los Angeles.

Houdini never had any luck presenting his magic show, but he performed some of his magic—including a version of Soo's Orange Tree Illusion—during his 1925–26 tour, which also included escapes and a lecture exposing Spiritualism. Houdini was appearing in Canada when he suffered a strange accident; he had been boasting about his abilities to tighten his stomach muscles and withstand punches. An enthusiastic fan offered a flurry of blows that ruptured the magician's appendix. He died of peritonitis on Halloween, 1926.

Adelaide Herrmann, the grand dame of magicians, survived them all, performing her vaudeville act through the 1920s. A disastrous warehouse fire destroyed her show shortly before her death in 1932.

Hugh V. Lee died in the early 1920s, and his widow, Bessie Smith Robinson Lee, survived into the 1930s. She operated her own beauty parlor in Portsmouth, Ohio.

—⁂—

Dot Robinson left Bradford suddenly in 1921, sailing on the *Baltic* and arriving in New York in September 1921. She was 58 years old. On the ship's log, she recorded her name as Olive Robinson, and her age as 40.

She settled in the Bronx, near her husband's family. Edward Willis Robinson, Rob's younger brother, had worked in Minneapolis as a book-shop manager but had returned to the Bronx with his wife and daughter several years earlier. Olive took an apartment on Edison Avenue.

It now seems remarkable how secretive and reclusive she became. Her friends in England lost track of her. She never contacted her old associates from America. The Houdinis were living several miles away in Harlem. Madame Herrmann was in a downtown New York hotel, at the end of a short subway ride. No one knew she was living in New York. If Olive had contacted her friends, the world of magicians would have embraced her—the world's greatest magic assistant and the star of three great magic shows.

But Olive was now embarrassed by the tragedy and the scandal that clung to the story of Chung Ling Soo. She lived her life quietly, as a former actress from England, seldom talking about her experiences.

In 1933 she was diagnosed with cancer of the uterus, and died on November 13, 1934, at the House of Calvary, a hospice in the Bronx. She was buried in the Robinson family plot in Woodlawn Cemetery, near the grave of James Campbell Robinson and just down the path from Alexander Herrmann. Her grave is unmarked. In death, as in life, she is invisible.

—⁓—

The Wood Green Empire was long considered cursed. In 1930, a man in the audience inexplicably chose the theater as the place to commit suicide, killing himself during a music hall performance. In 1939, the American illusionist Horace Goldin suffered a fatal heart attack the night after opening at Wood Green. Goldin had been an associate of Soo's, and the inventor of the cannon trick that Chung Ling Soo used in many shows. Coincidentally, Goldin had also performed the bullet-catching trick for many years.

Today the Wood Green Empire, like so many of the beautiful music halls, is gone. In its place is a building and loan office. Nearby is a modern multiplex movie theater. But part of the façade of the theater still exists: two masonry towers capped with small copper Moorish domes. They are just noticeable enough to provide distinctive landmarks. And then suddenly one can imagine the entire theater, the grand Matcham showplace, as it originally presided over the curve in the High Road: there had stood the exit where the audience stumbled into the street, the alley where Suee Seen followed the stretcher into the ambulance, the stage door where the Marvelous Chinese Conjurer's many crates of illusions were loaded onto a wagon for the last time

ACKNOWLEDGMENTS
AND NOTES

First, I'm grateful to Peter Lane. Over many years, Peter has become the expert on the subject of Chung Ling Soo. As the librarian of London's Magic Circle, a private club for magicians, he was able to guide me through the Circle's extensive collection of materials. But as a collector and historian in his own right, he was generous with the results of his own research. As he told me in our first phone conversation on the subject, "Soo's a puzzle. You'll find the answer to one question, and you'll be left with three more questions." Peter had gathered many pieces of the puzzle, and had amazing insights about the missing pieces. His help was essential to this book.

My good friend Mike Caveney has been supportive and accommodating in the way that only another writer and researcher can be. His wonderful Egyptian Hall collection was the source of dozens of letters, articles, and photographs. On one unsolicited bundle of papers, Mike wrote, "A few more grains of sand for your dune." Every grain was appreciated.

No researcher addresses the subject of magic—certainly the subject of British magic—without consulting Professor Edwin Dawes, the historian of the Magic Circle. His research is formidable, his books perceptive, and his enthusiasm inspiring. I thank Edwin and Amy Dawes for their hospitality and much important information.

Trevor Dawson has been meticulously unearthing the history of Chung Ling Soo, including the details behind the Ritherdon shop in Bolton. Trevor kindly volunteered essential facts, opinions, and suggestions. I sincerely thank him for his help.

Thanks are also due Todd Karr, author of *The Silence of Chung Ling Soo*; Brian McCullagh, author of *Chung Ling Soo's Mechanists,*

They Stayed Behind; Gary Frank, author of *Chung Ling Soo, The Man Behind the Legend* and *The Man of Mystery*; and Ben Robinson, author of *Twelve Have Died*, for guidance, advice, and important research on my behalf. Thanks to Bill Kalush and Steve Cuiffo for finding the files I couldn't.

Will Dexter's slender 1955 book, *The Riddle of Chung Ling Soo* (Arco, London, 1955), is the inspiration for many researchers, and Dexter's trademark chatty prose provides an insider's view of magic. I was grateful to have the use of Dexter's notes, thanks to James Hamilton and the Magic Circle Library, as well as various letters to and from Dexter written in the preparation of the book. Dexter knew the story of Robinson's mistress and children but left it out of his book; he was threatened with a lawsuit if he wrote about them, as Lou and the three children were still alive. Mary, in particular, did not wish her parentage discussed.

Times, and generations, have changed. I appreciated the assistance of Michael Robinson—the grandson of Chung Ling Soo and the son of Ellsworth Robinson—and his wife Catherine. They kindly trusted me with their family secrets and encouraged me to uncover new secrets.

Helpful "tour guides" provided paths through specific parts of Robinson's story. James Hamilton explained the history of the Herrmann family and their wonderful magic; Enrique Jiménez-Martínez has researched the Kellar and Herrmann feud through Mexico; Magic Christian described what it was like to watch Max Auzinger perform his innovative act.

This story could only be assembled through the kindest gesture offered an author—an open file cabinet. My sincere thanks to Patrick Albanese, Bruce Averbook, David Britland, Maurine Christopher and the Milbourne Christopher Collection, David Copperfield and the Copperfield Magic Collection, Sara Crasson, George Daily, Roger Dryer, Gabe Fajuri, Stephen Fenton, John Fisher, John Gaughan, Ray and Ann Goulet, Charles Green, Richard Hatch, David Hibberd, Ricky Jay, James Klodzen, Ken Klosterman, Joe Long, Elaine Lund and the American Museum of Magic, Jay Marshall, Max Maven,

Billy McComb, Bill Miesel, Stanley Palm, Charles Reynolds, Howard Ritherdon, David Stahl, Jacques Voignier, Byron Walker, and Chris Woodward.

Also to the collections at the British Library, Colindale; Harvard Theater Collection, Houghton Library, Harvard University; The Magic Circle Library and Museum; Billy Rose Collection, New York Public Library; the rare book room at the Doheny Memorial Library, University of Southern California; Woodlawn Cemetery, Bronx, New York, and the New York City Department of Records.

I've been grateful to my agent James Fitzgerald and for the folks at Carroll & Graf for their enthusiasm and insights. Executive editor Philip Turner and associate editor Keith Wallman made this book possible and then made it better.

And finally, thanks to my wife, Frankie Glass, for the objective opinion, the first read, and the continual encouragement that was essential for every page of this complicated journey.

—⁂—

Chapter 1, The Wood Green Empire

My account of the Wood Green Empire and Frank Matcham is drawn from Jack Read, *Empires, Hippodromes & Palaces* (Alderman Press, London, 1985) and Brian Walker, *Frank Matcham, Theater Architect* (Blackstaff Press, Dublin, 1980). The account of Soo's last show is from the official coroner's inquest transcript (Wood Green, March 28, 1918, A. M. M. Forbes, coroner), and the newspaper account in the *Sentinel, Finsbury Park to Finchley & Enfield Advertiser* (March 29, 1918), and Todd Karr, *The Silence of Chung Ling Soo* (The Miracle Factory, Seattle, 2001).

The remark, "An' jus' 'oo do you think I am? . . ." is from Val Andrews, *A Gift from the Gods* (Goodliffe Publications, Alcester, England, 1981). The Houdini correspondence is from David Copperfield.

McDonald Hastings, *The Other Mr. Churchill* (Dodd, Mead & Co., New York, 1965), mentions burning the gunpowder on the tray.

There are varied accounts of the final performance of the bullet-catching trick. Soo probably altered his procedure slightly during the years he performed it. Contrary to some accounts, Soo did not load the guns on the final night.

Chapter 2, Harry Hill's Saloon

The story of the Brooklyn Theater fire is from contemporary accounts in *The*

Brooklyn Union (December 6, 26, 1876, September 13, November 27, 1877), Percy MacKaye's *Epoch* (Boni and Liveright, New York, 1927), and Gerald Bordman's *American Theatre: A Chronicle of Comedy and Drama, 1869–1914* (Oxford University Press, New York, 1994).

Harry Hill's saloon is described in Herbert Asbury's *The Gangs of New York* (Knopf, New York, 1927), and Luc Sante's *Low Life* (Farrar, Straus and Giroux, New York, 1991). Additional material on Harry Hill is from his *New York Times* obituary (August 28, 1896), and the Billy Rose Collection, New York Public Library.

James Campbell Robinson information is from his obituary in the *New York Clipper* (March 28, 1903). The H. J. Campbell bill is in the David Copperfield collection. The Charley White information is from the Harvard Theater Collection.

Additional information on James Robinson and his family is taken from the U.S. census for 1870, 1880, and 1900.

Some previous accounts have erroneously claimed that William's father was a different James Robinson, an early British circus performer and acrobat.

Chapter 3, The Palace of Magic

The history of Angelo Lewis and *Modern Magic* is from Will Goldston's *The Magicians Annual, 1908–1909* (Gamage's, London), *The Linking Ring* magazine (July 1965) and Sidney W. Clarke, *The Annals of Conjuring* (Magico, New York, 1983), and Edwin A. Dawes's *Stanley Collins, Conjurer, Collector and Iconoclast* (Kaufman and Company, Washington, D.C., 2002).

Modern Magic was first published by George Routledge, London, 1876.

The account of the Martinkas is assembled from *The Linking Ring* (May 1954, April 1964), *Sphinx* magazine (June 1932, December, 1935, September 1937, September 1941), and the *Los Angeles Times*, August 6, 1902. Although Robinson's association with Martinka's has long been ignored, the *Los Angeles Times* article clearly stated that he was a "shopman."

Additional material on Robinson is from Henry Ridgely Evans, *The Old and New Magic* (Open Court, Chicago, 1909).

I've put together his show from material in *Modern Magic*, an early Robinson bill in the Christopher Collection, the magician's later remarks in *Mahatma* (1895–1898), and his article, "The Art of Magic," in Augustus Roterberg's *The Modern Wizard* (Roterberg, Chicago, 1894).

Chapter 4, The Great Herrmann

Material on the Herrmann family is from Evans, *The Old and New Magic*, Clarke, *The Annals of Conjuring*, and H. J. Burlingame, *Herrmann the Great* (Laird & Lee, Chicago, 1897). Also the *Sphinx* magazine (January 1937, July 1938, February 1943, November 1948).

The information on Bessie Smith is from the two William Robinson marriage licenses, and census and immigration records. The record of Annie in the 1900 census indicates that she's a granddaughter of James C. Robinson, but her mother is not Bessie. She is either the illegitimate daughter of William or his younger brother Edward. However, Edward, at 20, was unmarried and could have married the girl's mother.

Thauma is explained in many magic texts, including Hopkins, *Magic, Stage Illusions and Scientific Diversions* (Munn, New York, 1897), and ads in the *New York Clipper*.

Chapter 5, Olive Path

The early history of vaudeville is taken from Parker Zellers's *Tony Pastor, Dean of the Vaudeville Stage* (Eastern University Press, Ypsilanti, Michigan, 1971); Charles W. Stein, *American Vaudeville, As Seen by Its Contemporaries* (Da Capo, New York, 1984); Robert W. Snyder, *The Voice of the City* (Ivan R. Dee, Chicago, 1989); Douglas Gilbert, *American Vaudeville, Its Life and Times* (Dover, New York, 1963); and Susan Kattwinkel, *Tony Pastor Presents* (Greenwood Press, Westport, Connecticut, 1998). Harry Hill information is from his *New York Times* obituary.

A fascinating bill for Robinson's show with Bessie is in the Christopher Collection, and this lists the effects they performed.

The review of Robinson at Koster and Bial's is from the *New York Times*, April 27, 1885.

Elmore's birth return (without a first name) was filed in New York City on February 16, 1885.

James Campbell's obituary in the *New York Clipper* explained his work with Keith. The background on Keith is from the B. F. Keith files at the Harvard Theater Collection. Additional material is from Charles W. Stein, *American Vaudeville, As Seen by Its Contemporaries*.

The facts about Olive Path have long been a mystery. Her marriage certificate records the name Paff, but when I found her death certificate, it shows John Pfaff as the name of her father and Mary Steele as her mother. I found her through U.S. census records for 1870 and 1880.

In an April 4, 1918, letter from Dr. James Elliott to T. Nelson Downs, in the American Museum of Magic, Elliott suggested that Dot had been a showgirl in the worst sense of the term, a prostitute. "Dot was a gutter woman; she supported Rob," Elliott wrote, insisting that older New York magicians knew this story. This was certainly not the general assumption, although New York magicians may have resented the way Billy had left his wife and child for Dot. It's interesting to compare this rumor to the story of the Spiritualist's parlor in Chapter 10.

Chapter 6, The Black Art

Ben Ali Bey's act is also described in Ottokar Fischer's *Illustrated Magic* (New York, Macmillan, 1946), and Harry Houdini's *Conjurer's Monthly Magazine* (December 1907, May 1908, and subsequent letters).

Did Robinson see Ben Ali Bey's act? Robinson had been to Europe, including Germany, on several trips before 1896; Robinson's handwritten endorsement of Dr. Elliott, the Boston card magician, is in the Christopher Collection and mentions his travels. John Willmann's *Handel mit dem Wunderbaren* (Edition Volker Huber, Offenbach am Main, Germany, 1998) mentions a representative of Martinka's shop visiting Willmann at this time, but does not name Robinson.

I discussed the development of Black Art, and Lynn's patent, in *Two Lectures on Theatrical Illusions* (Burbank, Hahne, 2001). My friend Max Maven translated Lynn's visit to Japan from Toyokichi Hata, *Meiji Kijutsu-shi* (By the author, Tokyo, 1952).

A discussion of deKolta's use of Black Art is found in Houdini's *Conjurer's Monthly*, and also Peter Warlock's *Buatier deKolta, Genius of Illusion* (Pasadena, Magical Publications, 1993).

Robinson's Catholicism is discussed in the W. G. Craigen correspondence to Arthur Ivey, in the Magic Circle Museum.

The dates of Achmed Ben Ali's performances are taken from the *New York Clipper*. Additional material is from George O. Willard, *History of the Providence Stage* (Rhode Island News Company, Providence, 1891).

Chapter 7, Harry Kellar

The Cocoon is discussed in Warlock's *Buatier deKolta, Genius of Illusion*, and *Burlingame, Herrmann the Great*. Robinson's premiere in Providence is from *Mahatma* (June 1895).

Dates and reviews from Boston appeared in the *New York Clipper*. A record of Herrmann's route for those months is from a receipt book from Mike Caveney.

Harry Kellar's story is from Mike Caveney and Bill Miesel's *Kellar's Wonders* (Mike Caveney's Magic Words, Pasadena, 2003), and Harry Kellar and Phil Temple's *A Magician's Tour Revisited* (Phil Temple, San Rafael, California, 2000).

Herrmann's ad appears in the November 5, 1887, *Clipper*. "Ten times" is from the November 5, 1887, *Clipper*. Notices and reviews appear in that publication until December 10, 1887.

The note about Kellar's running commentary is from an undated review in the Kellar scrapbooks, David Copperfield collection. The dirty poem and Barney is from John Braun's *Of Legierdemaine and Diverse Juggling Knacks* (Salon de Magie, Loveland, Ohio, 1999).

Hugh and Bessie Lee is taken from the 1900, 1920, and 1930 U.S. census, and from *Mahatma*, June 1903.

Kellar wrote of the gun to Houdini in a 1918 letter in the Christopher Collection.

Chapter 8, Nana Sahib

Kellar and the broken box is from Sam Sharpe's *The Magic Play* (Magic Inc., Chicago, 1976). The levitation story is from Braun, *Of Legierdemaine and Diverse Juggling Knacks*. According to W. W. Durbin in *The Linking Ring* (December 1935), Kellar also bought shoes to apologize to his assistant Barry. By the end of a tour, Barney had trunks full of shoes.

D'Alvini is from Caveney and Miesel, *Kellar's Wonders*; Evans, *The Old and New Magic*; and *Mahatma* (November and December, 1900).

Timayenis and Thurnaer is from Caveney and Miesel, *Kellar's Wonders*, and the Kellar scrapbooks and David Copperfield.

The Mexico tour is from Michael B. Leavitt, *Fifty Years in Theatrical Management 1859–1909* (Broadway Publishing, New York, 1912), and Enrique Jiménez-Martínez's research into the subject.

The Herrmann quote about his rival is from the *Chicago Evening Post* (December 17, 1896). James Hamilton, Bill Kalush, Magic Christian, and Richard Hatch speculated on "Niemann."

Keyes is from *Mahatma* (April 1898) and John A. McKinven, *Roltair, Genius of Illusions* (Author, Lake Forest, Illinois, 1980) and *Linking Ring* (February 1937). The accounts of Astarte being rehearsed, and Kellar's premiere of the trick, as well as Annie Lloyd's appearance, are from the Kellar scrapbooks, David Copperfield collection.

John Mulholland wrote that Robinson left Kellar "for a personal reason unnecessary to mention and having nothing to do with his excellence as an assistant," in *Sphinx* (July 1944), but did not elaborate.

The mishap with the pistol is from a 1918 letter from Kellar to Houdini in the Christopher Collection.

Chapter 9, Abdul Khan

The Edna illusion is from bills in Caveney and Miesel, *Kellar's Wonders*, and accounts of the Steens with Kellar in the Kellar Scrapbooks, David Copperfield collection.

Herrmann's Theater is from T. Allston Brown, *A History of the New York Stage* (Dodd, Mead, New York, 1903), Bordman, *American Theatre: A Chronicle of Comedy and Drama, 1869–1914*, and Mary C. Henderson, *The City and the Theater* (James White, Clifton, New Jersey, 1971). Articles appear in the *New York Times* (August 17, September 5, 1890, and January 3, 1891).

The planned South American act is mentioned in the Will Dexter notes. Catskill resorts is from *Linking Ring* (December 1940). The hat production act is from Braun, *Of Legierdemaine and Diverse Juggling Knacks*. His teeth are mentioned in several places, including the magician Dick Ritson's personal memories in the Will Dexter notes. John Mulholland, in a letter to Dexter, repeated the common perception that Robinson was not a good speaker.

The palmed bird is from *The Wizard* (October 1908). Olive Robinson is from *Mahatma* (August 1903).

Chapter 10, Out of Sight

Kellar in second-class theaters is from *Sphinx* (March 1941), and the moustache story is in *Sphinx* (June 1950). The Philadelphia Egyptian Hall is recounted in Caveney and Miesel, *Kellar's Wonders*, and Thomas Ewing, *Kellar's Egyptian Hall* (Author, Pennsylvania, 1990).

Out of Sight, Gone, Flyto, and Cassadaga Propaganda are described in Hopkins, *Magic, Stage Illusions and Scientific Diversions*. The story of the chair is from *Sphinx* (March 1939). The spirit cabinet with the Robinsons is from a Houdini manuscript in the Christopher Collection, quoted in Dexter's notes.

Zanzic and Robinson's adventure is recounted by Houdini in *M-U-M* (September 1923) and David Price, *Magic, A Pictorial History of Conjurers in the Theater* (Cornwall Books, New York, 1985).

This is not the famous mindreader Zancig. Additional information on Zanzic is from *Mahatma* (January 1900), *New York Times* (December 18, 1899), and *Billboard* (September 28, 1918).

The mussel story is from Harry Leat, *Tragic Magic* (Author, London, 1925).

The Herrmann dinner was recounted in an unidentified clipping in the Magic Circle Museum. Accounts of Herrmann's illusions are from the Herrmann files, Harvard Theater Collection.

The quote about double-crossing is from Dr. Elliott's letter to T. Nelson Downs, in the American Museum of Magic.

Chapter 11, The Marvelous Bullet Catch

Herrmann's feat was described in the magazine *Magic* (December 1996) and in clippings in the Herrmann files, Harvard Theater Collection.

Accounts of the Bullet Catching Trick are from Jean Robert-Houdin (translated by Lascelle Wraxall), *Memoirs of Robert-Houdin, King of the Conjurers* (Dover, New York, 1954); H. J. Burlingame, *History of Magic and Magicians* (Burlingame, Chicago, 1895); Hoffmann's *Modern Magic*; Signor Blitz, *Fifty Years in the Magic Circle* (Belnap and Bliss, Hartford, Connecticut, 1871); and Ben Robinson's *Twelve Have Died* (Magic Art Book Company, Watertown, Massachusetts, 1986); and *Sphinx* (March 1946).

Dot's interview is from the December 25, 1895, *Oakland Examiner*.

The Montreal tour is from Caveney and Miesel, *Kellar's Wonders*.

Chapter 12, Escape from Sing Sing

Fuller and Madame Herrmann is from the *New York Clipper* (June 6, 1896), and Brown, *A History of the New York Stage*.

An account of The Artist's Dream is from a clipping in the Magic Circle Museum and *Linking Ring* (March 1937). The trunk mystery was described in the *Oakland Examiner* article. Escape from Sing Sing is from the *New York Times* (May 10, 1893) and Walter Gibson, *The Master Magicians* (Doubleday, Garden City, New York, 1966). Ya Ko Yo is described in *Linking Ring* (September 1933 and December 1940).

The account of Robinson as Herrmann is from *The Wizard* (October 1908), and James Hamilton has tied this to San Francisco.

Herrmann's secret was recounted in the *Boston Herald* (December 30, 1896) and *Mahatma* (September 1900). His doubts about the Bullet Catching Trick are relayed in clippings in the Herrmann files, Harvard Theater Collection.

Herrmann's health is discussed in the *New York Mirror* (December 26, 1896). The introduction of Leon is from an undated clipping from the *New York Dramatic Mirror* in the Herrmann files, Harvard Theater Collection.

The Sing Sing performance is recounted in the *New York Times* (July 2 and 4, 1896) and the *Washington Post* (July 12, 1896).

The magician's last day and his death were related by Burlingame, *Herrmann the Great*, the *Boston Evening Transcript* (June 20, 1899), *Chicago Tribune* (December 18, 1896), Evans, *The Old and New Magic*, and James Hamilton, *A Short Biography of Alexander Herrmann and Adelaide Herrmann* (Author, San Francisco, 1994).

The Martinka telegram is from Jay Marshall. The Kellar telegram is in the Magic Circle Museum.

The neck-and-neck race is quoted from *Mahatma* (October 1895).

Chapter 13, Ching Ling Foo

The auction is from Hamilton, *A Short Biography of Alexander Herrmann and Adelaide Herrmann*, and Adelaide's quote about her creditors is from James Hamilton, *The Queen of Magic* (Author, San Francisco, 1996). The Robinson remark on the old man is from a letter to Houdini, quoted in Todd Karr, *The Silence of Chung Ling Soo*. Adelaide's remark about Will not being a performer is from *The Magical Record* (April, 1918).

The quote about Robinson is from John Mulholland, *Sphinx* (July 1944).

The account of Adelaide's bullet-catching trick is from *New York Dramatic Mirror* (February 20, 1897). Leon is from W. W. Durbin in *Linking Ring* (February 1936).

James Campbell Robinson's information is from his *New York Clipper* obituary. Robinson's ads for Campbell's appear in *Mahatma* magazine. The *Mahatma* profile on Will and Dot appears in June 1895, followed by ads, news items, and articles sporadically until November 1899.

The Hopkins book, *Magic, Stage Illusions and Scientific Diversions*, is still in print. The Kellar letter is from David Copperfield.

Information on Ching Ling Foo is from Braun, *Of Legierdemaine and Diverse Juggling Knacks*; *Sphinx* (June 1938); Price, *Magic, A Pictorial History of Conjurers in the Theater*; *New York Dramatic Mirror* (June 3, 1899); *Stanyon's Magic* (March 1905); and *Sphinx* (April 1909).

Chapter 14, Keith's Union Square

The account of Thurston's performance appears in Thurston, *My Life of Magic*; Grace Thurston's *Thurston Scrapbook, the Grace Thurston Manuscript* (Phil Temple, San Rafael, California, 1985); the *Denver Post* (October 23, 1898); and Karr, *The Silence of Chung Ling Soo*.

I've attempted to reconcile these accounts, and the results are surprising. The Thurston trick became famous because the cards were named, not selected from the deck, but the reporter's account distinctly describes the cards as being selected. This must have been an earlier version of Thurston's ultimate trick, and it would not have been new to Robinson.

Robinson's books are reproduced in Karr, *The Silence of Chung Ling Soo*. *Spirit Slate Writing* was published by Munn and Company, New York, 1898.

The story of Keith's New York theater is from Zellers, *Tony Pastor, Dean of the Vaudeville Stage* and Gilbert, *American Vaudeville*. The *New York Clipper* notice appeared on March 25, 1899. The information on Ching Ling Foo's performance in New York is from his *New York Dramatic Mirror* interview. The accounts of Foo's successes are from the *Clipper*.

Chapter 15, The Folies Bergère

The information on Adelaide Herrmann's suit is from James Hamilton. The Newark interviews were described in Braun, *Of Legierdemaine and Diverse Juggling Knacks*. Leon's fate is described in Price, *Magic, A Pictorial History of Conjurers in the Theater*.

Foo's appearance at Keith's is from weekly descriptions in the *New York Clipper*. The challenge was described in Braun, *Of Legierdemaine and Diverse Juggling Knacks*, and *Mahatma*.

Mingus' goldfish trick was described in *Mahatma* (May and June, 1902) and Gibson, *The Master Magicians*. The Bedlams appear in the *New York Clipper* (February 6, 1897).

Michael Hatal's accident was described in *Mahatma* (November 1899).

Ike Rose's background is from his obituary in *Variety* (August 14, 1935).

Houdini described Ike Rose's negotiations at the Parisiana Theater in *M-U-M* (April 1918). His premiere is described in *Mahatma* (May 1900) and the *New York Clipper* (April 14, 1900). Jacques Voignier translated an account from Abel Blanche in *Le Journal de la Prestidigitation* (July–August 1936).

Another account of his premiere appears in *The Wizard* (November 1916). The imitators in Paris are described in *Mahatma* (July 1900).

Fred Culpitt described Soo's name in *The Magic Circular* (September 1942). Professor John W. Chang of The University of Southern California kindly provided information on translating this name.

Chapter 16, The Alhambra Theater

The account of Soo's early act is assembled from reviews and accounts in Karr, *The Silence of Chung Ling Soo*. Muller's quote is from Norman J. Girardot, *The Victorian Translation of China* (University of California Press, Berkeley, 2002). Dexter's comment is from Dexter, *The Riddle of Chung Ling Soo*. The comment about the ascending scale is from Jean Hugard, *M-U-M* (June 1951). The flag trick is described in Ellis Stanyon, *Magic* (May 1901). The patent process is described in *Magicol* (May 1971). The letter about Mapleton is from Peter Lane.

Peter Lane has the *Weekly Reporter* (April 9, 1900) and *Chums* (July 18, 1900) articles, as well as interviews with different hometowns. Culpitt's story is from *The Magic Circular* (September 1942), and the letter about mechanical tricks is in *The Encore* (July 31, 1902).

The account of meeting Houdini is from *M-U-M* (April 1918).

I wrote about Houdini in Steinmeyer, *Hiding the Elephant*, and discussed his background in magic and eventual success as an escape artist. The Houdini and Robinson correspondence appears in Karr, *The Silence of Chung Ling Soo*.

Chapter 17, The Great Lafayette

Soo's letter, giving the account of losing the job to Lafayette, is from Karr, *The Silence of Chung Ling Soo*.

Lafayette's act is from a handwritten account by Archie Maskelyne, from Ricky Jay. Another review appeared in Stanyon's *Magic* (January 1901). The newspaper quotes are from advertisements in the *Times* (September 1, 1900).

Lafayette's story is assembled from the following sources: Lafayette files in the Harvard Theater Collection; personal collections of Ricky Jay, Edwin Dawes, and David Copperfield; Stanley Palm, *The Linking Ring* (June–November 1931); "The Death of the Most Hated Magician that Ever Lived," by Brian Lead in *The Magic Circular* (serially from November 1986 to January 1991); U.S. immigration records; Edwin A. Dawes, *The Great Illusionists* (Chartwell Books, Secaucus, New Jersey, 1979); and Arthur Setterington, *The Life and Times of the Great Lafayette* (Abraxas, England, 1991).

The big-headed boy and Moss conversation is from clippings in the Harvard Theater Collection. The account, "I recall going with my uncle," is from the magician Cliff Osman, quoted by Brian Lead.

Soo's changes in program are described in Karr, *The Silence of Chung Ling Soo*, and *Mahatma* (January 1903). The letter quoted is to Stanyon, in Peter Lane's collection. *Fairy Tales from China* was mentioned in *The Showman* (July 26, 1901). The exhibit of materials was common at this time, for example, the review in the *Bristol Times Mirror* (August 1, 1905). The Bolton contract is from Stephen Fenton. The Houdini letters are quoted in Karr, *The Silence of Chung Ling Soo*.

James Campbell Robinson's death is from information in his *New York Clipper* obituary. *The Open Door* is advertised in *Mahatma* (September 1900). Some details of

Robinson's trip appeared in *Mahatma* (May, June 1903). The information on Hugh, Bessie, and Elmore Lee is from the 1900 census.

Chapter 18, Defying the Boxers

The ribbons are described in a letter from Percy Naldett, in the Dexter notes. Kametaro is described in reviews of the show and in Peter Lane's interview with Percy Mayhew. His crew and salary was reported in *Sphinx* (May 1904).

The information on Ritherdon is from Trevor Dawson and W. Buchanan Taylor's article, "The Mill of Magic," *The Sunday Chronicle* (August 28, 1908), quoted in Dexter. The Orange Tree Trick is described in contemporary reviews; Karr, *The Silence of Chung Ling Soo*; and by Percy Mayhew. The cannon is from contemporary reviews.

Did Ritherdon make the rifles? Trevor Dawson's research has led him to believe that a gunsmith manufactured the trick rifles, but Ritherdon's shop stored them and supplied Soo with powder and bullets.

The letter to Houdini is from Karr, *The Silence of Chung Ling Soo*.

Accounts record that Soo used between two and six rifles. Reviews in *The Magician Monthly* (December 1904) and Stanyon's *Magic* (August 1906) indicated that he closed the act with Defying the Boxers. But later this changed. Several authors have mistakenly written that it was intended as the closing trick when Soo was killed in 1918.

Chapter 19, The London Hippodrome

Ching Ling Foo's planned visit to England is discussed in *Mahatma* (July 1904). The Ching Ling Foo and Chung Ling Soo duel is drawn from accounts in Karr, *The Silence of Chung Ling Soo*; *Mahatma* (February 1905); and the Dexter notes. The Houdini correspondence and Houdini's comments on the event are from Karr, *The Silence of Chung Ling Soo*, and Harry Houdini and Clinton Burgess, *Elliott's Last Legacy* (Adams Press, New York, 1923). The story of the orchestra leader is from a letter from Leonard Williams to Will Dexter, Dexter notes. *The Era* ads are from Peter Lane.

Hilliard's comments are from *Sphinx* (March 1905). Raymond's comments are in *Linking Ring* (December 1940). The Tschin Mao troupe is mentioned in *Sphinx* (September 1905), and the boasts and explanations appeared in the *Weekly Reporter* (April 9, 1905).

The nest of boxes is from the review in Stanyon's *Magic* (July 1906), and Soo's comments on being a good showman are in a letter to Stanyon owned by Peter Lane.

Elliott, in his letter to Downs, also mentioned Robinson being a "terrible woman chaser."

Chapter 20, Tavistock Square

Readers of magic history may be surprised by this description of Lafayette's The Lion's Bride, described in *Sphinx* (March 1904).

Additional Lafayette references are taken from *Mahatma* (January 1902–January 1903) and *Sphinx* (December 1902–January 1906).

The description of Dot is from the letter from Leonard Williams to Will Dexter, Dexter notes, and Peter Lane's interview with Percy Mayhew. The trapdoor story is from W. Buchanan Taylor's article. The Wiley story is recounted in a note in Peter

Lane's collection. The boy down the trap is from Mayhew. The *Mahatma* story is from August 1903.

The man with the newspaper is taken from *Sphinx* (January 1907). The assistant foiling the trick is from *The Magician Monthly* (May 1908).

Soo's accident at the docks is reported in *The Wizard* (February 1907).

Information on Janet Louise Mary Blatchford is from Peter Lane, and his article in *The New Pentagram* (July 1988). I researched city directories in Plymouth for the family homes.

The difficulties with the bullet-catching trick are from an undated *World's Fair* article in Peter Lane's scrapbooks, quoting *The Football Post* (April 27, 1907).

Chapter 21, Lonsdale Road

The classified ad is noted in the *Daily News* (June 8, 1907).

I'm grateful to Peter Lane and Michael and Catherine Robinson for information on Kia Ora.

Nina Kametaro and the Chinese coin, and the *Entr'acte* article are noted in several reviews, including *The Magician Monthly* (March 1907).

The Chinese community watching Soo is described in Mayhew's interview, *The Magician Monthly* (October 1909), and *The Magic Wand* (August 1912).

Houdini's comments appear in *The Conjurer's Monthly Magazine* (September 1906–October 1907). Ritherdon's comment on Soo's illusions is from W. Buchanan Taylor's article.

Stevenson's memories are taken from *Top Hat* (The Official Organ of the Portsmouth and District Magic Circle) (Summer, 1951), and *The Model Engineer* (June 1949).

The Living Target was explained in contemporary reviews, and a rough description of the apparatus was given in John Northern Hilliard's *Greater Magic* (Carl Jones, Minneapolis, 1938).

The Crystal Lamp was described in Will Goldston, *More Exclusive Magical Secrets* (The Magician, London, 1921), and I wrote about the history and mechanics of this trick in Karr, *The Silence of Chung Ling Soo*.

The glass impaled on the stage is from Percy Mayhew.

The Cauldron is from contemporary reviews and Percy Mayhew. It was described in Will Goldston's *Exclusive Magical Secrets* (The Magician, London, 1912). Burns were described in W. Buchanan Taylor's article. The water poured on Suee Seen was described by Percy Mayhew.

Soo's bankbook was from *The Wizard* (October 1907). The contract is owned by Stephen Fenton. The petty cash was recalled by Will Goldston, *Secrets of Famous Illusionists* (John Long, London, 1933).

The quote about his article is from *The Wizard* (October 1907). Information on the photo of posters is from Peter Lane, who has studied the contents.

Charles Hand's exposure in the *Liverpool Theatrical News* was discussed by Stanley Collins in *Linking Ring* (October 1953) and subsequently researched by Trevor Dawson.

Chapter 22, Australia

Soo's attempts to play in America is from early notes in *The Conjurer's Magazine* and *Mahatma*, as well as *Linking Ring* (December 1940) and Theodore Bamberg's conversations with Robinson in Braun, *Of Legierdemaine and Diverse Juggling Knacks.*

Technical information about the tour and stages is from Peter Lane's interview with Percy Mayhew. Leat described his friendship with Soo in Harry Leat, *Forty Years In and Around Magic* (Leat, London, 1923).

Davies and Aldred were described in Brian McCullagh and J. Ernest Aldred's *Chung Ling Soo's Mechanists, They Stayed Behind* (McCullagh, Sydney, 1998).

Jurgen Neil Carlton has been researched by Peter Lane, and I've found additional records through the British census.

Information on Portsmouth and the new illusion is from Trevor Dawson. The Australian arrival and early shows is from McCullagh and Aldred, *Chung Ling Soo's Mechanists.* The Australian show was reviewed in Charles Waller, *Magical Nights at the Theater* (Gerald Taylor Publications, Melbourne, 1980). Additional accounts are from Frederic Culpitt in *The Magic Circular* (September 1942); *The Wizard* (September 1909); *Sphinx* (August 1909); *The Mirror* (The Official Organ of the Australian Society of Magicians) (April and August 1909); *The Illustrated Sporting and Dramatic News* (Melbourne, Sydney and Adelaide) (April 8, 15, 22, May 6, 13, 20, and August 26, 1909); and Karr, *The Silence of Chung Ling Soo.* I'm particularly grateful to Brian McCullagh for additional research in Australian archives.

Soo's return to London is noted in *The Wizard* (November 1909).

Chapter 23, Edinburgh

Soo and Lafayette on the Gibbons circuit is from *The Wizard* (December 1909). The Soo letter was to Ritherdon, supplied by Trevor Dawson and Howard Ritherdon.

I'm grateful for Stanley Palm for the research on Selbini, Pantzer, and Lafayette. This material is also quoted in Arthur Setterington, *The Life and Times of the Great Lafayette.*

The new version of The Lion's Bride is from *The Magician Monthly*, October 1908. The accident with the lion was described in *The Wizard* (July 1909).

Soo's decision to stop performing the bullet catch is described in *The Wizard* (May 1910). Dot's unease was described by Leonard Williams to Will Dexter.

Soo's letters to Stevenson are from Stephen Fenton. The Soo shop and model airplanes were described in *The Model Engineer* (June 1949). The letter to Houdini is from Karr, *The Silence of Chung Ling Soo.*

The information on Mary was recorded in *The New Pentagram* (July 1988). "Papa" was a recollection from Hector Robinson to Peter Lane.

Additional information on Lafayette and Beauty's death is from Alasdair Alpin MacGregor, *The Turbulent Years* (Methuen, London, 1945); *Magical World* (May 1911); *The Magician Monthly* (May 1911); the *New York Morning Telegraph* (May 10, 1911); and Brian Lead's timeline of the tragedy, *The Final Act* (by the author, 1991).

The recollection of the fireproof scenery is from Percy Mayhew.

Chapter 24, Asleep in the Air

Jarrett is quoted in Jarrett and Steinmeyer, *The Complete Jarrett.*

The Dream of Wealth is reconstructed from Peter Lane's interview with Percy Mayhew, *Sphinx* (August 1912), Goldston, *More Exclusive Magical Secrets,* and *The Magician Monthly* (November 1912).

An annotated program for the matinee—explaining the effect of every trick—is in Peter Lane's files. Edwin Dawes described the Reg Pocklington story in *The Magic Circular* (May 1972). Percy Mayhew described what it was like to prepare for the matinees.

Information on Goldston is taken from 1891 and 1901 census records and Edwin A. Dawes's *Glimpses of Goldston* (Author, Hull, 1999). Soo supporting Goldston is from *Top Hat* (Summer 1951). The Watson problem is explained in correspondence reproduced in Karr, *The Silence of Chung Ling Soo*. Additional material on Carter's tour is from Mike Caveney, *Carter the Great* (Mike Caveney's Magic Words, Pasadena, California, 1995), and *The Magical World* (June 1913).

Chinese Magic was advertised in *The Magician Monthly*. The apology was published in *The Magician Monthly* (March 1913).

Chapter 25, The Expanding Die

The information on Neil Carlton's death was supplied by Peter Lane and Michael and Catherine Robinson. Lane has found that the grave was changed several times, after Carlton's death and after Soo's, and inscriptions may have been changed at these times.

Professor Hoffmann's letter is from Peter Lane.

The backstage stories are based on Peter Lane's interview with Percy Mayhew. The story of the oboe player is from Harry Leat, *Forty Years In and Around Magic*.

Houdini's account of the séance is from a letter in the Christopher Collection, in the Dexter notes. The Robinson correspondence about The Expanding Die is quoted in Karr, *The Silence of Chung Ling Soo*, and Kenneth Silverman, *Houdini!!!* (Harper Collins, New York, 1996). The Die is described in Goldston, *Exclusive Magical Secrets*.

A Ziegfeld bill for Ching Ling Foo is from Mike Caveney. Accounts of his visit appear in magic journals, including *Sphinx* (April–September 1913).

The Burslem fire was described by Percy Mayhew.

Chapter 26, The World and Its People

The World and Its People was described from accounts in Leonard Williams's correspondence to Will Dexter, in the Dexter notes, and Peter Lane's interview with Percy Mayhew. Programs in Peter Lane's files show the way performances were scheduled.

Mike Caveney has a program from the London Palladium, September 16, 1915, showing The Charmed Bullets.

Information on Soo's performances for soldiers is from Leonard Williams's correspondence with Will Dexter and *The Magician Monthly* (March 1918). The account of the Palladium benefit is from a clipping in Peter Lane's collection.

Information on the projected tour is from a clipping of Peter Lane's, dated January 11, 1917, *The Performer* (February 22, March 15), and *The Magic Wand* (February and July 1917). Leonard Williams's memories are from his letter to Will Dexter, in the Dexter notes.

The Shanghai reference is from *The Magician Monthly* (September 1917). The *Australian Variety* article appeared April 12, 1918.

The information on Burrough Hay is from Hector Robinson's recollections to Peter Lane.

The letter about drunk assistants is from Stephen Fenton. Soo's story about watching Herrmann is from *The Magician Monthly* (March 1918) and Soo's attitude toward his assistants is reported by Percy Mayhew. The information on Crowley and Grossman is taken from inquest testimony.

Lyle's account is taken from the inquest, and reported in later papers. The callboy's story is from an article in Peter Lane's files.

Chapter 27, The Charmed Bullet

The account of the accident at the Wood Green Empire is taken from the testimony at the official inquest, *Sentinel, Finsbury Park to Finchley & Enfield Advertiser* (March 29, 1918); *Wood Green Weekly Herald* (March 29, 1918, reproduced in Frank, *Chung Ling Soo, The Man Behind the Legend*); *The Era* (March 27, 1918); Karr, *The Silence of Chung Ling Soo*; Hastings, *The Other Mr. Churchill*; and newspaper accounts in the Dexter notes.

The account of the blood-soaked curtain was relayed to Will Dexter by Chris Charlton and appears in Dexter's notes. Billy O'Connor's story was also in Dexter's notes.

The letters to Goldston are from Peter Lane. The letter to Stanley Collins is from Edwin Dawes.

Madame Herrmann's opinion appeared in the *Variety* obituary. The Houdini and Kellar correspondence is in the David Copperfield and Christopher collections.

Chapter 28, Death by Misadventure

In addition to inquest testimony and the contemporary accounts, Donald Stevenson offered his opinion about the accident in *Top Hat* (Summer 1951), including the information about the assistants' aim. Stevenson also wrote that coarse gunpowder was preferred, but only fine powder could be obtained during the war.

The suspicion about Dot was reported in a letter from Houdini to Kellar, in the Christopher Collection and recounted in Dexter's notes. The reporter's curiosity about Dot and Kametaro is from Craigen's correspondence, Magic Circle Museum.

The story about the ramrod is from an undated clipping from *The Performer*, in the Peter Lane collection.

Kellar's letters to Houdini are from the Christopher Collection.

The account of the funeral is from Karr, *The Silence of Chung Ling Soo*; *The Era* (April 3, 1918); and *The New Pentagram* (July 1988).

Peter Lane has found that the gravestone was changed, and perhaps the inscription added, some months after Soo's death. Dot told Houdini that she paid to have a sculpted harp at the top of the grave, but not long after this the sculpture was changed to that of an angel with a laurel wreath. That is how the grave appears today.

Epilogue

The April 4, 1918, letter from Elliott is in the American Museum of Magic. Leat's poem appears in *Leat, Tragic Magic*. Information on William Robinson's will is from Michael and Catherine Robinson and Peter Lane. Dot's show and Lou's show are recounted in issues of *The Magician Monthly*.

Information on William Robinson's will is from Michael and Catherine Robinson and Peter Lane.

The Frank Halse St. Claire information is from a January 1920 clipping from Peter Lane. Dot's ad in *The Encore* appeared on January 15, 1920.

Houdini's letters are in the Christopher Collection.

The auction catalog appears in a number of collections, including those of The Magic Circle and David Copperfield. Culpitt's account appeared in *The Magic Circular* (September 1942). The Houdini letter about the auction is from David Copperfield.

The information on Tom Warnock is from Michael and Catherine Robinson and Peter Lane.

Bason's story appears in *Fred Bason's Third Diary* (Andre Deutsch, London, 1955).

For many years the fate of Dot Robinson remained a mystery. Quite unexpectedly, when I enquired about the Robinson plot at Woodlawn Cemetery, I discovered that she was buried there in an unmarked grave.

LIST OF ILLUSTRATIONS

INDEX

ABOUT THE AUTHOR

Jim Steinmeyer has invented many of the famous illusions used by leading magicians from Ricky Jay to Siegfried & Roy. He created David Copperfield's vanish of the Statue of Liberty and has also designed magic for six Broadway shows and many other productions, including *Mary Poppins,* currently playing in London's West End. He is the author of *Hiding the Elephant, the Los Angeles Times* bestseller, which Teller hailed as "a radiant celebration of the genius, glamour, and gargantuan egos of stage magic."

Steinmeyer has researched and rediscovered many great illusions of the past and has written numerous technical books on magic history and the techniques of magic. He lectures on these subjects and is a contributing editor to *Magic* magazine, the leading independent magazine for magicians.

In addition, Steinmeyer has served as consultant and producer for magic television specials in the United States and Great Britain, and was a writer and producer for the A&E network's four-hour history of the art, *The Story of Magic.* For several years, he served as a consultant and concept designer for Walt Disney Imagineering, developing theme park attractions for The Walt Disney Company.

Jim Steinmeyer lives in Los Angeles with his wife, Frankie Glass, an independent television producer.

Also Available by Jim Steinmeyer
*From the magic world's leading historian, two essential books on
the fine art of deception and one of deception's finest artists*

Art & Artifice
and Other Essays on Illusion

From the author of *Hiding the Elephant* and *The Glorious Deception* comes a collection of essays that shows how history's great stage illusions were much more than the sum of their technical secrets. These illusions were integrally products of their times, were based on the traditions and fashions of the people, and were the offspring of incredible, inventive personalities such as Steele MacKaye, John Nevil Maskelyne, David Devant, P. T. Selbit, Horace Goldin, and Charles Morritt, touchstones to decades of magic history and ingenuity. Indeed, Steinmeyer reveals how such illusions as The Mascot Moth, Sawing a Lady in Halves, and Morritt's Disappearing Donkey required few secrets beyond those learned in grade-school science class, yet still, through art and artifice, left audiences with a profound sense of wonder.

Carroll & Graf Publishers / 208 pages / ISBN: 0-7867-1806-4 / $14.95

The Magic of Alan Wakeling

Alan Wakeling's acclaimed magic has been the "secret source" for leading professional magicians for years. His extensive career featured stage magic, illusions, close-up and stand-up effects, including several complete acts. Steinmeyer highlights some of the groundbreaking professional material developed by Wakeling, including clairvoyance, billiard ball tricks, and many large-scale illusions that the magicians, designers, and producers of today continue to integrate into their acts. Fully illustrated and beautifully designed, this book—endorsed by testimonials from Mark Wilson, Mike Caveney, Ricky Jay, and Channing Pollock—is a treasure for any aspiring magician.

Carroll & Graf Publishers / 352 pages / ISBN: 0-7867-1807-2 / $17.95

Available from all chain, independent, and online booksellers

Also Available
Hiding the Elephant
How Magicians Invented the Impossible and Learned to Disappear
Foreword by Teller

"A loving, engaging book about our . . . human need for wonder."—Michael Dirda, *Washington Post Book World*

"An enthralling history of great illusionists that reveals not only how magicians act but how they think." —Ricky Jay, author of *Learned Pigs & Fireproof Women*

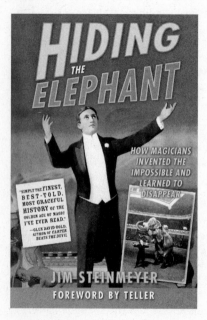

In this astonishing book, Jim Steinmeyer chronicles a half-century of illusionary innovation, backstage chicanery, and keen competition within the world of magicians. Lauded by today's finest magicians and critics, *Hiding the Elephant* is a cultural history of the efforts among legendary conjurers to make things materialize, levitate, and disappear. Steinmeyer unveils the secrets and life stories of the fascinating personalities behind optical marvels such as floating ghosts interacting with live actors, disembodied heads, and vanishing ladies. He demystifies Pepper's Ghost, Harry Kellar's Levitation of Princess Karnak, Charles Morritt's Disappearing Donkey, and Houdini's landmark vanishing of Jennie the elephant in 1918. This dramatic mix of science and history peers behind the curtain at the backstage story of magic.

"A loving celebration. . . . No author has ever better conveyed the way the love of conjuring consumes a magician's life with magic's joys, terrors and longings." —Teller, *New York Times Book Review*

"Simply the finest, best-told, most graceful history of the Golden Age of magic I've ever read." —Glen David Gold, author of *Carter Beats the Devil*

Carroll & Graf Publishers / 384 pages / ISBN 0-7867-1401-8 / $14.00
Available from all chain, independent, and online booksellers